… # THE ARDEN SHAKESPEARE

THIRD SERIES
General Editors: Richard Proudfoot, Ann Thompson,
David Scott Kastan and H.R. Woudhuysen

# THE TAMING OF
# THE SHREW

D1535294

# THE ARDEN SHAKESPEARE

* Second series

THE ARDEN SHAKESPEARE

# THE TAMING OF THE SHREW

Edited by
## BARBARA HODGDON

Bloomsbury Arden Shakespeare
An imprint of Bloomsbury Publishing Plc

BLOOMSBURY
LONDON · NEW DELHI · NEW YORK · SYDNEY

**Bloomsbury Arden Shakespeare**
An imprint of Bloomsbury Publishing Plc

Imprint previously known as Arden Shakespeare

| 50 Bedford Square | 1385 Broadway |
| London | New York |
| WC1B 3DP | NY 10018 |
| UK | USA |

www.bloomsbury.com

**BLOOMSBURY, THE ARDEN SHAKESPEARE and
the Diana logo are trademarks of Bloomsbury Publishing Plc**

This edition of *The Taming of the Shrew* by Barbara Hodgdon, first published
2010 by the Arden Shakespeare
Reprinted by Bloomsbury Arden Shakespeare 2014 (three times)

Editorial matter © 2010 Barbara Hodgdon

The general editors of the Arden Shakespeare have been
W. J. Craig and R. H. Case (first series 1899–1944)
Una Ellis-Fermor, Harold F. Brooks, Harold Jenkins and
Brian Morris (second series 1946–82)
Present general editors (third series)
Richard Proudfoot, Ann Thompson, David Scott Kastan
and H. R. Woudhuysen

**British Library Cataloguing-in-Publication Data**
A catalogue record for this book is available from the British Library.

ISBN: HB: 978-1-9034-3692-9
PB: 978-1-9034-3693-6

**Library of Congress Cataloging-in-Publication Data**
A catalog record for this book is available from the Library of Congress.

Series: The Arden Shakespeare Third Series

Printed and bound in Great Britain

*The Editor*

Barbara Hodgdon is Professor of English Language and Literature at the University of Michigan, Ann Arbor. Her publications include *The Shakespeare Trade: Performances and Appropriations*, *The End Crowns All: Closure and Contradiction in Shakespeare's History*, and many essays, primarily on performed Shakespeare, stage and film. With W.B. Worthen, she has edited *A Blackwell Companion to Shakespeare and Performance*.

'What I say,' said Eeyore, 'is that it's unsettling. I didn't want to come on this Expo – what Pooh said. I only came to oblige. But here I am.'
A.A. Milne, *Winnie the Pooh*

# CONTENTS

# LIST OF
# ILLUSTRATIONS

# GENERAL EDITORS' PREFACE

The earliest volume in the first Arden series, Edward Dowden's *Hamlet*, was published in 1899. Since then the Arden Shakespeare has been widely acknowledged as the pre-eminent Shakespeare edition, valued by scholars, students, actors and 'the great variety of readers' alike for its clearly presented and reliable texts, its full annotation and its richly informative introductions.

In the third Arden series we seek to maintain these well-established qualities and general characteristics, preserving our predecessors' commitment to presenting the play as it has been shaped in history. Each volume necessarily has its own particular emphasis which reflects the unique possibilities and problems posed by the work in question, and the series as a whole seeks to maintain the highest standards of scholarship, combined with attractive and accessible presentation.

Newly edited from the original Quarto and Folio editions, texts are presented in fully modernized form, with a textual apparatus that records all substantial divergences from those early printings. The notes and introductions focus on the conditions and possibilities of meaning that editors, critics and performers (on stage and screen) have discovered in the play. While building upon the rich history of scholarly activity that has long shaped our understanding of Shakespeare's works, this third series of the Arden Shakespeare is enlivened by a new generation's encounter with Shakespeare.

## THE TEXT

On each page of the play itself, readers will find a passage of text supported by commentary and textual notes. Act and scene divisions (seldom present in the early editions and often the product of eighteenth-century or later scholarship) have been retained for ease of reference, but have been given less prominence than in previous series. Editorial indications of location of the action have been removed to the textual notes or commentary.

In the text itself, unfamiliar typographic conventions have been avoided in order to minimize obstacles to the reader. Elided forms in the early texts are spelt out in full in verse lines wherever they indicate a usual late twentieth-century pronunciation that requires no special indication and wherever they occur in prose (except where they indicate non-standard pronunciation). In verse speeches, marks of elision are retained where they are necessary guides to the scansion and pronunciation of the line. Final -ed in past tense and participial forms of verbs is always printed as -ed, without accent, never as -'d, but wherever the required pronunciation diverges from modern usage a note in the commentary draws attention to the fact. Where the final -ed should be given syllabic value contrary to modern usage, e.g.

> Doth Silvia know that I am banished?
> (*TGV* 3.1.214)

the note will take the form

> 214 **banished** banishèd

Conventional lineation of divided verse lines shared by two or more speakers has been reconsidered and sometimes rearranged. Except for the familiar *Exit* and *Exeunt*, Latin forms in stage directions and speech prefixes have been translated into English and the original Latin forms recorded in the textual notes.

## COMMENTARY AND TEXTUAL NOTES

Notes in the commentary, for which a major source will be the *Oxford English Dictionary*, offer glossarial and other explication of verbal difficulties; they may also include discussion of points of interpretation and, in relevant cases, substantial extracts from Shakespeare's source material. Editors will not usually offer glossarial notes for words adequately defined in the latest edition of *The Concise Oxford Dictionary* or *Merriam-Webster's Collegiate Dictionary*, but in cases of doubt they will include notes. Attention, however, will be drawn to places where more than one likely interpretation can be proposed and to significant verbal and syntactic complexity. Notes preceded by * discuss editorial emendations or variant readings from the early edition(s) on which the text is based.

Headnotes to acts or scenes discuss, where appropriate, questions of scene location, Shakespeare's handling of his source materials, and major difficulties of staging. The list of roles (so headed to emphasize the play's status as a text for performance) is also considered in the commentary notes. These may include comment on plausible patterns of casting with the resources of an Elizabethan or Jacobean acting company and also on any variation in the description of roles in their speech prefixes in the early editions.

The textual notes are designed to let readers know when the edited text diverges from the early edition(s) or manuscript sources on which it is based. Wherever this happens the note will record the rejected reading of the early edition(s), in original spelling, and the source of the reading adopted in this edition. Other forms from the early edition(s) recorded in these notes will include some spellings of particular interest or significance and original forms of translated stage directions. Where two or more early editions are involved, for instance with *Othello*, the notes also record all important differences between them. The textual notes take a form that has been in use since the nineteenth century. This comprises, first: line reference, reading adopted in the text and closing square bracket; then: abbreviated reference, in italic, to the earliest edition to adopt the accepted reading, italic semicolon and noteworthy alternative reading(s), each with abbreviated italic reference to its source.

Conventions used in these textual notes include the following. The solidus / is used, in notes quoting verse or discussing verse lining, to indicate line endings. Distinctive spellings of the basic text (Q or F) follow the square bracket without indication of source and are enclosed in italic brackets. Names enclosed in italic brackets indicate originators of conjectural emendations when these did not originate in an edition of the text, or when the named edition records a conjecture not accepted into its text. Stage directions (SDs) are referred to by the number of the line within or immediately after which they are placed. Line numbers with a decimal point relate to centred entry SDs not falling within a verse line and to SDs more than one line long, with the number after the point indicating the line within the SD: e.g. 78.4 refers to the fourth line of the SD following line 78. Lines of SDs at the start of a scene are numbered 0.1, 0.2, etc. Where only a line number precedes a square bracket, e.g. 128], the note relates to the whole line; where SD is added to the number, it relates to the whole of a SD within or immediately following the line. Speech prefixes (SPs) follow similar conventions, 203 SP] referring to the speaker's name for line 203. Where a SP reference takes the form e.g. 38+ SP, it relates to all subsequent speeches assigned to that speaker in the scene in question.

Where, as with *King Henry V*, one of the early editions is a so-called 'bad quarto' (that is, a text either heavily adapted, or reconstructed from memory, or both), the divergences from the present edition are too great to be recorded in full in the notes. In these cases, with the exception of *Hamlet*, which prints an edited text of the quarto of 1603, the editions will include a reduced photographic facsimile of the 'bad quarto' in an appendix.

## INTRODUCTION

Both the introduction and the commentary are designed to present the plays as texts for performance, and make appropriate reference to stage, film and television versions, as well as introducing the reader to the range of critical approaches to the plays. They discuss the history of the reception of the texts within the theatre and scholarship and beyond, investigating the interdependency of the literary text and the surrounding 'cultural text' both at the time of the original production of Shakespeare's works and during their long and rich afterlife.

# PREFACE

Book covers, like introductions, offer interpretive cues, often by condensing the story into a single image, teasing a reader to look inside. This edition's cover also has a back-history: like the play, it has undergone several metamorphoses that, seen in sequence, trace *The Shrew*'s afterlives over the past half-century. The first, an abstract rendering of the iconic sun–moon scene in which Katherina agrees to humour Petruccio, featured three blobs of graduated sizes dotting a winding yellow road that stretched to the horizon; a blurred orb, half sun, half moon, presided over the scene, which might have been titled, 'The Three Lava Lamps Visit the Land of Oz'. A second cover of a faceless mannequin, enclosed by bars, evoked Katherina bound, if not bridled; a third erased the bars, revealing the mannequin, costumed in a vaguely Elizabethan bodice, waiting to be occupied by the next Katherina-actor. In the final image, Katherina, wearing her trademark red dress, extends one hand towards another, visible just at the frame's edge, that reaches for her: she almost seems to be dancing in tune to the play's perennial questions: shrew or not-shrew? Un-tamed or tamed?

One of the greatest pleasures of working on this remarkable play has been the generosity of colleagues, many of them women. Although there is little or no sense of women's community within the play, a wide-ranging network of present-day 'shrews' talk shrewdly about the play amongst themselves, with their students and in print. My introduction into that community began long ago when Lynda Boose shared her research on scolds' bridles and laughed with me about (re)performing shrews: I owe her deep thanks for generous support at the journey's beginnings. Just as Lynda's work represents a point of origin, more recent studies by Fran Dolan, Laurie Maguire, Carol Rutter and Liz Schafer, each of whom shared work prior to publication, have been invaluable resources: that their names frequently mark these pages seems small payment for so great an intellectual debt. In every sense, this book has been a collaborative endeavour. Among many others, I especially wish to single out Pam Brown, Margie Burns, Susan Carlson, Ann Christensen, Margie Ferguson, Penny Gay, Miriam Gilbert, Diana Henderson, Jean Howard, Leah Marcus, Margaret Maurer, Marianne Novy, Lena Orlin, Pat Parker, Ann Thompson, Val Wayne and Sarah Werner. For sharing their work on *A Shrew*, *The Shrew*'s 'sister play', my thanks to Alan Galey and Stephen Miller. I also am indebted to M.J. Kidnie and James Purkis, who gave essential late-summer advice at a crucial time. An admittedly incomplete list of significant others includes Giorgio Bertellini, Enoch Brater (for 'iambic pentempor-izing'), Ton Broos, Michael Cordner, Peter Holland (for the weasel story), Bill Ingram, Russell Jackson (for 'the tea time of the Shrew'), Mike Jensen, David Kathman, Ric Knowles, Ros Knutston, Jim Marino, Randall Martin, Jeff Masten, Yopie Prins, Cathy Sanok, Skip Shand, Robert Shaughnessy (for Sly-talk and the Spitfire story), Stephen Spiess, Terri Tinkle and Bill Worthen.

I have also been fortunate to have support from a number of institutions, libraries and archives. First, my thanks to Drake University's Center for the Humanities and the Department of English Language and Literature at the University of Michigan. Thanks also to Dartmouth College, the Shakespeare Association of America, the Modern Language Association, the University of Maryland's Center for Renaissance and Baroque Studies, The Shakespeare Institute and York University for providing occasions to share ongoing work. At Drake University's Cowles Library, Karl Schaefer sanctioned the long-term loan of a crucial book; at the University of Michigan's Hatcher Library, Peggy Daub and her staff in Special Collections helpfully produced key volumes time and time again; and at the Folger Shakespeare Library, Georgianna Ziegler, Betsy Walsh and her amazing staff always had answers to every question. I also want to thank Sylvia

Morris and Helen Hargest at The Shakespeare Centre Library; David Howells at the RSC Collections; James Shaw and Karin Brown at The Shakespeare Institute; Pamela Madsen at the Harvard Theatre Collection; Martin Durrant at the V&A Picture Library; David Schoonover, formerly at the University of Iowa Library; and Mary Robertson, Chief Curator of manuscripts at the Huntington Library, for details about 'Margery seynt John'. My thanks, also, to the Huntington Library for permission to reproduce *The Taming of a Shrew* in facsimile as Appendix 3.

Many thanks to Jessica Hodge and to Margaret Bartley, Arden's current publisher, for their patience, generosity and support, and to their team of assistants, including (most recently) Anna Brewer and Inderjeet Garcha. Thanks, too, to Kentston Bauman, my research assistant, for library travels and many hours spent checking references; and to Jocelyn Stockley for her keen-eyed proof-reading. Deepest thanks to Jane Armstrong, this book's tutelary wizard: her meticulous attention to detail and her editorial expertise have made *Shrew* a better book. Since Jane also worked on Brian Morris' Arden 2 *Shrew*, it seems especially appropriate to acknowledge his edition and her extraordinary talents together. Richard Proudfoot has taught me more than I can acknowledge here, not just by asking the right questions but also by generously agreeing that we disagree. The frequency with which (RP) occurs represents only the slightest trace of how much this edition owes to his immense store of knowledge, his excellent good sense and his discerning eye – as well as to his happy memories of a performance that made him fall in love with *The Taming of the Shrew* as a schoolboy.

My last and greatest debt is to my nearest collaborator and best and toughest reader, the in-house author and editor, expert sous-chef and maker of beautiful gardens, the 'without whom' who has lived with this play, witnessed repeated performances and watched over an oftimes more than usually shrewish Eeyore-editor. As ever and always, this book is for him, and his name is Richard Abel.

*Barbara Hodgdon*

# INTRODUCTION

## WHAT KIND OF PLAY?

*The Taming of the Shrew* is most certainly about courtship and marriage – the social rituals of wooing, winning and wedding that ground so-called festive comedy, the territory where it lives and breathes. But this particular play begins rather curiously, with an incident right out of early modern daily life (ripped, one might say, from the Warwickshire police report). The hostess of an alehouse threatens a drunken beggar with public punishment ('A pair of stocks', Ind.1.2) – he refuses to pay for some glasses he has broken – and fetches the local constable. The drunk (later named as Christopher Sly) calls her 'a baggage' (Ind.1.3), claims he's no rogue but has a pedigree ('Look in the Chronicles; we came in with Richard Conqueror', Ind.1.3–4), refuses to 'budge an inch' (Ind.1.13) and falls asleep. The title promises one shrew; the play's opening provides two: an uppity 'woman on top' and a disruptive lout, both behaving like scolds. A classic battle of the sexes? The set-up for a comedy of revenge? Who will prevail? What kind of play is this?

From its onset, *The Shrew* flaunts – and memorializes – its origins in the early modern theatre. Not only does it (mis)-quote Thomas Kyd's *Spanish Tragedy* ('Go by, Saint Jeronimy', Ind.1.8), an early modern box-office staple and the third most popular play of the period, reprinted in seven editions in twenty-five years, but the play's first gag – 'we came in with Richard Conqueror' – seems to refer to Shakespeare's English history plays and to Richard Burbage, the Lord Chamberlain's Men's chief tragedian, who played Richard III in Shakespeare's play (1597). *The Shrew* even hints at naming its author, for Christopher Sly's substitution of 'Richard' for 'William' Conqueror alludes to gossip – theatre's way of telling stories

1

about itself – that survives in a notorious anecdote from John Manningham's diary (13 March 1601; see also Race):

> Upon a tyme when Burbidge played Rich[ard] 3. there was a Citizen grewe soe farr in liking with him, that before shee went from the play shee appointed him to come that night unto hir by the name of Ri[chard] the 3. Shakespeare, overhearing their conclusion, went before, was intertained, and at his game ere Burbidge came. Then message being brought that Richard the 3ᵈ. was at the dore, Shakespeare caused returne to be made that William the Conquerour was before Rich[ard] the 3.
>
> (Manningham, 75)

If 'Richard Conqueror' combines Richard Burbage and William Shakespeare, then who is Christopher Sly? A Stephen Sly lived in Stratford during Shakespeare's time; William Sly was a player with Shakespeare's company. Is Christopher Sly another portmanteau name? And if, as usually understood, he is not a fully-fledged 'character', what is he? A hybrid of person and persona, similar to the Tarltonesque clown, the fictioning of the role as transparently bogus as 'Harry le Roy' (*H5* 4.1.49)? However tantalizing, the references to *The Spanish Tragedy* and Manningham's anecdote may simply be theatrical in-jokes – thrown out to *The Shrew*'s original audiences but appearing to its subsequent ones as just so much smoke and mirrors. Nonetheless, the tropes of ambiguous role-play, deception and pretence introduced in this first scene anticipate what is to come.

For as it turns out, no constable comes riding, and the Hostess never reappears (at least 'as herself'). Instead, a Lord and his huntsmen discover the drunken Christopher Sly and decide to play a joke on him. Servants dress him in fine clothes, tempt him with various wanton enticements and dupe him into believing that he has slept for fifteen years and that he is not (as he claims) a Warwickshire tinker from Barton-on-the-Heath, but a lord. Not only does his fantasy of gentlemanly birth (perhaps anticipating Shakespeare's own ambitious move to seek a coat of arms? It will recur in Bottom's dream and Falstaff's history and, transformed, in Lear's tragedy (Skura, 100)) seem to have come true, but he also learns that he has a wife – played by Bartholomew, the Lord's page. Another deception, another play? Or just another teaser worked up for a talented comic player?

A little later, however, *The Shrew* sets up another, less opaque, teaser:

SERVANT
> Your honour's players, hearing your amendment,
> Are come to play a pleasant comedy . . .

SLY           . . . Let them play it. Is not a comonty a
> Christmas gambol or a tumbling trick?

BARTHOLOMEW
> No, my good lord, it is more pleasing stuff.

SLY
> What, household stuff?

BARTHOLOMEW           It is a kind of history.
                              (Ind.2.125–6; 133–6)

At the point where Sly, who has 'never heard a play' (Ind.1.95), is about to see one put on by travelling players, *The Shrew* questions its own genre. Bartholomew, the Lord's page, dressed in borrowed robes as Sly's 'Madam wife', assures him that it is 'more pleasing stuff' – neither comedy, gambol nor tumbling trick but 'more pleasing stuff': 'a kind of history'. In a play where what someone (or something) is called takes on immense importance, it seems hardly accidental that genre itself is a slippery category. And in a theatre, where you are what you play, is it just coincidental that it is Bartholomew, who proleptically looks forward to Katherina Minola, the play's titular 'shrew' – a role also played in Shakespeare's theatre by a male actor – who renames the play and invites looking with a difference? Perhaps. As though speaking for the play's original moment as well as its subsequent theatrical – and critical – performances, Bartholomew seems to intuit that 'history' takes on various shapes and forms, even 'kinds' that include Sly's categories. For not only has *The Shrew* been seen as a pleasant comedy or commodity but it has also turned into a gambol or tumbling trick – a gag-filled romp that recycles the play's folk-tale roots, a knockabout farce featuring silly walks, cracking whips and custard pies. It has been read as a portrait of early modern marriage, as an historical treatise on the humiliation of women and as a Puritan polemic, and performed as a case history of a woman with a dangerous social neurosis in need of curing. It has even taken shape in genres unimagined by early moderns: gothic tragedy, problem play. Some *Shrew* visions and versions even play fast and loose with all these 'kinds', engaging in a merry war where the generic conventions of 'happy comedy' and the demands of high seriousness wage their own battle of the sexes. Gregory Doran (2003) found *The Shrew* especially difficult to stage because it can so easily either dissolve into gags or get buried by significance (CR). But his remark does not quite capture what is at stake, for it is not a case of either/or but of both/and – that is, the play is both great fun and greatly serious precisely because the gags and the significance often overlap, seeming at times to be one and the same.

The idea of game, sport or pastime, introduced in the opening as the Lord and his servants wager over hounds and then dupe Sly, echoes in the final scene, as Petruccio, Lucentio and Hortensio bet one hundred crowns on whose wife is most obedient. Wrapped up in this whirligig are tropes of gender, class and hierarchy – and what trumps them all, the power instated in the performance of social roles, which turns them all 'topsy-turvy down' (*1H4* 4.1.81). In *The Shrew*'s theatre of illusions, where the structure resembles a series of nested Chinese boxes, nothing stays stable for very long. Yet, like so much else in this play, one equivalence or identification serves both to fix and unfix another. Gender slips across bodies with amazing ease; Tranio turns into Lucentio, who, disguised as Cambio, woos Bianca; Hortensio (briefly) becomes Licio; the

Lord is equivalent to Petruccio, but so is Sly, who also mirrors or doubles Katherina (who is also called Katherine and Kate), as does Bartholomew, the Lord's page, the boy actor dressed in drag. 'Shrew' moves from Katherina to Petruccio and finally gathers up Bianca; class changes as easily as exchanging cloaks or, in Sly's temporary metamorphosis, experiencing the trappings of upper-class wealth – fine clothes (later denied to Katherina), sherris-sack, basins in which to wash, tapestries depicting Ovidian soft pornography, a wife called 'Madam' or 'Lady'. At times, you can't tell the players even with a programme (Maguire, *Names*, 100). Only Baptista, Grumio, Gremio and Biondello stay the same, though even they occasionally inhabit other roles. It is as though Kate's initial come-back to Petruccio, 'I knew you at the first / You were a movable' (2.1.195–6), governs the performances of nearly everyone in the play.

*The Shrew*'s first model of marriage – that of Sly and his Bartholomew-wife – sets up the terms of what, in Shakespeare's theatre, is an all-male mating game which juxtaposes images of how three other couples – Katherina and Petruccio, Bianca and Lucentio, Hortensio and his Widow – negotiate, and perform, marriage. But others also figure in these negotiations: Baptista Minola, father to Katherina and Bianca, and two other would-be suitors to Bianca – Gremio the old pantaloon and Tranio, Lucentio's servant, who disguises himself as Lucentio and woos Bianca in his name; in addition, Lucentio disguises himself as the Latin scholar 'Cambio' and Hortensio pretends to be the music teacher 'Licio'. But the central tale in this whirling dance – a kind of 'her-story' buried in 'his-tory' – is that of Katherina and Petruccio. In one sense, *The Shrew* is a two-hander, a froward, scrappy duet surrounded by an ensemble of other voices. Whether the play is presented as an exuberant marital farce, as a romantic comedy of fulfilled desire or (as it has been more recently) as a theatrical or critical performance that views the comedy as subversive and stresses the coercive harshness of the taming plot, the story of Katherina and Petruccio and the actors inhabiting their roles are the play's main attractions. The trajectory of their story, which puts on view, as in Shakespeare's English history plays, a series of resolutely masculinist scenarios, culminates in a finale where Katherina, the 'tamed' shrew, delineates the duties of husbands and wives in marriage. That speech – three times longer than any other in the play proper – has not only occasioned opinions ranging from praise to outrage, depending on the gender politics of a particular era, but also, through processes of metonymy, become detached from the scene of which it is a part and come to stand for the whole play. Overall, critical responses have ranged from complacent or delighted celebrations of the play's comic artistry and metatheatrical playfulness to troubled acknowledgement of its merged pleasures and dangers, including calls to remove it from circulation altogether as a brutally sexist polemic. Yet despite – or perhaps precisely because of – this deeply conflicted history, *The Taming of the Shrew* continues to be a perennially compelling favourite, even for latter-day cultures which espouse neither its marital ideologies nor its taming pedagogy. Moreover, the play is so inherently theatrical that, from its beginnings, it has spawned numerous and varied offspring, from John Fletcher's *The Woman's Prize; or, The Tamer Tamed* (*c.* 1611) to John Lacey's *Sauny the Scot; or, The Taming of the Shrew* (1698) and David Garrick's *Catharine and Petruchio* (1756), down to Cole Porter's *Kiss Me, Kate* (1948), Franco Zeffirelli's film starring Elizabeth Taylor and Richard Burton (1967), Gil Junger's film *10 Things I Hate About You* (1999), Amy Freed's *The Beard of Avon* (2003) and the BBC's *Shakespeare Retold* (Richards, 2005). Ultimately, the 'kind' of history that *The Shrew* tells will, like all history, depend on who tells its story, on how it is told and, in that specialized arena of historiography that has to do with theatre, on what those who perform it and those who witness its performances remember.

What happens to this brilliant, ambitious play as it criss-crosses centuries of theatrical witnessing is just one strand of its history, inseparable from and braided together with a tissue of other concerns. *The Shrew* is shot through with disguisings and 'supposings' (or confused identities), the latter idea deriving from George Gascoigne's *Supposes* (1566), which provides both an overall trope of disguise and metamorphosis and the ground-plan for the play's Bianca–Lucentio subplot (see pp. 65–9). While the writings of Ovid and John Lyly (among others) echo locally in the taming plot and the subplot, for the former, *The Shrew* also draws from a rich store of folklore materials, ballads, proverbial 'wisdom' turned into idiomatic speech, hawking manuals and the social customs and ceremonies surrounding early modern marriage. In both the subplot and the taming plot, strands of comic material are shaken and stirred together with the serious matter of marriage, the contract that grounds social life. Players and other theatre personnel, the material conditions of the Elizabethan theatre, the various companies through whose hands the play passed and the conditions of licensing: all enable and shape the play's histories. Outside the theatre are those responsible for remaking and refashioning the play, turning it into print for readers. *The Taming of the Shrew* is a product of shared performance, both in terms of the labour involved in writing and printing and in the work players do to (re)shape and (re)make that writing as performance.

## 'A KIND OF HISTORIE'

*The Taming of the Shrew* is intimately bound up with the anonymous play *The Taming of a Shrew* (Appendix 3), and existing narratives and counter-narratives about the relationship between the two continue to engender debates among textual scholars, critics and theatre historians without agreement about the degree or direction of influence joining the two. A present-day editor of *The Taming of the Shrew* is rather like a detective assigned to reopen a cold case, reassess the facts in the light of recent evidence and re-examine previous editorial scenarios. The search for a prime (or prior) suspect at the level of authorship as well as date has set up a longstanding cultural battle between 'Anon.' and Shakespeare – who may himself have been 'Anon.'

at one time, at least until Robert Greene's (and Henry Chettle's?) notorious 1592 allusion to 'an vpstart Crow, beautified with our feathers . . . [who] is in his owne conceit the onely Shake-scene in a countrey'[1] offered grounds for presuming that Shakespeare was by then known and resented as a play doctor. (With the publication of Francis Meres's comments on his comedies (*Palladis Tamia: Wit's Treasury*, 1598) and the appearance of his name on title-pages of quartos of his plays, Shakespeare's public visibility increased sharply.) If Greene's remark offers 'a stripped-down narrative in which the core of story-telling may be seen' (McMillin, *More*, 151) – at least in so far as it gestures towards textual traffic between *The True Tragedy of Richard Duke of York* (Octavo 1595) and *The Third Part of Henry the Sixth, with the death of the Duke of York* (Folio 1623) – exactly what the implications of that story-telling might be for *A Shrew* and *The Shrew* is less certain. Although the plays seem to know one another (see Appendix 4), the chain of that knowing remains intractable and cannot be precisely recovered.

A concise visual illustration of the two plays' tangled history appears on a poster for Trevor Nunn's 1967 Royal Shakespeare Company production, which reads (with Derridean crossings-out): 'RSC in The Taming of ~~the a~~ THE SHREW', the title of the play included in the 1623 First Folio. Yet this was not in fact quite the Folio's play, for this performance included *A Shrew*'s Sly 'interruptions' and closed with Christopher Sly awakening from 'the best dreame / That euer I had in my life' (*AS*, 1599–626), claiming that the play has taught him how to tame his own shrewish wife. By importing this ending to frame the taming, Nunn's production supplied what many readers and editors have assumed was missing, staging one of the most dominant theatrical formations of *The Shrew* (see pp. 82–5, 106–8). Yet if the RSC's poster not only suggests a playful indecisiveness about naming but also points to how parts of *A Shrew* have a long history of

---

1   Robert Greene, *Greene's Groatsworth of Wit* (1592), F2ᵛ.

becoming 'Shakespearean' (Marcus, *Unediting*, 101–31), especially in the theatre, early modern documents yield more complex, often contradictory stories. On the one hand, the existence of several plays based on the same narrative is consistent with the commercial strategy of playing companies, who regularly duplicated their competitors' popular offerings (Knutson, *Repertory*, 71). On the other, even though licensing authorities may have viewed a play as a title, plot and set of characters, and so 'habitually identified multiple plays on the same topic . . . as a single play and construed any revised text as part of the original work' (Marino, 'Oldcastle', 94, 104), to assume that playwrights and stage players did not discriminate between them seems not just unduly patronizing but highly doubtful. After all, playwrights and players, who held vested interests in their playbooks, found such issues significant – and so did publishers (WI).

At least up to a point, printing history distinguishes between the titles. The first mention of a *Shrew* play is a copyright entry in the Stationers' Register on 2 May 1594, for a play called '*A plesant Conceyted historie called 'the Tayminge of a shrowe*', entered to Peter Short. Existing in a single known copy (at the Huntington Library), its title-page (see p. 345) reads:

> A Pleasant Conceited Historie, called The taming of a Shrew. As it was sundry times acted by the *Right honorable the Earle of* Pembrook his seruants. Printed at London by Peter Short *and are to be sold by Cuthbert Burbie, at his* shop at the Royall Exchange. 1594.

*A Shrew* was reprinted in 1596 and re-entered in the Stationers' Register on 22 January 1607 (together with '*ROMEO and JULIETT* [and] *Loues Labour Loste*') to Nicholas Ling by a court order, with Burby's consent 'vnder his handwrytinge', and printed by Valentine Simmes. Later that year (19 November), a final entry documents a transfer of copyright for sixteen titles from Ling to John Smethwick, including *A Shrew*, '*ROMEO and JULIETT*',

'*Loues Labour Lost*' and 'a booke called HAMLETT' – the four Shakespearean titles Smethwick brought to the consortium which printed the 1623 First Folio (Greg, *Bibliography*, 1.24).

*The Taming of the Shrew* first appears in the 1623 First Folio as the eleventh play in the volume (see p. 309); it was not entered separately in the Stationers' Register. Although Smethwick's rights to *The Shrew* are not documented, it seems to have been assumed, given the entry for the First Folio made by Edward Blount and Isaac Jaggard (8 November 1623), which states that it pertained only to copies 'not formerly entred to other men', that Smethwick's rights to *A Shrew*, following its transfer to him from Nicholas Ling in 1596, also extended to *The Shrew*. Given the premise that a rewritten play with (virtually) the same title as one previously published automatically belonged to the copyright holder of the earlier text, Peter Blayney argues that *The Shrew* could not have been included in Folio without the consent of *A Shrew*'s owners ('Publication', 399; see also Greg, *Bibliography*, 1.33); Smethwick's name in Folio's colophon also suggests that his copyrights were made available to the consortium.

In 1631, Smethwick issued a quarto, printed by William Stansby, which adopted Folio's text of *The Shrew*, naming Shakespeare as its author on the title-page:

> A WITTIE AND PLEASANT COMEDIE Called *The Taming of the Shrew*. As it was acted by his Maiesties *Seruants at the* Blacke Friers *and the* Globe. *Written by* Will. Shakespearc. LONDON. Printed by *W.S.* for *John Smethwicke*, and are to be sold at his Shop in Saint *Dunstones* Churchyard vnder the Diall. 1631.

Given that *The Shrew* was performed both at Blackfriars, which the King's Men had acquired in August 1608, and at the Globe, it has been argued that the 1631 Quarto was to have been printed *c.* 1607 or 1609 but was 'stayed' by the author's intervention on behalf of himself and the company before being issued at the later date.[1] Accepting that hypothesis would suggest that '*The Taming of the Shrew* . . . by Will. Shakespeare' might have appeared in print before its publication in the 1623 Folio; however, given the lack of documentary support for a stay, it seems more reasonable to assume that the projected 1631 printing may have been simply an attempt to capitalize on Shakespeare's name.

This chronology suggests that the play available on London's bookstalls from 1594 to 1623 was *A Shrew*. Sir John Harington, who had a copy in his collection (Furnivall), writes in *The Metamorphoses of Ajax*:

> For the shrewd wife, reade the booke of taming a shrew, which hath made a number of us so perfect, that now every one can rule a shrew in our countrey, save he that hath her. But indeed there are but two good rules. One is, let them never have their willes; the other differs but a letter, let them ever have their willes, the first is the wiser, but the second is more in request, and therefore I make choice of it.
>
> (Harington, 153–4)

Harington's allusion to the proverbial 'Every man can rule a shrew but he that has her' (Dent, M106) not only marks the centrality of the shrew-figure in the early modern cultural imaginary (Boose, 'Scolding') but also suggests that a *Shrew* play (or plays) was a popular commodity. Some have cited Anthony Chute's *Beauty Dishonoured, Written Under the Title of Shore's Wife* (1593) – 'He calls his *Kate*, and she must come and kisse him', an action occurring twice in *The Shrew* though not in *A Shrew* – as proof of *The Shrew*'s priority (Moore, 55). Although Chute's allusion might derive from performance rather than print, it seems possible that 'Kate' may be cognate with 'Joan' as a generic name for any woman (especially for a servant); moreover,

---

1 Collier conjectures that the title-page was struck off subsequent to printing. Capell's copy (now in the library of Trinity College, Cambridge) is the only one with a perfect title-page (*First Folio*, vi, 2).

the assonance of the name with 'cate' (a delicacy) suggests that 'Kate' may resemble 'honey' or 'sweetie' in present-day idiom. Did the phrase 'Kiss me, Kate' circulate in the culture, perhaps even antedating both *Shrew* plays (WI; Maguire, *Names*, 124–5)?

Might *A Shrew* and *The Shrew* have existed in some form almost simultaneously? According to Richard Proudfoot, fragments of both appear in *A Knack to Know a Knave*, entered in the Stationers' Register on 7 January 1593/4, apparently following a 10 June 1592 performance – if indeed what Lord Strange's Men performed at the Rose, listed as 'ne' (new) in Henslowe's *Diary*, bore some relation to the 1594 printed text.[1] Yet neither the lines suggestive of *A Shrew* – 'Then will I haue rich Counterpoints and muske, / Calamon, and Casia, sweet smelling Amber Greece' (*Knack*, sig. F2$^r$, 1455–6; *AS*, 1296–7) – nor those evoking *The Shrew* – 'Besides a hundred Oxen fatly fed: / That euerie Winter feed within my stalles' (*Knack*, sig. D2$^{r-v}$, ll. 850–9; *TS* sig. T1$^r$, TLN 1239–40 (2.1.361–2)) – offer entirely convincing parallels; they are 'best accounted for as imitations or echoes' (*Knack*, vi). Moreover, *Knack* also echoes *A Looking Glass for London* (1594), *The Life and Death of Jack Straw* (1593–4) and *The True Tragedy of Richard III* (1594) as well as borrowing extensively from Lyly and Greene (Knutson, 'Shakespeare's', 349; Creizenach, 77, n. 4). In addition, Thomas Nashe's prefatory epistle to Robert Greene's *Menaphon* (1589) and *Menaphon* itself seem to satirize lines found in *A Shrew* but not in *The Shrew*, though the references may apply to another play (*TxC*, 110–11). Although the difficulty of tracking the symbiosis between *A Shrew* and *The Shrew* remains far from unique in the early modern theatrical marketplace, whether *Knack*'s references date to a 1592 performance or allude to whatever text lay behind the 1593/4 publication is unclear;

---

1  *Knack*, v–vii. Henslowe's *Diary* records seven performances at the Rose, on 10, 15 and 22 June 1592, 31 December 1592, 3 January 1592/3, 14 and 24 January 1593 (*Knack*, v).

neither option would require imagining the existence of *entire* texts of either *A Shrew* or *The Shrew*.

Finally, Francis Meres's *Palladis Tamia: Wit's Treasury* (entered in the Stationers' Register on 7 September 1598 and published by Cuthbert Burby, *A Shrew*'s publisher), often used to chart the chronology of Shakespeare's plays, lists neither *The Shrew* nor *A Shrew* among Shakespeare's comedies: 'his *Gentlemen of Verona*, his *Errors*, his *Loue labors lost*, his *Loue labours wonne*, his *Midsummers night dreame* & his *Merchant of Venice*' (Schoenbaum, 190). This lack has been explained either by assuming that Meres referred only to printed plays or by conjecturing that a lost printing of *The Shrew* under the title of *Loue labours wonne* existed by 1598. Although an Exeter Stationer's accounts record that such a title (never entered on the Stationer's Register) had reached print by summer 1603, since those accounts list 'taming of a shrew' as well as 'loves labor won', linking the latter to *The Shrew* seems highly unlikely. As H.R. Woudhuysen observes, although 'it was proverbial to lose one's labour, one wins a prize, not one's labour' (78–81).

If these scraps of evidence reveal gaps and uncertainties, the surviving documents of theatre history pose additional uncertainties about exactly when *A Shrew* and *The Shrew* were first performed and what playing company or companies were involved. *A Shrew*'s 1594 title-page links it to Pembroke's Men, a company with which Shakespeare may have been associated: the title-pages of two quartos without Shakespeare's name, *1 Contention* and *The True Tragedy of Richard, Duke of York* (Folio's *2* and *3 Henry VI*), as well as *Titus Andronicus*, also cite Pembroke's Men (McMillin, 'Casting'). Perhaps in part because of the plague closing London theatres and in part because of their declining fortunes in the London theatrical marketplace, Pembroke's Men 'broke and went into the country' in 1593–4 (Henslowe, 7).[1] One scenario assumes that 'broke'

---

1   Henslowe's phrase originally referred to the Queen's Men in 1593 (Gurr, *Playing*, 23, 272–3).

refers to bankruptcy (they had pawned their apparel); another that the company personnel dispersed, whether to form touring companies or to join other playing companies.[1] While relative dates remain uncertain, the mention of Pembroke's Men on *A Shrew*'s title-page, together with conjectures about the company's movements *c*. 1592–3, suggests that *A Shrew*'s initial performances probably occurred shortly before its publication on 2 May 1594. The first documentary evidence, however, comes from Henslowe's *Diary*, which lists 'the tamynge of A shrowe' as performed at Newington Butts on 11 June 1594 by an amalgamated company of players from 'my Lord Admeralle men & my Lorde chamberlen men', the latter apparently including players from Pembroke's Men. Although several documents list the principal members of the Lord Chamberlain's Men during its early years, none mentions Shakespeare, who was later associated with the company. If he was with them in 1594, perhaps working as their resident reviser, did he remake *A Shrew* 'anonymously'? Does 1594 mark a mysterious moment when *A Shrew* becomes *The Shrew*?

The desire to link Shakespeare, the Lord Chamberlain's Men and *The Shrew* has prompted commentators to invent theatre history in order to construct a master narrative of origins. Assuming that the linguistic difference between 'a' and 'the' was so minimal that substituting one for the other occurred regularly, some have argued that the Newington Butts performance was not *A Shrew* but *The Shrew*. Oliver's conjecture that the Lord Chamberlain's Men would not have performed *A Shrew* if they had had access to *The Shrew* – presumably the better play (30–2) – seems reasonable, yet no hard evidence supports it: moreover, nothing suggests that 'a company "preferred" Play A or B because it was artistically

---

1  David George argues that Pembroke's sold their playbooks in order to pay their debts; Roslyn Knutson claims that by the time of the sale, their bills were long past due and that a sale would have raised very little money ('Knows'). On Pembroke's touring, see Somerset; Knutson, 'Pembroke's'. On the company's later incarnation, see Gurr, *Playing*, 106–9, 272–3; Knutson, *Repertory*; McMillin & MacLean, 52.

superior to another available script . . . Not in 1594, anyway' (Knutson, 'Knows', 2). What can be said is that, in addition to *A Shrew*, the plays performed during June 1594 at Newington Butts by the combined company included 'andronicous' (presumably *Titus Andronicus*), *Hester and Ahasuerus* and a *Hamlet*-play. If that month also dates the beginnings of the Lord Chamberlain's Men, these entries suggest that the company began its commercial life with a repertory that included four second-hand plays, three of which later would be attributed to Shakespeare (Henslowe, 22; Knutson, *Repertory*, 59).

Since Henslowe does not list 'the tamynge of the shrowe' as 'ne', did the Newington Butts performance represent a revival? Although Henslowe's *Diary* does not record subsequent performances by the Lord Chamberlain's Men, Knutson supposes a 'continuation' from the 1594 Newington Butts run into the Lord Chamberlain's Men's 1594–5 repertory. On the evidence of a letter dated 8 October 1594 from the Lord Chamberlain to London's lord mayor asking permission for his company to perform at the Cross Keys Inn throughout the winter, it also is tempting to suppose that one play performed during that season was a *Shrew* play that opens by ousting a drunken tinker from a tavern (Chambers, *Stage*, 4.316; see also 'Dramatic records', 74; Gurr, *Playing*, 42). Since Henslowe lists 'Joronymo' on 7 January 1597 – a work which remained in repertory until October, when players from Pembroke's Men joined the company then performing at the Rose – it is possible to imagine that *The Shrew*'s allusions to *Spanish Tragedy* might be tied to revivals of that play as well as to *A Shrew*'s 1596 re-issue (Henslowe, 55–60). Subsequent reprints of *A Shrew* – recorded in the Stationers' Register on 22 January and 19 November 1607 – could also have coincided with revivals of a *Shrew* play, an hypothesis which fits with Malone's conjecture that *The Shrew* was revived in 1606–7 in conjunction with *A Shrew*'s republication, as well as supporting his guess that Nicholas Ling, who bought *A Shrew*, *Romeo and Juliet* and *Love's Labours*

*Lost* from Burby in January 1607 and who already owned a text of *Hamlet*, chose to publish only the *Shrew* play before selling all four plays to Smethwick ten months later (Knutson, *Repertory*, 11–12; Malone, 1.2, 292–3). Both publishers, having dealt previously with Shakespeare's plays, may possibly have known something about his involvement in *A Shrew*'s authorship that later historians can only guess at (McMillin & MacLean, 162).

If the narratives suggesting connections between *Shrew* plays, the 1590s repertories of Pembroke's Men and the Lord Chamberlain's Men and publishing history need to be seen as scenarios constructed around minimal evidence, later performance history moves from allusion to firmer document-ation. Chambers conjectured that lines from Samuel Rowlands's *A Whole Crew of Kind Gossips* (1609) – 'The chiefest Art I have I will bestow / About a worke cald taming of the Shrow' (E1ʳ) – may have referred to an early Jacobean revival of *The Shrew*, perhaps coinciding with performances of John Fletcher's *The Woman's Prize; or, The Tamer Tamed* (*c.* 1611), a sequel or response to *The Shrew*.[1] Although Rowlands's allusion carries little certainty, the idea of twinned performances anticipates a later instance when *The Shrew* and Fletcher's *Tamer Tamed* were performed, on 26 and 28 November 1633 respectively, for Charles I and Henrietta Maria at St James's palace. On that occasion, Sir Henry Herbert noted that *The Taming of the Shrew* was 'Likt' but *The Tamer Tamed* was 'Very well likt' – a minimalist review hinting at mid-century theatrical tastes (185). When Samuel Pepys went to the Theatre Royal thirty years later, on 9 April 1667, he saw the closest thing to Shakespeare's play currently on the boards, John Lacey's *Sauny the Scot; or, The Taming of the Shrew* (8.158, 516). Despite the incomprehensibility of Lacey's Scots accent, his *Shrew* play

1   Chambers, *Shakespeare*, 1.328. Sandra Clark dates *The Tamer Tamed* at 1604 (*Plays*, 176–7, n. 30; see also Sams, *Real*, 136–45); in 2009, the Malone Society published a facsimile of the Lambarde/Folger manuscript of *Tamer Tamed* (pressmark J.b.3); according to N.W. Bawcutt, comparisons with the 1647 Folio reveal why Henry Herbert called in and censored *Tamer Tamed* in 1633 (Herbert, 60–2).

had transformed its predecessor(s), superseded Shakespeare's play and required new licensing (Dobson, 23; Schafer, 7; see pp. 74–6).

Allusions to *Shrew* plays occur throughout the seventeenth century, but it sometimes remains unclear which *Shrew* is in question and whether such citations reference print or performance. A ballad entitled 'The Pleasant Wooing between Kit and Pegge' (STC 12725), attributed to Valentine Hamdulton (1630?), for instance, closely patterns Kate's initial encounter with Petruccio (*TS* 2.1) in the symmetry and content of its dialogue.[1] 'A new trick to tame a shrew', one section of John Taylor's *Crabtree Lectures* (1639), might refer to either *Shrew* play: when the narrator brags to his neighbour about taming his wife, the neighbour replies, 'But I pray you tell mee; did you not learne this at a play?' (214, 224–6). Christopher Sly well may have been his model, for by the mid- to late seventeenth century, he was much in evidence. A 1659 speech by Henry Cromwell alludes to the Sly frame: 'The Players have a Play, where they bring in a Tinker, and make him believe himself a Lord, and when they have satisfied their humour they made him a plain Tinker again' (Thorn-Drury, 11); twenty years later, the Prologue to Edward Ravenscroft's *The London Cuckolds* (pub. 1682) also recalls him: 'Then waking (like the Tinker in the Play) / She finds the golden Vision fled away' (Thorn-Drury, 27). If, as Montague Summers suggests, a staging lies behind Ravenscroft's reference, and if, as H.W. Crundell supposes, *The Shrew* was sometimes performed with *A Shrew*'s Sly ending (both cited in Schafer, 7), the seventeenth century's latter decades may have marked a referential shift – a moment when, in performance, parts of *A Shrew* became 'Shakespearean'. Curiously, *A Shrew* and *The Shrew* appear, at times juxtaposed,

---

1 A note in *STC* conjectures that the printer (as opposed to Henry Gosson, the seller) may have been Elizabeth Allde, who took over her husband's printing business; countering that implication, part 2 claims to be printed by W I – who could be William Jaggard (active 1594–1623) or, more likely, William Jones III (active 1601–39). Alternatively, the ballad might date to the 1620s (BRS).

in the unexpected running-titles of subsequent Folios: in the Second Folio (1632), two pages (S3$^r$, S4$^r$) have '*The Taming of a the Shrew*'; the title '*The Taming of a Shrew*' appears on nine pages (S3$^{r-v}$; T1$^{r-v}$; T3$^{r-v}$; U2$^{r-v}$; V1$^r$) of the Third Folio (1663; re-issued 1664); and in the repaginated Fourth Folio (1685), the title '*The Taming of a Shrew*' appears on facing pages (corresponding to F, TLN 197–483). By memorializing, in print, how the titles were interwoven in compositorial as well as in cultural memory, these 'mistakes' offer an uncanny premonition of future conflations – in print as well as in performance (Danks; see also pp. 116–18).

### Enter the editors

Conflating the two plays continued throughout the eighteenth century. That master narrative re-begins with Nicholas Rowe, ostensibly Shakespeare's first editor (but see Massai, *Rise*), whose 1709 (and 1714) editions of *The Shrew* (based on the Fourth Folio, 1685) imported stage directions and business from *A Shrew* that ensuing editions have fossilized. A playwright and poet laureate, Rowe seems to have relied on contemporary *Shrew* stagings – probably Lacey's *Sauny* – to authorize features of his editorial practice (see pp. 336–7). Drawing on both plays, his edition resembles modern readers' texts of *King Lear* which incorporate *The History of King Lear* (Q) and *The Tragedy of King Lear* (F). Indeed, *The Shrew* that readers encounter in most modern editions, which bears traces of *A Shrew*'s stage directions (silently attributed to Rowe himself), belongs as much to Rowe and other eighteenth-century editors as to Shakespeare (Hodgdon, 'Who'; see also Maurer). Although Alexander Pope did not believe that Shakespeare had written *A Shrew* (Preface to 1723–5 edition, B3$^v$–B4$^r$), he added most of *A Shrew*'s Sly episodes to his 1723–5 edition, making textual changes that bred textual traditions: following Pope, Lewis Theobald (1733), Thomas Hanmer (1744), William Warburton (1747), Samuel Johnson (1765) and Edward Capell (1768) drew in some or all of the Sly materials, thus tacitly accepting them as Shakespearean. In the 1747 Warburton edition, the Sly interpolations reached their height: eliminating the second and third Sly passages (*AS*, 1216–17, 1219, 1329–39), it not only added the first and fourth as well as the Sly ending (510–19, 1413–20, 1599–626), combining the two plays seamlessly into one, but also imported dialogue mentioning stage properties ('a shoulder of mutton . . . and a little vinegre to make our Deuill rore', 83–4), generated additional SDs and produced a 'new' version of *The Shrew*'s penultimate scene.

The question of attribution, however, remained troubling. Although 'Anonymous' was hardly a problematic label in the early modern theatrical marketplace (Silver), later editors and commentators attributed *A Shrew* to Marlowe, Greene, Peele and Samuel Rowley – as well as to nearly every contemporary writer save Nashe and Lyly – a situation somewhat resembling the credits for Franco Zeffirelli's 1966 film of *The Shrew*: 'Screenplay by Paul Dehn, Suso Cecchi D'Amico, and Franco Zeffirelli with acknowledgements to William Shakespeare, without whom they would have been at a loss for words' (cited in Hutcheon, 93). But from the end of the eighteenth century onwards, it became increasingly important to the textual–critical enterprise to clarify the relation between the two texts, to fix an order of priority, determine a date of composition and, with the rise of the New Bibliography, to establish, through emendation, the best text available, given a (supposedly) objective examination of the existing evidence (Maguire, *Suspect*, 21–71). Behind those issues lay questions of *A Shrew*'s authorship – and, consequently, its authority: was it merely a local habitation without a name? Or could it, as the history of overlaps, conflations and theatrical transmutations between the two *Shrew* texts suggests, merit a Shakespearean name? Beginning centuries ago and continuing to the present day, three major editorial scenarios have addressed these questions (Maguire, *Suspect*, 310; see also Morris, 12–50; Oliver, 13–57; Thompson, 9–17, 160–85; *TxC*, 109–11, 169–71).

19

1  *A Shrew*, the original anonymous play, was reworked by Shakespeare and thus constitutes a principal, even direct source for *The Shrew*. A variant might argue that, since at one point Shakespeare himself was 'anonymous', he may have authored both plays.

2  *The Shrew* is the original play, beside which *A Shrew* stands as one of the 'stolne and surreptitious copies' alluded to in the First Folio's Preface (sig. A3) – a 'bad quarto', either an adaptation of *The Shrew* or of a lost play, possibly though not necessarily Shakespearean, or a compilation drawing on both. A version of this account argues that both *A Shrew* and *The Shrew* derive from a lost Shakespearean 'original' – the *ur-Shrew* theory.

3  *A Shrew* is a memorial reconstruction – that is, it represents, or approaches, something like what may have appeared onstage – which shows evidence of 'conscious originality' (Hosley, 'Sources', 293). *A Shrew* has been considered to represent (a) a report of *The Shrew* made by members of the Queen's Men, with or without a writer's assistance (Honigmann, 'Lost'; Morris, 46); (b) a 'derivative text dependent on *The Shrew* but . . . rewritten more extensively (especially in the sub-plot) than is usually the case with memorially reconstructed texts' (Thompson, 182); or (c) a memorial reconstruction and thorough adaptation of *The Shrew* (Miller, 11).

Over time, interweaving these scenarios has created a thick palimpsest. This account offers a selective history of a complex textual debate that dates from Edmond Malone's 1790 edition which, by removing the Sly scenes, separated the two *Shrew*s that Rowe, Pope and others had joined together. In what now appears to have been a protectionist effort to save Shakespeare from what then were considered *A Shrew*'s indifferent plotting, excessive Marlovian borrowings and unsophisticated verse, Malone believed that *A Shrew* was not Shakespeare's but a source play – an assumption grounding a plausible narrative starring Shakespeare as the better playwright.[1] In 1850, however, Samuel Hickson's (limited) comparison of both texts concluded that *A Shrew* was an unworthy 'imitation' or pirated version of *The Shrew*. Some fifty years later, R. Warwick Bond stood on the uncertainty principle: calling *A Shrew*'s anonymous author an 'intermediate' or 'Marlowe-esque' adapter, Bond argued for the possibility of Shakespeare's hand in *A Shrew* (xli–xliv). By the 1920s, however, distancing *A Shrew* from *The Shrew* took firmer hold when several scholars, primarily Peter Alexander (see also Wilson, 97–126; Dam), dubbed *A Shrew* a 'bad quarto' ('*Shrew*', 614)[2] and proposed that *A Shrew*'s compiler gave up trying to follow *The Shrew*'s complicated subplot and fell back on love scenes ('Original', 114). Some, notably E.K. Chambers (*Shakespeare*, 1.372) and Leo Kirschbaum (43), dissented, but most embraced (with occasional caveats) Alexander's notion, which hardened into a master narrative. By the 1940s, a variation of the bad quarto theory, put forward by Raymond Houk and G.I. Duthie (with whom it is associated), argued that *A Shrew* derives not from F's *The Shrew* but from an early (Shakespearean) *Shrew* play with a romantic subplot more closely resembling that of *A Shrew*. This *ur-Shrew* theory provided a solution to a perceived loss of control over what was and was not Shakespearean by imagining texts that Shakespeare did not write.

As the debate over what seemed a classic instance of the chicken-and-egg dilemma oscillated between the source theory, the bad quarto theory and the *ur-Shrew* theory, by mid-century the idea began to take hold that not only did *A Shrew* fail to meet

---

1  See Boas. *A Shrew* is absent from Pollard's list of folios and quartos. The 1821 Malone–Boswell edition relegated much of *A Shrew* to notes; Steevens's final footnote in that edition explains his decision to preserve them, 'though they really compose no part of it, being not published in the folio of 1623' (5.523).

2  Blayney cites Humphrey Moseley's preface to his edition of Fletcher's plays, which states that plays were usually markedly abridged for performance, as a commonplace origin for the idea of bad quartos ('Publication', 393–4); the moment when Pembroke's Men 'broke' (1593), selling their playbooks to printers, has also supported the bad quarto theory.

the usual criteria for a bad quarto but it also, when disentangled from *The Shrew*, appeared to be a play worth considering in its own right. Although Richard Hosley considered *A Shrew* 'more original than other bad-quarto texts' ('Sources', 43; see also Schroeder), several 1980s editors – Morris (12–50), Oliver (13–57) and Thompson (9–17, 160–85) – still favoured the bad quarto theory; only Oliver (following Hibbard) leaned towards the *ur-Shrew* theory, which Wells and Taylor, putting forward a theory of internal revision in 1987, effectively wrote out of the textual debate (Wells & Taylor, 351–70). Each edition provides a detailed account of what, after nearly a century, remains an issue with no global (or local) answers. By the 1990s, Leah S. Marcus's apt assessment – that *A Shrew* constitutes an anomaly, 'too regular and original to be a "bad quarto," yet somehow too derivative and uncouth to be acceptable Shakespeare' – seems an accurate description of the *Shrew* problem – at least within mainstream twentieth-century textual studies (*Unediting*, 107). Simultaneously, however, Paul Werstine, arguing that the bad quarto theory ran counter to current ideas of early modern authorship and textual transmission, contested the idea of bad quartos, calling the label itself into question ('Narratives', 'Century'; see also Allen & Muir, xv; Greg, *Folio*, 210–16). Eliminating *A Shrew* as a bad quarto engenders a newly entangled tale: if *A Shrew* is not a bad quarto, what is it exactly?

Intent on representing *A Shrew* as independent, a viable play in its own right, Stephen Roy Miller, its most recent editor, assumed *The Shrew*'s priority but proposed variations on previous editorial scenarios (see also Honigmann, 'New', 82). Conjecturing that 'an early staging of *The Shrew* might have revealed an overly wrought play . . . [that challenged] . . . current ideas of popular comedy', Miller imagined a 'play doctor' who crafted a 'creative response' to *The Shrew* aimed at appealing to audiences mesmerized by Marlowe's sounds and sensations and engaged by Robert Greene's intricately plotted romances (10–11). Miller assumed that this play doctor toned down *The Shrew*'s subplot, generating a more conservative (and class-inflected) comedy, but considered that the Kate–Ferando material may have derived from memorial reconstruction, a view Laurie Maguire shares, though with reservations (*Suspect*, 310, 337–8). Yet imagining player-compiler-author-adapters who on the one hand were remembering bits and pieces of a play (perhaps working from actors' parts?) but on the other were also, in effect, writing (whether from scratch or returning to Gascoigne) the better part of a *new* play, seems not just overly inventive but counter-intuitive, especially to theatre historians. While scholars have little evidence with which to construct scenarios of repertory acquisition, Miller's narrative raises some questions. Did the playing company to whom his supposed adapter(s) offered *A Shrew* already own a *Shrew* play, and if so, why might that company (or another) want to acquire a duplicate play (Knutson, 'Knows')? Moreover, Miller seems to assume that early 1590s audiences had somewhat limited tastes – a notion belied by the repertories of established companies, and even that of the newly formed (1594) Lord Chamberlain's Men.

### *'Inductions dangerous': to frame or not to frame?*

Reading Shakespeare through an eighteenth-century aesthetic of classical decorum, Pope applied the label 'Induction' to *The Shrew*'s initial scenes. Turning to *A Shrew* provided the play's conclusion; moreover, Pope found the 'latter part of the last Act, manifestly better . . . clear of . . . impertinent Prolixity' (B3$^v$–B4$^r$). But what if the first scenes represent a true beginning, however liminal: would the play look different without the label? (Daniell, 23–4). While it might be tempting to remove 'Induction' altogether (Marcus, 'Editor'), the history of the term 'induction' calls that choice into question. In early modern usage, 'induction' appears to be a fluid category, applying to dramatized scenes and to prologues as well as to prologue-like initial speeches (Greenfield, esp. 97–104). Richard III's 'Plots have I laid, inductions dangerous' (1.1.32) picks up the definition (now obsolete) of 'induction' as 'the initial step in any undertaking' (*OED n.* 3c); Q and F texts of *2 Henry IV* label Rumour's prologue-like speech 'Induction' – the only time the word labels a scene before 1600 (Compositor B, who set *The Shrew*'s initial pages, also set this page of *2 Henry IV*). From 1565 to 1592, ninety per cent of printed plays had some kind of framing device, whether consisting of 'a dramatized scene "without" the play' (Greg's definition of an induction), a prologue and/or epilogue (both usually in verse) or some combination of all three. Moreover, not all plays with induction-like materials, prologues or prologue-like materials had epilogues – *1* and *2 Troublesome Reign of King John* (*c.* 1591–2) and Lyly's *Midas* (1592) are examples. Focusing only on plays for which some evidence of performance exists, Richard Hosley found that over half (26 of 45) lacked a dramatized epilogue ('Epilogue'); notoriously, too, epilogues can be both variable and detachable: that for *2 Henry IV* combines passages thought to have been spoken on three different occasions; Q and F printings of *2 Henry IV* perhaps point to performance variants. Throughout the 1590s, inductions or induction-like materials (except those in *2 Henry IV*) are not labelled as such, nor are they divided or distinguished from the rest of the text – again, with one exception, Robert Greene's *James IV* (1598), where an (unlabelled) prose induction is set apart from '*Attus primus. Scena prima.*', which begins on a new page.

Defining 'induction' as a *metadramatic* action narrows the sample even further. *A Shrew* is the first *printed* play where the induction material is neither set apart nor labelled; the second, Jonson's *Every Man Out of His Humour* (1600), contains a verse and prose induction (labelled '*Inductio, sono Secondo.*' ('second sounding')) played by characters who intervene throughout (the play also has a prologue), but since the quarto title-page notes that the play '*Contain[s] more then hath been publickely spoken or acte[d]*', these materials may or may not have been performed. Thereafter, Marston's *Antonio and Mellida* (1602) and *The Malcontent* (1604) feature more elaborate metadramatic frames: in *Antonio*, eight actors enter with 'parts in their hands: hauing cloakes cast ouer their apparell' (A3ʳ) to explain their roles; while an induction written by John Webster for a Globe performance of *The Malcontent* distinguishes the play from that acted by the Children of the Queen's Revels at Blackfriars. This set piece features John Sincler and Will Sly, who come on stage dressed as gallants and demand to see 'Harry Condell, Dick Burbage and Will Sly' (Ind.11–12): Condell, Burbage and John Lowin then appear as themselves – players in the King's Men. Since these in-jokes – Sly asking to meet himself, doffing his hat, Osric-like, to Burbage and insisting that he be seated on the stage – depend upon spectators' knowledge of the players and their previous roles, it is tempting to imagine that Will Sly once sat upon a stage in the guise of a spectator called Christopher Sly (McMillin, 'Casting', 157; Berry, 191–7; Honigmann & Brock, 80).

Although similar metadramatic material appears in Jonson's *Bartholomew Fair* (1614) and *The Magnetic Lady* (1632) and Middleton's *A Game at Chess* (1624), it also faced criticism: the prologue to Beaumont and Fletcher's *The Woman Hater* (1606–7) claims that 'Inductions are out of date, and a Prologue in Verse is as stale as a blacke Velvet Cloake, and a Bay Garland' (1–3). Something similar might be said of *The Shrew*'s induction, which has passed in and out of theatrical (as well as cinematic) fashion throughout subsequent centuries (see pp. 79–80). Were both inductions (especially dramatized material?) and prologues transforming into paratextual materials such as prefatory arguments and printers' epistles to the reader (Stern, 166)?

Given this history, neither *The Shrew* nor *A Shrew* is unusual in including dramatized induction-like materials. While *A Shrew* follows the same form as plays such as *The Rare Triumphs of Love and Fortune* (1589, ascribed to Kyd) or Kyd's *Spanish Tragedy*, which feature 'interludes' where the frame characters return as well as a dramatized epilogue, *The Shrew* appears decidedly unorthodox: not only does it have *two* fully dramatized scenes that preface the 'play proper', but Sly's role creates an expectational (and performative) excess which feeds the desire to see him return. Yet he does not. Most modern editors adopt a scenario that sees *A Shrew*'s more conventional epilogue-ending as evidence that *A Shrew* post-dates *The Shrew*; in at least one editorial narrative, desiring Sly's return equates with desiring to find Shakespeare's authorial hand. Arguing that *The Shrew* should be grouped with *The Spanish Tragedy* (1587), Peele's *Old Wives Tale* (1591–4) and Beaumont's *Knight of the Burning Pestle* (1607), Morris conjectured that *A Shrew*'s Sly interludes and epilogue, 'however garbled, are witnesses to their presence in Shakespeare's holograph' (41, 45). Wells and Taylor float a variant premise: that *The Shrew* '*as acted* . . . included a continuation or rounding-off of the Sly framework written by Shakespeare himself at a later stage of composition than that represented by the Folio text, and that the corresponding episodes in *A Shrew* derive from these' (*TxC*, 169, my emphasis).

Once imaginary performance enters the story, further questions arise. Was Sly's disappearance at the end of *The Shrew* (in which he is last heard from at 1.1.247–9) a casualty of Shakespeare's revision (Wentersdorf; Oliver, 28–9, 40–3)? Since dropping Sly decreases the number of necessary players, some have conjectured that *The Shrew* represents a text prepared for touring, a view supporting the idea that Sly himself represents the quintessential provincial spectator, nodding off at any entertainment other than a 'Christmas gambold' (Maguire, *Suspect*, 329). Yet no hard evidence suggests that provincial playgoers preferred comic foolery over other entertainments: recent work belies that notion and troubles conventional assumptions about touring (Knutson, 'Pembroke's'). Although no documentary evidence suggests that Sly might have re-appeared in another role, some late twentieth- and early twenty-first-century performances have exploited that potential (see pp. 399–400). Perhaps, as Sears Jayne suggested, *The Shrew* contains no Sly ending because such material was played *extempore*, improvised as part of the final jig; as though anticipating some later performances, he views the inner play as Sly's dream and imagines doubling Sly and Petruccio (43; see also Schafer, 97–8). In intuiting material playing conditions, such conjectures offer an instance of how playhouse circumstances, so often ignored or repressed, blossom into favour once they become convenient to shoring up a textual argument. That also pertains to accounts that marry genre and authorship. Oliver thought the Sly epilogue anticlimactic: 'One does not improve a farce by ending it with the reminder that it may have been only a farce; far better to let the audience make that judgement' (43; see also Hosley, 'Epilogue').

Not only does *The Shrew*'s lack of an epilogue prove to be the most intransigent textual question, generating no answer except from performance (see pp. 116–18), but it also impacts on the desire to recover evidence of Shakespeare's hand and fix the play's date of composition. For both, the indications are sketchy and inconclusive. Internal features such as rhyme and word usage are contradictory and inconclusive: although stylometric analysis uncovers no suggestive links between *The Shrew* and any play post-1596, metrical evidence places *The Shrew* closest to *The Comedy of Errors* and reveals rare vocabulary links with *Love's Labour's Lost* – figures that trouble an early date for *The Shrew* but would support composition by 1594–5, immediately following *A Shrew*'s publication (*TxC*, 69–107, 110–11; Miller, x; see also Mincoff). Just as fixing *A Shrew*'s date remains contingent on that assumed for Marlowe's *Doctor Faustus* (performed *c*. 1589–91?), which it quotes, *The Shrew* presumably post-dates *The Spanish Tragedy* (*c*. 1582–92, probably later rather than earlier during that span). However, performance dates for both *Doctor Faustus* and *The Spanish Tragedy* are hypothetical, and the vexed printing history of both offers minimal support for precise dating (Rasmussen, *Textual*). Although Miller conjectures between mid-1592 and spring 1594 as the likeliest range for *A Shrew*'s compilation and performance, no firm evidence supports the further inference that *A Shrew* represents either a memorial reconstruction or an adaptation of a longer play, which may or may not be Folio's *The Shrew*. Indeed, any hypothesis about possible origins troubles the idea of origins altogether. Moreover, during the last century, conjectures about *The Shrew*'s date have ranged from 1589 (Morris, 57, 65) to 1604–5 (Sams, *Real*, 136–45). If recent textual scholars and editors seem to favour the story that *The Shrew* must have existed before the closure of the theatres in January 1593 and probably existed before 1592, that narrative is haunted by the aura of memorial reconstruction as well as by vestigial assumptions about bad quartos, theories that have served to support a desire for *The Shrew*'s priority and thus to sustain myths of Shakespeare's immanent authority.

In the context of what we now believe were the conditions under which early modern plays developed and were 'open to penetration and alteration not only by Shakespeare himself and by his fellow players but also by multiple theatrical and extra-theatrical scriveners, by theatrical annotators, adapters and revisers (who might cut or add), by censors, and by compositors and proofreaders' (Werstine, 'Narratives', 86; see also 84), looking just for 'Mr Shakespeare' or fixating upon the binary of a Shakespearean or non-Shakespearean DNA may obscure, at the level of authorship and publishing practices, what Paul Werstine calls the 'close contriving' within playing companies between playwright, players, book-keepers and annotators during the composition of plays ('Close', 5; see also Masten) – and, I would add, the circumstances surrounding the movements of players and playbooks between companies. How, then, does theatrical evidence offer insights into the problematics of *The Shrew*'s origins?

### Players' names, playing companies and textual evidence

The idea that the presence of players' names has significance for dating as well as for tracking how texts might have moved among playing companies and publishers has a long history within textual studies. For *The Shrew*, that history began in 1928, when John Dover Wilson matched references to players' names, among them '*Fel.*' (William Felle), '*Curtis*' (Curtis Greville), '*Par.*' (William Parr) and '*Sincklo*' (John Sincler) (see also Bentley; Nungezer; Kathman, 'Index'). Supposing that Petruccio's servants may have used their own names and that *The Shrew*'s cast was rich in boy players, Wilson identified '*Nicke*' as Nicholas Tooley, Richard Burbage's boy (Tooley's will refers to Burbage as his former 'master') and imagined him playing both a servant and Biondello. Based on a principle of 'follow man find master', he conjectured that, if Tooley's name in *The Shrew* dates back to 1592–4 and therefore to his membership in Pembroke's Men, it is 'natural enough' that Burbage also was with Pembroke's (115–19) – an hypothesis which not only implies that Burbage may have played Petruccio but also supports an early date for *The Shrew* on the back of invented theatre history. Gurr notes, however, that the occurrence of a player's name does not necessarily mean that he belonged to the company for whom the play was written (*Stage*, 248, n. 25); moreover, Tooley would have been eight in 1591 (a bit early for him to be an apprentice), 14 in 1597 (Kathman, 'Grocers'). While Wilson's conjectures allow the desire for Shakespearean priority to drive the interpretation of evidence, theatre historians have recently brought forward evidence about *The Shrew*'s most puzzling instance of naming – the SP '*Sincklo*' (TLN 98) – that has put considerable pressure on existing textual scenarios.

'*Sincklo*' undoubtedly refers to the player John Sincler (Sinclo, Sinclair), named as a beadle in the 1600 Quarto of *2 Henry IV*, a gallant in *The Malcontent*'s induction (1603–4) and a gamekeeper in Folio *3 Henry VI* (3.1); he also appears as a 'keeper' in the plot of *The Second Seven Deadly Sins*, an anonymous work (which represents Henry VI's history in morality form) preserved in Dulwich College and long associated with Edward Alleyn (Mahood, 1; see also Gaw; Eccles). Judging from these minor roles and from the absence of his name on royal patents or in lists of principal players, Sincler was a hired man, not a sharer. In *The Shrew*, his name is bound to another role: the Lord remembers one of the Players as having acted 'a farmer's eldest son' who 'wooed the gentlewoman so well' but has forgotten his name (Ind.1.82–5); the Player responds, 'I think 'twas Soto that your honour means' (Ind.1.87). The Sincklo–Soto connection seems to be another theatrical in-joke: remembering Sincklo's performance but not his character's name glances not just at the vagaries of performance memory but also, perhaps, at the practices of provincial touring. The best 'match' referring to such a role in a *surviving* play occurs in John Fletcher's *Women Pleased* (*c*. 1619–23, a version of *The Wife of Bath's Tale*), where Soto, a trickster servant who is indeed a farmer's eldest son, attempts, while disguised (in a masque-like Morris-dancers' entry, 4.1), to woo Lady Belvidere for his master – an action which, oddly and aptly, aligns with Tranio's (more successful) wooing of Bianca on Lucentio's behalf. A 1935 performance of *The Shrew* made that connection: the Lord addressed the player who would act Tranio, 'lifting his domino to see his face' (Schafer, 88). Yet since Fletcher's play – considered to be in the King's Men's repertory (1619–23) but not published until 1627 – clearly post-dates Shakespeare's death, the Sincklo–Soto connection troubles the theory that *The Shrew* pre-dates *A Shrew*.

Several narratives aimed at preserving *The Shrew*'s priority have addressed this disparity in dates. One supposes that, as a topical allusion, the Soto reference represents a late addition dating from a revival preceding the First Folio's publication in 1623; another (originating with Wilson) conjectures that Fletcher's play was based upon an earlier lost text owned by the Chamberlain's Men – an adaptation of the fall-back position which invents *ur*-texts in order to explain puzzling evidence (or its lack) and thus to control Shakespearean authority. After all, many early modern plays have been lost (though the circumstances under which such losses may have occurred have not as yet been thoroughly explored); moreover, not only is the idea of a servant wooing a gentlewoman a frequent plot device, but one Soto may not be the only Soto (a character by that name appears in Middleton and Rowley's *The Spanish Gypsy* (1653), even later than *Women Pleased*). Recent editors have rehearsed (and sometimes combined) both scenarios. Favouring a 'lost Elizabethan play later adapted by Fletcher', Wells and Taylor imagine an *ur*-Soto and link those assumptions to a general theory of textual revision 'undertaken during composition', floating the (somewhat unlikely) idea that the Soto reference constitutes Shakespeare's 'hint', which Fletcher later expanded (*TxC*, 169–70). Eric Sams accounts for Sincklo by positing a *c*. 1604 revision ('Timing', 33–45) – a notion Wells and Taylor consider arbitrary, though they concede that Folio's induction material may date from a Jacobean revival (*TxC*, 170). Extending the range of possible dates for Shakespeare's and Fletcher's plays, Hans Walter Gabler suggests that if *The Shrew*'s date were brought forward 'by some ten years to around 1613', the original composition of *Women Pleased* might be similarly dated (Beaumont & Fletcher, 5.444–5). Other accounts have used Sincklo as evidence of Shakespeare's hand and supposed that Shakespeare wrote roles for individual players, even hired men (Morris, 6; Oliver, 4–5).

Although a minor player during his lifetime, Sincklo's posthumous career has given him a starring role in scenarios of *The Shrew*'s history. Those roles associated with Sincklo suggest that his career spanned the 1590s and the first decade of the seventeenth century; based on his supposed physical characteristics, Gurr would extend his career to *c*. 1606 (*Company*, 241). Given this range, his name could support either a pre- or post-1594 date for *The Shrew*. Evidence for an early date comes from the plot for *The Second Seven Deadly Sins*. Although that plot nowhere mentions the company which performed the play, theatre historians have assumed, based on the Dulwich connection, that it was some version of the Lord Strange's Men that included Edward Alleyn of the Admiral's Men – a scenario first put forward by F.G. Fleay (supported by Chambers and Greg), and one that has become fetishized by textual scholars as well as theatre historians (Fleay, 83; Chambers, *Stage*, 3.497; Greg, *Documents*, 12–24). Examining the traffic between playing companies in the early 1590s for evidence of casting the *Henry VI* Quartos and *A Shrew*, Scott McMillin conjectured that the players named in the *Sins* plot represented a large company which later divided and that some of the younger personnel reflected in the texts of plays performed by Pembroke's Men – among them Alexander Cooke, Henry Condell, John Holland, John Sincklo, Nicholas Tooley and perhaps Will Sly – became members of the newly formed Lord Chamberlain's Men in 1594 ('Casting', 155–9; Knutson, *Repertory*; Gurr, *Stage*, 24–8). Although Sincklo's name does not appear in any version of an existing play known to have belonged to Pembroke's, it does appear in those plays which made up the Chamberlain's Men's initial repertory – plays that historians assume were 're-wrighted' by and for that company. Not all of the players named as King's Men in Folio's list could trace their professional history back either to the *Sins* company or to Pembroke's, but it seems possible to assume that Sincler, Cooke, Sly and perhaps Tooley may have performed in both *A Shrew* and *The Shrew*.

Reconsidering the Fleay-Chambers-Greg scenario some twenty years later, McMillin suggested that the *Sins* plot belonged, not to Strange's Men in the early 1590s, but to the Lord Chamberlain's Men in the later 1590s ('Building'). More recently, David Kathman has not only questioned the provenance of the *Sins* plot (further troubling the connection to Strange's Men and Alleyn) but has also argued persuasively that the plot's list of principal players, all known to have been associated with the Chamberlain's Men from the mid to late 1590s, represents evidence best accounted for by assuming that the plot originated with the Chamberlain's Men, *c.* 1597–8 – at about the time they were first performing *The Merchant of Venice* and *1* and *2 Henry IV*; identifying 'T. Belt' as Thomas Belt, apprenticed to Heminges on 12 November 1595, offers the most persuasive bit of evidence ('Reconsidering', esp. 14–18, 25–6, 33–4). Both the Fleay-Chambers-Greg and Kathman scenarios connect a number of dots on the complicated theatrical map of the 1590s; each offers plausible accounts of the evidence.[1] Whereas the Fleay-Chambers-Greg scenario privileges an early date for *The Shrew*, Kathman's account points to a date range from after 1594 to *c*. 1604 – a span coinciding with the print documentation of Sincklo's professional history. Moreover, re-dating the *Sins* plot suggests that Francis Meres's failure to document *The Shrew*'s pre-1598 existence may not have been a mistaken omission from his (supposedly selective) list of Shakespeare's comedies.

If the document that has figured as 'proof' of Sincklo's early 1590s career post-dates 1594, then all surviving documentation associates him with the Chamberlain's Men and, later, with the King's Men. Arguing for a Sincklo–Shakespeare connection, James Marino points out that Sincklo's name appears in print only in plays 'which have somehow entered the Chamberlain's/ King's repertory from that of another company. *The Shrew* and *3 Henry VI* had been Pembroke's Men's plays before they belonged to the Chamberlain's Men; the Queen's Men's *Famous Victories of Henry V* had staged Falstaff (under his previous name, Oldcastle) and the theatrical reformation of the future *Henry V* before the *Henry IV* plays did so.' Moreover, *The Malcontent*'s Induction (where Sincklo again appears) clearly differentiates the King's Men's performance from the play formerly belonging to the Children of Blackfriars ('Anachronistic', 42). Rather than guaranteeing a pre-1594 date for *The Shrew*, he argues, Sincklo's name 'might be better construed as a sign of the Chamberlain's

---

1  Theatre historians who have questioned Kathman's work include Gurr, *Company*, 18, n. 26, and 'Work', 71–80; Manley, 'Reconsidering'; at the time of writing, Kathman plans to rebut Gurr's arguments.

Men's possession and the consolidation of their ownership' ('Anachronistic', 43; see also Marino, *Owning*).

Following Marino's logic, is Soto, then, also a sign of the King's Men's possession? Since the Sincklo–Soto connection occurs only in *The Shrew*'s Induction, perhaps their joint appearance serves to differentiate *The Shrew* from *A Shrew*. After all, if the King's Men commissioned and performed a new Induction to *The Malcontent* – claiming it as their own, apparently as revenge against the Children of Blackfriars for their theft of 'Jeronimo'[1] – it is possible to imagine that some agent or agents for that same company had a hand in *The Shrew*'s Induction, a conjecture at least as viable as assuming that a pre-existing *Women Pleased* was touched up for the 1620s. Since *The Shrew*'s publication date occurs near the end of Fletcher's career with the King's Men, it would be convenient to account him responsible. Editorial accounts, however, have tended to protect *The Shrew* from post-Shakespearean revision, preferring to attribute textual 'confusions' to carelessness during original composition, thus closing off further possibilities (Marino, 31–4, 39–40; see also *TxC*, 170). It is, however, hardly necessary to identify a 'revising hand', one need only think, as Werstine and others do, of early modern plays as being open to revising and reworking, entailing collaborations by various agents ('Close', 5; Masten). Although Marino finds it strange that such 'mistakes' (if that is what they are) went uncorrected during the years *The Shrew* remained in the Lord Chamberlain's repertory (44), that assumes that the printed play bore an equivalent relationship to the performed play. It is, of course, back-handed to argue from a later legacy, yet *The Shrew*'s performance history has consistently countered the myth of textual fidelity. Indeed, *The Shrew* offers an instance of the proposition that a performance is not a performance *of*

---

1    Knutson, 42. This may refer to *1 Jeronimo*, Q1605 ('Hieronimo in Decimosexto'). Knutson notes, 'The playlists of Richard Rogers and William Ley (1656), Edward Archer (1656), and Francis Kirkman (1661) include an item entitled "Hieronimo, both parts"' (171, n.9).

the text – neither in the early modern period nor in subsequent centuries (Gurr, 'Maximal'; Worthen).

## *Reconsidering* The Shrew

*The Shrew* is one of the most malleable early modern plays, and its textual condition is, to say the least, extremely complex. Both the Fleay-Chambers-Greg argument and Kathman's scenario play into competing accounts of the relationship between *A Shrew* and *The Shrew* as well as competing conditions of possibility for dating *The Shrew*. In reconsidering origin stories, which scenario seems most plausible? Until more information becomes available, neither the argument about *Sins*'s date nor Marino's speculation situating *The Shrew* within 'a narrative of revision driven by the needs of playing companies' has hardened into fact. All that can be said with high probability is that '[t]his text is not the product of any discrete historical moment. It was not written at one time. It is not an integral text' (Marino, 'Anachronistic', 46). Although my rehearsal of the evidence leads to arguing that the play we identify as *The Shrew* post-dates *A Shrew* and came into being after 1594, it seems neither responsible nor possible, lacking further evidence, to determine a more decisive date for *The Shrew*. What might such evidence be? While textual critics freely imagine *ur*-texts, theatre historians are considerably more circumspect. Straddling the two, my choice for such *ur*-evidence would include a full Henslowe-like account of the Lord Chamberlain's and King's Men's professional activities, including play titles, cast lists (play by play), performance dates and box-office figures. An even more extravagant fantasy would ask for photographic stills as well as audio and video records of what was spoken and seen on early modern stages.

However, considering the textual and theatrical evidence as well as the lack of information concerning early modern performances, the most conservative reading of that evidence suggests that a *Shrew* play, by whatever name, was part of the early modern repertory, moved between playing companies and was subject to changes in company personnel, practices and playing venues, both in London and on provincial tours. Shifting shape during its travels, that play remained alert and responsive to theatrical tastes, to minor revolutions in playing styles and to changing attitudes towards comedy. Last but not least, that play also exhibits shifts in conceptions of and ideologies grounding gender and sex relations: on the one hand, circulating Elizabethan notions of hierarchy within marriage; on the other, alluding to Jacobean ideologies of companionate relations between women and men. Certainly *The Shrew* shares with other plays – *Doctor Faustus*, *The Spanish Tragedy*, *Mucedorus* – an early history revealing evidence of revision, but precisely when such revision(s) occurred is difficult to determine: each of these three plays as well as a *Shrew* might be considered 'Jacobean' rather than 'Elizabethan' (Hattaway; Proudfoot).

I view the two *Shrew* plays as representing different stages of an ongoing theatrical 'commodity' that was formed at some point in the early 1590s and has been undergoing mutations ever since (Levenson, 103–4, 124–5). This edition, then, considers *A Shrew* and *The Shrew* as separate textual entities which are bound together, especially though not exclusively in theatrical practice, in an inter- or intra-textual relationship, 'a cluster or network of related texts that can be fruitfully read together and against each other as "Shakespeare"' (Marcus, *Unediting*, 124). Parallel texts, of course, could best represent such a network; an electronic environment might also include *Sauny*, *Catharine and Petruchio* and *The Tamer Tamed* – later responses to or continuations of sixteenth- and seventeeth-century *Shrew* plays.

Departing from editorial tradition which appends *A Shrew*'s Sly materials as 'additional passages' – a label admitting Sly into the conversation but holding him at arm's length – this edition reprints the complete text of *A Shrew* in facsimile as Appendix 3, followed by a summary of the similarities and differences between it and *The Shrew* (Appendix 4). Although most modern editions reference *A Shrew* in the commentary, this edition does so only infrequently. For one, scholarly editions of *A Shrew* edited by Stephen Roy Miller (1998) and co-edited by Graham Holderness and Bryan Loughrey (1992) map out the idiosyncratic relationships between the two texts, coming to slightly variant conclusions; and Alan Galey is currently working on an electronic edition ('Signal to Noise'; http://ise.uvic. ca). For another, appending *only* the Sly materials, seemingly a straightforward choice (adopted by, among others, Ard$^2$, Cam$^2$, Oxf$^1$ and Oxf), oversimplifies what is at stake. For to view *A Shrew* primarily as a way to add 'more (probable) Shakespeare' to an already (presumably) Shakespearean *The Shrew* is not only to see it as a play traditionally denied authority but also to counter current thinking about early modern compositional practices and the conditions under which plays moved between playing companies (Marcus, *Unediting*; Galey, 48). Resistant to including 'additional passages' (or spare parts) in modern editions, Alan Dessen calls the practice a 'do-it-yourself-kit' which invites readers and practitioners into a world of 'what you will' (187–8; see also Miller, 8–12).

Yet the idea of every-reader-her-or-his-own-*Shrew*-editor consorts with what I understand to be the various ways in which readers as well as theatrical practitioners, less wedded to notions of textual stability and fixedness, process plays. Moreover, in a present-day textual–critical culture which increasingly recognizes that editorial and playhouse intervention and invention may (and often do) twin one another, what gets printed and what gets performed already inhabit such a world: the sound of *A Shrew* and *The Shrew* in conversation with one another, speaking from different scripts in varied voices, has existed for some centuries, modelled in the varied textual and theatrical guises in which the play we choose to call *The Taming of the Shrew* has appeared. To list a few: Folio *The Shrew*, *The Shrew* without Sly, *The Shrew* with *A Shrew*'s Sly ending, *The*

*Shrew* with most (or all) of the Sly materials, *The Shrew* with all the Sly materials and a re-scripted 'Induction' (Alexander, 1992) and *The Shrew* with directorially or collaboratively rewritten frames (Marowitz, 1973; Bogdanov, 1978). The matter of difference(s) – textual, sexual, social, political and performative – suggests that *The Taming of the Shrew* has been and continues to be a *texte combinatoire* – a phenomenon which can be readily observed in the equally layered fabric stretching through the play's performance and critical histories (see pp. 71–131). That the practice (and theory) of change has been integral to the twinned histories of *A Shrew* and *The Shrew* since the 1590s seems particularly apt: suiting the tropes of metamorphosis and 'supposing' that trace through both texts, such playfulness remains a major hallmark of the *Shrew* complex or syndrome.

## *SHREW*-SOURCES

### *'Margery seynt John ys a shrew'*

So reads an inscription written in an early sixteenth-century hand on the preliminary flyleaves of the Ellesmere Chaucer manuscript. Although the manuscript's ownership at that time is not known, archivists speculate that Margery is most probably 'George Waldegrave's niece after her marriage to John St. John of Bledsoe, although the "Margery" signatures also might belong to her daughter Margery (d. 1562)' (Dutschke, 1.49; David, 314). Did someone, reading the Epilogue to Chaucer's *Merchant's Tale*, where the first recorded usage of 'shrew' applied to a woman appears – 'But oh hir tonge, a lobbying shrewe is she' (2428) – recognize Margery's blabbing tongue? Or, reading *The Wife of Bath's Tale*, discern her desire for 'maistrie [and] al the soveraynctee' there? (Prologue, 818). Or was this simply idle mischief? Whatever the case, English shrews existed long before Katherina Minola, even before Chaucer's not-so-good women, with whom Shakespeare was familiar (Bergeron; Thompson, *Chaucer*, 84). He might have seen shrews staged, from Noah's wife in the medieval mystery plays (Bradbrook, 134) to figures in Tudor plays such as John Heywood's *Merry Play between John John the Husband, Tyb his Wife and Sir John the Priest* (1533) and the anonymous *Tom Tyler and his Wife* (1555); he also knew of Socrates' Xanthippe, a stereotypical shrewish wife, named in Petruccio's catalogue of potential wives (1.2.68–70). He may even have remembered seeing images of marital conflict in Stratford-upon-Avon's Holy Trinity Church, where several fifteenth-century misericords depict husband- and wife-beating (White, 8–9). One shows three women's faces, the first with an oversized tongue, a second grimacing, a third with a bit in her mouth, bridled like an animal – a traditional punishment for scolds, the legal term for a woman accused of instigating domestic violence (see Fig. 1). Such images bred a legacy: John Taylor's *Crabtree Lectures* (1639) lists 'Certaine signes to know a Shrew by': 'Take heede of a sowre Lasse, whose wrinkles in her forehead comes neare her eye-browes . . . Take heede of a Hawks eye, a sharpe nose . . . Take heede of one, who hath a long white hand; for shee will doe no huswifry, for feare she should spoyle her fine fingers' (226–7).

What are the traits of the shrew, the shrewish wife? Originally, 'shrew' referred to an animal (now described as genus *Sorex*) – according to Edward Topsell, a creature with a venomous bite that 'beareth a cruell minde, desiring to hurt any thing . . . [and] feared of al' (536) – a description modified by later naturalists, who stressed the animal's aggressive behaviour and loud squeaking noise (Corbet, 106–10; Crowcroft, 20–62). Pronounced in the late medieval and early modern periods to rhyme with 'show', by the mid-thirteenth century 'shrew' had come to mean 'a wicked, evil-disposed, or malignant man', a definition which by the end of the fourteenth century had expanded to refer to the devil. In Chaucer's time, the term swerved between the genders, also denoting a 'woman given to railing or scolding'; by the sixteenth century, the latter meaning had become dominant. Yet the devilish connotation remained: derivatives such as 'shrewd'

1  Fifteenth-century misericord of scolds; Holy Trinity Church, Stratford-upon-Avon

or 'shrewish' – terms evoked throughout Shakespeare's play – originally meant 'rascally' or 'villainous', and the verbal form 'to shrew' meant 'to curse' (as in 'beshrew'). How, then, does this shrew–scold nexus work to define 'Katherina Minola, / Renowned in Padua for her scolding tongue' (1.2.98–9)?

Early on, Gremio thinks her 'too rough for me' (1.1.55), a 'fiend of hell' who 'may go to the devil's dam' (1.1.88, 105); Hortensio dubs her 'Katherine the Curst' (1.2.126); (before meeting her) Petruccio calls her as 'an irksome brawling scold' (1.2.186), later likening her to a stinging wasp (2.1.214); and Tranio speaks of her 'chattering tongue' (4.2.59). Noisy, irascible and aggressive, Katherina is defined by sound – countering the play's other music? – and by behaviour evoking a range of gendered references. Yet many derogatory terms applied to her – 'devil', 'froward', 'shrew', 'scold', 'wildcat' – come from hearsay: is 'shrew' just (theatrical) disguise? Notably, the play offers no *explicit* motivation for her shrewishness. Beatrice, in

Shakespeare's later *Much Ado About Nothing*, shares her shrewd speech (Benedick calls her 'my Lady Tongue', 2.1.252), yet is considered witty – not quite shrew, not quite not shrew. But Katherina is not all shrew all the time, for although her quick tongue characterizes her, once she arrives at Petruccio's house, she says little until, at the play's end, she talks – and talks and talks.

## Cultural horizons

Although it has been customary to confine discussion primarily to *literary* sources and/or analogues, the notion of 'source' has expanded considerably in recent years. Shakespeare's plays constitute elaborate memory systems: there seems to be no end to uncovering possible recollections – some tantalizingly apt, others accidental and of minor substantive significance – of printed or written materials (including his own work), structures, tropes and verbal echoes that travel between plays. Always, however, it is as useful to note where Shakespeare reorders or counters materials as when he follows them rigorously. When, in 1981, Brian Morris wrote, 'The real sources of *The Taming of the Shrew* rise in Shakespeare's experience of Warwickshire, of the town houses of mercantile London, of the taverns and streets, and of all sorts and conditions of women, their expectations, frustrations, conquests and surrenders' (69), he marked a paradigm shift in the critical climate that considers plays in relation to a wider range of written as well as visual materials, materials that reveal the plays' connections to elite as well as popular discourses, social customs and ways of seeing and speaking in the early modern period. Although I consider literary sources later, I turn, first, to those materials that, however tangentially, shaped the cultural codings of the shrew-taming narrative that lies at the play's centre. Given recent interest in recuperating early modern women's histories, noting how the play negotiates between the shrew-taming tradition and early modern women's lived experience becomes crucial both to

41

conjecturing how *The Shrew* may have worked on its first readers and spectators and to understanding how it works on present-day readers and spectators.

'Every man can rule a shrew but he that has her' went just one of the many proverbial taunts that demonized the shrew (or shrewish wife), positioning her 'as the test obstacle essential for positing the culture's terms for male dominance not only over women but over other men as well' (Dent, M106; Boose, 'Husbandry', 214). Her figure's centrality emerges in a boisterous shrew-taming tradition that includes proverbs, jokes, ballads (see Wiltenburg) and oral folklore as well as plays. All presume a hierarchical domestic order where women are subordinate to men, an order overturned by the shrew and righted by her tamer and that 'is organized around a double standard for domestic violence' (Dolan, 'Household', 206–7; Fletcher, 21) – that is, just as tradition represents the shrewish woman as engendering domestic violence, so it assumes that her behaviour justifies her husband in reasserting his mastery through reciprocal violence.

Perhaps the most famous example of this tradition, a lengthy ballad entitled 'A Merry Jest of a Shrewd and Curst Wife, Lapped in Morel's Skin, for Her Good Behaviour' (*c.* 1550) centres, like *The Shrew*, on a family with two sisters: the younger her father's favourite, pursued by suitors; the elder shrewish and considered unmarriageable – at least until a gullible suitor motivated by financial gain appears, at which point the story details this couple's courtship and marriage (Hazlitt, 4.415–48; Dolan, *Shrew*, 257–88; see also Hosley, 'Sources', 289). Unlike *The Shrew*, 'Merry Jest' features a shrewish mother who has trained her firstborn daughter to seek mastery over her husband (Woodbridge, 203; Mikesell, 150–2). While wrestling with her in the nuptial bed, the husband hits his wife, promising not to do so again as long as she agrees 'in all sports to abide my will' (l. 516), but when she refuses to perform household duties, speaks lewdly and beats him 'as [she] had been a man' (l. 710), he retaliates by beating her bared back with rods, drawing blood; then, having killed black Morel, his blind, lame horse, and salted the hide, he wraps her raw and bleeding body in it, threatening to keep her there. Only when she promises 'to do nothing that may pretend / To displease you' (ll. 1005–6) does he release her – which leads to a communal feast where she performs like a proper hostess and agrees to obey her husband 'in presence of people, and eke alone' (l. 1010). The tale concludes with an *envoi* resembling Petruccio's 'He that knows better how to tame a shrew, / Now let him speak' (4.1.199–200), also hinting at the play's final wager (5.2).

Aside from briefly exploring the mother's and eldest daughter's agency as 'women on top', 'Merry Jest' sides with the husband, affirming his dominance in the gender hierarchy and suggesting that violence 'seems to be a masculine prerogative that shrews usurp; when they insist on wearing the breeches, they also seize the rod' (Dolan, 'Household', 207). In contrast to beating one's wife and wrapping her bloody body in a salted horse-hide (disciplinary actions 'real' women might not survive), Petruccio's tactics – withholding food, sleep and new clothes – indeed seem designed to 'kill [or tame] a wife with kindness'. Distinct differences pertain, however, between representations of (supposedly) comic shrew-taming and the more complicated history of domestic violence in the early modern period. Wife-beating was not illegal, but male violence was increasingly being questioned and monitored; conduct books and sermons advised that good household government should not involve physical strife. Despite those who argued that 'euen blows', when provoked or deserved, 'may well stand with the dearest kindnesses of matrimony', such conduct was increasingly viewed as incompatible with ideals of companionate marriage (Whately, 108; see also Bryson).

Even stronger structural resemblances to the taming plot surface in oral folklore traditions. Jan Harold Brunvand's exhaustive study of Tale Type 901 (as classified by Aarne–Thompson), a narrative that occurs throughout the Indo-European world, presents a compelling map of *The Shrew*'s plot events as well as a comprehensive catalogue of local detail. Surveying 35 literary versions and 383 oral versions representing thirty countries or national groups, Brunvand identified a wide range of 'motif-complexes' and 'free-floating narrative elements' common to such tales:

- The taming is a play within a play or story within a story (Ind.1–2).
- The shrew is usually the elder of two daughters (1.1) and is identified with the devil.
- The father, a wealthy man, warns the prospective suitor and offers a large dowry (1.2; 2.1).
- The suitor claims that he can tame the shrew and lays a bet that he can do so (1.2; 2.1; 5.2).
- At the wedding, the groom arrives late, is dressed poorly and rides an old nag; he has a falcon; he behaves boorishly and refuses to stay before beginning the trip home, during which bride and groom ride on one horse or the husband rides while the wife walks (3.2; 4.1).
- The taming occurs at the couple's home or on a trip to visit the wife's parents. The husband beats his servants and/or punishes his dog for a supposed fault as a warning to his wife (4.1).
- There is a school where husbands learn shrew-taming (4.2.55).
- Taming tactics include depriving the wife of food and getting her to agree to her husband's absurd statements: several tales include the husband calling the sun the moon and a man a woman (4.3; 4.5).
- The test of the wife's obedience takes place after dinner at the father-in-law's house; during the test, the wife looks over some new clothes; the reward is a prize offered by the father-in-law (4.3; 5.2).

- The wife comes at once when called and is polite to all; she throws her cap on the floor and steps on it, pulls off her husband's boots to clean them, places her hand under his foot, brings other wives in and lectures them, kisses her husband (5.2).
- Others concede that the shrew's husband has won the victory (5.2).[1]

Claiming that the basic tale reaches back to early medieval exemplum literature, Brunvand makes a strong case that Shakespeare adapted traditional English versions to suit the conditions of his stage (*Oral*, 122–6, 185–6); treating the shrew-taming tradition as culminating in Shakespeare, he argues that *The Shrew* remains closer to oral traditions than *A Shrew*, which Thompson views as evidence of *The Shrew*'s priority (13). Although no definite proof suggests that oral tradition offered the primary model for Shakespeare, the discovery of variant shrew-taming tales throughout Northern Europe and the British Isles suggests that early modern audiences might have been pre-conditioned to enjoy the taming spectacle (Oliver, xviii).

Several folk-tale motifs do not appear in *The Shrew*: in one variant of the tale's conclusion, the couple reach an understanding that the husband will in future give back whatever treatment she gives him – a shred of equality or a hint that the shrew-wife is never well and truly tamed? And just as Petruccio does not physically abuse Katherina, there is no mention of killing or torturing recalcitrant animals as an object lesson, nor does he break her arm or require that she carry the horse's saddle. Nonetheless, ballads, verse tales and folk literature sought, as Joy Wiltenburg observes, to pressure women to avoid rebellion in favour of submissiveness (125). Arguably, even those who complied with the culture's prescriptions for wifely behaviour may have seen their own rebellious desires mirrored in these tales:

---

1 Brunvand, *Oral*, esp. 171–211, 217–22, 250–1, 257–67. Hosley ('Sources', 302) mentions a wager episode in *The Book of the Knight of La Tour-Landry* (1372–3, translated into English by Caxton, 1484).

if so, they also must have been aware of the legal consequences (see Hunt, esp. 27; Wiltenburg, 128) and of the formal public punishments for scolds. Men as well as women were either put in the stocks (see Fig. 2), incarcerated in the town 'cage', or, occasionally, carted and paraded round the town (Ingram, 68). Such communal rituals, in which neighbours mocked offensive behaviour, were festive occasions and, like ballads and folk-tales, often ended with public atonement or reconciliation: like many plays, where a final speech attempts to impose a (rhetorical) order, these staged lessons in the proprieties of gender relations offered one model for healing the social fabric.

By the early seventeenth century, cucking – binding the offender to a stool and dunking her in water – had become the typical shaming ritual and may have been responsible in part for establishing 'scold' as a legal category adjudicated by secular courts (Ingram, 59; Underdown). Behaviour that could result

*Published Oct.' 1.'1796 by D. Akenhead & Sons, Newcastle upon Tyne*

2   Scold's bridle-cage and barrel stocks, from Ralph Gardiner, *England's Grievance Discovered* (1655)

in cucking included: 'brawling or abuse, indiscriminate slander, tale-bearing, the stirring up of strife, the deliberate sowing of discord between neighbours, and . . . the pursuit of quarrels through needless lawsuits and legal chicanery' (Ingram, 68), but the most common offence, detailed in the ballad 'The Cucking of a Scold' (*c.* 1615–30), was transgressive and insulting speech. One cucked scold, according to *The Anatomy of a Woman's Tongue* (1638), though unable to talk while under water, 'spoke' her resistance with a time-honoured gesture, signifying that although 'She had no power, but yet she had a will, / That, if she could, she would have scolded still' (*Tongue*, 4.278); a similar story occurs in a collection of scolds' speeches entitled *A Curtain Lecture* (1637, attributed to Thomas Heywood, and cited in Dolan, *Shrew*, 325–6). Less dangerous than cucking, which risked drowning, was the practice, followed primarily in the north of England, of bridling scolds, a punishment which addressed verbal belligerence at the source; made of metal, bridles either covered the mouth or inserted a prong, or brank (sometimes sharp or tooth-edged), to hold down the tongue (see Fig. 2; Boose, 'Scolding'; Ingram, 58, 62).

If making the offending woman a public spectacle seems an excessive reaction to insulting speech, it is important to remember that flaunting, rebellious behaviour jeopardized the communal order for men and women alike. As historians and critics suggest, these tales reinforce patriarchal prerogatives by objectifying women, yet it is also wise to remember that early modern patriarchy, as constructed by modern interpreters, was hardly a monolithic entity: women sought accommodations that would 'afford them some measure of autonomy and space, and a limited degree of authority' (Capp, 25). Although both folklore and social custom represent the unruly woman primarily as a collection of faults – laziness, vanity, gossiping, consorting with other men, husband-beating – as in 'The Cruel Shrew, or the Patient Man's Woe' (*c.* 1600–50, cited in Dolan, *Shrew*, 247–50) – nowhere is shrewish behaviour endorsed or lionized. Although popular and semi-official discourses aimed at subordinating scolds authorize silencing and shaming rituals, the equally 'unruly' male tongues that spoke out against women railed just as loudly and insistently – and had more legitimate cultural power. Ironically, those voices gave the shrew or scold her own form of cultural power within a curious double standard in which men and women acted out forms of aggression within a coded domestic terrain in a self-sustaining, never-ending cycle.

In that *The Shrew* partially subscribes to folk-tale traditions but skirts historical practices such as cucking and bridling, both elements figure as deep historical though dramatically invisible background, evidence of how early modern women were wrapped in stereotypes as strait-jacketing as the punishments worked out on them. In the tales as in the drama, inversion is the name of the game that makes domestic violence funny – a tradition that survives in farce, puppet shows and film and television situation comedy, where the 'woman on top', however badly treated, is usually accorded remarkable powers of recovery (Shershow, 161–82; Hodgdon, 'Bound', 24–5). Yet if opting for the festive comic perspective endorsing heterosexual marriage neglects the very real lived differences in early modern husbands' and wives' access to socio-economic power, in the theatre, farce – if indeed *The Shrew* can be considered one – always plays at deadly, intensely serious games.

### Taming domestic violence

In contrast to the vulgarity of oral tradition and the cruelty of public punishments for talking 'big', Shakespeare's play differs markedly from that of its 'sister-plays', *A Shrew* and Fletcher's *Tamer Tamed*, in the level of physical violence it stages and that to which it alludes. While *A Shrew*'s Ferando beats his servants in front of Kate, who then hits his servant, and *Tamer Tamed* explicitly invokes wife-beating, *The Shrew* invites a more historically situated reading than that which views Petruccio as 'performing shrewishness' – showing Katherina to herself, as in a mirror. As conduct literature preached against violence as a means of resolving domestic discord, violence between husband and wife became redirected towards more acceptable, subordinate, targets – servants and social inferiors (Dolan, *Marriage*, 120–7; Dolan, 'Household', 208–17; see also Dolan, 'Plot', 324; Burnett). Petruccio wrings Grumio's ears for misunderstanding and failing to obey him (1.2); cuffs the priest; throws winesops at the sexton (3.2); beats Grumio because Kate's horse stumbled; either kicks, strikes and throws food at his servants or threatens to do so (4.1). Both at the wedding and at Petruccio's house, Katherina responds as though the violence is aimed at and threatening to her. As Lady Mary Chudleigh's poem 'To the Ladies' put it, 'Wife and Servant are the same, / But only differ in the name' (ll. 1–2).[1] A rhetorician adept at 'rope tricks', Petruccio dominates by using words as weapons, but he does not attempt to punish Katherina's 'railing'; rather, he seems intrigued by her – 'Now, by the world, it is a lusty wench; / I love her ten times more than e'er I did. / O, how I long to have some chat with her' (2.1.159–61) – an attitude placing her within the tradition of 'spirited English lasses' and resonating with the proverbial 'better a shrew than a sheep' (Tilley, S412, S414, S415; Brown, 118–19, 178–217). Moreover, any potentially violent impulses Petruccio harbours get worked out not on Katherina's body, as in folk-tales, but on her clothes – and are displaced further down the social scale when Grumio threatens his subordinate, the lowly Tailor (4.3).

Yet *The Shrew* does offer evidence of Katherina's domineering disposition: she threatens Hortensio with a three-legged stool and breaks a lute over Hortensio–Licio's head; and she ties up and strikes Bianca and strikes Petruccio (2.1) – aligning her with folk-tale shrews. Later, having learned the appropriate codes of

---

1   One of the Folger Library's First Folios (copy 23) bears the bookplate of William Brocket (1719–91), of the Middle Temple, London, and Spains Hall in Essex. His unmarried aunt Elizabeth Brocket (1681–1759) signed her name at the top of the recto of one of the front flyleaves, and on the facing verso page inscribed Chudleigh's twenty-four-line poem. She signed her name three more times as Elizabeth Brockett on the next flyleaf, with three dates, 1695, 1711 and 1712 (GZ).

domestic violence, Kate mimics Petruccio and beats Grumio for refusing her food – actions sanctioned by her authority within the household and considered 'chastisement' necessary for maintaining domestic order, 'agreeable to Gods will, [as] is euident out of the Prouerbs' (Dod & Cleaver, sig. D4$^v$). *The Shrew*, then, dramatizes a shift from 'Kate the Curst' – constructed as refusing and abusing authority – to a Katherina who learns from Petruccio how to remodel her speech and actions in accordance with the authority marriage confers on her (Boose, 'Husbandry'; Kahn, 108; Burt, 299, 302). By the play's final scene, she calls the Widow to account and '[s]winge[s]' Bianca and the Widow 'soundly forth unto their husbands' (5.2.110): both have become acceptable targets. But it is not through physical violence that Katherina's 'domineering' becomes apparent but through her final speech – the longest (and most controversial) in the play. Given that she responds to Petruccio's command to instruct the 'froward' Bianca and Widow on their place within the marital hierarchy, it is hardly surprising that her language encompasses an inherited discourse expressing the culture's ideologies. Copious, filled with *sententiae*, her speech is didactic but also affective, designed, like its precedents, to instruct and to move, effecting a metamorphosis upon both speaker and listeners (Ong, *Rhetoric*, 25, 29–30; see also *2H4* 2.3.9–46). Nor is it surprising that this speech accounts for *The Shrew*'s central place in social histories of early modern England and histories of marriage (Underdown, 117; Fletcher, 114; Dolan, *Marriage*, 120–7).

Commentators have identified verbal parallels with two of Erasmus' Colloquies and with two works by Juan Vives, *The Office and Duty of an Husband* (trans. Thomas Paynell, 1553) and *A Very Fruitful and Pleasant Book Called the Instruction of a Christian Woman* (trans. Richard Hyrde, 1529) – texts that echo the idea of women's dependence on men for food, shelter and comfort (Hosley, 'Sources', 299–302; see also Muir, 20–1). In his colloquy *Senatulus*, Erasmus, adopting a female persona, speaks of men's 'Maintenance for their Families', 'scamper[ing] thro all the Parts of the Earth by Land and Sea . . . while we sit at home in Safety' (cited in Thompson, 14) – language resembling Katherina's claim that a husband 'cares for thee / And for thy maintenance; commits his body / To painful labour both by sea and land . . . / Whilst thou liest warm at home, secure and safe' (5.2.153–7). Although the colloquy was not translated until 1725 – and although Petruccio has not been travelling but has been busy at home, running his 'taming school' – the parallel remains striking, and Shakespeare might have known it since Erasmus' *Colloquies* were part of the curriculum at the King's New School at Stratford-upon-Avon, which he probably attended. As part of this training, a student learned (and performed) such texts, uttering 'the dialogue liuely' as if he 'were the person which did speake' – that is, he played at 'becoming' a woman, a skill as pertinent to a playwright as to a boy actor performing the 'woman's part' (see Baldwin, 1.491–2, 2.193–4; Rutter, 'Learning'). Another text, the anonymous *Frederyke of Jennen* (*c.* 1560), included in Captain Cox's collection of popular literature and one source for *Cymbeline*'s wager, contains an even more pertinent analogue in a passage spoken by the misogynistic John of Florence: 'And we labour dayly both in wynde and in raine and put often our liues in ieopardy and in auenture on the sea for to fynde them withal & our wyues syt at home and make good chere with other good felowes, & geue the parte of the money that we get' (sig. A3ᵛ, cited in Bullough, 8.65; VW).

Yet in terms of influence on plot and verbal detail, several other texts prove even more significant. The *Book of Common Prayer* of 1559, recording Anglican liturgies and prayers, maps a physical conception of marriage based on obedience – 'Wilt thou obey him and serve him, love, honor, and keep him' – and on 'knitting them together' (292, 296), echoing the notion that man and woman originally shared the same flesh and implying that, following their vows, man and wife (again) become one flesh. The *Book of Common Prayer* also requires that 'after the Gospel shall be said a sermon' (a procedure instituted by Edward VI) or that the minister read passages entailing the duties of husbands towards their wives, and wives toward their husbands: 'Ye husbands . . . [give] honor unto the wife as unto the weaker vessel (1 Pet. 3) . . . Ye wives submit yourselves unto your own husbands, as it is convenient in the Lord (Col. 3)' (297–8). Just as details of Katherina's speech seem tailored to this text, the *Book of Common Prayer* also supports Petruccio's control over what Katherina may or may not wear as well as his ideas of proper apparel as 'honest mean habiliments' (4.3.169–73): 'let [the wives' apparel] not be outward, with broided hair and trimming about with gold, [or] in putting on of gorgeous apparel' (298–9; see also 1 Peter, 3.5). (It seems uncannily apt that *The Shrew* features a tailor.) Similar ideas appear in the *Homily of the State of Matrimony*, printed in *The Second Tome of Homilies* (*Homilies*, sigs Gg3ᵛ–Hh4ᵛ), a collection of sermons by dignitaries of the Anglican church, compiled under Bishop John Jewel's editorship, which was available in all churches and easily consulted (Klein). Since regular church attendance was obligatory (those who refused could be fined or imprisoned), most English subjects would probably have heard the *Homily of the State of Matrimony* or an equivalent: many ministers drew from the sermons available in the *Homilies* or spoke the one given in the *Book of Common Prayer*. Circulating an *ideologically* dominant view of marriage (one not necessarily adhered to in practice; see Dolan, *Shrew*, 171–3),[1] the *Homily* represents marriage as an 'honourable and comfortable' condition but also warns that each spouse's 'desire to rule' (sig. Gg4ʳ) – the Wife of Bath's 'maistrie' – presented a danger, one pertinent to *The Shrew*. And as the *Homily* prescribes the duties of husbands and wives to each other, it speaks with a forked tongue, advising husbands not to beat their wives while offering abused wives 'a great reward' from God for patiently enduring their suffering (sig. Gg6ᵛ).

1   *An Homily against Disobedience and Wilful Rebellion* (*Homilies*, sigs Ll4ʳ–Pp6ʳ), reiterating the importance of obedience to civil authorities and representing rebellion, whether against God's ordinances or human laws, as the most dangerous violation of all God's commandments, also echoes in Katherina's final speech (5.2.142–51, 179–80).

Two sections of the *Homily* seem especially attuned to *The Shrew*'s concern with prescribing conduct that will ensure wifely obedience and maintain domestic concord. Drawing primarily from 1 Peter, 3, the *Homily* tells husbands to be 'the leader and authour of loue' and to 'vse measurableness and not tyranny', yielding at times to the woman, for 'honest natures wil sooner be reteyned to do their duetie, rather by gentle wordes, then by stripes' (sig. Gg5ʳ). The *Homily* is more explicit, however, concerning the wife's duties:

> Ye wiues, be ye in subiection to obey your owne husband . . . [T]hem must they obey, and cease from commanding, and performe subiection. For this surely doth nourishe concorde very muche . . . But on the contrary parte, when the wiues be stubburne, froward, and malepert, their husbandes are compelled therby to abhorre and flee from their own houses
>
> (sigs Gg5ᵛ, Hh1ʳ)

Both the *Book of Common Prayer* and the *Homily of the State of Matrimony* define and value marriage as a social contract. So does *The Shrew*. But as it so happens, Katherina's speech ventriloquizing the culture's prerogatives is out of place. Katherina's and Petruccio's wedding is not staged but reported by Gremio as a 'mad marriage' (3.2.181). However much his account departs from any expectation of what a wedding should be, the prescribed sermon is that ceremony's most significant omission (Jeaffreson, 262–4; Hodgdon, 'Bride-ing', 75–6). Although the *Homily* accords Petruccio, as husband, the ideological upper hand, *The Shrew* breaks apart the narrative order of a sacrament to put the last word(s) on scriptural matters into a woman's mouth – and then, shrewdly, gives her even more to say. Just as the wedding substitutes a Petruccian taming regime for church ritual (jamming the two together in a radical rewriting), the sermon is not only delayed but doubly displaced, occurring at the play's close and – in an equally radical rewriting – spoken not by a male priest and not in church but by Katherina, *ex cathedra*, at Bianca's wedding feast. In speaking thus, she – or, on the early modern stage, he as she – invades the domain of masculine biblical interpretation by preaching – a potentially transgressive act associated with Lollardy.[1] Although the convention of an all-male stage may have suppressed potential objections to giving a woman the authority to preach, quoting St Paul would hardly have raised many eyebrows. Nonetheless, the association with preaching not only enhances the social and theatrical power accorded to Katherina, but also suits the shrew figure's outspokenness. Exactly how *The Shrew* invites readers and spectators to value the marriages it dramatizes remains somewhat ambiguous, though the conclusion suggests that Katherina's and Petruccio's 'mad' match wins out – 'We three are married, but you two are sped' (5.2.191). But is this because Kate has become 'conformable' to the (official) ideology of wifely obedience, or does their relationship edge towards an early modern model of a (more) modern mutuality? Characteristically, Shakespeare refuses to say. Nor does studying historical materials provide any definitive answer. Given the imaginative range Katherina's sermon evokes, her words cannot be enclosed entirely within their early modern historical moment: the questions of and about marriage which *The Shrew* raises open the play out to its audiences, inviting their responses.

### Taming matters

In negotiating between comic shrew-taming traditions and socio-historical contexts, *The Shrew* walks a fine line, setting up double terms for reading – and playing. That also pertains to the dominant source for the taming narrative. Although verbal detail in the play circulates animal metaphors evoking folk-tale

---

1   Lollardy held that all faithful persons were effectively 'good priests', and was often associated with women preaching. Women do preach in medieval verse drama (e.g. the Digby *Mary Magdalene* (in David Bevington, ed., *Medieval Drama* (Boston, 1975), ll. 1481–1526)), but a difficult distinction pertains between preaching and teaching (see Blamires).

origins, the strategies Petruccio adopts, rather than aligning Katherina with her animal counterpart – a small, squeaking rodent – or with the bridled scold paraded through the streets like a horse, identify her with a haggard, or wild female hawk. His scheme of 'watching' her – that is, keeping her awake – and starving her reproduces methods minutely described in early modern falconry manuals on taming, and designed to train the bird to answer to the falconer's commands, to know and come to her keeper's call. As with the play's staging of physical violence, these references also engage with a deeply gendered history.

Half a century after Shakespeare's play, 'watching' was practised on those accused of witchcraft, predominantly women, with the aim of getting them to confess – leading to hanging if the confession came (see Hopkins, sig. B1$^r$; Ady, 99–100, 105–6; see also Schuler; Clark, *Demons*). However similar they might appear, 'watching' a 'hag' and 'watching' a 'haggard' were poles apart: watching a witch came from the legal prosecution of witches; watching a hawk from sport. Yet whether practices dealing with suspected witches were aimed at subordinating strong and 'naturally' rebellious women or those marked as supernaturally 'other', both watching procedures involved breaking a wild spirit (Hartwig; Roberts). Two works on falconry are especially pertinent: George Turberville's *The Book of Falconry or Hawking; For the Only Delight and Pleasure of All Noblemen and Gentlemen* (1575, 1611) and Simon Latham's *Latham's Falconry, or The Falcon's Lure and Cure* (four editions, 1614–58). Turberville served as Queen Elizabeth's ambassador to the Emperor of Russia; Latham, a professional falconer, had trained under the grandson of Elizabeth's 'grand falconer' and was an officer under the master of the hawks (Dolan, *Shrew*, 305). Focusing on the male falcon, the 'tassell gentle', Turberville's work is as much a self-fashioning manual that praises the sport's social and homosocial virtues as it is about hawks and hawking. When the Lord's servants convince

Sly that he is not a tinker but a gentleman, their references to hawks and hounds align with Turberville's notion of sport as asserting gentlemanliness and social status. Latham, however, speaks of the more 'deserving' female haggard who 'preys for herself' (3–8). There is more than one 'haggard' in *The Shrew*. Hortensio calls Bianca 'this proud disdainful haggard' (4.2.39); that neither he nor Lucentio can tame her while Petruccio seems successful not only differentiates the men but also becomes a means for Petruccio to win the final sporting wager. *The Shrew*'s vocabulary of falconry is shared among men but closed to women; in other *Shrew* plays the 'manning of the haggard' is also something that women do to men. In Garrick's *Catharine and Petruchio* (1756), Catharine vows to 'make her husband stoop unto her lure' (1.279); and *Tamer Tamed*'s Maria calls herself a 'free Haggard . . . [who will] look out ev'ry pleasure . . . till her pitch command / What she desires' (1.2.150–6).

As Latham explains it, taming a hawk is not a one-way street, for it requires that the falconer suffer the same hardships as the bird – going without sleep, watching for at least three nights or until the bird stops her 'bating' – beating her wings in order to free herself from the jesses restraining her legs (8). If falconry suggests the strategies of Petruccio's 'taming school' (see Taylor, *Divers Crabtree Lectures*, 224–6), it also maps out an intimate relationship between man and bird which mimics Petruccio's 'kindness' as he plays tassell gentle, 'naturall and chiefest companion' to Katherina's haggard (Latham, 5; Ranald, *Social*, 28). Not only does the falconer speak a language of love, but Latham advises him to stroke the bird gently with a feather and to 'lure her vsing your voice, with a bitte or two of meate bestowed on her . . . for that wil make her eager, and to loue your voice, because shee sees nothing to crosse that humor in her' (10). Even more specific to *The Shrew*, however, is the link between food and obedience: as with Katherina, it is the hawk's stomach that 'keepes her in subiection to the man' (10–11).

Arguing that 'only the kindness of the keeper and the consequent gratitude or indebtedness of the bird can keep it under control', Margaret Loftus Ranald sees reciprocity and equality in the relationship comparable to that between Katherina and Petruccio (*Social*, 120). Dolan, however, sees little if any equality, but suggests that the bond between falconer and hawk, in paralleling the marital bond, offers a positive role model for monogamous marriage (*Shrew*, 306–8; see Fig. 3). Although both positions seem viable, neither is prescriptive; most significantly, Latham's treatise and *The Shrew* weave

3    A gentleman taming his falcon, from George Turberville, *The Book of Falconry or Hawking* (1611)

taming and the performance of obedience together: when the haggard (or wife) is wild, she is one thing; once tamed, quite another.

## Local colourings

*The Shrew*'s first instance of 'appropriate' marital relations is a theatrical fantasy – Sly's 'madam wife', played by Bartholomew, the Lord's page, represents Shakespeare's addition to a folk-tale widespread throughout Europe and the near Middle East. Its best-known form, identified in Aarne–Thompson's *The Types of the Folktale* as 'The Man who thinks he has been in Heaven' (Type 1531; see also Types 1313*, 1526), where a sleeper, or drunken man, awaking to find himself finely dressed, is duped into believing that he is a lord, occurs in *The Arabian Nights*. Although the stories comprising *The Arabian Nights* probably originated in the thirteenth century (or earlier) in Arabo-Byzantine materials that travelled from the Eastern Empire to the West, they were not collected until the eighteenth century.[1] No printed version of the dreamer story pre-dates Shakespeare except Heuterus' *De Rebus Burgundicis* (1584), but that was not translated from Latin into French until *c*. 1600 (by Simon Goulart) and did not appear in English until Edward Grimeston's 1607 translation, where the story becomes a moral fable.[2] In Grimeston's retelling, Philip the Good, Duke of Burgundy, while attending the marriage of Eleonora, sister to the King of Portugal, disguises himself, walks about the town, finds a drunken 'Artisan' in the street and has him carried to his palace, dressed in fine clothes, waited on, taken hunting and hawking and entertained with 'a pleasant Comedie', then returned to the street.

1   Chaucer's knowledge of the 'matter of Araby', evident in *The Squire's Tale*, probably came from French romances (Metlitzki, 140–1, 159–61, 241–3; see also Lynch).
2   See Bullough, 1.109–10. A similar story appeared in Richard Barckley's *A Discourse on the Felicity of Man* (1598), 24. Thomas Warton mentions seeing, in the library of William Collins of Colchester, a black-letter collection of short comic stories, 'sett forth by maister Richard Edwardes mayster of her maiesties reuels' (3.293), of which this story was one; that book, however, has disappeared.

The parallels between this story and both *Shrew*s' Sly materials seem temptingly close, but whether Shakespeare knew the tale remains uncertain. However, ballads such as 'The Waking Man's Dream' and 'The Frolicsome Duke, or the Tinker's Good Fortune' (Morris, 77) rehearse the tale, and though their printed versions also post-date the play, that does not preclude the tale's oral circulation within the period. In addition, Baskervill mentions a ballad, 'Alas the poor tinker' (1591), and a jig, 'A pleasant jig between a tinker and a clown', as well as Jan van Arp's 'Singhende Klucht, van Droncke Goosen' ('A singing lament for drunkards'; Amsterdam, 1639), in which a tinker, thrown out of a tavern, is left to sleep on the cold ground (315). The latter may be a direct echo: Helmer Jon Helmers's study of Dutch adaptations of early modern English plays cites Abraham Sybant's play *De Drolle Bruyloft* (*The Mad Wedding*), published in 1654, as 'after Shakespeare's *The Taming of the Shrew*'.[1]

Commentators also have proposed sources or analogues for later incidents in *The Shrew*. According to Morris, a story somewhat resembling Petruccio's anger at the tailor for making Kate's gown with fantastical, highly fashionable sleeves (4.3) appears in Gerard Legh's *Accidence of Armory* (1562). Sir Philip Caulthorp of Norwich (living in the reign of Henry VII) commissions his tailor to make a gown from fine French tawny. Seeing the material, a shoemaker asks for a similarly styled gown, but when Sir Philip discovers the second gown is for a mere shoemaker, he orders his own to be 'made as full of cuts as thy sheres can make it' – and so the tailor slashes the sleeves of the second. When the shoemaker berates the tailor, 'I have done nothing quoth the Tailor, but that you bade mee, for as sir Philip Caltrops is, even so have I made yours' (Hosley, 'Sources', 302). Although folk-tale

---

1  Helmers also mentions two anonymous 'farcelets' called *Pots van Kees Krollen* (*Kees Krollen's Trick*; Leiden, 1649) and Melchior Fockens's more elaborate *Klucht van Dronkken Hansje* (*The Farce of Drunken Hansie*; 1657); since the former has stage directions resembling those in *The Shrew*, Helmers conjectures that the writer was influenced by visiting English players.

tradition includes stories about tailors (Aarne–Thompson Types 1096, 1574–1574C, 1631, 1640), Morris remains unconvinced that this tale was available to Shakespeare. Yet it is intriguing that both Legh's story and *The Shrew*, where the tailor scene hammers home Petruccio's authority over subordinates, concern class relations; given his desire for a coat of arms, had Shakespeare read Legh's volume? Another item, from *El Conde Lucanor* (*The Book of Count Lucanor*), a collection of stories made by Don Juan Manuel, Infante of Castile (1335–47), also constitutes a deep analogue: in a tale paralleling the moments when Katherina agrees to call the sun the moon and Vincentio a 'Young budding virgin' (4.5.38), Vascuñana, to prove her obedience, agrees with her husband Don Alvar that a herd of cows is a herd of mares (and vice versa) and that a river is flowing backwards to its source. Folk-tale or/and oral tradition may lie behind both tales: given the broad reach of analogues and anecdotes, there is no definitive answer to what Shakespeare knew and how he knew it (Hosley, 'Sources', 302; Brunvand, 'Folktale', 349–50).

More generally, *The Shrew* seems alert to a range of folk customs associated with courtship. When Katherina complains to her father, 'I must dance barefoot on [Bianca's] wedding day / And, for your love to her, lead apes in hell' (2.1.33–4), her reference to an old wives' tale underlines 'the folkloristic nature of [her] position' (Thompson, 89). And Petruccio's mention of throwing himself 'into this maze' (1.2.54) refers to an Elizabethan dance pattern (Baskervill, 193–4, 214; West, 65–73); claiming that 'wealth is burden [refrain] of my wooing dance' (1.2.67), he evokes the proverbial 'Love is potent but money is omnipotent' marking the mercenary 'Smithfield match', in which the prime negotiator was called a cattle dealer.[1] Later, Petruccio's 'every

---

1  See Jeaffreson, 1.309. Arguably, Bianca's marriage might also be called a 'Smithfield match', but, unlike Katherina's, hers is a clandestine marriage, for which there were heavy fines (Holt, 23); in *The Shrew*, however, both fathers' pardons excuse any transgression. Despite the custom of arranged marriage, particularly among the gentry, *Tell-Troth's New Year's Gift* (1593) denounces constrained marriages as against God's word, especially when marriage functioned as a business deal (A3ʳ–A4ᵛ).

day I cannot come to woo' (2.1.114) echoes the sixteenth-century ballad, 'The Wooing of John and Joan'; 'We will be married o'Sunday' (2.1.328) alludes to several popular ballads, including one sung in Nicholas Udall's *Ralph Roister Doister* (*c.* 1550); and 'Where is the life that late I led' (4.1.126) also apparently derives from a now-lost ballad. Thompson notes that these references to country practices suggest class origins at odds with Paduan bourgeois culture (13), yet such rituals surrounding weddings may have crossed class boundaries. When, about to spirit Kate away, Petruccio instructs the company to 'revel and domineer, / Carouse full measure to her maidenhead, / Be mad and merry' (3.2.225–7), his words align with opinions concerning the 'barbarous customs' and 'public and disorderly banquets' marring the 'great and serious matter' of marriage (Erasmus, *Guide to Christian Matrimony*, cited in Coulton, 439–40). Henry Bullinger, for instance, strongly disapproved of dancing on such occasions: 'Then there is such a lyftinge up and discoueringe of damsels clothes and of other wemens apparel, that a man might thinke, all these dauncers had cast all shame behinde them' (*Christian State of Matrimony*, cited in Jeaffreson, 1.24).

*The Shrew* also appears unusually attuned to proverbs, some of which, such as 'Women are always desirous of sovereignty' (Dent, W697), lie just beneath the surface, implicit in the taming plot. Shakespeare is clearly indebted to Lyly, whose *Euphues, The Anatomy of Wit* (1578) created a fashion for proverbs in polite conversation, but this does not mean that Lyly was entirely responsible for Shakespeare's usage, for many of Lyly's metaphors and similes were already proverbial coin before he used them in *Euphues* (Tilley, *Lore*, 47–8). A partial list includes: 'Let the world slip' (Ind.2.138); 'Haply to wive and thrive' (1.2.55; *Euph.*, 1. 454); 'Old maids lead apes in hell' (2.1.34; *Euph.* 1. 60); 'To take one napping' (4.2.46; *Euph.* 1. 72); others, such as 'Hap what hap may' (4.4.105) and 'Better once than never' (5.1.141), appear in George Pettie's collection of stories, *The Petite Palace of Pettie his Pleasure* (1576). Although proverbs sound like (and indeed are) clichés, they may well have sounded different to early modern ears, for Renaissance rhetoricians advocated their use as a form of received wisdom. Henry Peacham, in *The Garden of Eloquence* (1593), calls them 'amongst all the excellent formes of speech . . . none other more brief, more significant, more euident or more excellent, than apt Prouerbs' (15). It would be wrong to consider proverbs as 'low' speech, for in the period, common idiom and proverbial lore were thought no less substantive than fine sayings, or *sententiae*: proverbs especially were considered to be inventive and to have aesthetic value in terms of developing and amplifying arguments, for persuasion and as an important type of proof, appealing to emotion (Wilson, *Art*, 143, 149; Peacham, 36). Providing language that sharpened exchange, proverbs not only offered means of self-assertion and a storehouse of authorities but also 'charactered' the speaker. When Hortensio and Gremio discuss finding a suitor for Katherina so that they will again 'have access to our fair mistress and be happy rivals in Bianca's love' (1.1.105–44), both speakers rely on idiom as fact or generalized wisdom to express power relations within their social roles, to evoke precedents for decision-making and action – and also to say something without saying something and so to remain civil to one another (Sinfield, 78; Magnusson).

### *Shakespeare's reading*

So far, *The Shrew*'s sources inhabit a region governed by Touchstone's 'if', a territory comprised of folklore, socio-historical documents and cultural contexts. When commentators imagine the range of Shakespeare's reading, they include the tale of Patient Griselda, recounted by Boccaccio in the last story of the last day of *The Decameron*, retold in Petrarch's *A Fable of Wifely Obedience and Devotion* (*c*. 1373) (upon which Chaucer relied for *The Clerk's Tale*), in John Phillips's moral interlude *The Comedy of Patient and Meek Griselda* (*c*. 1559) and in Thomas Dekker, Henry Chettle and William Haughton's

*Patient Griselda*, performed by the Admiral's Men in 1600 (Chambers, *Stage*, 2.292; Henslowe, 125, 128–30).[1] In this extremely popular story, Griselda, a peasant, weds Walter, a prince – a marriage made possible only after he has stripped her naked, reclothing her as a suitable bride; later, he strips away her rich gown and sends her home in her shift. The anti-type of the shrew-wife, Griselda is so overly obedient that she also agrees to her children's (supposed) deaths at the hands of her husband; when she is recalled to the palace to witness Walter's (supposed) remarriage, he acknowledges that his behaviour was a pretence to try her virtue, praises her patience and honours her as his true wife and his children's mother (Bond, xxviii–xxix, liii; on the 'Griselda complex', see Brown, 178–217). Not only does Petruccio allude to Griselda's story when describing Katherina ('For patience she will prove a second Grissel', 2.1.298), but several of Walter's remarks – 'her beautie shin[es] through those weedes'; 'such poore abilments'; 'the sun will break through slender clouds and vertue shine in base array' – closely echo his philosophy of clothing (4.3.168–73). Moreover, in Dekker's play, Griselda's shift, which she wore when first meeting Walter, is hung up on the stage and repeatedly referred to – a material mnemonic signifying the distance between her origins and those of her husband (Jones & Stallybrass, 13, 220–4). While Dekker's Griselda is doubly stripped, doubly divested of finery, Katherina is only teased with (and refused) a rich gown. These allusions invite thinking of *The Shrew*'s Katherina as framed between Patient Griselda and *Tamer Tamed*'s feisty Maria, who provides Petruccio with demands countering his past treatment of Kate, including 'Liberty and clothes' (2.5.136).

## Supposings and metamorphoses

If Patient Griselda offers a counter touchstone for Katherina and the taming plot, for the story of Bianca and her suitors as

1 Henslowe's *Diary* (19 July 1602) mentions another Dekker play (now lost), 'a comody called a medyson for a curste wiffe', perhaps part of the *Shrew*-play tradition (204).

well as for tropes governing the entire play, the idea of 'source' not only retains its literary meaning but also pertains more directly to Shakespeare's reading. All commentators agree that he drew on George Gascoigne's *Supposes*, described on its title-page as 'a Comedie written in the Italian tongue by Ariosto and Englished by George Gascoygne of Grayes Inne Esquire, and there presented 1566' and representing a translation of Ariosto's *Gli Suppositi*, performed at Ferrara (1509) and at the Vatican (1519). Considered the first English drama in prose (pre-dating John Lyly's plays by nearly twenty years), Gascoigne's play appeared in two collections to which Shakespeare could have had access: *The Posies of George Gascoigne Esquire. Corrected, Perfected and Augmented by the Author* (1575) and *The Whole Works of G. Gascoigne* (1587). It appears to have been fairly well known, at least among educated, fashionable young men at a time when everything Italian – forks and fashions, poetry and classical Roman comedy – was the rage: Chambers records a probable private performance in 1582 at Trinity College, Oxford, where, apparently, the play was 'handeled in y$^c$ haul [hall] indifferently' (*Stage*, 3.321). According to Gascoigne's Prologue, a 'Suppose' is 'but a mistaking or imagination of one thing for another. For you shall see the master supposed for the servant, the servant for the master: the freeman for a slave, and the bondslave for a freeman: the stranger for a well-known friend, and the familiar for a stranger' (14–19; see also Morris, 78–80). Twenty-four false suppositions or mistaken identities occur, each signalled by a marginal note; following classical models by Plautus and Terence, *Supposes* observes the unities of time and place, but its extremely complex plot makes *The Shrew*'s confusions of masters and servants, true and false fathers, shrews and non-shrews pale by comparison.[1]

---

1 On Plautus and Terence, see Hosley, 'Formal'; for a plot summary, see Seronsy, esp. 16. Bond catalogues Gascoigne's departures from Ariosto (*Early*, lv–lxiii); see also Morris, 82–3; Oliver, 45–8; Hutson, 209–23.

In a partial catalogue of *The Shrew*'s 'supposes' (whether that entails assuming another's identity – Lucentio and Tranio exchanging places (1.1.205–8), Lucentio inventing a life-threatening situation that explains his disguise to Biondello (1.1.226–30) or Tranio inventing a deceptive disguise for the Merchant (4.2.80–6)), Lucentio's 'While counterfeit supposes bleared thine eyne' (5.1.108) is the most obvious homage to *Supposes*. Yet Shakespeare also borrows two names, 'Petrucio' and 'Lytio' (Hortensio's *alter ego*), both servants; and the scene unravelling the subplot's 'mistakings' (5.1) contains structural and verbal echoes of Gascoigne. The real Vincentio knocking at his son's lodging and false Vincentio looking out of the window also seem to be direct borrowings, as does the Vincentio–Biondello exchange – 'What, have you forgot me?' 'Forgot you? No sir. I could not forget you, for I never saw you before in all my life' – and Vincentio's 'Tell me, thou villain, where is my son Lucentio?' (5.1.43–6, 81–2). More significant, however, are Shakespeare's departures from Gascoigne. *The Shrew* not only discards the unities but also dramatizes events that *Supposes* reports, such as Erostrato's (Lucentio's) arrival and sudden infatuation with Polynesta (Bianca) and his account of meeting the Sienese (the Merchant/falseVincentio), which grounds Biondello's description of spying the 'ancient angel coming down the hill' (*Supposes*, 1.1; *TS* 4.2.62). Changes in characterization also occur. Unlike Erostrato, Lucentio is not a fortune-seeker (a trait transferred to Petruccio), nor does he gain access to Bianca through a nurse (reminiscent of *Romeo and Juliet*) or seduce (and impregnate) her; rather, *The Shrew*'s Bianca is a virginal heroine whose romance and clandestine marriage are set off against those of Katherina. One striking difference between the two plays is that, in contrast to Gascoigne's Polynesta, Bianca's dutiful submission to her father and her 'pretty' manners offer a pre-psychological explanation for Katherina's shrewish behaviour. Although exchanging one persona or 'suppose' for another is not confined to the subplot alone, Bianca's role constitutes a major link between the wooing plots: by controlling her competing suitors (3.2, 4.2), she gains a mastery over them that results in her own metamorphosis, countering Katherina's, from 'good girl' to proto-shrew. Yet despite such frank borrowings or adaptive strategies, there are interpretive stakes in assuming that Gascoigne's play grounds – and explains – *The Shrew*'s whirligig of shifting identities. On the one hand, doing so supports the age-old binary between reality and illusion, leading to the notion that, since play-acted fictions are not truth but lies, *The Shrew* can be dismissed as trivial fun – just entertainment, a good night out. On the other, *The Shrew* plays with perhaps the most fundamental question of human – and theatrical – consciousness: 'Who am I?' The viewpoints are interrelated, and the play repeatedly see-saws between them, beginning with 'Am not I Christopher Sly . . . ?' (Ind. 2.16–17). Indeed, the idea of 'supposings', social as well as theatrical, first arises in Sly's transformation from a tinker to a lord, within a context drawn from Ovid's *Metamorphoses*.

Readily available (and widely read) in Arthur Golding's 1567 translation, *Metamorphoses* constituted a rich storehouse of classical mythology. Part of the Humanist inheritance essential to the period, Ovid, in Latin and English, was schoolroom reading for Shakespeare and his contemporaries, and perhaps the first 'sexual' or 'seduction' text schoolboys encountered (Baldwin, 1.511–13, 2.417–55; Ong, *Rhetoric*; Rutter, 'Learning'). A belief in myths and classical texts as vestiges of the much-admired classical Golden Age characterized early modern thought and pervades Elizabethan and Jacobean texts, providing *exempla* for nearly every occasion. Marlowe drew heavily from Ovid, as did Lyly, whose *Euphues* makes use of Ovid in incidental allusions and occasional passages of sustained imitation. Like Marlowe and Lyly, Ovid himself was an inveterate borrower, and Shakespeare follows that tradition in his use of Ovidian texts (Bate, 32–6).

Ovid's mythological world first appears when the Lord's servants tempt Sly with 'wanton pictures' (Ind.1.46) – 'Adonis painted by a running brook . . . Cytherea all in sedges hid . . . Io as she was a maid . . . Daphne roaming through a thorny wood . . . / And at that sight shall sad Apollo weep, / So workmanly the blood and tears are drawn' (Ind.2.48–58). 'Almost a programme for Shakespeare's subsequent Ovidianism', this passage catches up *The Merry Wives of Windsor*, *Titus Andronicus*, *A Midsummer Night's Dream* and *Lucrece*: as the figures seem to lift off the paintings and move, 'we are', writes Bate, 'on the road to Shakespeare's most astonishing Ovidian coup, Hermione's statue, so "lively painted" that it comes to life' (119–20). Ovid's tales do not, as a rule, have happy endings, yet in *The Shrew* (and other Shakespearean comedies), although violence may threaten, its dangers undergo their own metamorphoses to bring about the weddings and reunions associated with comic closure. Even such reassuring signs of fulfilment, however, can seem unstable: rather than all ending well all the time, it's often a case of all ending more or less well.

Announcing that he has come to Padua to study 'Virtue and . . . philosophy' (1.1.18), Lucentio seems bent on pursuing a Euphuistic regime similar to the course of study proposed to the young men at Navarre's court (*LLL*), yet it takes hardly any time – some twenty lines and the sight of Bianca – to shatter his resolve. Warning against such restrictive study – 'Let's be no stoics nor no stocks, I pray, / Or so devote to Aristotle's checks / As Ovid be an outcast quite abjured' (1.1.31–3) – Tranio brushes away *Euphues* – a moral fable teaching the young man to reject erotic desire and return to the academy – and Aristotle's *Ethics* to opt for Ovid. Advising Lucentio to pursue pleasure rather than profit and to 'study what you most affect' (1.1.40) suggests that he knows Lucentio's desires well enough to direct his master not to Ovid's *Metamorphoses* but to his *Ars Amatoria*, *The Art of Love*. Moments later, the Lucentio–Tranio switch of identities operates like an Ovidian see-saw: the master achieves a descending metamorphosis, from gentleman to schoolmaster, while the servant assumes nobler status. Yet despite his 'declension', Lucentio wins his love, while Tranio, even when elevated to gentility, briefly competes for Bianca's hand but loses out (see Gilbert, 323–8). Finally, as identities are revealed (5.1), Ovid's *Metamorphoses* intertwines with *Ars Amatoria* when Bianca and Lucentio explain to Vincentio that 'Cambio is changed into Lucentio' and that 'Love wrought these miracles' (5.1.113–14).

*The Shrew*'s most extended reference to Ovid's writings occurs in the Latin lesson (3.1.28–43, 50–3).[1] The primary text here, however, is neither the *Metamorphoses* nor *Ars Amatoria* but the *Heroides* (1.33–4). Since the matter comes from a letter written by Penelope, complaining of being plagued by unwelcome suitors (precisely Bianca's situation), the passage bears a contextual irony. However, she turns Lucentio's citation to her advantage, re-'constering' the Latin to express her own desires and preferences. As several have noted, she is no 'breeching scholar' but an accomplished student of Ovidian erotic arts – perhaps even over-mastering Lucentio: she withholds ('presume not') and gives ('despair not'), anticipating Beatrice in her mastery of word-play as well as looking ahead to Cressida. And when Lucentio reassures her that he is a gentleman, not a schoolmaster, with an allusion that ratifies his lineage – 'Aeacides / Was Ajax, called so from his grandfather' (50–1) – her half-mocking response – 'I must believe my master; else . . . / I should be arguing still upon that doubt' (52–3) – suggests that she may have heard the 'Englished' Latin names as an 'ass' and 'a jakes' (Parker, 'Construing'; see also Maurer & Gaines; Bate, 127). When Lucentio comes again to the schoolroom, he avoids 'construing' altogether and instead

---

1  Bond (72) cites two other echoes: Middleton's *The Witch* (2.2) and Nashe's *Four Letters Confuted* (1592); Hosley conjectures that R.W.'s *The Three Lords and Three Ladies of London* (*c.* 1589, published 1590) affords an analogue ('Sources', 306). Touches of 'schoolmasterly' Latin appear in *LLL* (4.2); *MW* also stages a Latin lesson (4.1).

is well armed with Ovid's *Ars Amatoria* – or, rather, with its title, for its 'wanton matter' was not thought appropriate either for Elizabethan grammar school students or for young ladies. Although a tradition of allegorizing and moralizing Ovid's explicitly erotic tales extended into the late seventeenth century, Shakespeare in all probability went directly to Ovid rather than to contemporary mythographies (Bate, 32). In any case, Lucentio does not read out passages, though the (knowing) Bianca clearly understands his reference (see Fig. 4). Did she, perhaps, learn the (playful) arts of seduction not just from Ovid but also from Shakespeare's immensely popular, equally erotic, *Venus and Adonis?*

Although most of *The Shrew*'s Ovidian allusions are confined to the initial Sly scenes and the Bianca–Lucentio plot, Bate suggests that Petruccio bases his taming on a precept from *Ars Amatoria*: '*Vim licet appelles: grata est vis ista puellis*' – 'You may use what is termed force: girls like you to use it' (1.673). But this seems a 'fatal misreading', for the precept illustrates the art of winning a lover (Book 1), not the art of keeping her (Book 2), which advises the 'tamer' to remain in charge by not crossing the woman – 'And let her count'nance be to thine a law, / To keep thy actions and thy looks in awe' (Heywood's 1625 translation of 2.201–2; see also Bate, 128–9). Might Katherina have read those sections of Ovid? Perhaps. Although Bianca apparently desires Lucentio to be 'master' (at least of the art of love), what she says is undercut by her apparent 'reversion' – call it an Ovidian declension? – into shrew-dom at the play's close. Nonetheless, these references to *Ars Amatoria* encapsulate both couples' attitudes to the negotiations over 'mastery' that occur within marriage (Bate, 124–5; see also Roberts). But whether either pair has achieved some reciprocal or mutual understanding takes place in an Ovidian space beyond the stage.

If, as sometimes occurs in the theatre, *A Shrew*'s Sly ending is imported to close off the performance, Bianca and

4   Lucentio (Anthony Higgins) wooing Bianca (Zoë Wanamaker), directed by
Michael Bogdanov for the Royal Shakespeare Company, 1978

Lucentio's story drops away, for Sly's selective memory focuses
only on Petruccio's taming of Kate, which he reads as a dream.
Yet, although Sly may think he can become a shrew-tamer, the
Tapster's warning – 'your wife will course you for dreming
here tonight' (*AS*, 1618) – suggests that once he gets home,
he may expect a beating from his wife. Attaching the Sly
ending diminishes the idea of metamorphosis governing Kate's
taming. If *The Shrew* was merely, as Puck says, a 'weak and idle
theme, / No more yielding but a dream' (*MND* 5.1.421–2), it
has no bearing on the waking world, whether that of official
discourses on marital duties, that of folk-tale and ballad, where
shrews live on and on, or that of early modern (or twenty-first-
century) mercantile society, where ambitious young men (and
women) marry for money. Yet if the Sly ending is discarded,

the play may become, not perhaps, as Hamlet maintains, 'the thing / Wherein I'll catch the conscience of the King' (2.2.539–40), but a thing that catches the consciousness of a culture four centuries away, where Petruccio's 'taming school' and the metamorphosis it seems to achieve could be seen as an idealized pedagogical exercise – an Ovidian–Shakespearean 'commodity'.

## PERFORMANCE AND CRITICAL HISTORIES

This chronicle of *The Shrew*'s afterlives interweaves critical with theatrical, cinematic and televisual performances, where, re-textualized and re-textured by players' bodies and voices, *The Shrew* appears in its most material form. Although performed most frequently in England, the United States, Canada and Australia, *The Shrew* has also travelled to stages in many other countries, including France, Germany, the Czech Republic, the Soviet Union/Russian Federation, Turkey, Denmark, Japan, China and India. Taking a slice through deep *Shrew*-histories, my account focuses on English, American and Canadian performances – those occurring in the English-speaking West. One trajectory explores how *The Shrew*'s generic indecisiveness (see pp. 3–6) becomes even more kaleidoscopic, taking form as farce, romantic comedy, black comedy, satire, problem play, male fantasy, macho history, women's history or any combination of these all at once; another traces several pressure points, among them the fortunes of Christopher Sly, Petruccio and Katherina Minola and the play's ending, especially Katherina's notorious final speech. Although the story begins chronologically, it is neither a strictly linear history nor a tale of progress, but recounts an ongoing conversation between theatrical and critical cultures.

Since my own theatre-going figures in this story, I give more attention to *The Shrew*'s most recent fortunes than to its distant past. My experience of *The Shrew* in performance is framed by two RSC productions, Michael Bogdanov's (1978) and Gregory Doran's (2003), the latter played in tandem – to my knowledge for the first time since the seventeenth century – with Fletcher's *Tamer Tamed*. Bogdanov's production marked a high moment of synergy between theatrical and critical cultures – less a direct dialogue than a continuing conversation across spaces – in which *The Shrew* assumed a heavy burden of socio-historical responsibility. During the ensuing decades, the play became highly over-invested real estate, a property without boundary markers, a test site for examining the abrasive relations among early modern contexts and contemporary feminisms and post-feminisms. Yet even before Doran's staging – in which the play underwent another generic shift, returning to laughter – critical and theatrical performances were beginning to tell *Shrew*-stories different from those understanding it as a dark tale of domestic violence centred on a woman's ruthless subjection.

## *First beginners*

*The Shrew* opens by calling attention to plays, players and playing in gags that book-end Shakespeare's play between the 1590s and the early decade(s) of the seventeenth century, offering tantalizing hints about its first performances (see pp. 1–3, 72–3); nothing more, however, is known. Yet just as it is possible to fantasize an early modern cast of known players, it is also possible to imagine, with Lesley Wade Soule, that Petruccio's and Katherina's roles were played by master and apprentice, and that audiences might have seen in their relationship Petruccio not only courting and subduing a fictive shrew but also taming and training a miscreant boy player, the pair collaborating in a 'duet of comic combat – [aimed at] achieving and demonstrating a successful theatrical partnership as both characters and players'. Moving through several acting tutorials towards the boy player's impersonation of a gentlewoman (cued by his performance of femininity as Sly's 'wife'), the play comes 'full circle to rest its vitality on the skill of the performer, the actor's physical presence and performative display – notions that *The Shrew*'s canny theatricality serves well' (Soule, 173, 178–9; see also Bradbrook, 134).

Soule's conjectures leap across time, anticipating subsequent theatrical and critical history. From these beginnings, *The Shrew* soon fell into parts: not only did the Sly scenes become a disposable commodity, but with the appearance of John Fletcher's *The Woman's Prize; or, The Tamer Tamed* (*c.* 1611), which reverses *The Shrew*'s terms to regenerate Petruchio as a 'new man' and lovable husband, *The Shrew* claimed the honour of being one among several Shakespearean plays[1] to provoke 'a theatrical "reply" in his own lifetime' (Thompson, 17–18). Katherina the shrew has died but is not forgotten: remembering her makes Petruchio 'start in's sleep, cry for cudgels, / And hide his breeches out of fear her ghost / Should walk, and wear 'em yet' (1.1.34–6). Moreover, Petruchio's taming fame becomes a public lie: his new wife, the supposedly mild Maria, turns out to be another Kate: taking on '*Petruchio Furioso*' like a mask, she re-performs his behaviour and insists on remaining a 'free haggard' unless he meets her conditions – liberty and clothes, horses and hawks, a remodelled house and gardens. In a version of *Lysistrata*'s sex-strike plot, she barricades herself in a bedroom on their wedding night with her cousin Biancha who, as commander-in-chief of what becomes a Monstrous Regiment of Women, extends Maria's personal rebellion into principles for resisting patriarchal power. The subplot, involving a romantic heroine, Maria's younger sister Livia, and two suitors – Moroso, a wealthy old man approved by her father, and Rowland, whom Livia loves – recirculates *The*

---

1 The anonymous *Thomas of Woodstock* (1591–5) might be considered a reply to *Richard II*; *Sir John Oldcastle* (1600, also anonymous) to the *Henry IV* plays and *Henry V*; conversely, *As You Like It* replies to the Chettle/Munday *Huntingdon* plays (1601), as does *Henry VIII* to Samuel Rowley's *When You See Me You Know Me* (1605) (RP).

*Shrew*'s bride-bargaining over Bianca, but with a difference, for Livia claims, 'no man shall make use of me; / My beauty was born free, and free I'll give it / To him that loves not buys me' (1.2.37–9).

While *The Shrew*'s Petruccio rules the stage, *Tamer Tamed* cabins, cribs and confines him, echoing *The Shrew*'s taming tactics in a spatial register: he moves from the main stage to the locked house and later, pretending death, to a coffin. In contrast, women claim the full stage – most spectacularly when, led by a tanner's wife (a vestige of the nightmare folk-tale shrew-figure), they join in a charivari, beating out their defiance with tools of the wife's trade (see Fig. 5). However, their subversive proto-feminist collective is absorbed in a celebratory finale which rewrites but also echoes *The Shrew*'s close.[1] Promising no more tricks, Maria vows to love and serve Petruchio, who claims to be reborn; in a Rosalind-like epilogue, Maria speaks for the play as 'being aptly meant / To teach both sexes due equality; / And, as they stand bound, to love mutually' (Ep.6–8). In reimagining marriage as a companionate undertaking, valuing women's sexual desires and domestic pleasures, and even destabilizing if not erasing 'shrew', *Tamer Tamed*'s critique of *The Shrew*'s marital politics sets the ongoing debate on the role and status of women firmly on the early modern public stage (Smith, 'Response'; Crocker).

It was, however, a momentary interruption, for masculine control resurfaced in John Lacey's *Sauny the Scot: or, The Taming of the Shrew* (performed 1667; pub. 1698). Mimicking *Tamer Tamed*, *Sauny* transfers Shakespeare's Italianate comedy to London and, like many Restoration plays, sets up a dialogue between life and the stage, mentioning London locales and touching on topical events and issues. Although *Sauny*'s concluding couplet – 'I've *Tam'd the Shrew*, but will not be asham'd / If next you see the very *Tamer Tam'd*' (5.1.435–6)

---

1    *Tamer Tamed* also echoes other Shakespearean plays, among them *Henry V*, *Troilus and Cressida*, *Much Ado*, *Othello*, *King Lear* and *Antony and Cleopatra*.

5   Maria (Alexandra Gilbreath) leads the women's dance in *The Woman's Prize;
or, The Tamer Tamed*, directed by Gregory Doran for the Royal Shakespeare
Company, 2003

– seems designed as a teaser for Fletcher's play,[1] it is less a
companion piece than *Tamer*'s anti-type, for despite its upper-
class London setting, vestiges of the brutality present in *The
Shrew*'s folk-tale origins surface. As played by Lacey, an actor
best described as a Restoration Will Kempe, Sauny (*The Shrew*'s
Grumio figure) becomes a Sly-like Scottish footman who speaks
a salacious, lubricious language that combines Lacey's additions
(or ad libs) with Shakespearean borrowings in a collaborative
palimpsest, a downmarket *Shrew* that prefigures some twentieth-
and twenty-first-century performances (see Aebischer; Osborne;
and Hodgdon, *Trade*, 23–7). Petruchio forces Meg to drink beer
and smoke tobacco and, declaring her dead when she refuses to
speak, threatens to bury her alive. Reviving, she wins the wager
for Petruchio, begs his pardon and speaks a single scolding line –

1   See Dobson, 22–3, 23n.; see also Spencer, 280; Sprague, *Restoration*, 46; Staves,
133–4. Pepys's diary entry for 9 April 1667 records *Sauny*'s earliest performance.

'Fie, Ladies, for shame. How dare you infringe that Duty which you justly owe your Husbands; they are our Lords and we must pay 'em Service' (5.1.426–8) – before *Sauny* concludes with song and dance.

Although *Sauny*'s finale papers over the questions it raises, Lacey's comic talents together with Petruchio's and Sauny's class-crossing doubles act, an unusual 'grammar of actions' (MC) on the Restoration stage, ensured its nearly seventy-year-long stage life. Their act had an even longer afterlife, for the frontispiece for Rowe's 1709 edition of *The Shrew* reproduces the dinner scene at 'Petruchio's country house' (4.1) from the *Shrew* the engraver knew, in which Petruchio throws a joint and Sauny stands ready to catch it (see Fig. 6). (The 1747 Tonson reprint of Rowe's edition also features this frontispiece, though with a different background, possibly representing later staging.) Not incidentally, the scene preserves a SD – '*Throws meat at 'em, Sauny gets it*' – which, especially when *The Shrew* turns towards knockabout farce, makes ghostly reappearances.

Although *Tamer Tamed* and *Sauny* dispensed with or refashioned the Sly material, which has differed markedly in its level of fixity (see Stern), several early eighteenth-century plays turned Sly's story into a clown-play or droll, a *Shrew* subgenre or offshoot (Cohn, 3–4). Two rival farces, one by Christopher Bullock, the other by Charles Johnson, both titled *The Cobbler of Preston* and produced in 1716, look backwards to *A Shrew* and forward to twentieth- and twenty-first-century performances which, like them, bring in Mrs Sly (mentioned in *A Shrew*) at the play's ending (see Schafer, 59–60). Bullock's play retains vestiges of the taming plot in a class-based revenge farce with a slapstick-stuffed ending. Toby Guzzle (*The Shrew*'s Sly), having become a justice of the peace, sentences his wife Dorcas and Dame Hacket, an alewife to whom he owes money (both played by men), to be ducked in the river; when Guzzle awakes, however, the bedraggled women beat him, claiming that they

6   Petruchio and Katherina at dinner; frontispiece from Nicholas Rowe's
edition of *The Taming of the Shrew* (1709)

are the justices now; but when Guzzle beats them, they settle for
peace – made possible when Guzzle discovers a purse that pays
his score with Dame Hacket. By contrast, Johnson's play directly
addressed contemporary politics and later became a musical farce,
performed at Drury Lane (29 September 1817), a premonition
of *Kiss Me Kate* (Sidney, 1953; see Schafer, 8–9) and of James
Worsdale's farce-opera *Cure for a Scold* (1735), which, although
claiming to 'abbreviate' Shakespeare (see Dobson, 112–13),
instead remembers *Sauny*. Ballads cap and extend most scenes,
sweetening a condensed taming plot that also evokes *The Shrew*'s

folklore sources. As Margaret grows silent and is threatened, like her namesake in *Sauny*, with tooth-drawing, her husband (aptly named Manly) calls in a surgeon to 'bleed her plentifully under the tongue' (*Cure for a Scold*, 35); this reminder of the scold's bridle prompts her recovery, and, after promising to alter her behaviour, she breaks into a duet with Manly, 'Rapture crowns the Marriage State, / When equal Affection unite them' (36). An epilogue, spoken by the Margaret-actor, calls Shakespeare to task, suggesting that he 'should study Nature, [for] how few / In Life, resemble those our Author drew' (40).

Margaret's apology for her 'unwomanly . . . Part' as well as her critique of Shakespeare not only offers the first evidence of friction between the shrew's fictional role and the culture's sense of 'real' women's nature but also serves as prologue to David Garrick's *Catharine and Petruchio*. This was the most popular shrew-play in England from 1754 to 1844 and until 1887 in America, travelling into a Frederic Reynolds opera (1828), with an overture appropriated from Rossini and songs raided from other Shakespearean plays (Dobson, 184). Condensed to an afterpiece and played beside *Florizel and Perdita*, Garrick's adaptation of *The Winter's Tale*, *Catharine and Petruchio* amplifies the gestures towards 'equal affection' which had suited *The Shrew* to changing times. Catharine's first speech is an aside approving of Petruchio ('the Man's a Man', 8); two further asides voicing her decision to marry – and tame – him (and take revenge on Bianca) make her resistance to Petruchio seem more like a performance or mask of shrewishness than an attempt to remain, like *Tamer Tamed*'s Maria, a 'free haggard'. As for Petruchio, he finally confesses to having put on an 'honest Mask' to play the shrew-taming role of 'lordly Husband' which he 'throw[s] off with Pleasure' (34–5), opting for mutual love. Not only does this sense of savouring gender performances and then giving up the role for the 'real' travel into later critical and theatrical performances, but Garrick's strategy of sweetening

Shakespeare with sentiment generates a kinder, gentler – and more gentrified – *Shrew*. With its 'outright feudal masculinism' tamed down in favour of guardedly egalitarian, and specifically private, contemporary versions of sympathy and domestic virtue, *Catharine and Petruchio* becomes 'family entertainment for the 1750s', giving audiences a 'Shakespeare they wish to recognize as their own' (Dobson, 188–9, 195). In Dobson's apt phrase, early cinematic *Shrew*s, twentieth-century television sitcoms such as *Moonlighting*'s *Shrew* episode and adaptations such as *10 Things I Hate About You* (Junger, 1999) are not very far away (Hodgdon, *Trade*, 23–7).

Overall, Garrick's play anticipates the 'key scene, key image, key phrase' strategy of late nineteenth-century stagings and early twentieth-century Shakespeare films (Pearson & Uricchio; Hodgdon, *Trade*, 9–12). Its highly telescoped plotting and time frame rearrange the play's final moves, so that in the sun–moon exchange it is not Vincentio but Baptista whom Catharine misrecognizes as a maiden, which leads directly to the 'proofs' of her taming. As Catharine kneels to ask pardon for her mad mistaking, Baptista, telling her to rise, asks, 'How lik'st thou Wedlock? Ar't not alter'd Kate?', to which she replies, 'Indeed I am. I am transform'd to Stone' (33) – as if in anticipated reversal of Shaw's *Pygmalion* (RP). If evoking *The Winter's Tale*'s statue scene neatly ties *Catharine and Petruchio* to *Florizel and Perdita*, it also raises several questions. Does marriage turn a woman to stone? Does Garrick's play really affirm mutuality? Although Catharine is not asked to throw down or tread on her cap, Petruchio not only interrupts Catharine's final speech but, '*Go[ing] forward with Catharine in his Hand*', he turns her into an exhibit, speaks her lines on the subject's duty to a prince and concludes the play with 'How shameful 'tis when Women are so simple / To offer War where they should kneel for Peace; / Or seek for Rule, Supremacy and Sway, / Where bound to love, to honour and obey' (35) – suggesting that her homily indeed has been ventriloquizing what properly belongs to a male speaker (see pp. 120–1). However it may domesticate *Shrew*'s marital politics, Garrick's play remains faithful to the ideal of male dominance while simultaneously bending its absolutist contours. In January 1790, the acclaimed actress Sarah Siddons arranged and starred in back-to-back performances of *Henry VIII* and *Catharine and Petruchio*: did she, perhaps, perceive the irony of Garrick's play seen as a corollary of Shakespeare's? After all, Queen Katherine receives divorce and banishment for the obedience that Katherina Minola offers to Petruccio (Richmond, 44). Or did Siddons view (or perform) Garrick's Catharine as a sister to Shakespeare's Queen Katherine in matters of womanly conduct?

Whatever the case with Siddons, comments on *Catharine and Petruchio*'s original players, Kitty Clive and Henry Woodward, intimate that Clive, whose 'talons, tongue and passion were very expressive to the eyes of all beholders', was 'perfect mistress of Catharine's humour' but 'overborne by the . . . triumphant grotesque of Woodward' (Tate Wilkinson, cited in Winter, *Stage*, 499). Known to dislike each other, the pair reportedly played out their offstage quarrels in stage roles: 'in one of [Petruchio's] mad fits, when he and his bride are at supper, Woodward stuck a fork . . . in Mrs. Clive's finger; and in pushing her off the stage he was so much in earnest that he threw her down' (Davies, *Garrick*, 1.312). If such behaviour recalls Soule's conjecture about the master–apprentice relationship, it also offers a prototype for future husband-and-wife teams of performers – from Constance and Frank Benson to Mary Pickford and Douglas Fairbanks, Lynne Fontanne and Alfred Lunt, Elizabeth Taylor and Richard Burton, and even to Patricia Morison and Alfred Drake in *Kiss Me, Kate* and Cybill Shepherd and Bruce Willis from *Moonlighting* – whose star presences, by linking 'real couples' to fictional roles, would not only double *The Shrew*'s pleasures but also invite viewing theatre as a peculiar form of marital therapy. Indeed, the idea of one performance citing another well describes *Catharine and Petruchio*'s theatrical legacy as a memory archive for subsequent *Shrews*.

During the near-century that *Catharine and Petruchio* controlled the stage, Sly had gone missing, a casualty, perhaps, of gentrification. Even in 1774, John Bell had demeaned Sly: 'This introductory scrap is surely too trifling and insignificant, to deserve utterance or notice' (6.73). Yet he was not altogether gone, but had moved outside the theatre, where Robert Smirke's engraving for the Boydell Shakespeare series of 1801–3 commemorated his fantasy (see Fig. 7). Evoking the oriental milieu of the Sly material's source, *The Arabian Nights*, it presents Sly as a pasha, his slightly pouty face resembling that of a netsuke figurine; costume maps his double history as beggar and would-be 'king': he wears a decorously ragged undergarment that exposes his muscular body and bare chest, and over it an ermine-trimmed cloak. The image serves as a

7   Christopher Sly ensconced in splendour; engraving by Robert Smirke, Boydell Shakespeare Gallery (1801–3) (Folio, vol. 1)

kind of place-filler for the resolutely lower-class Sly who would appear on nineteenth- and early twentieth-century stages: 'a man purely sensual and animal, brutish in appetite, and with a mind unleavened by fancy' (Henry Morley, 6 December 1856, cited in Salgado, 76–7). In another solo vehicle for Sly, Ermanno Wolf-Ferrari's 1927 tragic opera *Sly*, he becomes a Hoffman-like character – a debt-ridden, hard-drinking poet and balladeer who delights habitués of London's Falcon tavern with his songs. When he discovers that he has been tricked into believing he is a count, he slashes his wrists, and, in an echo of *Romeo and Juliet*, his mistress Dolly arrives too late to save him.

When Sly resurfaced in the mid-nineteenth century, he was hardly recognizable either as this figure or as the one who ruled eighteenth-century ballad-farces and drolls. On 27 March 1844, at the Theatre Royal Haymarket, Sly had become reattached to what the playbill described as 'the original text as acted divers times at the Globe and Blackfriars Playhouses, 1606' (see Fig. 8), in a version of present-day 'original practices' staging. Not only were the scenes that Charles Knight considered 'one of the most precious gems in Shaxspere's casket' restored, but the production, conceived by Benjamin Webster and designed by J.R. Planché, paid homage to its author with a 'Shakespearian overture . . . with entre-act and incidental music, selected from Works of Festa, Wilbye and Popular Melodies of the 16th century' and to its historical moment in a preface showing illustrations of 'London in The Olden Time – composed and painted (from Hollar's celebrated print)', among them depictions of Bankside, the Globe, Old London Bridge, Old Saint Paul's and the Tower (Planché, 2.83–9; see also MacDonald, 'Haymarket', esp. 160, 163). In every sense, this was to be 'the real thing'. And in supplying a substitute for the decorated stage to which audiences had grown accustomed, Planché harnessed the popular diorama to theatre in a proto-cinematic move – offering perhaps the first 'multi-media' *Shrew*.

8    Playbill for *The Taming of the Shrew*, 27 March 1844, directed by Benjamin Webster, advised by J.R. Planché

The idea was to have only two scenes, the alehouse and the bedroom, where 'strolling players' acted the comedy without scenery; in a proto-Brechtian move, written placards informed audiences of changing locales (Fig. 9). Seated in a great chair, Sly witnessed a performance in which three actors were made up to resemble Shakespeare, Ben Jonson and Richard Tarlton – recalling *The Malcontent*'s Induction, where members of the King's Men played themselves (see pp. 24–5). As music played between acts, servants brought Sly wine and refreshments, so that during Act 5, he fell into a drunken stupor. After the actors had bowed, servants lifted Sly out of his chair and carried him to the door as the curtain slowly fell. Justifying this solution to the problem of how to end the play, Charles Knight observed:

SCENE FROM "TAMING THE SHREW," AT THE HAYMARKET THEATRE.

9    *The Taming of the Shrew*, Haymarket Theatre, 1844, directed by Benjamin
     Webster, advised by J.R. Planché

'We doubt whether [the] Sly ending ever was produced, and
whether Shaxspere did not exhibit his usual judgment in letting
the curtain drop upon honest Christopher, when his wish [had
been] accomplished at the end of the comedy ["would 'twere
done"]' (cited in Planché, 2.84).

Reviving 'this curiosity of dramatic construction' – which
lasted a long three and a half hours (though short for Victorian
audiences) of pantomime moments – was a somewhat hazardous
experiment, especially for Webster, whose Petruccio was not
admired. Instead, the evening belonged to Charles Strickland's
Sly, praised for his by-play, and to Mrs Nisbett (then Lady
Boothby) – considered the best Katherina since Mrs Charles
Kemble because her performance offered 'practical proof that
woman's ascendancy is never more absolute than when she

seems to relinquish it' (*Athenaeum*, 30 October 1847). Although Nisbett's Katherina matched the era's ideal of woman, critics were less sure about Planché's Sly 'innovation': *The Times* thought it a pity that he 'could not have been allowed to indulge in a running commentary upon what he "doubly sees" which would be a great relief to the monotony of the scene' (cited in MacDonald, 'Haymarket', 160). Yet even if Sly remained an added-on attraction, the Webster–Planché *Shrew* initiated a conversation between critical and theatrical culture that earns it a place in the story.

An even more influential late nineteenth-century landmark, Augustin Daly's 1887 New York staging, rivalled and displaced *Catharine and Petruchio*. A stunning commercial success, Daly's *Shrew* played for 121 consecutive performances and toured internationally, performing a benefit for the Library Fund of Stratford's Shakespeare Memorial Theatre on 3 August 1888. Representing the first attempt to stage something like Shakespeare's original in America, Daly's revival established *The Shrew* as a popular play, capable of competing with modern comedy (*Harper's*, June 1887, 152); The *Epoch*'s critic praised the performers' ability to 'mark a delicate line between the boisterousness of farce and the intelligence of romantic comedy' (11 February 1887). And by casting Ada Rehan, an actress 'well aware that the essence of farcical acting is absolute gravity, and sometimes the semblance of passionate ardor, in comically preposterous situations', the production made Katherina Minola a star part (Winter, *Rehan*, 516–17).[1] Daly's playing text, printed in illustrated commemorative copies as well as in a 'prompter's copy' with introductory materials by Daly, Rehan and William Winter, offers the first fully documented behind-the-scenes record of a *Shrew* performance.

Advertising his fidelity to 'pure' Shakespeare, Daly retained the opening Sly scenes – a novelty for American audiences

---

1    Rehan's portrait hangs in the RSC Collection.

familiar only with Garrick's adaptation. Fidelity and purity, however, were slippery terms, for Daly 'improved' Shakespearean dramaturgy by telescoping scenes, thus restricting the taming process, which Daly thought tedious (especially, one might say, for Katherina) to a single scene. Nine scenes represented eight different locales, a bow to theatrical practicality (and audiences' patience) that minimized scene and costume changes for the lavish, opulent sets and elaborate dresses endemic to the age of pictorial or decorated Shakespeare, when 'realizing' famous paintings was a common practice (Meisel). Modelled on Paolo Veronese's *Wedding Feast at Cana* (1562–3), the final scene (see Fig. 10) included song and dance: 'Miss Quentin and a choir of boys' performed Henry Rowley Bishop's 'Should He Upbraid' (lyrics from 2.1), originally composed for Covent Garden stagings (*c.* 1821). Given its epic-sized cast of extras, Daly's revival must have looked at times like a proto-musical, proto-Cecil B. DeMille *Shrew*.

Paring Shakespeare's script to 2,000 lines, 200 of which were taken from Garrick or represented slight variations of Shakespeare's text – 'Garrick adulterated by Shakespear', in George Bernard Shaw's phrase (186–7) – Daly shrank Petruccio's role considerably and expanded Katherina's to Petruccian size, either by creating Garrick-derived speeches (with Fletcherian echoes) or by reordering and transposing passages in order to provide her with curtain speeches (Winter, *Stage*, 524–5). At the end of Petruccio's severely curtailed taming attempt (4.1), Katherina crept back in: seeing her, he laughed quietly and exited, leaving her alone onstage, a silent presence, offered up for audience contemplation – and consumption. As recrafted around Rehan's figure, Katherina was, in every sense, both the shrew and the show.

There had been outstanding Katherinas before this: Sarah Siddons had acted the role with John Philip Kemble's Petruccio in Garrick's adaptation – a revival that (famously) introduced Petruccio's whip, which would define his figure for nearly

10 Finale of *The Taming of the Shrew*, modelled on Paolo Veronese's *Wedding Feast at Cana* (1562–3), directed by Augustin Daly in 1887

two centuries (see pp. 98–9). But never like Rehan's. She was sensational: 'fêted, sought, eulogized, idolized', her gestures and movement were captured in laudatory verses (Winter, *Rehan*, 58, 59–63). Called 'glorious', 'magnificent' and 'savage' – terms usually reserved for the reigning queens of tragedy, Sarah Bernhardt and Eleanora Duse – Rehan's performance established the contours of the quintessential Katherina the Shrew. 'No one', wrote Odell, 'will ever forget . . . her first tiger-like entry' (delayed until Act 2), when she swept in, driving Bianca with her (Odell, 2.439; Daly, 110–11, 352; see Fig. 11). Even her costume haunted spectators' memories:

> She wore ruddy golden hair, short and curly. Her first dress, dark red in color, consisted of a short skirt of velvet; an over-skirt of stiff, heavy, flowered silk, looped up at the left side, with a gold cord, so as to expose the velvet skirt; a short train; a long-bodied waist; inner sleeves, fitted close to the arms; and over-sleeves depending from the shoulders almost to the knees, with flame-colored lining. Around her neck she wore a single, close-fitting string of large, heavy, dark-ruddy beads. On her head was a small red cap, and from her ears depended massy gold ornaments. Her shoes were of satin, dark red in color, to match the dress.
>
> (Winter, *Stage*, 521–2)

In a consumer society where the presence of some playgoers would be noted in the next day's society papers, Winter's description might have come straight from the fashion pages of *Queen*, the *Lady* or the *Lady's Pictorial*, publications that regularly represented the playhouses as fashion showrooms, sites where theatrical costume offered back images of spectators' own wealth and power in a 'commercial interplay of stage and stalls' (Kaplan & Stowell, 10–11). Rehan's performance – and her dress – cast a long shadow. For more than a century, subsequent

11    Ada Rehan as Katherina in *The Taming of the Shrew*, directed by Augustin
      Daly in 1877

Katherinas would wear red: in place of that perennial Elizabethan
signifier, the ruff, red fabric accomplishes good shrewish – and
shrewd – work, releasing all the transgressive labels attached to
her figure (Hodgdon, 'Bride-ing', 77–8).

Psychologizing her role, Rehan spoke of Katherina as
'externally a virago, but the loveliest qualities of womanhood
are latent in her . . . [she] turns the whole divine force within
her to exemplifying the perfection of human obedience and
dependence' (Rehan, vi–vii). However operatically overstated,

Rehan's words point to the task facing the Katherina-actor, especially but not exclusively in the nineteenth century: that of embodying on the one hand scornful shrewishness and on the other the virtues of 'true' or 'civilized' femininity expected of the respectable, 'womanly' woman. Explaining *The Shrew*'s appeal, Rehan writes: '[t]he more a heroine is made to suffer, the greater is her triumph with her public, if, as Katherina does, she passes through fire, and comes out pure gold' (vi, x). Although she seems to see herself as a passive object for audience consumption, a token expression of male mastery, she also hints at a dynamic tension between that and her desire to show herself off and so to achieve professional celebrity (Glenn, 2–4, 20–3). Although perhaps not as legendary as her entry, her final moments on stage revealed that 'she was seen to be unmistakably the same woman, only now her actual self' (Winter, *Stage*, 525). Rather than kneeling to place her hand beneath Petruchio's foot, she made *him* rise to stand beside her, equals both; as she spoke the homily's last words, she threw her cap under his foot. John Drew's Petruchio, a version of Garrick's citified fop, cast off his mask of 'lordly husband', knelt and kissed her hand. Was this the taming *of* the shrew or, as in Fletcher, taming *by* the shrew? It would be hard to say. Whether wittingly or unwittingly, in fashioning a 'modern' Katherina, Rehan's performance represented a self-invention that contributed to defining the twentieth-century social and sexual terrain of the role.

## Send in the clowns

Garrick – or Garrick plus Daly – took on new, if slightly different life, in Frank and Constance (Fetherstonhaugh) Benson's staging, which opened in 1889–90 (Manchester and London) before moving to Stratford's Memorial Theatre in 1893 – where it was played through the twentieth century's second decade – and appearing sporadically, in various venues, until 1932. Although Benson cut Sly, he adopted Daly's strategies, transposing scenes, deleting potentially offensive language and severely telescoping the Bianca subplot; as in *Catharine and Petruchio*, the focus was on the taming game. Where Daly had psychologized *The Shrew*'s farcical elements, the Bensons' revivals were all farce – all the time. The prompt copy (of uncertain date), stuffed with marginal notations for business that threaten to obscure the text, offers a print metaphor for this venture: Constance Benson's memoirs confirm that, although business was added and/or elaborated continually, some set pieces, such as the frantic dinner scene (4.1) and the often shrewishly stubborn donkey that carried Katherina home to Padua, remained constant.[1] Petruccio's household was far from serene: food and dishes cascaded through the air, crockery got smashed, flour was thrown about 'in a pantomime rally' and Frank Benson leapt over the furniture, finally seating himself in a chair he had hoisted onto the table (Crosse, *Diaries*, 2.8). To the *Daily World*, Benson's Petruccio became a violent 'knock-about artist' who overstepped 'the limit even of Elizabethan crudity': 'there is no reason why [the scene] should be ear-splitting, nerve-torturing, senseless, barbarous, brutal' (William Archer, undated clipping, SMT *Theatre Records*). Constance Benson's Katherina, an 'undisguised, unpoeticized Shrew', laid about with a crutch-handled stick, chased Bianca, knocked over chairs and bit Petruccio (2.1); 'clutch[ing] a knife to stab Petruccio [4.3], [she] saw his mocking smile, thrust the blade into the table and fell at his feet in tears' (Crosse, *Playgoing*, 29; Trewin, *Benson*, 65). Inevitably, critics thought her best when delivering 'a fine moral sermon dressed in language of the loftiest poetry' (unidentified clipping, SMT *Theatre Records*), but Benson's ludicrous excesses, shot through with amateurish acting, not only outplayed her but overwhelmed the play. Although his

---

1 Benson, 86–7. In 1911, Will Barker filmed the Bensons' *Shrew* (RJ); several stills (including one of the donkey) from the film, itself now lost, survive in The Shakespeare Centre Library archives. See Russell Jackson, 'Staging and storytelling, theatre and film: *Richard III* at Stratford, 1910', *New Theatre Quarterly*, 16.2 (2000), 107–21.

antic athleticism appealed chiefly to the groundlings (those perennial surrogates for the Sly-like spectator), it 'seemed to scandalize a section of the house, who received his exuberance with some slight hissing' (*The Times*, cited in Trewin, *Benson*, 65). In setting a clownishly vulgar Petruccio opposite an almost painfully realistic Katherina, the Bensons' staging not only see-sawed between 'gambold', comedy and history – a pattern that carried forward into the Pickford–Fairbanks (Taylor, 1929) and Taylor–Burton (Zeffirelli, 1967) films – but revealed fault lines at the level of reception.

In May 1909, when Stratford-upon-Avon's annual Festival highlighted *Cymbeline*, Shakespeare's other wife-wagering play, as well as *The Shrew*, audience members who just days before had witnessed women's suffrage protests surrounding a Stratford by-election were confronted with Benson's spectacle of wife-taming – a conjunction that put *The Shrew* at the centre of an ongoing debate over the rights and roles of women. Five years previously, R. Warwick Bond had written, 'It will be many a day, I think, ere men cease to need, or women to admire, the example of Petruchio' (lviii), but that day apparently had arrived sooner than expected. Although some critics defended Benson's playing on the grounds that Shakespeare 'wrote to amuse', others were troubled by the combination of shrew-taming high jinks and the serious implications of 'the lord-of-creation moral implied in the wager and the speech put into the woman's own mouth' (Shaw, 187–8). Enlisting Shakespeare as 'the common ground upon which all English-speaking peoples may meet without encountering the disturbing influences of religion and politics', Benson maintained that his staging licensed audience laughter at domestic manipulation and abuse. Only much later did Constance Benson voice some hesitancy: remembering *The Shrew* as 'one of our most successful plays and invariably a favourite, especially with the men' (86), she anticipated later critics who have argued that the play caters to male spectators' pleasure.

Unwittingly, the Bensons' *Shrew* engendered a debate that extended beyond the theatre – to the London Shakespeare League's forum on 'What Shakespeare Thought of Women' and an address to the Stratford Shakespeare Club, 'Shakespeare – Women – Human Nature', making *The Shrew* central to women's claims for full citizenship (Carlson, 93–102). Back in the theatre, however, desiring the shrewishness of the shrew was still alive: when the avowed suffrage activist Violet Vanbrugh replaced Constance Benson as Katherina in 1912, she was faulted for being not 'a real flesh and blood shrew . . . [but] a frightened prisoner . . . rather than the fire-eating wife that needed breaking in, all the time'; one critic, however, remarked that her homily could scarcely 'be endorsed in these days of women's suffrage' (all quotations cited in Carlson, 93–102). *The Shrew* swung between art and life, mobilized on the one hand to shore up the rights of farce, and on the other recruited to promote 'real' women's rights. The contours of a play that, by the late twentieth century, feminist, new historicist and cultural materialist critics would claim as their own territory was beginning to emerge, born out of farce.

Although 1909 represented a watershed moment, the conversation that engaged *The Shrew* with women's histories had begun much earlier when, in 1878, Francis Power Cobbe, citing *The Shrew* as evidence that the English condoned wife-beating, argued that giving women the vote might reduce domestic violence (Carlson, 96). Yet some eighty years later Kenneth Tynan, reviewing John Barton's 1960 SMT staging, waxed nostalgic: 'Petruchio's violence, however extreme, is at least attentive. He cares, though he cares cruelly, and to this [Katherina] responds, cautiously blossoming until she becomes what he wants her to be. The process is surprisingly touching, and Dame Peggy [Ashcroft] plays the last scene . . . with an eager, sensible radiance that almost prompts one to regret the triumph of the suffragette movement' (*Observer*, 26 June 1960).

## Horseplay

By the 1930s, with a second world war pending, farce claimed its rights on New York and London stages. In 1935, another husband and wife team, Alfred Lunt and Lynne Fontanne, staged perhaps the most successful mid-twentieth-century *Shrew*, a Theatre Guild performance that toured the United States (Schafer, 30). Casting reverence for Shakespeare aside, the Fontanne–Lunt *Shrew* offered 'a lavish exhibition of the Bard in his underpants' stuffed with tumblers, beer-garden music, horseplay and one-offs (Percy Hammond, *New York Herald Tribune*, 1 October 1935, cited in Haring-Smith, 129; Brooks Atkinson, *New York Times*, 1 October 1935). Katherina threw objects onstage just before her entrance (which was delayed, as in Daly's staging, until just before the wooing scene (2.1)), shot off a blunderbuss that brought down a goose from the rafters, got roundly spanked by Petruccio at their initial meeting and stuffed sausages down the front of her dress (4.3). These and other bits of comic business survive in *Kiss Me, Kate* (1948): in the theatre, nothing ever occurs for the first time (Schafer, 32–3; see also Roach, 2–4). The *pièce de résistance* of this three-ring circus, however, was an outrageously joyous *deus ex machina* finale, in which the happy couple, surrounded by a sunburst and accompanied by a grand chorus, ascended into the heavens in a golden chariot drawn by the two dwarfs who had served as Bianca's bodyguards and Katherina's bridesmaids (*San Francisco News*, 14 November 1939, cited in Schafer, 31).

Back across the Atlantic, the Bensons' famous donkey sired a stableful of horses. In 1937, spectators at the New Theatre saw the best *Shrew* 'fantastication' that Londoners had yet seen (see Fig. 12). Its most inspired feature, a magnificent steed played by J. Sproll and Richard Beamish – 'by Panto out of Mime', 'straight from the stables of the Griffith Brothers' (*Observer*, 7 April 1937; *Daily Mail*, 24 March 1937)[1] – that danced solo to

---

1 Horses and *Shrew* have a lasting affinity: the panto horse, one eye missing, returned in Bogdanov (1978); Bruce Willis's Petruccio rode into church on a real horse, who wore sunglasses (*Moonlighting*, 1986).

12   The wedding journey; Katherina (Edith Evans) astride a pantomime horse (J. Sproll and Richard Beamish), Petruccio (Leslie Banks) and Grumio (Mark Daly), directed by Claud Gurney at the New Theatre, London, 1937

orchestral accompaniment, prompted rapturous Shakespearean parodies: 'O happy horse, to bear the weight of Katherine! Do bravely horse! For wot'st thou whom thou movest?' (*The Times*, 24 March 1937). This amazing animal was only one among many exaggerations: Petruccio's whip was twelve feet long; his servants played rugger with a joint of mutton; there was a Spanish dance with castanets. Getting resonantly drunk in an immense revolving bed, Sly presided over a wordless bedroom scene where Petruccio and his servants, dressed up as ghosts, 'haunted, teased and bereft [Katherina] of all covering but a shift' (*Tatler*, 14 April 1937, 66–7) – an instance of abjection-through-fashion that would appear in later productions (Barton, 1960; Alexander, 1992). Scenery and costumes were delightfully absurd: 'It is obviously Easter Sunday and everybody in Padua has got a new mantua' (*Sunday Times*, 28 March 1937): hats resembled fantasy skateboards decorated with whole ostriches of feathers à la Carmen Miranda's banana-infested creations; costumes ran the gamut from Elizabethan doublet and hose to *commedia*-inspired overskirts for the men, all tossed together in an early technicolour palette.[1]

All in all, it was a good night out: 'so long as the piece goes with a swing, none but the dustiest greybeard will be a stickler for the text' (*The Times*, 24 March 1937). Although most seemed delighted that, in George VI's Coronation year, visitors from abroad could see 'so thoroughly distinctive and distinguished a production of a Shakespeare play' (W.A. Darlington, *Daily Times*, 24 March 1937), others viewed the pantomime and revue-like interruptions as signs 'that [*The Shrew*] is not a good play and that something must be done about it'. Upholding a high-art Shakespeare, Herbert Farjeon objected to the ending, where, 'after the three couples make their final wedding-night exit through three curtains, they then thrust out their hands through the folds and put out six pairs of boots and shoes for the night' – which, he found, 'if not the worst, is, I think, the *commonest* thing I have ever seen done in any Shakespearean production' (*Bystander*, 7 April 1937, 10).

Yet silly costumes and equine *lazzi* were not the entire show: amidst all the frippery, 'the heart of the revival keeps true to Shakespeare's meaning as none other has done since the days of Ada Rehan' (*The Times*, 24 March 1937). Not only was Edith

---

1    Rouben Mamoulian's *Becky Sharp* (RKO, 1935) was the first feature-length film to use the three-strip process; Disney's *Snow White* followed in 1937.

Evans 'the Shrew that Shakespeare drew – a virago indeed, and yet a woman' (*Sketch*, 7 April 1937) but Leslie Banks's Petruccio had 'a lightness of attack that preserv[ed the play] as a fierce, swift piece for the theatre . . . saving it from being the pageant with clowning that it now and then threatens to become' (*Daily Mail*, 24 March 1937). As with previous performances, especially when a great comic performer embodies Katherina, her presence tends to pull against farce, particularly at the ending, where *The Shrew* suddenly shifts ground. It is as though that which Shakespeare seems interested in exploring cannot be developed fully within the conventions of farce: pushing conventional boundaries, *Shrew* not only counters them but also plays with them.[1] As the *Daily Mail* observed, Evans's Katherina 'comes dangerously near revealing the weakness of the play . . . when she gets to the final homily to wives. She speaks the lines beautifully, of course – and in doing so throws into relief all the tinsel shallowness of what has gone before' (24 March 1937). By the mid-twentieth century, the line between high seriousness and high farce was becoming ever more sharply drawn in terms of gender. That ambivalence, which marks farce male, has spawned costume design as well as choices of locale that not only preserve but also enhance and exaggerate a masculinist perspective. Any move such as this would not burst, *sui generis*, from the imagination of the theatrical designer, but can be traced to *The Shrew*'s written language of costume.

Among Shakespeare's plays, *The Shrew* makes a major investment in wardrobe, especially in second-hand clothes, which constitute its stock in theatrical trade, performing their own supposings. The play even jokes about it: when, setting out for Padua, Petruccio instructs Grumio, 'bring our horses unto Long-lane end' (4.3.184), the action suddenly swerves from fictive Italy to the Elizabethan London locale where

---

1 Based on Plautine sources, *The Comedy of Errors* is Shakespeare's prime example of farce; Shakespeare never again called on farce when exploring marital abuse: Iago's wife Emilia inhabits a tragedy (LEM).

brokers and second-hand clothes dealers hawked their wares (see Stow, 2.122; Jones & Stallybrass, 192–3). In a play where metamorphosis is not just a piece of plot machinery but also part of the costume plot, clothes, obeying early modern culture's sumptuary codes, label their wearers by gender, class, occupation and station (see the *Homily Against Excess of Apparel* (1563), *Homilies*, O3$^r$–P2$^v$; Stubbes, 1.34). So, too, do theatrical clothes. *The Shrew*'s male wardrobe is remarkably full, if occasionally loosely described, as in '*the habit of a mean man*' (Lucentio's disguise as Cambio, 2.1.38.1–2) or '*brave*' (Tranio's showy Lucentio-dressing, 1.2.216.1). But for Petruccio's wedding attire, Shakespeare writes precise instructions: 'a new hat and an old jerkin, a pair of old breeches thrice-turned; a pair of boots that have been candle-cases, one buckled, another laced' – there is, of course, even more about his horse (3.2.43–6). Similarly, Grumio wears 'a linen stock on one leg and a kersey boot-hose on the other, gartered with a red and blue list' – poor motley-wear, topped with 'an old hat, and the humour of forty fancies pricked in't for a feather' – a simulacrum ornament (3.2.64–7). In a theatre of male performers, the men's fully-stocked closets demonstrate how the play is about looking at (as well as listening to) early modern men behaving badly: whether dressed up (Sly) or down (Petruccio), they are the centre of *The Shrew*'s fashion spectacle. Arguably, the scrambling of visual codes in Biondello's description of Petruccio's (and Grumio's) wedding attire has licensed a range of farcical looks, antic posturings and performative behaviour (Hodgdon, 'Bride-ing', 72–4).

Was Petruccio's whip – a property with perhaps as long a performative afterlife as such famous Shakespearean stage properties as the dagger, skull and handkerchief – *The Shrew*'s 'original' farcical exaggeration?[1] When Philip Kemble's alteration

---

1  The whip's ancestor, the riding crop, was not always gendered male: in 1559, Benedict Spinola presented Queen Elizabeth with a New Year's gift of an 'Riding rodde garnished with Golde Silke and pearle', 'all in a Case of Woode covered with grene vellat embrauderid with Silver' (Arnold, 141).

of *Catharine and Petruchio* was performed at Covent Garden (*c.* 1810), audiences heard the whip crack first offstage, as Biondello finished describing Petruchio, then again as Petruchio exited – 'What ho! My Kate! My Kate!' – moments memorialized in the drawing by Robert Cruikshank which appeared as the frontispiece of Kemble's performance edition (1815). Sometimes grown to great length, as in Claud Gurney's 1937 New Theatre staging or in *Kiss Me Kate* (see Fig. 13), the whip has appeared with great regularity ever since; Katherina has also brandished a whip, as in the Pickford–Fairbanks film (Taylor, 1929, see Fig. 14), but Pickford later discards it, marking one stage of Petruccio's taming. Productions have expanded Petruccian excess to other roles and to stage fashions that are the material equivalents of Shakespeare's topical language.

13   Petruccio (Howard Keel) whipping Katherina (Kathryn Grayson) in *Kiss Me Kate*, directed by George Sidney (1953)

14   Whip in hand, Katherina (Mary Pickford) confronts Petruccio (Douglas
Fairbanks), in Sam Taylor's film version (1929)

In Barry Jackson's modern-dress production (30 April 1928,
Court, London), Petruccio turned up in a battered top hat, a
fairisle jersey, torn hunting breeches and a morning coat; others'
clothing and behaviour stirred up an eclectic disarray of one-off
jokes: Grumio was a Fascist, Tranio had a cockney accent, and
Katherina and Petruccio left the wedding in a Harry Tate car with
whirling wheels, comic scenery flying past them. Appropriating
his established screen image of romantic manliness, Douglas
Fairbanks (Taylor, 1929), a Robin-Hood-Black-Pirate Petruccio

dressed in rags and motley with an upside-down jackboot on his head, slouched against a column at the wedding, crunching an apple. Marc Singer's bare-chested Petruccio, wearing skin-tight white tights, swung in 'like a Renaissance Tarzan' (Schafer, 72) in William Ball's *commedia*-inspired *Shrew* (1973, televised 1976), where *lazzi* and running in-jokes pushed minor roles towards stereotypes, wrapping the play in pure style. Wearing a raggedy-fibre sarong and a huge brimmed hat sprouting straw and weeds, Julie Taymor's 1988 Petruccio, Sam Tsoustsouvras, resembled a pirate gone native (Blumenthal, 127–9).

In the late twentieth century and the first decade of the twenty-first, cartoon-like chauvinism gave way to a series of manic postmodern fashion shows. Mark Lockyer's Tranio, in Gale Edwards's 1992 *Shrew*, resembled the rock star formerly known as Prince; Michael Siberry's Petruccio sported torn black leathers with skateboarder's knee-pads, a boxing glove, a huge feathered ruff and a hawk-beaked, plumed headdress, parodying those worn at Elizabeth I's Accession Day Tilts, which anticipated his hawk-taming strategy; Robin Nedwell's Grumio, in a pink tutu and Doc Martens, helped to spirit away Josie Lawrence's Katherina, splendid in white silk brocade, in a flame-decorated red Mini car (see Fig. 15). In the BBC's *Shakespeare Retold* (2007) Rufus Sewell did a quick change from morning dress to punked-up drag for his wedding – a premonition, perhaps, of his role-switch to MP Katherina's 'house husband' (see Kidnie, 'Problem', 103–39). Costumes for Ed Hall's Propeller *Shrew* (Richards, 2005) signposted (and sent up) hyper-masculinities. Tam Williams's matador-Lucentio had 'a nearly complete suit of lights' (*The Times*, 20 September 2006), and Dugald Bruce-Lockhart's Petruccio wore 'tight red jeans and open red leather jacket, festooned with chains like something from a Michael Jackson video, under which he wore only a chunky gold necklace', and showed up for the wedding in 'cowboy boots, a Stetson hat (into which he relieved himself before putting it back on his head), a brown fringed jacket and a

15   Petruccio (Michael Siberry) in his wedding attire, with Baptista (Clifford
     Rose) and Grumio (Robin Nedwell), directed by Gale Edwards for the
     Royal Shakespeare Company, 1995

leopard-skin thong'. The production's half *commedia*, half pure
camp design created a bizarre aesthetic that undermined an
attitude 'which seemed convinced of the [play's] oppression and
injustice' (Smith, 'Review', 65–6).

   If costume deflects the play's potential unpleasantness and
stifles *The Shrew*'s taming story, so does a locale such as the
American Wild West. Setting the play at a time when 'men were
men and women were women' gives comic permission to macho
masculinity and violent taming tactics (whips being *de rigueur*),
seen through an optic of nostalgia. Just as Shakespeare's Italy
is always a version of England, setting *The Shrew* elsewhere
offers the advantage of a displaced locale where anything goes.
Both the idea of the 'Wild' West and its iconography became
available first, not in the theatre but in dime novels, landscape
paintings and early cinema (Abel). Perhaps the very first *Shrew*-
western was Selig Polyscope's 1911 *The Cow Boy and the Shrew*,

in which Hank Wilson, a good-natured Cow Puncher, develops a strategy for 'roping' his runaway bride who has caused considerable annoyance in the town – an instance, according to the film's synopsis, of love being 'forced to the surface through trying circumstances'. Later, the Rodgers–Hammerstein team's first musical success, *Oklahoma* (1943), which displaced the Second World War into the American West, may well have prompted Michael Benthall's 1948 Wild West *Shrew*, set in 1880s Oklahoma and observed by Sly and his 'wife' from a giant bed. Costumes from various periods and styles came out of a basket: Petruccio resembled a cowboy; Katherina (Diana Wynard) was at some points a Wild West heroine, at others a Lily Langtry figure; the rest of the cast looked like survivors from eighteenth-century comedy (Beauman, 191). The fashion for westernized *Shrews* even travelled to Ireland and Canada, with John Ford's film *The Quiet Man* (1952), starring John Wayne and Maureen O'Hara, and Stratford, Ontario's first comedy western (1964), before returning to 'Padua, Arizona' in Trevor Nunn's 1967 RSC staging, which featured a Katherina who resembled a somewhat Elizabethan Annie Oakley. In 1990, A.J. Antoon's *Shrew*-western at New York's Public Theater, starring Tracey Ullman and Morgan Freeman, firmly reappropriated the West for North America, as did Miles Potter's cartoon-inspired 2003 Stratford, Ontario *Shrew*, a tale of two social misfits set in a spaghetti western milieu, in which Petruccio resembled Clint Eastwood's smouldering gun-slinger – 'ankle-length cattle-coat, saddle in hand, cigarette in the corner of his mouth, dusty hat pulled low over his eyes, six-shooter at his hip' – his entrance accompanied by a guitar sting sounding like a rattlesnake's warning (Shand, 'Romancing', 230).

Slap- or whip-happy stagings from the Bensons' onward prove that *The Shrew* is a tough and accommodating play and that farce – even when over-the-top – has special privileges as a major epistemological category: in more than one sense, it makes the play 'work' (see Saccio; Heilman; Moisan). One advantage of farce is that 'it spares us the necessity of thinking. The story of the wooing, wedding and taming of a shrew by a man of stronger will than her own then comes over to us comfortably as a high-spirited exploitation of the age-long humour of strange bedfellows' (Anthony Cookman, *Tatler*, 3 April 1960). In this view, espoused by critics who read *The Shrew* through its wagering tropes as game or sport (Leggatt, 41–62; Huston; Novy, *Argument*, 264n., 265, 279–80), farce magically (if not mysteriously) provides a way of laughing back at the play and, by gaining mastery over it, preserves it (and Shakespeare) from reproach. Or so one story goes. For George Bernard Shaw, however, nothing could 'make the spectacle of a man cracking a heavy whip at a starving woman other than disgusting and unmanly' (187). His bitter assessment has given *The Shrew* a difficult topicality, grounding a wave of responses exemplified by Shirley Nelson Garner, who views Katherina as well as herself as butts of the joke Freud describes that bonds the teller of a dirty joke and his male audience (see also Skura, 103), and for whom nothing redeems *The Shrew* from its hard opinions. Mapping a context in which *The Shrew* could be seen as social comedy, Alan Bott, reporting that, in 1920, a headmistress barred *The Shrew* from her New Hampshire girls' seminary because it 'gave the young an improper idea of man's relation to woman', thought such censorship patently absurd in 'depriv[ing] female students of a Shakespearean he-man, when a hundred well-known comedies showed the triumph of the she-woman, from *Love's Labour's Lost* and *Merry Wives*, by way of *She Stoops to Conquer*, to *What Every Woman Knows* and nearly every play adorned in London by Miss Marie Tempest or in New York by Miss Helen Hayes' (*Tatler*, 14 April 1937, 66–7). Another strand to this story, however, sees the Sly scenes as *The Shrew*'s saving grace. For by framing the taming, the story of the night told over can turn what Michael Billington saw as a brutally sexist polemic 'totally offensive to our age and society' (*Guardian*, 5 May 1978) into 'just a play' – a theatrical fantasy born of the playwright's (or Sly's) idle, wishful brain with little purchase on or address to either an early modern or a later social reality. That story is one which twentieth- and twenty-first-century performance and critical histories have not only mined but also called into question.

## *Sly-ing Christopher Sly*

By the early decades of the twentieth century, critical debates turned to formal concerns with *The Shrew*'s structure, particularly the questions raised by *A Shrew*'s 'epilogue'. Was Shakespeare's play incomplete? Or was Sly's disappearance deliberate? Including *A Shrew*'s epilogue not only resolves what textual scholars and theatrical practitioners have viewed as *The Shrew*'s incomplete textual condition (see pp. 25–7) but also encloses and distances the taming story. In this view, freedom is the name of the frame, permitting viewers to dissolve *The Shrew*'s gender politics into a ludic space where social roles slide into theatrical ones. Yet although the opening Sly scenes introduce tropes that the inset play develops – gendered identities, social mobility, hierarchical relations, economies of masculine desire and class (Rutter, 'Kate'; see also Shapiro, 143–66; Quilligan, 209–24; Orlin; and Marcus, *Unediting*) – as the dramatic fiction proceeds, it takes hold in and of itself, pulling audiences closer to its performance, which no longer needs a frame but instead opens out to address, even confront its offstage audience (Burns; see also Burt). To Sly or not to Sly? Whichever choice one espouses, Sly, once so detachable, has become the key to re-viewing and re-staging the scene of taming and a site for its critique.

In the wake of the Webster–Planché experiment, Sly became a signifier of the Elizabethan past in performances ranging from antiquarian revivals to those fusing Edwardian experiments with Elizabethan practices and the New Stagecraft associated with Max Reinhardt. Martin Harvey's 1913 staging featured a permanent locale, the Lord's manor house, and itinerant players carrying a wagonload of props, screens and curtains: seated at the edge of a sunken apron stage, Sly served as intermediary between the travelling players and the modern audience (see Mazer; MacDonald, 'Unholy'). Often played by a star comic, Sly appeared sporadically in London during the 1930s – parked in a gallery or upper room (Old Vic, 1931) or enthroned on the stage with servants and his 'wife' (New Theatre, 1937) – yet he was hardly known at Stratford between the two world wars, where even William Bridges-Adams, known as 'Unabridges Adams' for his penchant of playing everything written, cut Sly from his 1933 staging (Trewin, *Going*, 53). He also disappeared from the Pickford–Fairbanks film (Taylor, 1929) and Broadway's *Kiss Me, Kate* (1948); each, however, replaced him with another illusionary framework: the film with a Punch and Judy show, *Kate* with the familiar trope of making a musical about a musical, which equates a couple's ability to perform together onstage with their successful offstage sexual performance.

George Devine's SMT staging (1953) brought Sly back. Played on an elaborate open set, its expanded frame included a troupe of players and 'nudging, guffawing actor-spectators', chief among them Sly, who risked becoming more important than the inset play, and an epilogue in which the disbelieving Hostess accompanied Sly to hear his dream (*Nottingham Guardian*, 11 June 1953; Harold Conway, *Evening Standard*, 10 June 1953). As they left, Sly turned back to see the strolling players crossing the stage, with Katherina and Petruccio (Yvonne Mitchell and Marius Goring), at the procession's end – her head resting on his shoulder, his arms embracing her – a moment one critic thought 'magical' while another fantasized a new life for Sly (promptbook; *Spectator*, 12 June 1953; *Western Daily Press*, 11 June 1953). Devine's staging resembles the 'happy *Shrew*s' prevalent in mid-twentieth-century negotiated readings that reconciled a joyous conclusion with the coercive means through which it is reached – extreme versions of 'the end justifies the means'. In *Love's Labour's Lost*, *Much Ado* and *All's Well*, women 'cure' or refashion male behaviour, but *The Shrew*'s Katherina must be transformed from a challenger of patriarchal order to its most eloquent female spokesperson. Wresting pleasure from this scenario, critics not only viewed Katherina as undergoing a metamorphosis enabling her to engage pleasurably in the games of love and marriage (Leggatt; Huston, 58–93) but also read *The Shrew* as chronicling the achievement of a loving mutuality consonant with early modern ideas of companionate marriage (see e.g. Hibbard, 'Social'; Mikesell; see also Daniell; Miola). The story of the tempestuous woman, a nonconformist desiring mutuality on her own terms or on terms mutually defined, can easily turn *The Shrew* into *The Philadelphia Story* (1940) or *Bringing up Baby* (1938) – screwball comedies of remarriage which destabilize gender roles and neatly deflect and resolve any potential threats to heterosexual union by comic closure (see Cavell; Shand, 'Romancing').

Some features of Devine's staging reappeared, considerably magnified, in John Barton's 1960 SMT *Shrew*, which was part of a season designed to show 'the range, development and paradox of Shakespearean Comedy' (programme note; see also Holderness, 49–72). *The Shrew* was one of Barton's first ventures into using theatre as a laboratory for scholarship and into writing Shakespearean pastiche (his re-scripted *The Wars of the Roses* came three years later). He included *A Shrew*'s Sly 'interruptions', added bits from *A Shrew* to the opening (Third Player (later Katherina) asked for a shoulder of mutton as a property; introducing the inset play, First Player (later Baptista) remarked, ''Tis a good lesson for us . . . that are married men'), cut topical references, pared the subplot to a minimum and supplanted the play's concluding lines with *A Shrew*'s epilogue.

Alix Stone's 'rabbit hutch' set (*Spectator*, 15 July 1960), designed to reproduce an Elizabethan country inn yard, was set on a revolve that allowed spectators to see backstage action – actors consulting scripts, changing costumes, rushing up and down stairs and swigging ale; an invented 'Prompter', seated under a staircase, thumbed his promptbook and appeared occasionally in minor roles (see Fig. 16). However authentic, this prototype for later stagings at London's Shakespeare's Globe seemed at times to 'bear some resemblance to Piccadilly Circus in the rush hour' (Lisa Gordon, *Plays and Players* (n.d.), *Theatre Records*, Shakespeare Centre Library). Heavily stressing the proscenium confined the playing area, distancing the taming play as though it were a picture or painting: the result was 'a picture-frame stage with a quasi-Elizabethan stage set within it and within this, again, one finds the play' (*Education*, 1 July 1960), so that the emphasis was on varying levels of illusion. Outdoing William Poel, Barton's 'gently amusing antiquarian spectacle' (*The Times*, 22 June 1960), an Extreme Elizabethan *Shrew* obsessed with metatheatricality, repeatedly called attention to the frame: on entering, Lucentio and Tranio bowed to Sly, who responded to jokes about class and proverbial language; as Petruccio concluded his taming soliloquy, he bowed to Sly, who rose, acknowledging him; Sly's reactions to Katherina's homily were also carefully choreographed (promptbook). Played by the engaging Jack MacGowran, Sly became *The Shrew*'s 'inevitable hero' (*Stratford-upon-Avon Herald*, 27 April 1962). Moving from one balcony or window to another to watch from different angles, thus keying spectators to look *at* and *with* him, he resembled the court masque's designated spectator, the 'king' of this Sly-*Shrew*-show. Yet even though some thought that Sly overwhelmed the taming play (J.C. Trewin, *Illustrated London News*, 25 July 1960), Peggy Ashcroft's and Peter O'Toole's performances, which followed the joyous transformation model, made the production extremely popular: O'Toole's Petruccio, 'a gentleman posing as a virtuoso in shrew-taming . . . show[ed] no particle of ill-humour', and Ashcroft's Katherina, 'waiting for a man of spirit and an even stronger will than her own . . . contriv[ed] to tame racy, boisterous farce into rather touching sentimental comedy' (Anthony Cookman, *Tatler*, 3 August 1960).

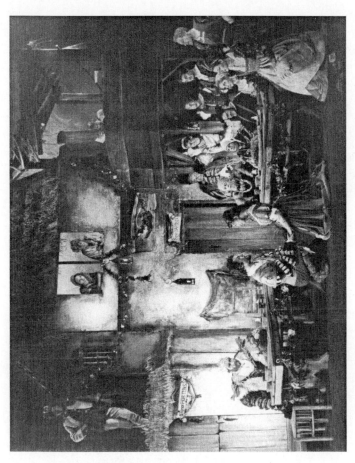

16  Finale of *The Taming of the Shrew*; Katherina (Peggy Ashcroft) and Petruccio (Peter O'Toole), directed by John Barton at the Shakespeare Memorial Theatre, 1960

Barton's refashioning returned *The Shrew* to its performative 'origins'; Michael Bogdanov's 1978 RSC staging moved in the opposite direction, marking a watershed moment for Sly and for *The Shrew*. Onstage was a Zeffirelli-esque view of Padua in perspective, somewhat surprising in an era of minimalist stage design. A commotion began in the front stalls, where a drunk theatregoer argued with a woman usher who threatened him with the police and asked him to leave. Shouting, 'No bloody woman pushes me about. I'm not taking orders from any snotty cow in a uniform . . . I'll soon sort you out' (promptbook), he leapt onto the stage, knocked over pillars, overturned fruit-laden baskets, demolished a balcony and pulled apart a statue of Diana; two flats fell over him, emptying the stage of its Italian-operatic scenery (see Fig. 17).[1] As lights came up, hunting horns sounded and men dressed in impeccable hunting pinks walked downstage out of swirling mist to discover the fallen drunk, a bloodied fox-skin thrown over his sleeping form, and to play out *The Shrew*'s opening moves, interweaving Shakespeare's language with Sly's invented colloquialisms. Having produced Sly out of an everyday battle of the sexes, this performance further unwrapped and doubled up identities, blurring distinctions between onstage and offstage, one role and another, one history and another. Jonathan Pryce's drunk changed from Sly the hunted to Petruccio the hunter (entering on a motorcycle); the argumentative usher, Paola Dionisotti, reappeared as Katherina. Scrawled on a backstage wall, the words 'SHREW Kills!' remained for some years, documenting the occasion.

This sensational *coup de théâtre* offers a chronotope of *The Shrew*'s theatrical culture – an organizing, historicizing moment, a complex theatrical signifier of the play's gender and class

---

1   At initial performances, some audience members left to ring the police. An early modern precedent occurred in a performance of *Periander* in 1608, during which an actor-spectator who began a disturbance from the audience was nearly thrown out and punished by the real audience, 'but as soone as it once appeared that hee was an actor their disdaine and anger turned to much pleasure and Content' (John Sansbury, *Periander*, in *The Christmas Prince* (Oxford, 1922), 286, 228; cited in Greenfield, 11).

17   Italianate set being demolished; Royal Shakespeare Company, 1978, directed by Michael Bogdanov

politics. Teasing spectators with memories of *Shrews* past, Bogdanov stripped away that stylistic inheritance: no scenic splendours or gorgeous period costumes softened the edges of this event set in a modern, mercantile milieu where, echoing the programme's image repertoire, women became objects of the male gaze, prisoners of their own images, matter for the pages of *Penthouse* or bodice-ripper novels, perhaps the most commodified sites for circulating romantic victimization (see Radway). Arguing that Shakespeare was a proto-feminist who exposed the social strictures of his era, Bogdanov held that *The Shrew* could no longer be considered a domestic marital comedy, but should be understood as 'the ruthless subduing of a woman by a man in a violent excess of male savagery, couched in the form of a class wish-fulfilment dream of revenge' (*Shakespeare*, 1.133–4, 138–9). Yet despite viewing the Sly scenes as encoding clues to *The Shrew*'s 'real nature', Bogdanov's staging ended not with *A Shrew*'s epilogue but with a reminder of the opening frame:

As the characters sit around the table . . . we hear faintly, stealing in from a far distance, the sounds of hunters' horns, of hounds baying . . . to which that Lord, so long ago now, almost in some other country, discovered the comatose body of a certain drunken tinker. We had forgotten: These solid events of shrew-taming have been only an insubstantial pageant. It is like an elaborately painted scrim, back-lit, shimmering and becoming transparent . . . like the end of *The Tempest*.

(Julia Novick, *Village Voice*, 25 September 1978, 130)

Recrossing the frame to speak their own gender politics, some critics overwrote that sense of ending. Although most, echoing Bogdanov, read his staging as 'a male supremacist's fantasy, the longed-for revenge of the Sly clan upon its uppity women' (*New Statesman*, 12 May 1978), many (male) critics stood apart from Sly, reserving their praise for Petruccio – or, rather, for Jonathan Pryce's Petruccio: 'a tearaway performance'; a 'manic chauvinist pig' who brings 'tense alertness, grating determination and happy flamboyance to the job of shrew-taming' (*Observer*, 7 May 1978; *Guardian*, 5 May 1978; *Listener*, 11 May 1978). For most, Dionisotti's Katherina was all shrew: a 'hard-faced bitch with a strident voice [and] a mean temper'; 'a hot-tempered, strong-chinned, minor Magnani' (*New Statesman*, 12 May 1978; *Guardian*, 5 May 1978); only Jane Ellison noted how attitudes sympathetic to Katherina were fully justified in this atmosphere of commodity dealing, where 'her sour refusal to be sold to the highest bidder is seen as frustration and rebellion against the marriage market' (*Evening Standard*, 5 May 1978). Wincing at the dark overtones of domestic violence, Michael Billington, ventriloquizing George Bernard Shaw, concluded that this 'barbaric, disgusting play' should be shelved, never again performed (*Guardian*, 5 May 1978).

Although it is tempting to imagine a cause-and-effect relationship which would give theatre priority over literary culture, what can be said is that Bogdanov's staging anticipated feminist, new historicist and cultural materialist criticism that, during the twentieth century's last decades, would shine an increasingly brilliant spotlight on *The Shrew*. From the first, feminist/gender studies and performance studies, two emergent critical 'ghettos', converged around *The Shrew* (Ranald, 'Performance'). Cued in part by Betty Friedan's *The Feminine Mystique* (1963), the first wave of feminist critics argued that the new critical orthodoxy of reading *The Shrew* through a comic lens ignored real differences in husbands' and wives' access to economic and socio-cultural power in the early modern period. Moreover, a post-Vietnam climate of political engagement brought an urgent need to reclaim *The Shrew* from Petruccio and for women – if not for their pleasure then as a means of understanding their past history and their position in present-day patriarchies. Arguing that the play is less about taming a shrew than about exposing how a society conditions men to believe that women need taming, Coppélia Kahn viewed Katherina as finding, in marriage, a newly-fashioned subjectivity which gave her the power to (re)create Petruccio as a good man (104; see also Dusinberre; Bean; Perret). Carol Thomas Neely acknowledged a double perspective: although 'feminists cannot . . . fail to rejoice at the spirit, wit and joy with which Kate accommodates herself to her wifely role', neither can they 'fail to note the radical asymmetry and inequality of the comic reconciliation and wish for Kate, as for [themselves], that choices were less limited, roles less rigid and unequal, accommodations more mutual and less coerced' (218–19; see also Novy, *Argument*). With the figure of the patriarchal bard squarely in view, Kathleen McLuskie's seminal account of feminist and historicist reading strategies (92–3) engendered others (see especially Woodbridge; Newman, esp. 42); by the 1980s, it seemed that there was oppression, no end of oppression – and especially for women;[1] or, as Ann

---

1 Adapting Stephen Greenblatt's 'There is subversion, no end of subversion, only not for us' ('Invisible bullets', 45).

Thompson wrote, 'The real problem lies outside the play in the fact that the subjection of women to men, although patently unfair and unjustifiable, is still virtually universal. It is the world that offends us, not Shakespeare' (41).

More recent criticism has expanded the boundaries of feminist enquiry: Joel Fineman, Patricia Parker (*Margins*) and Laurie Maguire (*Names*) have mined *The Shrew*'s linguistic twists, turns and tropes of identity and subjectivity; Marianne Novy's essay collections have considered how historically situated women readers have responded to Shakespeare, and *The Shrew* (*Re-Visions*; see also Fleming). Situating *The Shrew* in its early modern contexts – including debates over the nature of women (see e.g. Martin), women's legal status, the contours of the domestic household – critics searched for the voices that spoke into it from the Elizabethan–Jacobean social imaginary. Historical enquiry is always an interested process, especially when examining sites and sights of gender struggle, and sustained investigations such as Frances E. Dolan's exemplary work (*Taming*; *Marriage*) have been responsible for engendering a new orthodoxy that has positioned *The Shrew* as a limit text for women's histories.

Perhaps one of the most influential landmarks among such studies, Lynda Boose's article on the scold's bridle and its restrictions on women's speech embraces a double perspective, balancing meanings pertinent to *The Shrew*'s original historical moment against the liberating potential of performance ('Scolding'). Exploring a related context, that of the agricultural problems of land enclosure, Boose situates *The Shrew* as a 'middle- and lower-class male viewer's fused fantasies of erotic reward, financial success and upward social mobility', fantasies which eventually impact on Katherina ('Husbandry', 215, 219). Following her lead and turning to *A Shrew*'s tropes of class and gender, Jean Howard points to how Sly's claim that he knows how to tame a shrew suggests that 'there is always something lower than a beggar – a beggar's wife' (139). Others have explored material domesticity: situating the play in the proto-commodity culture of the late 1580s and 1590s, in which the housewife becomes a consumer rather than a producer, Natasha Korda draws on Marxian notions to reveal how the housewife's subjectivity is constructed in relation to status objects: Katherina, she argues, must learn to indulge, not in excessive language but in an excess of things (71–5). Rather than opposing language and things, Lena Orlin links them: arguing that things have social as well as theatrical life and that both work as forms of exchange, she explores how self-identity and subjectivity are connected to possessions and class distinctions, leading to rivalries and metamorphoses (167–8, 172–5; see also Christensen). Although all this work engages with aspects of recent performances, Boose's and Howard's work in particular seems almost tailor-made to provide an extra-theatrical framework for Bogdanov's staging as well as a lens for situating Bill Alexander's 1992 *Shrew*, which, by interweaving *A Shrew*'s conventional treatment of class and social hierarchy with *The Shrew*'s emphasis on hierarchical gender relations (see Holderness & Loughrey, 33), gave fresh theatrical prominence to ideas currently circulating in critical culture.

Alexander's *Shrew* ousted Sly from the Ugly Duckling, a wink at Stratford's Dirty Duck, the pub across the road from the theatre. But another joke was also afoot, as a group the programme identified as 'Lord Simon's party' stumbled upon the sleeping Sly: deciding that 'the drunk needs teaching a lesson . . . We'll mess with his mind for a bit' (promptbook), Simon took Sly to his Elizabethan manor house to join the audience for a St Valentine's Day entertainment. Dressed in theatrical versions of working-men's gear, the hired players resembled Sly (or the RSC on tour), but when they returned, dressed in sumptuous period costumes, they began acting like surrogates of their patrons, who were seated on an upstage raised dais beside a Sly now resplendent in a brocade dressing-gown. *The Shrew* itself also doubled up, played out between Katherina (Amanda Harris) and Petruccio (Anton Lesser) and Lady Sarah Ormsby and Lord Simon, between aristos and actors, and between Shakespeare's taming scenarios and Alexander's restructured opening which, like Bogdanov's, wrote present-day idiom onto early modern text (Rutter, 'Kate', 203–9).

Juxtaposing a (more or less) early modern *Shrew* to a present-day parallel narrative and emphasizing class dynamics was not precisely new. Lashing sexual and social scenarios together, Charles Marowitz's 1974 *Shrew*-collage, conceived as a 'head-on confrontation with the [play's] intellectual substructure' (24) and a challenge to its classical status, alternated Shakespearean scenes with exchanges between a bourgeois young woman and her working-class lover, exploiting the possibility of reading the one through the other (Hodgdon, *Trade*, 4). Later, Di Trevis (1985–6) set *The Shrew* side by side with Bertolt Brecht's and Elisabeth Hauptmann's *Happy End*, cross-casting the two plays. Played in Brechtian style on a traverse stage by Victorian strolling players, the performance – bannered as 'A Kind Of History' – heavily stressed class distinctions. That was especially striking at the close, where, after the Lord threw coins at Sly and exited, laughing, Sly saw the actor who had played Katherina scrubbing the floor, her baby strapped to her chest: as the lights faded, the two stared at one another, as though recognizing that the Lord had exploited them equally (Cousin; Schafer, *Ms-Directing*, 57–72). Putting a new twist on such scenarios, Alexander's staging closed the gap between parallel narratives and played the frame *against* the taming play, a frame-breaking move which created a community of onstage and offstage interpreters grounded in Sly as a unique interpretive subject (AR) – a strategy echoing but also exceeding Barton's and Bogdanov's stagings and one that, in a 1990s post-Thatcherite Britain deep in recession, fashioned a critique of *The Shrew* aimed at commodity-obsessed upper-class audiences (see Boose, 'Husbandry', 213n.).

The friction between frame and fiction, engendering recognitions and misrecognitions among onstage and offstage audiences, came to a head at several points. At Petruccio's house, the actors pulled the watchers into the fiction, casting Lady Sarah as Katherina and the rest as Petruccio's servants, with Grumio as prompter-MC (4.1). Verbally and physically disempowered, the aristos became so many Slys, victimized by the scripts forced on them and by an authoritarian Petruccio who kicked Lady Sarah as she tried to remove his boot (promptbook) – an instance of class revenge which nearly convinced Peter Holland that *The Shrew* is 'about class and that male subjugation of women is only an example of masters' oppression of servants' (*English*, 90; see also Dolan, *Marriage*; pp. 48–50). Had Alexander chosen to play out the logic of his transfictional framing device before enclosing it, Lady Sarah might have been handed Katherina's homily and either spoken or stumbled through it (Rutter, 'Kate', 208–9). Alexander, however, displaced any potential critique away from the play onto the watchers in a strategically choreographed close. After Katherina and Petruccio left, hand in hand, the watchers shook hands with the actors, and Ruth, the one among Lord Simon's party who had crossed the frame most decisively, joined the Hortensio-actor – a choice that not only critiqued her place in the class system but also suggested that performance offers a utopian space where socio–economic dynamics may be muted or forgotten: as Petruccio had put it, when Sly objected to Vincentio's being sent to prison (5.1): 'It's all right. It's only a play' (echoing *A Shrew*, 1330). However, when Lady Sarah and Lord Simon started to exit, rather than echoing Katherina and Petruccio's happy union, Sarah rejected Simon's embrace and (upstaging Big Daddy) left on her own. Sly, again in workman's clothes, was brought in; the Ugly Duckling's Hostess exited with him, but as they left, the lights faded on an exchange of looks between Sly and the players – a moment resembling the ending of Ridley Scott's *Thelma and Louise* (1991) or of Julie Taymor's *Titus* (2000), where a freeze-frame marks how the issues raised by the performance hang suspended, ripe for resolving within the larger cultural debate.

### *Katherina on behalf of the play*[1]

For performers, directors and critics alike, Katherina's last speech, which caps her history and renegotiates her role, is a fatal attraction, a locus of obsessive attention in a scene that is 'riddled with visible and invisible bullets . . . fraught with sexual and social implication' (Bogdanov, *Shakespeare*, 1.145). Just as early modern law courts relied on rhetoric as an instrument of civil order, so did the stage: the ending of *The Shrew* resembles a trial, in which providing a credible story is one way of establishing the 'truth' (Cunningham). And even as publicly staging Katherina's Pauline homily (see pp. 50–4) valorizes women's speech and crowns the play, it also tests the performance and, especially, the performer. On the page, her speech is both noisy and mute, for just at the moment when she seems most 'readable', in that her autonomy becomes most fully realized, her presence also can seem most opaque, its meanings released only by an historically situated performer or reader. How Shakespeare's original performers negotiated these moments and how audiences heard and responded remain purely conjectural. For subsequent performers, however, the speech sets up a tension between the historicity of Katherina's inherited rhetoric and its address to a culture (or cultures) that has, especially since the latter half of the twentieth century, either rewritten or questioned its forms and pressures.

The roles, attributes and ideologies of gender circulating in any era provide coded meanings that performers and critics mobilize to construct – or deconstruct – the story of Katherina's speech. Even the earliest commentary, 'Something pretty might be made of this in pastorale' – an anonymous annotation made *c*. 1670 in a copy of the First Folio (Hackel, 150; see also Blayney,

---

1    Playing on Kenneth Burke's 'Antony in behalf of the play'.

'Introduction') – hints at a widening gap between *The Shrew*'s Elizabethan–Jacobean moment and the late seventeenth century. A century later, Bell's 1774 edition noted: 'This speech must ever stamp credit on its author . . . and we wish that, not only every unmarried, but also married lady, were perfect in the words and practice.' Deeming the speech too long, Bell thought it (and the play) should end with 'When we are bound to serve, love, and obey', for what follows 'is monstrously insipid' (sigs H3$^v$–H4$^r$). That both comments view the speech as detachable (somewhat like Sly?) – the one positioning it in an Arcadian (if not Edenic) genre, the latter appropriating its pedagogy – aligns with a common eighteenth-century practice of printing the speech separately, circulating it as a sermon (Marcus, *Unediting*, 125; see also Novy, *Re-Visions*, 7).

In the wake of America's Civil War, Ada Rehan (1887) evoked General Sherman's remark that Katherina reminded him of a soldier as she 'braced herself for her last grand fight, and fought it with vigor. Being defeated . . . her submission was absolute, and she acknowledged her conqueror as frankly as she had defied him' (Daly, x). William Winter maps the trajectory of Rehan's military model: she 'show[ed] pride, scorn, sarcasm, anger, bewilderment, terrified amazement, and, at the last, sweetly feminine tenderness'; in her closing speech, 'she was seen to be unmistakably the same woman, only now her actual self' (*Stage*, 525). His account points towards what more recent Katherinas – Paola Dionisotti (Bogdanov, 1978), Sinead Cusack (Kyle, 1982) and Fiona Shaw (Miller, 1987) – have described as the actorly labour of negotiating the transformation from shrew to not-shrew, the problems of reconciling textual obligation, directorial concepts and their own gender politics to reach the end-point which Winter's phrase describes as a schizoid subjectivity.[1]

---

1 See Rutter, *Clamorous*, 1–25. Other than in (unrecorded) Q&A sessions or brief interviews, no more recent Katherina has commented on performing the role; Michael Siberry (Edwards, 1995), however, has written about his Petruccio (see Smallwood, 45–59).

Much late twentieth-century criticism begins with and on what has come to be called Katherina's 'speech of submission' and reads the play backwards through it – a quirk of critical practice that tends to erase the layering of the speech, detaching it from a scene that troubles comic form and cultural custom where the final stage picture sets Katherina (however performed) against two conventional (perhaps even misaligned) couples who represent the *status quo* (Dolan, 'Household', 218–19). Moreover, discussions of the speech often split it apart, separating those lines evoking biblical texts and the *Book of Common Prayer* from what follows. That Katherina speaks in two voices (if not from two bodies) suggests a double subjectivity: on the one hand, she ventriloquizes the culture's prerogatives; on the other, she formulates an exegesis of those prerogatives. Viewing *The Shrew* as brushing against the worlds of the history plays, David Daniell reads her speech as resembling those of contentious claimants to the throne (31). Moreover, not only does its scriptural content accord the speech cultural power, but its strong rhythms generate a formal mode of containment – what Gayatri Spivak (following Fredric Jameson) calls the prison-house of patriarchal language (176). For Lynda Boose, Katherina speaks her 'self-deposition, where – in a performance not unlike Richard II's – she moves center stage to dramatize her own similarly theatrical rendition of "Mark, how I will undo myself"' ('Scolding', 179).

Setting Katherina's homily beside *A Shrew*'s more conventional articulation of gender hierarchy puts that extremist position in perspective. Whereas *A Shrew*'s speech argues that women must submit to men not only because, as creatures made from Adam's rib, God created them as inferior but also because they were responsible for man's Fall from Paradise, apologists for Shakespeare's version argue that it expresses an attitude of 'humanistic' mutuality consonant with the Protestant ideal of companionate marriage (see Miola, 27–33). That was made visible in Jonathan Miller's 1980–1 BBC production, which closed with a community of celebrants singing Psalm 128, which praises a peaceful family life, from partbooks. If, as is often the case with present-day stagings, the interval follows Petruccio's soliloquy on shrew-taming, Katherina's speech offers a structural rhyme that not only tests the efficacy of his project but also, by giving her equal pride of place, supports such mutuality.

Another critical strategy focuses on the speech's final section, where Katherina refers to the female body – a moment that, given the convention of the all-male stage, poses questions about whether or not gender is grounded in the body. In the opening Sly scenes, gender slips easily between sexed bodies: the logic of the early modern stage suggests that gender roles bear no relation to 'natural' bodies but are simply play-acting. Arguing that appending *A Shrew*'s epilogue undercuts the discourse of the body in Katherina's final speech, Maureen Quilligan observes that, without it, the fiction of her femaleness remains intact, permitting early modern audiences to imagine that what they see is a 'real' woman choosing a wifely role, not a male fantasy of that role (223). Situating these lines within the context of women's history, Natasha Korda reads them as articulating a 'new division of labour' that erases the idea of housework as work and 'renders the housewife perpetually indebted to her husband, as her "love, fair looks" and true obedience are insufficient payment for the material comforts in which she is passively "kept"' (72). Paul Yachnin extends Korda's thinking by connecting consumption to the commercial theatre; viewing the trajectory of Katherina's role as 'homologous with the situation of many Elizabethan cultural consumers, especially with regard to their ambivalence toward the status hierarchy', he reads across two histories, on the one hand acknowledging the 'poignant loss of freedom attendant on gaining social legitimacy that has made the play important to modern bourgeois culture', and on the other conjecturing that what Elizabethan audiences understood was that 'submission to her socially mandated place as lady and obedient wife gives *her* pleasure, even erotic pleasure'. In expressing a desire, whether conscious or unconscious, for the tamer, Katherina not only becomes a perfectly obedient subject but, like her counterpart, Sly, delights in the bodily erotics of social masquerade (60–1).

By introducing the trope of pleasure, Yachnin speaks for a segment of the interpretive community that willingly affirms a sincere Katherina who means what she says. However, desiring the tamer is one thing; desiring the taming, quite another. Critical as well as theatrical performances construct apologies for the play in order to reconcile the two, whether putting pressure on the Sly frame to insulate the action or emphasizing the delights of 'shrewd and kindly farce' (Saccio). Yet the playing-field that dreams a joyful finale is far from even: Katherina and Petruccio travel a rocky road to reach an ending: Fiona Shaw (Miller, 1987) sees their journey as 'almost medieval . . . like all those journeys of people who go through a terrible ordeal' (cited in Rutter, *Clamorous*, 25). Performances that emphasize the brutality of the taming process and situate Katherina as the victim of patriarchal (or Petruccian) tyranny turn *The Shrew* into just such an ordeal, robbing the play of any potential pleasure. The most biting critiques foreground the shrew-figure's psychic destruction, trapping Katherina in a sado-masochistic dynamic, as in Charles Marowitz's 1974 *Shrew*-collage, a Grimms' fairy-tale of sinister archetypes and hopeless victims that invoked the Stockholm syndrome (see Detmer, esp. 287), ending with a dream sequence drawn from *A Shrew*'s Sly materials. Following the sun–moon scene, Petruccio commanded Katherina, 'Madam, undress you and come now to bed'. When she asked to be spared for a night or two, Baptista and servants held Katherina down; Petruccio 'whips up her skirts ready to do buggery . . . [and] an ear-piercing, electronic whistle rises to crescendo pitch; Kate's mouth is wild and open, and it appears as if the sound issues from her lungs'. Following a blackout, lights came up on a surreal tribunal where Katherina, dressed in a shapeless institutional garment and seemingly mesmerized, delivered her speech, Petruccio frequently prompting her. As she concluded, the couple from the present-day parallel plot, dressed in formal attire and smiling out at invisible photographers for a wedding photo, framed her figure – a juxtaposition suggesting that marriage legitimates psycho-social and psycho-sexual abuse (Marowitz, *Shrew*, 179–80). Yücel Erten's Turkish adaptation of *The Shrew* (1986) pushed Marowitz's ending even further: as Katherina concluded her speech, she sank to the floor, her shawl slipping from her shoulders and arms to reveal that she had slit her wrists – a martyrdom some Turkish feminists viewed as protest against *The Shrew*'s traditional conclusion while others thought it far too extreme (Zeynep Oral, cited in Elsom, 74–5).

Some thirty years after Marowitz, Edward Hall's all-male *Shrew* (Propeller, 2006–7) also emphasized brute-force taming. When Dugald Bruce-Lockhart's hyper-macho Petruccio ripped the Tailor's gown from Simon Scardifield's punked-up Katherina and lashed her body, she went limp, terrified. Even Baptista joined in, slamming Katherina's nose in a door, forcing Bianca indoors and beating Tranio and Biondello, who appeared wearing bandages covered with blood – an omen of the finale. Summoned to speak, Katherina hesitated; then, sensing that she would be beaten again if she did not comply, she '[laid] it on thick . . . not daring to look at anyone', until, at Petruccio's 'Why, there's a wench', she glanced towards her father, as though begging him to intervene. When he ignored her, she seemed destroyed – 'the victimised moral centre of a grotesque and misogynistic world into which she can fit only through self-abnegation' (Sam Marlowe, *The Times*, 20 September 2006). Overall, commanding central performances and inventive farcical detail lightened the taming's impact, producing the sense of a stag party seen through a high-camp lens during the first half, but as the physical cruelty intensified, laughter faded into guilty silence. Critical opinion wavered: Peter Smith called it a 'courageous reading' ('Review', 66); Sandy Holt thought it intriguing that 'in today's post-feminism world audiences are less likely to feel ill at ease seeing a man abuse his wife, if his wife is played by a male actor' (*Stratford-upon-Avon Herald*, 9 November 2006).

Perhaps. Yet such an attitude not only strains at wishful thinking but also off-handedly licenses male–male violence. Would an all-female *Shrew* invite a similar logic? David Ultz's *The Taming of the Shrew: The Women's Version* (1985) for the Theatre Royal Stratford East first tested that proposition. Set within the context of a feminist theatre group meeting, the action unfolded on a scaffolded stage lit like a film studio: neo-Brechtian captions displayed the play's themes; characters burst through paper screens; spray-painted cartoons outlined Katherina and Bianca, marking them, respectively, as devil and saint. Mining *The Shrew*'s deep historical contexts as well as Marowitz's concept of brainwashing, Fiona Victory's Petruccio encased Katherina in a muzzle labelled 'Scold' and perused a falconry manual while subjecting her 'to a barrage of flashing lights'. At the final banquet, Katherina (Susan Cox) stepped off the stage and shouted out her speech, which was 'passed off as an hysterical brainstorm' (*Guardian*, 15 March 1985): stifled by cast members, she was bundled in a blanket, recalling her folklore fate in 'A Merry Jest of a Shrewd and Curst Wife' (see pp. 42–3). Reflecting on what read as a bitterly satirical 'feminist tract about the depersonalisation of women' (Suzie Mackenzie, *Time Out*, 14 March 1985), Francis King imagined that 'A true women's version of *The Taming of the Shrew* would surely be to reverse the sexes and show how a woman can break the spirit of a man and subject him to her own will' (*Sunday Telegraph*, 17 March 1985) – a play, of course, that existed in other guises, among them Fletcher's *Tamer Tamed*. Carole Woddis, however, found herself 'still waiting for the real "women's version", directed by a woman' (*City Limits*, 15 March 1985).

The idea that a woman director might make *The Shrew* speak with a difference suggests a somewhat naive – and essentialized – assumption that a woman possesses a magical key to unlock the play. Staged as part of 2003's 'Season of Regime Change' at

Shakespeare's Globe, Phyllida Lloyd's *Shrew* raised the ante on that assumption with single-sex casting in which, according to its prologue, 'The girls do get the chance to wear the codpiece'. In a doubles act packed with physical comedy that verged on sado-masochistic farce, Janet McTeer's commanding Petruccio – 'a triumph of cross-dressing and cross-being' (Nicholas de Jongh, *Evening Standard*, 22 August 2003) – and Kathryn Hunter's diminutive, waif-like Katherina seemed bent on mounting a feminist critique by 'guying the rituals and mannerisms of men' (Lyn Gardner, *Guardian*, 23 August 2003) as well as mocking the rites of taming. That strategy culminated when Hunter delivered Katherina's speech 'like a spoof preacher or a parody fanatic' (de Jongh). Breaking the speech into beats, Hunter played each transition as a false ending (to the relief of the onstage 'men') followed by a renewed (and unwelcome) beginning; finally, she and the other wives, giggling uncontrollably, prostrated themselves before their husbands. Refusing to kiss Petruccio, Katherina left, unnoticed by Petruccio or the others, robbing him of a triumphal exit – a counter-echo of Zeffirelli's film, where Elizabeth Taylor's Katherina disappeared, leaving Richard Burton's Petruccio ensnared by a mob of admiring women. With no Sly to frame or enclose the action, a substitute epilogue in Italian, played on the Globe's upper level, staged Katherina and Petruccio in a full-blown domestic quarrel – 'a sort of *Punch and Judy Meet The Sopranos*' (Shand, 'Guying', esp. 556–7, 559–60). If the finale sent up Katherina's homily by girling the guys, the epilogue, seemingly designed to mock the Slys among the audience with hints of what's in store for them, underpinned an all too familiar everyday scenario: ultimately, joining over-the-top farcical exaggerations to a post-feminist moment blunted or neutralized any potential critical edge.

Although Petruccio's ideal of 'awful rule and right supremacy' may be somewhat dated, Katherina-players have a long history of speaking back to ideology by delivering her homily as a performance. Perhaps the most famous instance occurred in the Pickford–Fairbanks *Shrew* (Taylor, 1929), where Pickford's Katherina delivered the homily standing behind a self-satisfied Petruccio: each knew that she was humouring him. Making that visible, Katherina gave a broad wink, directed at the viewer and Bianca, who acknowledged it – a scenario which assumes an unspoken understanding that joins sisters under the skin, engendering a community of secret sharers that even includes the absent Sly. In William Ball's all-*commedia*-all-the-time *Shrew* (1973), Fredi Olster's Katherina borrowed Pickford's wink but directed it only to the audience; it was she who embraced Petruccio on 'Kiss me, Kate' – a line Cybill Shepherd (*Moonlighting*, 1986) changed to 'Kiss me, Petruccio'.

Nearly fifty years later, Paola Dionisotti's Katherina (Bogdanov, 1978) took Pickford's wink even further: simultaneously taking the speech literally and mocking the ideals of male dominance it expresses, she exposed them as mere fantasy (Kahn, 116). 'Confronted with the logic of his own actions, [Petruccio] quails, and when she ventures to kiss his shoe, he instantly withdraws his foot . . . It is the best interpretation of this scene I remember, but one has to wade through a lot of wife-beating to get to it' (Michael Billington, *Guardian*, 5 May 1978). Some, however, not only missed the irony but aligned the performance with their own beliefs and desires: 'how superbly Miss Dionisotti accommodates all kinds of duty until her own most moving total submissiveness to her master' (Desmond Pratt, *Yorkshire Post*, 6 May 1978); 'the pair have fallen in love' (John Barber, *Daily Telegraph*, 6 May 1978); 'her great anti-Women's Lib speech [made it clear that] she is lost forever' (B.A. Young, *Financial Times*, 5 May 1978). Yet there was little ambiguity about what followed. Petruccio left, a 20,000–crown cheque in his hand, Katherina trailing after him: as Dionisotti put it, 'He's as trapped now by society as she was in the beginning . . . The last image was of two very lonely people' (cited in Rutter, *Clamorous*, 23). Still caught in this *Shrew*'s mercantile world of traffic in

18 Katherina (Paola Dionisotti) kneels before Petruccio (Jonathan Pryce), directed by Michael Bogdanov for the Royal Shakespeare Company, 1978

women, the rest – including Grumio, who retrieved the money Katherina had won for his master – hardly noticed their exit.

Gale Edwards (RSC, 1995) pushed Bogdanov's idea of *The Shrew* as a masculine dream of power further but, by hollowing out that dream from within, set it on a collision course with nightmare. Playing Katherina's homily as an improvisational aria, Josie Lawrence, star of the comedy game show *Whose Line Is It Anyway?* (a question Katherina might ask of her final speech), deconstructed the speech: showing how it was made, she marked out a 'space apart', as though observing Katherina from a (Brechtian) distance. As she sank to the floor, stretching out her hand, Petruccio stumbled and knelt beside her. But rather than leaving with the money and Katherina, he bowed his head, acknowledging the space of shame Katherina had redefined as his own. In the production's epilogue, Petruccio (re-dressed as Sly) again knelt before Katherina, dressed as Sly's wife, 'Kate Hacket', who touched his head and shoulder, perhaps in forgiveness. Did an apology from the Petruccio/ Slys of the world rewrite *Shrew*-history? Lawrence's Kate Hacket seemed unsure (see Hodgdon, *Trade*, 33–8; Schafer, *Ms-Directing*, 67–72; Werner, 81–95).

After twenty years of calling Katherina's homily to account, the twentieth century closed on a growing consensus that her speech 'could not be left as an unquestioned celebration of the taming of a shrew into the delights of normative matrimony, unless the production was to shirk its responsibilities both to the play and to its modern audience' (Holland, 'Shakespeare', 204). Yet even before the millennium turned, there were signs of a sea-change. No longer was *The Shrew* being viewed primarily as the patriarchal manifesto recuperated by recent critical and theatrical cultures – the story of a woman's humiliation wrapped in the glittering tissue paper of farce. It would be facile, however, to assume that the era of confrontational gender politics had been swept away by an emergent post-feminist world view (see Brooks), for angry *Shrew*s bent on serving up patriarchal tyranny as a main course were still being staged throughout the twenty-first century's first decade. Nor could this shift be read as nostalgia for another genre that would reify a past *Shrew*-history. Rather than pigeonholing *The Shrew* into one particular genre – farcical taming play, fine romance, feminist tract or masculine dream of power – Julie Taymor's staging for New York's Theatre for a New Audience (1988) consciously viewed the play through various lenses. Stressing the other characters' conventionality, her staging set Katherina and Petruccio off against them, playing the erotic excitement of their intellectual compatibility and their shared delight in games as leading to a mutual equality, capped by Sheila Dabney's Katherina delivering her homily from atop the banqueting table: 'Much as it might hurt her pride, [she was] willing to play the woman because she loved him. The gesture was grand, and it moved him' (Taymor, cited in Blumenthal, 127–8; see also Lanier).

Taymor's strategy anticipates that of Gregory Doran's RSC staging (2003), which, like Bogdanov's, represents a chronotope, an historicizing moment – one that remembered and regenerated an ending other than the one that cannot forget the psychic destruction of the woman. Doran took risks both with the central couple (Alexandra Gilbreath and Jasper Britton) and with the play's theatrical and critical baggage. Eliminating Sly removed the frame that either insulates the taming or turns *The Shrew* into just another story of 'The Boys from Padua', and the play became the story of two psychologically vulnerable people: a Katherina cast aside by her father, a Petruccio still mourning his father's death. And, just as Ada Rehan's red dress (also worn by many others) became material for interpretation (thus resembling a written text), costume also figured in the ending. Cracking theatrical codes, Gilbreath's Katherina, unlike her predecessors, did not wear a Big Dress that shouted her conformity to social customs: rather, she appeared 'as herself', a kind of counter-culture figure wearing mismatched clothes. Having discarded her muddied wedding dress (as outrageous as Petruccio's attire), she wore only its under-dress, tucked up to show leggings (a substitute for breeches, one sign of the early modern shrewish woman; see Woodbridge, 217), brown boots – and the cap (defining the married woman), flipped inside out. Her costume remembered Petruccio's logic ('is the jay more precious than the lark / Because his feathers are more beautiful?', 4.3.174–5) and realized it on her back, a material sign of his philosophy. So dressed, she was neither the obedient wife of masculine desire nor the resistant shrewish woman but a learned metamorphosis (Hodgdon, 'Bride-ing'). Taking centre stage, she controlled the space, playing to – and with – her auditors (see Fig. 19). Yet when she extended her hand ('My hand is ready'), she paused: surprised, Petruccio also paused, after 'Why, there's a wench', raised his foot ('Come on') – and

19 Katherina (Alexandra Gilbreath) takes centre stage, directed by Gregory Doran for the Royal Shakespeare Company, 2003

waited. So did Katherina. But as she started to kneel before him, Petruccio swept her into his arms for a big romantic kiss (Gilbert, 333–4). At the end, the woman who had mistaken herself for a shrew and put on a surprising performance by dressing down her audience exited with Petruccio, cheek by jowl.

For many critics and viewers, *The Shrew* ends neither with spoken words nor with an exit (or exits) but in a space beyond the play. Far from empty, that space, as densely inhabited with variant readings as the play's finale, constitutes a not-so-invisible frame filled with speculative, subjective performances that cannot be precisely named or analysed. There are good reasons why comedies end at a point where marriage is still just over the horizon. As Feste knows, 'What's to come is still unsure'. There are even better reasons why *The Shrew*, which explicitly evokes the words of the marriage ceremony, ends where it does (see Burns, 91–102). For as the play opens out to its audiences, it teases them with memory and desire, invites them to consider what a marriage – or remarriage – is, how 'peace . . . and love, and quiet life [and] what not that's sweet and happy' might be achieved, and what wonders might lie ahead.

# THE TAMING
# OF THE SHREW

# LIST OF ROLES

## THE INDUCTION

| | | |
|---|---|---:|
| Christopher SLY | *a tinker* | |
| HOSTESS | *an alewife* | |
| LORD | | |
| BARTHOLOMEW | *the Lord's page* | |
| HUNTSMEN ⎫ | *attending the Lord* | 5 |
| SERVANTS ⎭ | | |
| PLAYERS | | |

## THE PLAY-WITHIN-THE-PLAY

| | | |
|---|---|---:|
| BAPTISTA Minola | *a rich citizen of Padua* | |
| KATHERINA | *his elder daughter* | |
| BIANCA | *his younger daughter* | 10 |
| PETRUCCIO | *a gentleman of Verona* | |
| GRUMIO | *his groom* | |
| HORTENSIO | *Petruccio's friend, suitor to Bianca* | |
| LUCENTIO | *a gentleman of Pisa, suitor to Bianca* | |
| TRANIO ⎫ | *Lucentio's servants* | 15 |
| BIONDELLO ⎭ | | |
| GREMIO | *a rich old man, suitor to Bianca* | |
| VINCENTIO | *Lucentio's father* | |
| MERCHANT | *from Mantua* | |
| WIDOW | *Hortensio's wife* | 20 |
| CURTIS | *Petruccio's steward* | |
| NATHANIEL ⎫ | | |
| PHILIP ⎪ | | |
| JOSEPH ⎬ | *Petruccio's servants* | |
| NICHOLAS ⎪ | | 25 |
| PETER ⎭ | | |
| TAILOR | | |
| HABERDASHER | | |

Attendants, Servants (Walter, Sugarsop, Gregory,
Gabriel, Adam, Rafe), Officer      30

LIST OF ROLES Rowe was the first editor to provide a cast-list; it gives male roles first, followed by female roles, a practice that continued well into the 20th century. When the first two scenes (Induction) are performed, doubling between them and the inset play often occurs, though the practice varies widely, depending on whether Sly remains onstage and whether *AS*'s so-called epilogue is imported to frame the action. T.J. King estimates 24 players (81); David Bradley, 15–17 (233); Oxf[1], 16 (41); Cam[2], 10 men and 4 boys; Hosley, 12–13 players ('Epilogue', 30–1); except for King, who includes non-speaking parts, all are concerned to demonstrate the minimum number of players required for the main parts, not to claim that such a number would always have been used when more players were available. See Appendix 5, pp. 399–402.

1 **Christopher** SLY In F's SDs and SPs, Sly = '*Begger*'; some editors, following Rowe, raise his status to 'tinker', perhaps playing off the drunken tinker as a type of beggar (as in Thomas Harman's *A Caveat or Warning for Common Cursitors*, 1567). He names himself 'Christophero Sly' (Ind.2.5), then 'Christopher Sly' (Ind.2.17, 71), and describes his changing professions at Ind.2.17–19. William Sly is among the actors in F's list of the King's Men; the name Stephen Sly appears in Warwickshire records (1615). In performances where Sly does not remain to watch the play, his doubles have included Petruccio, the Merchant, Vincentio and Grumio (Schafer, 79).

2 HOSTESS the first image of 'woman' in the play. Women as well as men managed alehouses in the period; alewives were stock characters in popular works – John Skelton's *The Tunning of Elinor Rumming* (*c.* 1508) is a famous example. In *AS*, it is a (male) Tapster who ousts Sly from the tavern.

3 LORD In *AS*, the Lord = 'Simon' or 'Sim' when in disguise as a servant.

4 BARTHOLOMEW The Induction's plot invites spectators to remain aware of Bartholomew *as* Bartholomew, but the text replaces 'Bartholomew' with 'Lady' (Jones & Stallybrass, 215). He is named at Ind.1.104; disguised, he appears as '*Lady*': F's SD at Ind.2.96.1–2 reads '*Enter Lady with Attendants.*' (*AS* reads '*Enter the boy in Womans attire*', 142); SPs read '*Lady.*' or '*La.*' In the early modern period the role was probably played by a boy actor; in more recent performances, the actor's age has varied (see Schafer, 79).

5 HUNTSMEN The actors who play the Huntsmen usually double as the Lord's and Petruccio's servants. See 6n.

6 SERVANTS Doubling the servants in the Lord's and Petruccio's households also supports doubling Sly and Petruccio (Mahood, 46, 269–70). *AS* implicitly suggests this doubling.

7 PLAYERS The troupe of players who enter at Ind.1.77 presumably number at least 10. At this point, they are only identified by number; some performances (e.g. Alexander, 1992), largely by casting 'stars' or well-known actors in some or most parts – Katherina, Petruccio, Grumio, Baptista, Bianca, Tranio, Hortensio – make their roles in the inset play immediately apparent.

8 BAPTISTA **Minola** Mantuan, *LLL*'s Holofernes's favourite Humanist poet and supplier of Latin verse to Elizabethan schoolboys, was in fact Baptista Spagnuola of Mantua. Quite possibly, the collocation of Baptista, Mantua and schoolmasters in *TS* suggests him as a potential source for Signor Minola's name (RP).

9 KATHERINA Naming figures significantly in constructing the character variously called 'Katerina', 'Katherina', 'Katherine' and 'Kate'. The names 'Katherina' (or Katherine) and 'Kate' seem to represent a kind of verbal doubling that identifies two personalities (even national identities, swerving from 'Shakespearean Italian' 'Katherina' to English 'Katherine'/'Kate'), ones that cue different behaviour (e.g. public/private). At her initial entry, F reads

'*Katerina*' (1.1.47.1); at 1.1.52, she is '*Katherina*'; SPs throughout identify her as '*Kate*.' or '*Kat*.'; she first refers to herself as '*Katerine*' (2.1.183); Petruccio 'rechristens' her '*Kate*' (2.1.181). Throughout F, these spelling variants appear interchangeable, bearing no relation to the shift from Compositor B to Compositor C. F's variant spellings find echoes in modern editions and performances; this edition adopts the 'Italianate' 'Katherina' as a SP. In the spoken text, 'Kate' dominates (58 instances, all but three spoken by Petruccio); 'Katherine' or 'Katerina' occurs only 19 times. Maguire comments that 'the name Kate assumes an almost generic quality and becomes a synecdoche for "woman"' ('Household', 130). 'Katherine' and 'Kate' occur elsewhere in Shakespeare (*LLL*, *1H4*, *2H4*, *H5*, *MM* (Mistress Kate Keepdown) and *H8*); in each case, as in *TS*, the diminutive 'Kate' appears to be used either as a 'pet name' or, especially in the speech of Petruccio in *TS* and King Henry in *H5*, as a means of domestication and control (Maguire, *Names*, 123–4). Positive as well as negative, or downmarket, resonances of Kate's name extend into John Fletcher's *Tamer Tamed* (*c.* 1611). A reference to St Catherine of Alexandria, who declared to her parents that she would only marry someone who surpassed her in reputation, wealth, beauty and wisdom, is tempting to consider as lying behind the name. *AS* reads 'Kate' throughout; Garrick (1756), 'Catharine'; *Sauny* (first performed in 1667), 'Margaret'.

10 BIANCA The name means 'white', suggesting purity. It may sometimes, however, have suggested that only the exterior was fair. In *Oth*, Bianca is a prostitute. Middleton dramatized the story of the notorious Venetian courtesan Bianca Capello (1548–87) in *Women Beware Women* (*c.* 1620); her figure also may lie behind the murderous adulteress in Webster's *The White Devil* (1612).

11 PETRUCCIO The name, meaning 'little Peter', probably derives from Gascoigne's *Supposes* (written 1566; published 1575), where Petrucio – ironically (given *The Shrew*), a non-speaking part – is listed as a servant to the Sienese (a gentleman stranger), though his name does not appear elsewhere in the text; or from Ariosto's *Suppositi* (1509), where his role is described as '*Servo*' or '*Famiglio*'. Shakespeare seems to have conflated servant and master, making Petruccio a gentleman stranger. F's spelling, 'Petruchio', which has been followed by most editors, is an early modern phonetic spelling indicating Italian pronunciation. Shakespeare may have thought of the name as having potentially four syllables, not three, as in Italian (cf. *MA*'s 'Borachio'), although in most contexts, three syllables best fit the metre; only three lines (3.2.246, 5.2.64 and 117) require four syllables. This edition follows *Oxf*'s spelling.

There was one prominent Petruccio in London, Petrucchio Ubaldini, two of whose works are plausibly associated with *Edward III* (RP). In *AS*, Petruccio = Ferando.

12 GRUMIO possibly deriving from Plautus' *Mostellaria*, where a character called 'Grumio' is a countryman, though it seems equally possible that the name simply represents 'groom' in 'Shakespearean Italian'. In *AS*, Grumio = Sander; in *Sauny*, Grumio = Sauny, the star role.

13 HORTENSIO The name does not appear in either Ariosto or Gascoigne's *Supposes*; the latter has no equivalent for Hortensio's role. The name 'Licio', Hortensio's name in his disguise as music master, occurs in both. *Supposes* uses the form 'Litio' for a character who is a servant to Phylogano, a Sicilian gentleman; 'Licio' names a transgressive servant in Lyly's *Midas* (1592). Most modern editions of *TS* standardize to 'Litio', even though F reads 'Litio' 3 times (2.1.60, 3.1.54, 3.2.146) as against 'Lisio' 4 times (4.2.1, 15, 16 and 49); Rowe opts for

F2's 'Licio' (2.1.60). Hosley identifies 'Litio' as a variant spelling of 'Lizio' and views the nickname as 'apparently a joke in the New Comedy tradition of significant names, for *lizio* is an old Italian word for garlic' ('Sources', 291). Conjecturing that 'Lisio' or 'Licio' puns on 'licere' (to license or allow), which occurs in a famous line in the so-called Golden Age chorus from Torquato Tasso's *Aminta* (1573; trans. 1591), Margaret Ferguson views this multilingual punning (which playgoers and readers might or might not have been aware of, depending on their linguistic capital) as 'pertinent to the disputes in early modern culture over the boundaries servants *and* masters may transgress, and with what consequences, as they engage in the work/play of courtship' (1–2). *TN* alludes to such transgressions: fantasizing a changed status, Malvolio imagines himself 'Count Malvolio', offering an 'example for't. The Lady of the Strachy married the yeoman of the wardrobe' (2.5.34, 38–9). On the confusions with Hortensio's SPs at 3.1 and 4.2, see pp. 313–16.

14 LUCENTIO 'Cambio' (meaning 'I change' or 'exchange' in Italian), Lucentio's schoolmasterly *alias*, alludes to Ovid, whose *Ars Amatoria* and *Heroides* Lucentio/Cambio uses as a pretext for wooing Bianca at 3.1. In *AS*, Lucentio = Aurelius; in *Sauny*, Winlove.

15 TRANIO The name may derive from Plautus, *Mostellaria*, 3.2, where it is given to a clever townsman; Hibbard conjectures an association with 'train' = deceit, trickery, artifice (*OED n.*[2]1b); the figurative connotation of the verb 'train' = 'to allure, entice, decoy', to 'take in' (*OED v.*[1] 4) seems equally appealing. Except for '*Tronio*' at 5.1.75, always spelled 'Tranio' in dialogue; SD variants read '*Triano*' (1.1.0.1) and '*Trayno*' (2.1.277.1).

16 BIONDELLO The name may derive from Boccaccio's *Decameron*, Day 9, Tale 8, which tells how Biondello, a prankster, gulls the gluttonous Ciacco and is later beaten; he is described as 'a little fellow, always extremely well dressed and neater than a fly, with a cap on his head of long, blond hair, done up in such a way that not a strand of hair was out of place' (588). The name does not appear in either Gascoigne or Ariosto but is borne by a doctor in Aretino's *Lo Ipocrito* (1542) and by a servant in an English comedy of uncertain authorship, *The Buggbears* (*c.* 1562–5), which Ard[1] suggests Shakespeare may have seen revived (xxviii).

17 GREMIO 'the old pantaloon' (3.1.36, also '*pantaloon*' at 1.1.47.2). A stock comic figure in the Italian *commedia dell'arte*, the pantaloon was an old, often miserly, man, usually fearful of being cuckolded; *pantaloon* refers to his baggy trousers. In *Sauny*, Gremio = Woodall.

18 VINCENTIO The Vincentio perhaps best known to early modern Londoners was Vincentio Saviolo (d. 1598/9); his fencing school is mentioned by John Florio in 1591 as being 'in the little street where the well is . . . at the sign of the red Lyon'. Saviolo wrote the first treatises on fencing in English, *Vincentio Saviolo, His Practice, in Two Books, the First Entreating of the Use of the Rapier and Dagger, the Second of Honor and Honorable Quarrels* (1595). Although any precise connection to Vincentio's role in *TS* seems far-fetched, a topical connection or theatrical in-joke seems possible. The name Vincentio recurs in the *dramatis personae* list for *MM*, where it is assigned to the Duke (though absent from the text).

19 MERCHANT At 4.2.64, Biondello refers to this figure as 'a Marcantant or a pedant', offering a choice of identities. F reads '*Pedant*' at 4.2.72.1 and in all subsequent SDs and SPs. From his statements about his 'bills for money by exchange' (4.2.90), he is clearly a merchant, as are the corresponding characters in Ariosto's *Suppositi* and Gascoigne's *Supposes* (Hosley, 'Sources', 305). Cam[2] speculates that the copyist chose 'pedant' instead of 'marcantant' because the latter term, a corruption of the Italian *mercatante* (*OED*), obs.

rare), was unfamiliar (64). Although no pedant appears among the masks for *zanni* in *commedia dell'arte*, such a character does figure prominently in Flaminio Scala's *Il Pedante* (pub. 1611; a possible source for Molière's *Tartuffe*): in Act 1, the pedant Cataldo acts as a mediator between Oratio and his father Pantalone (a rich and dissolute merchant) – a role not unlike that played by the Merchant (Smith, *Commedia*, 3.161–3). Shakespeare's pedants – *LLL*'s Holofernes and *CE*'s Pinch – however, seem distant relatives of the Italian predecessor. Whether called 'Pedant' or 'Merchant', he has often been played as drunk.

20 WIDOW F's SPs read '*Wid.*' (also used as SP for Lady Grey in F *3H6*); SDs and dialogue read '*Widdow*'. The widow is a character stereotype, a role with no name, simply a designation of gender and social status. On the status of widows in the period, see Mendelson & Crawford, 174–84.

21 CURTIS Given the cuckolding joke at 4.1.24–5, Curtis would seem to be male; in the early modern period, the name could be either a given name or a surname. The role was first played by a woman in Garrick's *Catharine and Petruchio* (1756), a practice that has been followed in some subsequent performances, in which Curtis has often been 'an old woman, a gossip and occasionally tipsy' (Schafer, 80). Given *TS*'s other references to specific players, 'Curtis' may allude to Curtis Greville, often referred to simply as Curtis, who may have been a member of the King's Men (or simply a hired actor) in the early 1620s; he had a minor role in a *c.* 1625 revival of *TNK* (Cam[1],

118).

22–6 NATHANIEL. . . . PETER Petruccio's 'Italian' manor house is staffed by servants with English names; the confusion/conflation of England and Italy mirrors the confusions between masters and servants.

27 TAILOR in the period, a maker of men's and women's outer garments; historically, a tailor was a cutter; in the trade, however, the tailor is the man who sews and makes up what the cutter has shaped (*OED n.* B1a). Tailors, whether for women or men, were figures of derision on the early modern stage, as is Francis Feeble, the 'woman's tailor' Falstaff recruits in *2H4* 3.2.148–70, who inspires a sexual pun over 'prick' = to prick the name on a list/penis. Hulme suggests that 'tailor' had the sense of 'penis' or 'pudendum' in Elizabethan idiom (99–102); the proverbial 'the tailor makes the man' (Dent, T17) catches the sexual sense of *tailor*/'penis'. Women's tailors were also associated with effeminacy, as is the foolish Nick Stuffe in Jonson's *New Inn* (1629).

28 HABERDASHER 'Haberdash' = petty merchandise, small wares, including caps; by the 16th century, the trade was split into two: dealers or makers of hats and caps, and dealers in small articles of dress, such as thread, tape, ribbons, etc. (*OED n.*). In performance, the Haberdasher's role is sometimes conflated with that of the Tailor.

29–30 **Walter . . . Rafe** These are not speaking roles; their status as 'citational servants' seems designed to inflate Petruccio's household staff.

# THE TAMING
# OF THE SHREW

**[Induction 1]**          *Enter* Christopher SLY
                                *and* Hostess.

SLY    I'll feeze you, in faith.

HOSTESS    A pair of stocks, you rogue!

SLY    You're a baggage, the Slys are no rogues. Look in

TITLE *A Pleasant Conceited History, Called The Taming of a Shrew, as it was Sundry Times Acted by the Right Honorable the Earle of Pembrook His Servants*, entered on the Stationers' Register on 2 May 1594, has long been considered a quarto version of Shakespeare's comedy. The full text of *A Shrew* (*AS*) appears as Appendix 3. Although the two plays resemble one another at certain points, this edition considers them as textually, though not theatrically, independent.

Ind.1 Pope first called the two Sly scenes an 'Induction', a label that marks them as a framing device, not, as in F, the first episodes of the play. Setting these scenes apart has, on the one hand, made them vulnerable to cutting (Schafer, 83) and, on the other, encouraged adding *AS*'s so-called epilogue to complete the frame (see pp. 17–23). Both scenes allude to theatrical practices, players associated with several acting companies and plays that are touchstones of early modern theatrical history from the 1590s to the 1620s (see pp. 28–35). The imagined settings, the exterior of a tavern or alehouse and, subsequently, outside the Lord's house nearby (Ind.2.17–20, 87 and nn.) suggest a Warwickshire location.

0.1–2 The Hostess's implied action (throwing Sly out of her tavern) and her threat ('A pair of stocks') anticipate

behaviour attributed to scolds or 'shrews' and later to Katherina (1.1) and Petruccio (4.1). See definitions of 'shrew', pp. 38–41; on the term's gender markers, see 4.1.76n.

1 SP See LR, 1n.

1 **feeze** 'do for', 'beat, flog' (*OED v.*[1] 3a, 3b); proverbial: 'I will vease thee' (Dent, V22). Spelled 'pheeze' in F, the word originally meant to drive off or frighten away (*OED v.*[1] 1); proverbial usage develops a more abusive sense.
   **in faith** in truth, really (*OED* faith *n.* 12a)

2 **A . . . stocks** heavy timber frame with holes for the ankles. Stocking was a common public punishment for minor offences – and for scolds or shrews.
   **rogue** vagrant, person of no fixed abode – terms that counter Sly's protestations of gentility

3 **baggage** good-for-nothing woman, prostitute

3–4 **Look . . . Conqueror** proverbial: 'I came in with the conqueror' (Dent, C594). Sly's claim to aristocratic descent ironically anticipates the Lord's 'practice' (see 35); Oxf[1] comments that Sly may understand *Conqueror* as a surname. Substituting *Richard* for 'William' may allude to Richard Burbage, the chief tragedian of the Lord Chamberlain's Men from 1594 (see pp. 1–2).

Induction 1] *Pope; Actus primus. Scaena Prima. F; Padua. A publicke Place. / Capell*    0.1–2] *Rowe; Enter Begger and Hostes, Christophero Sly. F*    1+ SP] *Rowe; Beg[ger]. F*    3 You're] *(Y'are)*

139

the Chronicles; we came in with Richard Conqueror:
therefore *paucas pallabris*, let the world slide. Sessa!    5
HOSTESS    You will not pay for the glasses you have
burst?
SLY    No, not a denier. Go by, Saint Jeronimy, go to thy cold
bed and warm thee.
HOSTESS    I know my remedy; I must go fetch the    10
headborough.    [*Exit.*]
SLY    Third, or fourth, or fifth borough, I'll answer him
by law. I'll not budge an inch, boy. Let him come, and

---

5    *paucas pallabris* few words; a corruption of Spanish *pocas palabras*, perhaps recalling Kyd's *Spanish Tragedy*
(1592), 3.14.118: '*Pocas palabras!* mild
as the lamb', where Hieronimo cau-
tions himself against revealing his plan
for revenge. In *commedia dell'arte*, the
braggart captain usually spoke Spanish
(Fava, 129).
   **let . . . slide** 'Let the world go, why
worry?' Sly repeats the proverbial
phrase (Dent, W879) at Ind.2.138.
   **Sessa** 'Be off with you, be quiet'; a
cry of encouragement from hunting
or fencing. Possibly from French *cessez*
(cease), as in *KL*, where it has the former
meaning at 3.6.71 ('sese', F) and the
latter at 3.4.98 ('caese', Q; '*Sesey*', F).
7    **burst** broken, shattered (*OED ppl.a.*
1a)
8    **denier** French coin of small value
   **Go . . . Jeronimy** a contemptuous
dismissal; the phrase is proverbial:
'Let it go by' (Dent, GG6). Sly
confuses St Jerome (Hieronymus)
with *Spanish Tragedy*'s Hieronimo,
misquoting 'Hieronimo, beware: go
by, go by' (3.12.31). Sly's obsession
with fragments from Kyd's play, and its
status as an overwhelming popular hit,
allows this kind of allusion, even from
such a lowly figure. Brian Vickers has
recently floated the conjecture that Kyd
was one of the co-authors of *1H6* and
*E3* ('Kyd', 13–15).

8–9    **go . . . thee** Edgar, disguised as Poor
Tom the beggar, uses the same phrase
(*KL* 3.4.46–7); the similarity of the
settings suggests that it may have been
traditionally associated with vagrancy
(Ard²). There may also be an allusion to
Hieronimo's 'What outcries pluck me
from my naked bed' (*Spanish Tragedy*,
2.5.1). Sly effectively contradicts his
denial at 3 that he is a *rogue*; then
reverts (12–13) to a pretence of higher
status, threatening legal action.
11    **headborough** petty constable. Sly's
reply at 12 has prompted emendation
to 'thirdborough', making the joke
explicit. In secretary hand, 'he[a]d'
and 'thrd' easily might be confused
(RP). The terms have equivalent early
modern meanings; given Sly's history,
he might well know the precise titles of
law officers.
13    **by law** in the law courts
   **I'll . . . inch** proverbial: 'He will not
yield, budge an inch' (Dent, 152)
   **boy** insulting term of address (though
not always, see 18). Perhaps as in the
modern 'old boy' = 'good fellow',
'old chap'. This single Shakespearean
instance of addressing a woman as *boy*
may be a typically Sly-like reference,
calling attention to the boy actor's body
beneath the role; cf. *AC* 5.2.219: 'Some
squeaking Cleopatra boy my greatness'.
13–14    **and kindly** and welcome; or *kindly*
= agreeably (*OED adv.* 3)

---

8 by,] *Theobald;* by *F*    11 headborough] thirdborough *Pope² (Theobald)*    SD] *Rowe*

kindly. *Falls asleep.*

*Wind horns. Enter* Lord *from hunting* [, *two* Huntsmen
*and others*].

LORD

Huntsman, I charge thee, tender well my hounds:          15
Breathe Merriman – the poor cur is embossed –
And couple Clowder with the deep-mouthed brach.
Sawst thou not, boy, how Silver made it good
At the hedge corner, in the coldest fault?
I would not lose the dog for twenty pound.               20

1 HUNTSMAN

Why, Belman is as good as he, my lord:
He cried upon it at the merest loss,

14.1 *Wind horns* Blow the horns. This SD occurs frequently in Shakespeare. Green costumes may have signalled hunting visually (Dessen & Thomson, 118).

15–28 Were real dogs included in the Lord's train? *TGV*'s Crab is justly famous; real dogs appear in SDs in Jonson's *Every Man Out of His Humour* (1599) ('one leading a dog', 3.2.0.1) and Middleton and Dekker's *The Roaring Girl* (1611) ('*Enter . . . with water spaniels and a duck*', sc. 4, 414.2–3), among others (Carroll, 67–8). Petruccio's spaniel Troilus (4.1.136) usually, though not always, remains offstage. For a similar description of hunting, cf. *MND* 4.1.102–26; see also Ind.2.39–44.

15 **tender well** take good care of

16 *Breathe Merriman i.e. 'give the dog time to recover its breath'. Emending to *Breathe* picks up the meaning of *embossed* = 'driven to extremity; foaming at the mouth from exhaustion' (*OED ppl.a.*²); but F's 'Brach' also

makes sense (see 17), for *Merriman* might be a bitch-hound, especially in a theatre where men play women and women behave like men.

17 **couple** leash together, usually in threes; the leashes, or 'slips', were constructed so that hounds could be let go immediately (Winter, *England*, 348–9).

**deep-mouthed brach** bitch hound with deep baying voice

18–19 **made . . . fault** 'picked up the scent at the hedge corner when it was nearly lost'. A *fault* = 'a break in the line of scent' (*OED n.* 8a); *coldest* intensifies the sense.

20 proverbial (Dent, P516.1); the suggestion of a wager over a dog anticipates the wagering over wives at 5.2.66–76, which begins at *twenty crowns*.

22 'despite the fact that the scent seemed completely lost, he bayed to declare he had picked it up again'; *merest* = most complete, absolute

14 SD] *Falls from off his bench and sleeps. / Capell; Lies down on the ground, and falls asleep. / Malone*   14.1–2 *two* Huntsmen *and others*] *this edn; with his train. F; train . . . of Huntsmen and Servingmen. Cam*²   16 Breathe] *Sisson;* Brach *F; Leech Hanmer; Bathe (Johnson);* Trash *Dyce;* Broach *Cam¹*   cur is] cur, is *Grant White*   20 lose] *(loose)*   21 SP] *Q; Hunts. F*

And twice today picked out the dullest scent.
Trust me, I take him for the better dog.

LORD

Thou art a fool. If Echo were as fleet                                    25
I would esteem him worth a dozen such.
But sup them well, and look unto them all:
Tomorrow I intend to hunt again.

1 HUNTSMAN

I will, my lord.

LORD

What's here? One dead, or drunk? See, doth he breathe?     30

2 HUNTSMAN

He breathes, my lord. Were he not warmed with ale,
This were a bed but cold to sleep so soundly.

LORD

O monstrous beast, how like a swine he lies!
Grim death, how foul and loathsome is thine image.
Sirs, I will practise on this drunken man.                           35
What think you, if he were conveyed to bed,
Wrapped in sweet clothes, rings put upon his fingers,
A most delicious banquet by his bed
And brave attendants near him when he wakes,
Would not the beggar then forget himself?                        40

1 HUNTSMAN

Believe me, lord, I think he cannot choose.

---

27  **sup them well** feed them a good supper
29  Some editors instruct 1 Huntsman to exit here; the discovery of Sly may deflect his attention.
34  **image** likeness. Sleep as the image of death is proverbial (Dent, S527), as is comparing a drunken man to a beast (Dent, B152.1).
35  **practise on** play a practical joke on. The pretence that Sly is a gentleman is the first instance of sliding social identities or 'supposings'; for a possible

source for the Lord's trick, see pp. 58–9.
36  **conveyed** made away with, taken off
37  **sweet** i.e. scented or perfumed; cf. *WT* 4.4.251: 'a pair of sweet gloves'.
38  **banquet** not the meal but the sweetmeats and *conserves* (Ind.2.3, 7) following it or served separately (*OED n.*[1] 3)
39  **brave** finely dressed
41  **cannot choose** is bound to. Given 40, Oxf[1] suggests a play on the proverbial 'Beggars cannot be choosers' (Dent,

31–2] *Rowe; prose F*

2 HUNTSMAN

It would seem strange unto him when he waked.

LORD

Even as a flattering dream or worthless fancy.
Then take him up, and manage well the jest:
Carry him gently to my fairest chamber,                    45
And hang it round with all my wanton pictures;
Balm his foul head in warm distilled waters
And burn sweet wood to make the lodging sweet;
Procure me music ready when he wakes
To make a dulcet and a heavenly sound;                    50
An if he chance to speak, be ready straight
And with a low submissive reverence
Say, 'What is it your honour will command?'
Let one attend him with a silver basin
Full of rose-water and bestrewed with flowers;            55

B247); other proverbial expressions –
'cannot choose but' (Dent, CC11) and
'to forget oneself' (Dent, FF9) – also
apply.

43 **flattering . . . fancy** The aristocratic
Theseus (*MND* 5.1.2–22) dismisses
dreams and fancy, or 'imagination'; so
does Mercutio (*RJ* 1.4.50–103). Here,
*flattering* = pleasurable, 'pleasing to
the imagination' (*OED ppl.a.* 2a); *fancy*
= 'delusive imagination'; 'creative
or productive imagination' (*OED
n.* 3; 4a). On dream and imagination
in *TS*, see p. 27.

45–64 The Lord's 'practice' here and in
Ind.2 reveals his own desires (and his
conspicuous consumption) as well as his
sense of *jest* (44). On *TS*, obsession with
material possessions, see Orlin, Korda.

46 **wanton pictures** paintings or
tapestries (hung in chambers) woven
with biblical or mythological scenes;
*wanton* = gay, lively in colour, but
also lewd, lascivious (*OED a.* 3d; 2).
Presumably these works represent

the kind of 'wantonness' condemned
by anti-theatrical polemicists. See
Ind.2.47–58 and n.

47 **Balm** bathe, anoint
**distilled** distillèd; concentrated,
perhaps perfumed, like the *rose-water*
at **55**

48 **sweet wood . . . sweet** Juniper,
which gives off a pungent smell when
burned, was used to 'purify' indoor air.

49 **music** as entertainment but also to
cure mental distraction; cf. *KL* 4.7,
*Per* 5.1. On music in *TS*, see Waldo &
Herbert.

50 **dulcet** sweet, melodious
**heavenly** i.e. the music imitates that of
the heavenly spheres, cf. *MV* 5.1.60–5.
For the idea, see Sir John Davies,
'Orchestra, or a Poem of Dancing'
(*Works*).

51 **An . . . speak** 'If he should chance
to speak'; *an if* = a conditional
construction
**straight** immediately

52 **reverence** deep bow

43 flattering] *(flatt'ring)*   47 Balm] Bath *(Capell)*   head] hide *(Capell)*   51 An] *(And)*

Another bear the ewer, the third a diaper,
And say, 'Will't please your lordship cool your hands?'
Some one be ready with a costly suit
And ask him what apparel he will wear;
Another tell him of his hounds and horse          60
And that his lady mourns at his disease.
Persuade him that he hath been lunatic,
And when he says he is, say that he dreams,
For he is nothing but a mighty lord.
This do, and do it kindly, gentle sirs,          65
It will be pastime passing excellent,
If it be husbanded with modesty.

1 HUNTSMAN

My lord, I warrant you we will play our part
As he shall think by our true diligence
He is no less than what we say he is.          70

LORD

Take him up gently and to bed with him,
And each one to his office when he wakes.

*[Some carry Sly out.] Sound trumpets.*

56 **ewer** pitcher with wide spout, used to bring water for washing hands (*OED* ewer² 1)
**diaper** towel or napkin, usually of fine linen
58 **Some one** 'one of you servants'
60 **horse** probably the old generic plural, now only used of troops, 'the foot and the horse' (Oxf¹)
61 **disease** mental derangement rather than physical disorder
63 **when . . . is** 'when he says he must be mad'. Some editors emend F's reading: the most persuasive, though metrically less satisfactory suggestion, Johnson's 'when he says he is Sly', is supported by Sly's play on his name (Ind.2.5–6, 16–17). Although Sly's name has not been mentioned since the Lord

entered, in performance audiences may easily accept that the Lord shares their knowledge of it (Ard²).
65 **kindly** naturally, spontaneously
**gentle** well born, belonging to a family of position (*OED* gentle *a.* 1a); the Huntsmen are the Lord's equals.
66 **passing** surpassingly, exceedingly (*OED adv.* a)
67 **husbanded with modesty** managed with restraint; cf. Petruccio's 'practice' on Katherina, 'done in reverend care of her' (4.1.193).
69 **As** so that
72 **to his office** perform his duty or part; see *MND* 2.2.8: 'Then to your offices'.
72 SD Greg conjectures that *Sound trumpets* is one of several SDs added by the book-keeper (*Folio*, 213).

63 he is, say] he is poor, say *Rowe*; what he is *Collier*; he is Sly, say *Cam¹ (Johnson)*     72 SD *Some . . . out.*] *Theobald (Some bear out Sly.)*

Sirrah, go see what trumpet 'tis that sounds.

[*Exit a Servant.*]

Belike some noble gentleman that means,

Travelling some journey, to repose him here.                    75

*Enter* Servant.

How now? Who is it?

SERVANT                          An't please your honour,

Players that offer service to your lordship.

*Enter* Players.

LORD

Bid them come near. –

Now, fellows, you are welcome.

PLAYERS

We thank your honour.

LORD

Do you intend to stay with me tonight?                    80

1 PLAYER

So please your lordship to accept our duty.

---

73 **Sirrah** term of address to a social inferior
74 **Belike** likely, probably
75.1 **Servant** one of the *others* specified in 14.1, or a Huntsman (see LR, 5n., 6n.)
76 **An't** if it
77 **Players** a travelling troupe of actors, such as those in *Hamlet*. Like Hamlet, the Lord recalls an actor in a particular role (82–6; *Ham* 2.2.433–6), though he neither mentions rewriting a play to suit his own occasion nor asks the player to re-perform the role. Since *TS* may date from 1592–4, when plague closed London theatres, forcing acting companies to tour the provinces, this may be a topical reference.
77.1 The Players' entry follows the first

half of 76 in Ard²; in theatrical practice, timing of entries and exits responds to particular performance spaces.
78 **come near** approach; F's 'neere' can mean either 'near' or 'nearer'.
79 **welcome** literally, well come: possible stress on both syllables (common in Shakespeare)
81 SP F reads '*Sincklo*', identified as the player John Sincler. Emended in all modern editions, here to 1 PLAYER (probably the troupe's leader). See also LR, 7n., and p. 400.
   **So please** if it please
   **duty** due respect, but also function. What they offer is, of course, a performance, so the line also implies 'if you are willing to allow us to perform for you'.

---

73 SD] *Theobald subst.* 75.1] *(Enter Servingman.)*   76 SP] *(Ser.)*   76–7 An't . . . lordship.] *F lines* Players / Lordship. /   77 that offer] that come to offer *Capell*   77.1] *after* near. *78 Ard²*   81 SP] *Ard¹; 2. Player. F; First Player. Ard²*

LORD

    With all my heart. This fellow I remember

    Since once he played a farmer's eldest son –

    'Twas where you wooed the gentlewoman so well.

    I have forgot your name, but sure that part         85

    Was aptly fitted and naturally performed.

2 PLAYER

    I think 'twas Soto that your honour means.

LORD

    'Tis very true; thou didst it excellent.

    – Well, you are come to me in happy time,

    The rather for I have some sport in hand         90

    Wherein your cunning can assist me much.

    There is a lord will hear you play tonight;

    But I am doubtful of your modesties

    Lest, over-eyeing of his odd behaviour –

    For yet his honour never heard a play –         95

    You break into some merry passion

    And so offend him; for I tell you, sirs,

    If you should smile, he grows impatient.

1 PLAYER

    Fear not, my lord, we can contain ourselves

    Were he the veriest antic in the world.         100

LORD

    Go, sirrah, take them to the buttery

---

83 **Since once** since a time when

86 **aptly . . . performed** well cast and convincingly played; cf. Hamlet's advice to the players (3.2.1–44).

87 **Soto** On the Sincklo–Soto connection, see pp. 28–35.

88 **excellent** splendidly

89 **in happy time** opportunely

90 **The rather for** the more so since

91 **cunning** professional skill

93 **modesties** discretion, self-restraint

94 **over-eyeing of** observing; staring transfixedly at

95 **yet** before now (Abbott, 76)

96 **merry passion** laughing fit (scansion suggests *passion* is trisyllabic here)

98 **impatient** scansion invites pronouncing as four syllables

100 **veriest antic** oddest or most absurd fellow (*OED* antic *n.* B 4)

101 **buttery** store-room or pantry for liquor and provisions

87 SP] *Oxf; Sincklo F; Sin. F2; Sim. F3; Play. / Hanmer; 1. Play. / Capell ; A Player. Ard¹; Second Player. Ard²*   99 SP] *Ard¹; Plai. F; First Player. / Capell*

And give them friendly welcome every one;
Let them want nothing that my house affords.

*Exit one with the Players.*

– Sirrah, go you to Barthol'mew my page
And see him dressed in all suits like a lady.                105
That done, conduct him to the drunkard's chamber,
And call him 'Madam', do him obeisance.
Tell him from me, as he will win my love,
He bear himself with honourable action
Such as he hath observed in noble ladies                    110
Unto their lords by them accomplished.
Such duty to the drunkard let him do,
With soft low tongue and lowly courtesy,
And say, 'What is't your honour will command,
Wherein your lady and your humble wife                      115
May show her duty and make known her love?'
And then with kind embracements, tempting kisses
And with declining head into his bosom,
Bid him shed tears, as being overjoyed
To see her noble lord restored to health,                   120

---

103 **want** lack
104 **Barthol'mew**     pronounced 'Bartlemy' in the early modern period
105–34 The Lord gives directions that reflect the gender conventions of the professional stage. In voicing assumptions about the ideal woman or wife ('soft low tongue and lowly courtesy', 113), the Lord aligns with Petruccio; in anticipating Katherina's 'performance' of wifely obedience (5.2.142–85), the passage sets up a structural rhyme; and in outlining a plan, the Lord's speech parallels Petruccio's strategies for taming Katherina at 4.1.177–200.
105 **in all suits** in every detail, punning on 'suits of clothes'
107 **do him obeisance** show him (i.e. the page) dutiful respect
108 **as . . . love** if he wishes to win my favour
109 **bear . . . action** act in a dignified, appropriately aristocratic manner
111 **accomplished**     accomplishèd; performed
113 **soft low tongue** Cf. *KL* 5.3.270–1: 'Her voice was ever soft, / Gentle and low, an excellent thing in woman'.
   **courtesy** curtsy (*OED n.* 8)
118 **with . . . bosom** The pronoun *his* is ambiguous: Morris suggests either 'leaning upon his (Sly's) breast' or 'hanging his head', preferring the latter.

109 bear] bare *Q*   113 low] slow *Malone*   114 will] doth *Q*

Who for this seven years hath esteemed him
No better than a poor and loathsome beggar.
And if the boy have not a woman's gift
To rain a shower of commanded tears,
An onion will do well for such a shift,                          125
Which in a napkin being close conveyed
Shall in despite enforce a watery eye.
See this dispatched with all the haste thou canst;
Anon I'll give thee more instructions.          *Exit a Servant.*
I know the boy will well usurp the grace,                       130
Voice, gait and action of a gentlewoman.
I long to hear him call the drunkard 'husband',
And how my men will stay themselves from laughter
When they do homage to this simple peasant.
I'll in to counsel them: haply my presence                      135
May well abate the over-merry spleen
Which otherwise would grow into extremes.       *[Exeunt.]*

121 **seven years** proverbial (Dent, Y25);
a common time span in folklore and
fairy tales, and a holy number in
scripture (e.g. the seven lean years of
Pharaoh's dream). Theobald emended
to 'twice seven' in order to approximate
Ind.2.77's *fifteen*, but there Falstaffian
exaggeration, as at *1H4* 2.4.155–
223, seems the point. Here, *years* is
pronounced as two syllables.
**esteemed him** thought himself
123 **And if** 'An if' is a possible alternative
(RP).
124 **commanded** calculated, produced
on demand
125 proverbial: 'To weep (it may serve)
with an onion' (Dent, O67). Cf. *AW*
5.3.314: 'Mine eyes smell onions; I shall
weep anon'.
**shift**, trick, device (*OED n.* III 4a)
126 **napkin** handkerchief (probably)
**close conveyed** secretly brought close
(to the eyes)

127 **in despite enforce** produce willy-
nilly
129 **Anon** very soon
**instructions** Four-syllable pronunciation completes the metrical line.
130–1 **usurp . . . gentlewoman** assume
a gentlewoman's behaviour, voice and
body movements
133 **stay . . . laughter** restrain their
laughter, evoking the proverbial sense
of 'to contain oneself' (Dent, CC17)
134 **simple** of low rank or position;
common (*OED a.* 4a)
135 **I'll in** I'll go in
**haply** perhaps; 'if luck is with us'
136 **over-merry spleen** excessive impulse
to laughter. Early modern writers on
physiology also considered the spleen as
the seat of melancholy and irritability.
137 **grow into extremes** get out of hand
**Ind.2** The imagined location is a chamber
in the Lord's house.

121 this] twice *Theobald*   him] himself *Rowe*   129 SD] *(Exit a Servingman.)*   134 peasant.]
*Johnson;* peasant, *F;* peasant; *Rowe*   137 SD] *Bell; Exit Lord. / Theobald*

**[Induction 2]**     *Enter aloft* [SLY] *the drunkard*
*and three* Servants – *with apparel, basin and ewer,*
*and other appurtenances – and* Lord.

SLY     For God's sake, a pot of small ale.

1 SERVANT

Will't please your lordship drink a cup of sack?

2 SERVANT

Will't please your honour taste of these conserves?

3 SERVANT

What raiment will your honour wear today?

SLY     I am Christophero Sly – call not me 'honour' nor     5
'lordship'. I ne'er drank sack in my life, and if you give
me any conserves, give me conserves of beef. Ne'er ask
me what raiment I'll wear, for I have no more doublets
than backs, no more stockings than legs, nor no more

---

0.1 *aloft* F's placement suggests the gallery above the tiring-house wall, oddly distant for a substantial, elaborate scene requiring at least six and possibly nine actors. For conjectural early modern stagings, see Hibbard (66–7) and Hodges (56–65). Modern performances choosing to keep Sly on stage throughout have placed Sly *aloft* on an Elizabethan-style balcony (Dews, 1981) or on an upstage platform (Alexander, 1992). See also Barton, 1960.

0.2–3 *apparel . . . appurtenances* The Lord specifies the *basin*, *ewer* and *apparel* (Ind.1.54–9); *'other appurtenances'* might include whatever food and drink is offered to Sly as well as musical instruments (33 SD).

0.3 The Lord's re-entry is somewhat unusual; such immediate re-entries rarely occur, except where, at dates after 1610, they straddle an act-break (RP).

1 **small ale** weakest (and cheapest) ale

2–4, 24–5 This Tweedledum–Tweedledee vaudeville-like routine tempts Sly with precisely those commodities – drink, food, fine clothes – that Petruccio later withholds from Katherina (4.1.146–54; 4.3.65–95); 24–5 builds further on the repetitious routine.

2 **sack** white wine imported from Spain and the Canaries

3 **conserves** candied fruits (see Ind.1.38n.)

4 **raiment** clothing, apparel – heightened speech

5 **Christophero** mock-Spanish for Christopher

7 **conserves of beef** preserved (salted) beef; like the *ale/sack* contrast (1–2), marking class distinctions

8–11 Sly says he needs no clothes except those he's wearing; proverbial: 'All his wardrobe is on his back' (Dent, W61).

8 **doublets** A doublet was a close-fitting body-garment, with or without sleeves, worn by men (*OED* 1a).

**Induction 2]** *Capell*     0.1 SLY] *Rowe*     0.2 *three* Servants] *this edn; attendants* F     1+ SP] *Rowe; Beg.*
F     2 SP] *(1. Ser.)*     2 lordship] *Q;* Lord F*;* Lordship F2     3 SP] *(2. Ser.)*     4 SP] *(3. Ser.)*

shoes than feet – nay, sometime more feet than shoes, or          10
such shoes as my toes look through the over-leather.

LORD

Heaven cease this idle humour in your honour!
O, that a mighty man of such descent,
Of such possessions and so high esteem,
Should be infused with so foul a spirit.          15

SLY    What, would you make me mad? Am not I Christopher Sly, old Sly's son of Burton Heath, by birth a
pedlar, by education a cardmaker, by transmutation a
bear-herd and now by present profession a tinker? Ask
Marian Hacket, the fat ale-wife of Wincot, if she know          20
me not. If she say I am not fourteen pence on the score
for sheer ale, score me up for the lying'st knave in

11  **over-leather** uppers
12–15  The Lord apparently assumes a servant's role.
12  **cease** stop; transitive use of a verb now exclusively intransitive (Abbott, 291)
**idle humour** trifling, incoherent, empty fantasy (*OED* idle *a*. 2a, 2b). Elizabethans believed that relative proportions of four humours (blood, phlegm, bile and melancholy) determined a person's physical or mental health.
15  **infused . . . spirit** infusèd; filled with delusions, possessed by such an evil spirit
16–17  **Am . . . Christopher Sly** In questioning his identity, Sly introduces an idea central to human and theatrical consciousness: 'Who am I?' (see p. 66).
17–20  **Burton . . . Wincot** Barton-on-the-Heath and Wincot are villages near Stratford-upon-Avon. The first was the home of Shakespeare's aunt, Joan Lambert; the parish register shows Hackets living at Wincot in 1591; *Cicely Hacket* is mentioned at 87.
18–19  **pedlar . . . tinker** Although both are marginal occupations, Sly considers himself a 'professional'. Cf. *WT*'s

Autolycus, who claims to be a pedlar who has been 'an ape-bearer . . . and married a tinker's wife' (4.3.93–5). Rehearsing such facts about oneself was (and remains) a common test for sanity; the catalogue may also play on genealogical formulae for establishing one's right to display a coat of arms.
18  **cardmaker** maker of iron 'cards', toothed instruments used for separating wool fibres before spinning (*OED* card *n*.[1] 2a). The wool industry contributed significantly to Warwickshire's economy.
**transmutation** change of condition (*OED* 1)
19  **bear-herd** keeper and exhibitor of a (tame) performing bear
20  **ale-wife** alehouse-keeper, barmaid
21  **on the score** in debt; charges for drink were scored or notched on the ale-wife's tally-stick.
22  **sheer ale** just ale taken alone without solid food (*OED* sheer *a*. 7b)
**score** mark
22–3  **lying'st . . . Christendom** Gloucester speaks exactly these words to Simpcox (*2H6* 2.1.121–2).

10 sometime] sometimes *F3*    17 Sly's] *Q (Slies)*; Sies *F*    Burton Heath] *(Burton-Heath)*    21 fourteen pence] *(xiiii.d.)*    22 sheer ale] Warwickshire ale *Collier*

Christendom. What, I am not bestraught: here's –

3 SERVANT

O, this it is that makes your lady mourn.

2 SERVANT

O, this is it that makes your servants droop.                    25

LORD

Hence comes it that your kindred shuns your house,
As beaten hence by your strange lunacy.
O noble lord, bethink thee of thy birth,
Call home thy ancient thoughts from banishment
And banish hence these abject lowly dreams.                      30
Look how thy servants do attend on thee,
Each in his office ready at thy beck.
Wilt thou have music? (*Music*) Hark, Apollo plays,
And twenty caged nightingales do sing.
Or wilt thou sleep? We'll have thee to a couch                   35
Softer and sweeter than the lustful bed
On purpose trimmed up for Semiramis.
Say thou wilt walk, we will bestrew the ground.
Or wilt thou ride? Thy horses shall be trapped,
Their harness studded all with gold and pearl.                   40

---

23 **bestraught** distracted; bereft (of wits) (*OED v.* 1)
   **here's** – Sly may produce material proof of his identity (or may realize he has none); alternatively, 3 Servant interrupts him at 24; or, Sly offers a toast.
25 **droop** become despondent, despair
28 **bethink thee** recall, consider
29 **ancient thoughts** former (sane) state of mind; perhaps also suggesting that Sly recall his (imaginary) 'noble' lineage; cf. *H5* 1.2.102, 'Look back into your mighty ancestors'.
31 **Look** see
32 **in his office** according to his assigned responsibility

**beck** nod; other silent signal of command (Oxf¹)
33 **Apollo** Greek god of music and song, associated especially with stringed instruments
34 **caged** cagèd
36 **lustful** lust-arousing
37 **trimmed up** arrayed (*OED* trim *v.* 7)
   **Semiramis** legendary Assyrian queen, known for voluptuous sexuality; stresses on second and fourth syllables
38 **bestrew** cover
39 **trapped** provided with a decorated bridle and saddle
40 **all** all over

24+ SP] *Capell subst.; 3 Man. F*   25+ SP] *Capell subst.; 2 Man. F*   25 is it] it is *Rowe*   26 shuns] shun *Rowe*   33 SD] *Oxf¹; opp. 33 F*   38 bestrew] (bestrow)

Dost thou love hawking? Thou hast hawks will soar
Above the morning lark. Or wilt thou hunt?
Thy hounds shall make the welkin answer them
And fetch shrill echoes from the hollow earth.

1 SERVANT

Say thou wilt course, thy greyhounds are as swift                    45
As breathed stags – ay, fleeter than the roe.

2 SERVANT

Dost thou love pictures? We will fetch thee straight
Adonis painted by a running brook
And Cytherea all in sedges hid,
Which seem to move and wanton with her breath                   50
Even as the waving sedges play with wind.

LORD

We'll show thee Io as she was a maid,
And how she was beguiled and surprised,
As lively painted as the deed was done.

---

41 **hawking** a popular aristocratic sport.
*2H6* 2.1 stages a hawking. Petruccio
uses hawking terms to describe his
taming strategy at 4.1.179–85 (see
pp. 54–8).

43 **welkin** sky, heavens

45 **course** hunt hares with greyhounds

46 **breathed** breathèd; strong-winded.
See Ind.1.16 and n.
**fleeter . . . roe** swifter than a small
deer; proverbial: 'As swift as a roe'
(Dent, R158)

47–58 Presumably these are the
Lord's *wanton pictures* (Ind.1.46);
the descriptions of Adonis, Io
and Daphne come from Ovid's
*Metamorphoses*, a popular source of
erotica which Shakespeare knew both
in Latin and in Arthur Golding's
translation (1567). On Ovidian
references, see pp. 66–9.

48 **Adonis** beautiful youth desired by

Venus (Cytherea) and killed by a boar
while hunting (Ovid, *Met.*, 10.596–
863). Shakespeare's popular narrative
poem *Venus and Adonis* was published
in 1593.

49 Ovid's account of Venus and
Adonis does not mention this detail,
though the tale of Salmacis and
Hermaphroditus is similar (*Met.*,
4.352–481). Hibbard suggests
Spenser's *FQ*, 3.1.34–8 as a possible
source. Cf. *TGV* 2.7.29: 'Giving a
gentle kiss to every sedge'.

50 **wanton** sway seductively

52 **Io** The maiden Io was raped by Jove
(who concealed himself in a mist) and
afterwards transformed into a heifer
(Ovid, *Met.*, 1.701–943).

53 **beguiled** beguilèd; deceived, deluded
(*OED ppl.a.* b); also, taken by surprise

54 'so that the painting is a life-like
representation of the act'

45+ SP] *Capell subst.*; *1. Man. F*     47+ SP] *Capell subst.*; *2. M. F*     51 with] *wi' th' Alexander*

3 SERVANT

    Or Daphne roaming through a thorny wood,       55
    Scratching her legs that one shall swear she bleeds,
    And at that sight shall sad Apollo weep,
    So workmanly the blood and tears are drawn.

LORD

    Thou art a lord, and nothing but a lord.
    Thou hast a lady far more beautiful          60
    Than any woman in this waning age.

1 SERVANT

    And till the tears that she hath shed for thee
    Like envious floods o'er-ran her lovely face
    She was the fairest creature in the world –
    And yet she is inferior to none.             65

SLY

    Am I a lord, and have I such a lady?
    Or do I dream? Or have I dreamed till now?
    I do not sleep. I see, I hear, I speak,
    I smell sweet savours and I feel soft things.
    Upon my life, I am a lord indeed,        70

55 **Daphne** wood nymph beloved by Apollo and changed into a laurel tree to preserve her from being raped by him (Ovid, *Met.*, 1.545–700)

60 **a lady** Cam[2] observes that the Lord 'cunningly introduces the topic of Sly's "wife" as the climax of these descriptions' of Ovidian seduction and rape.

61 **this waning age** Oxf[1] notes: 'An allusion – deliberately pretentious – to the widely held belief that the world had consistently deteriorated from the Golden Age (or, in the Christian version, the Garden of Eden).'

63 **envious** spiteful

65 **yet** still, even now

66–73 Beginning to believe himself a lord, Sly moves from prose into verse;

at 72 he uses the royal plural (*our lady*) – yet still insists on *smallest ale* (73). Brian Vickers compares Eliza Doolittle's switch into Received Standard English in Shaw's 1913 *Pygmalion* (*Artistry*, 13–14). Noting that the script seems intent on placing Sly within a verse-speaking culture where all the servants speak verse, G.B. Shand suggests that, played as a conscious choice, the shift into verse marks Sly as opportunely adopting his sudden upward mobility ('Reading', 251–2). On *TS*'s play with and on slippages between social categories, see pp. 65–6; 1.1.206n.

68–9 Sly's checklist of senses resembles Lear's at *KL* 4.7.63–8.

69 **savours** scents (*OED* savour, savor *n.* 2)

61 waning] *(waining)*   63 o'er-ran] *this edn (RP):* o'errun *F*

153

And not a tinker, nor Christopher Sly.
Well, bring our lady hither to our sight,
And once again a pot o'th' smallest ale.

2 SERVANT

Will't please your mightiness to wash your hands?
O, how we joy to see your wit restored;                                              75
O, that once more you knew but what you are.
These fifteen years you have been in a dream,
Or when you waked, so waked as if you slept.

SLY

These fifteen years – by my fay, a goodly nap.
But did I never speak of all that time?                                              80

1 SERVANT

O yes, my lord, but very idle words;
For though you lay here in this goodly chamber,
Yet would you say ye were beaten out of door,
And rail upon the hostess of the house
And say you would present her at the leet                                            85
Because she brought stone jugs and no sealed quarts.
Sometimes you would call out for Cicely Hacket.

SLY     Ay, the woman's maid of the house.

---

71 **Christopher** Ard[1] and Ard[2] unnecessarily follow F2's 'Christophero',
making F's metrical line unmetrical;
precise scansion invites hearing the
fourth foot as dactylic (RP).

73 Some editors generously attend to
Sly's requests for drink. Assuming an
immediate response, Cam[2] adds '*Exit
a Servingman*'; Hibbard reads this as
asking for a refill.

75 **wit** understanding, senses

76 **knew but** only knew

77 **fifteen years** 2 Servant escalates the
Lord's *seven years* – see Ind.1.121
and n.

79 **fay** faith
**goodly** considerable, long (*OED a.* 2)

80 **of** during

81 **idle** See 12n.

82 **goodly** splendid, well proportioned
(*OED a.* 1)

84 **rail . . . house** abuse the alehouse-
keeper

85 **present . . . leet** bring her to trial
at the local court; the *leet* court, a
predecessor of the modern police or
magistrate's court, could indict all
crimes and punish trivial ones.

86 **sealed quarts** vessels containing a
quart of liquid (a quarter of a gallon),
officially sealed as proof that they
contained full measure; stone jugs had
no seals.

87 **Cicely Hacket** See 17–20n.

88 **woman's . . . house** landlady's maid
(Hope, 1.1.4)

---

71 Christopher] Christophero *F2*

3 SERVANT

Why, sir, you know no house nor no such maid
Nor no such men as you have reckoned up –          90
As Stephen Sly and old John Naps of Greet,
And Peter Turph and Henry Pimpernell –
And twenty more such names and men as these,
Which never were, nor no man ever saw.

SLY

Now Lord be thanked for my good amends.          95

ALL

Amen.

SLY          I thank thee, thou shalt not lose by it.

*Enter* [BARTHOLOMEW the Page *as*] *Lady,*
*with Attendants.*

BARTHOLOMEW

How fares my noble Lord?

---

89, 90 **nor no . . . Nor no** Elizabethan
use of double negative for emphasis
(Hope, 2.1.9)
90 **reckoned up** enumerated
91 **Stephen . . . Greet** A Stephen
Sly lived in Stratford-upon-Avon
during Shakespeare's day. Greet
is a Gloucestershire village near
Stratford; given other local references
(17–20), F's 'Greece' is probably a
misreading. Editors who do not emend
conjecture that 'John Naps' anglicizes
a Greek name; the name may pun
on 'Jackanapes' = 'impertinent fellow'
(*OED n.* 2c).
95 **thanked** thankèd (?); such
'aristocratic' pronunciation might
suggest Sly's (ironic?) acceptance of
his new status.
**amends** recovery

96 **I . . . it** Sly thanks the Servants for
their devoted service during his
'illness' and promises future rewards
for it.
96.1–2 F reads '*Enter Lady with*
*Attendants.*', and the SPs hereafter
consistently read '*Lady.*'; but this must
be *Barthol'mew my page* (Ind.1.104).
Boys transformed into women were
thought dangerous (Rainolds, 34).
Cam[2] places this entry following 96
and adds '*one of whom gives Sly a pot of*
*ale*', providing a specific reference for
Sly's remarks at 96 and 98.
97–8 **fares . . . cheer** Sly puns: he *fares*
well because of the good 'fare' (*cheer*)
– i.e. the ale. At 4.3.36–7, *fares* and
*cheer* are addressed to Katherina, who
is denied food and drink.

---

91 of Greet] *of* Greete *(Halliwell);* of Greece F; o'th' Green *Hanmer*     96.1–2] *Oxf; Enter Lady with*
*Attendants. F after Amen.; Enter Page as lady, attended. / Capell; Enter Bartholomew, a page, dressed as*
*a lady, with Attendants, one of whom gives Sly a pot of ale. Cam[2] (Hibbard)*     97+ SP] *Cam[2]; La[dy].*
*F; Page. / Capell*

SLY

> Marry, I fare well, for here is cheer enough.
> Where is my wife?

BARTHOLOMEW

> Here, noble lord. What is thy will with her?                    100

SLY

> Are you my wife, and will not call me 'husband'?
> My men should call me 'lord'; I am your goodman.

BARTHOLOMEW

> My husband and my lord, my lord and husband,
> I am your wife in all obedience.

SLY    I know it well. – What must I call her?                    105

LORD    'Madam.'

SLY    'Al'ce madam'? Or 'Joan madam'?

LORD

> 'Madam', and nothing else. So lords call ladies.

SLY

> Madam wife, they say that I have dreamed
> And slept above some fifteen year or more.                    110

BARTHOLOMEW

> Ay, and the time seems thirty unto me,
> Being all this time abandoned from your bed.

---

98 **Marry** indeed; an attenuated oath, 'by the Virgin Mary'

100 **What . . . her?**    Bartholomew's question is echoed in Katherina's response to Petruccio at 5.2.106.

102 **goodman** form in which lower-class wives addressed their husbands. RP observes that metre invites stressing the second syllable.

104 anticipates Katherina at 5.2.142–85; see also Ind.1.105–34n.

105–8 Sly's questions about how to address his *wife* introduce the trope of naming; at 2.1.181–8, as Petruccio 're-christens' Katherina as Kate, this becomes a strategy of control, as it is also at 4.5, where, at Petruccio's cue, sun and moon become interchangeable.

107 **Al'ce . . . Joan** names common to serving-women; Shakespeare had an aunt named Joan.

109 **Madam wife** Despite the Lord's advice, Sly creates his own title for Bartholomew.

112 **abandoned** banished (*OED v.* IV)

98–9] *prose Pope*    98 enough.] enough. *He drinks. / Hibbard*    102 goodman] *(good-man)*    107 Al'ce] *(Alce)*    109–10] *prose Pope*    110 above] about *F4*

SLY

    'Tis much. Servants, leave me and her alone.

                         *[Exeunt Lord and Servants.]*

    Madam, undress you and come now to bed.

BARTHOLOMEW

    Thrice-noble lord, let me entreat of you                115

    To pardon me yet for a night or two,

    Or if not so, until the sun be set.

    For your physicians have expressly charged,

    In peril to incur your former malady,

    That I should yet absent me from your bed.                120

    I hope this reason stands for my excuse.

SLY    Ay, it stands so that I may hardly tarry so long; but

    I would be loath to fall into my dreams again. I will

    therefore tarry in despite of the flesh and the blood.

                 *Enter a* Servant.

SERVANT

    Your honour's players, hearing your amendment,                125

    Are come to play a pleasant comedy;

    For so your doctors hold it very meet,

---

113–21 Sly's command to be left alone with his *wife* anticipates later distinctions between private and public (e.g. at 2.1.308–9); although Bartholomew has expressed obedience at 103–4, 'her' request to delay going to bed with Sly (115–21) not only disobeys Sly's second command but also glances at the play's delayed wedding and bedding.

113 SD Some editors leave the Lord and Servants to watch the play with Sly and his 'wife'.

119 'because of the danger that you will have a relapse'

120 **absent** In current British usage, the stress falls on the second syllable.

122 **it stands** Sly picks up Bartholomew's *stands* = is acceptable, seems valid (121) and turns it into a sexual pun, often emphasized by stage business.

**tarry** stay, linger; restrain (myself)

124.1 Hibbard suggests that it is the Lord who returns here, an optional doubling which echoes Sly's upward social mobility in reverse; a more likely alternative is that 'Servant' ('*Mess.*', F) is one of the Lord's attendants (Mahood, 46). On doubling the servants in the Lord's and Petruccio's households, see LR, 5n., and Appendix 5, pp. 399–402.

127 **meet** suitable, fitting

---

113 SD] *Hibbard (Exeunt Lord and Servingmen.); The servants withdraw. Cam¹* 115 Thrice-noble] *(*Thrice noble*)* 119 In] On *Capell* 124.1 Servant] *Oxf¹ (Servingman); Messenger F; Lord as a Messenger / Hibbard*

Seeing too much sadness hath congealed your blood –
And melancholy is the nurse of frenzy –
Therefore they thought it good you hear a play                    130
And frame your mind to mirth and merriment,
Which bars a thousand harms and lengthens life.

SLY    Marry, I will. Let them play it. Is not a comonty a
Christmas gambol or a tumbling trick?

BARTHOLOMEW

No, my good lord, it is more pleasing stuff.                       135

SLY

What, household stuff?

BARTHOLOMEW                      It is a kind of history.

SLY

Well, we'll see't. Come, madam wife, sit by my side

---

128–32 Elizabethans believed that melancholy resulted from a thickening of the blood. In *The Anatomy of Melancholy* (1621), Robert Burton writes: 'Stage-plays [among other entertainments] . . . if opportunely and soberly used, may justly be approved' as a cure; however, he recommends study as the best recreation or distraction (2, 2.2.4.1.82). Proverbial: 'Melancholy is the pathway to madness' (Dent, M866). Cam[2] suggests that repeated references to the humours are an attempt to overwhelm Sly with scientific learning.

129  **nurse** nourisher

130  **hear** should hear

132  **bars** prevents (*OED v.* 6a)

133  **Marry . . . it** Oxf emends to 'I will let them play it' and comments, 'F1's reading suits Sly's growing lordliness'. Textual notes offer other options.
     **comonty** Often read as Sly's malapropism; the term slips between 'comedy' and 'commodity' = object of trade, a thing produced for use or sale (*OED* 6a). 'Commonty fire' was

a fire provided at common expense in a fellow's rooms at Cambridge; the term also applied to the after-dinner gathering around that fire (*OED* commonty *n.* 7).

134  **Christmas gambol . . . tumbling trick** leaping dance . . . acrobatic performance. Both were popular entertainments, the former associated with mumming plays performed during the Christmas holidays. Ard[2] observes that F's 'gambold' may suggest Sly's pronunciation.

136  **household stuff** furnishings, punning on *stuff* in the sense of 'matter' at 135.
     **history** story, whether factual, as in the Chronicles (see Ind.1.4), or fictional, as in drama. On *TS* as domestic history, see Dolan, *Marriage*.

137–8 Ard[2] finds it appropriate for Sly to be 'left at the end of the scene in prose', but retaining F's lineation gives Sly a doubly classed verbal identity; turning from prose to verse at 133–4 (see 66–73n.) emphasizes his acceptance of

---

128 too much] so much *Rowe*    133 will . . . Is] *Capell subst.*; will let them play, it is not *F*; will, let them play, it is *F3*; will, let them play, is it *F4*; play; is it *Theobald*    comonty] commodity *Pope*    134 gambol] (gambold)    136] *Oxf*; *F lines* stuffe. / history. /    137–8] *Oxf*; *F lines* see't: / side, / yonger. / ; *prose Pope*

And let the world slip: we shall ne'er be younger.

[1.1]    *Flourish. Enter* LUCENTIO *and his man* TRANIO.

LUCENTIO
Tranio, since for the great desire I had
To see fair Padua, nursery of arts,
I am arrived for fruitful Lombardy,
The pleasant garden of great Italy,
And by my father's love and leave am armed                5

imagined nobility, while the awkward scansion here seems appropriate to the unpractised Sly. Bell's SD, '*Seating her for the play*', suggests a more gentlemanly Sly.

138 **let . . . slip** See Ind.1.5 and n. Sly combines two proverbs: 'Let the world wag (or pass)' (Dent, W879) and 'You shall never be younger' (Dent, Y36). Some editors add '*They sit down*' or a similar direction for Bartholomew only. In some stagings, Sly has remained to watch the play – whether from a box, the orchestra, an Elizabethan stage or, on occasion, from a magnificent bed (Gurney, 1937; see also Schafer, 91). In others, this is the last spectators see of Sly and company – or, more accurately, their last appearance in these roles (see Appendix 5, pp. 399–402).

1.1 Capell reads '*Padua. A publick Place.*' When the Sly scenes are not played, this constitutes the play's opening scene.

0.1 *Flourish* a trumpet flourish announcing the play's opening. Even though the two scenes are contiguous and the Sly scenes are often omitted, some editors place the SD after Ind.2.138.

TRANIO F's '*Triano*' and the spelling '*Trayno*' both occur in later SDs, though not in dialogue. Misreading the name would have been easy: similar errors typically affect proper names

early in the typesetting; cf. '*Butonio*' in 1.2 (RP). Cam[1] believes a different hand was responsible for SDs in printing-house copy.

1  **for** because of

2  **Padua . . . arts** Padua, a commune of north-eastern Italy west of Venice, was famous for its ancient university, a centre of Aristotelianism. In *MV* 4.1.105–6, 119, the Duke sends to Padua for the learned doctor Bellario.

3  **am arrived for** 'have arrived in'; idiomatic (Abbott, 295)
   **Lombardy** Padua is not in Lombardy, but Elizabethans may have thought it was; Ard[2] notes that Ortelius' map of Europe has 'Lombardy' written across northern Italy. Although Shakespeare shared with his contemporaries a somewhat imprecise knowledge of Mediterranean geography, the relative positions of Padua, Mantua, Verona and Venice in *TS* are fairly accurate. For an overview, see Hoenselaars.

4  **garden . . . Italy**     proverbial: 'Lombardy is the garden of the world' (Dent, L414), possibly deriving from John Florio's manual for the study of Italian, *Florio's Second Fruits* (1591): '*La Lombardia è il giardino del mondo*'. Shakespeare may have drawn on Florio for the Italian words and phrases in this scene and the next (Praz, 105).

1.1] *Pope*    0.1 TRANIO] *F2; Triano F*    3 for] from *Theobald; in Capell (Heath);* fore *Oxf*    Lombardy] *(Lumbardie)*

With his good will and thy good company –
My trusty servant, well approved in all –
Here let us breathe and haply institute
A course of learning and ingenious studies.
Pisa, renowned for grave citizens,                               10
Gave me my being and my father first –
A merchant of great traffic through the world –
Vincentio, come of the Bentivogli.
Vincentio's son, brought up in Florence,
It shall become to serve all hopes conceived        15
To deck his fortune with his virtuous deeds:
And therefore, Tranio, for the time I study,

---

7  **approved** tested, reliable
8  **breathe** pause, take a rest (*OED v.* 5)
   **haply** perhaps; also, with (anticipated)
   good luck or fortune
   **institute** begin. Oxf[1] suggests that
   Lucentio is perhaps being pedantic: the
   word also meant 'educate', 'establish in
   principle' (*OED v.* 3).
9  **ingenious** appropriate. Johnson
   comments: 'I rather think it was
   written *ingenuous studies* but of this
   and a thousand such observations there
   is little certainty.' The words were
   spelled identically; the meaning here is
   'befitting a well-born person, liberal',
   which *OED* gives as an obsolete sense
   of 'ingenuous' (*a.* 6).
10 Oxf[1] cites Boswell-Stone, who
   compares the reference in Greene's
   *Royal Exchange* (trans. from Italian,
   1590) to Pisa, 'famous for honorable
   Citizens'.
   **renowned** renownèd; metre invites
   trisyllabic pronunciation.
11 **first** before me
12 **traffic** business, trade
13 **come of** descended from
   **Bentivogli** The 15th-century
   Bentivogli family was powerful in
   Bologna, not Pisa (see Machiavelli,

*History of Florence*, Book 6, 1525, trans.
1595). Shakespeare abbreviates the
name to Benvolio in *RJ*.
14–16 'It shall become me, as Vincentio's
son, brought up in Florence, to fulfil
all the hopes conceived by my father by
adding virtuous deeds to what fortune
already has given.'
14 **Florence** centre of banking, and home
to mercantile dynasties such as the
Medici (see Jardine, 93–132)
16 [1]**his** Vincentio's
   [2]**his** Lucentio's
17–24 Young Englishmen often travelled
to Italy, considered the seat of
Humanist learning, to seek education
and – for those who were not aristocrats
but were upwardly mobile – to
fashion themselves as gentlemen (see
Castiglione's *Book of the Courtier*, 1528,
trans. Sir Thomas Hoby, 1561). Some
English Protestant writers feared the
influence of travel in a Catholic country
(see Harrison, *Description*, 74–5, 114–
15). Tranio describes a course of study
at 28–40; in *TGV* 1.1.2, Valentine tells
Proteus: 'Home-keeping youth have
ever homely wits'.
17 **time** i.e. period during which I study
here

---

9 ingenious] ingenuous *Cam*[2] *(Johnson)*    13 Vincentio] *Hanmer; Vincentio's F*    Bentivogli]
*(Bentivolij)*    14 Vincentio's son] Vincentio his son *Pope;* Lucentio his son *Tyrwhitt*

Virtue and that part of philosophy
Will I apply that treats of happiness
By virtue specially to be achieved.                    20
Tell me thy mind, for I have Pisa left
And am to Padua come, as he that leaves
A shallow plash to plunge him in the deep,
And with satiety seeks to quench his thirst.

TRANIO

*Mi perdonato*, gentle master mine,                    25
I am in all affected as yourself,
Glad that you thus continue your resolve
To suck the sweets of sweet philosophy.
Only, good master, while we do admire
This virtue and this moral discipline,                    30
Let's be no stoics nor no stocks, I pray,
Or so devote to Aristotle's checks
As Ovid be an outcast quite abjured.

19 **apply** pursue, study
   **treats of** discusses, deals with a subject
   in writing (*OED v.* 2b)
19–20 **happiness . . . achieved** The idea
   that virtue begets happiness is central
   to Aristotle's *Ethics*, especially Books
   1 and 2.
23 **plash** puddle, pool (*OED n.*[1])
   **plunge him in** dive into
24 **satiety** *OED* notes the pronunciation
   'society' well into the 19th century;
   RP observes that *t* and *c* were
   interchangeable in such words in the
   early modern period.
25 *Mi perdonato* Pardon me; with
   apologies. Not perfect Italian, though
   near enough. Other Italian words and
   phrases occur at 197 and at 1.2.24–6
   and 281; they probably derive from
   *Florio's First* and *Second Fruits* (1578,
   1591). With the exception of *marcantant*
   (4.2.64), Italian words occur only in Act
   1, perhaps emphasizing the Italianate

setting, in contrast to the Induction's
Warwickshire locale.
26 'I am exactly of the same opinion as
   you'
29 **admire** marvel at, respect, revere
   (*OED v.* 3a)
30 **moral discipline** moral philosophy
31 **stoics . . . stocks** *stoics* put aside
   pleasure and desire; *stocks* are blockheads.
   For the word-play, see Kökeritz, 83, 223.
32 **devote** devoted (Abbott, 342)
   **Aristotle's checks** the self-restraint
   advocated in Aristotle's *Ethics* or
   Seneca's *Epistolae Morales*. Although
   Lucentio claims his devotion to
   Aristotelean Humanism (17–20),
   Tranio reminds him that virtue is not
   his major concern.
33 **Ovid** author of *Ars Amatoria* (*The
   Art to Love*), which Lucentio mentions
   at 4.2.8. In *Remedia Amoris* (not part
   of the official Humanist curriculum),
   Ovid calls himself 'Professor of Love'.

24 satiety] *(sacietie)*    25 *Mi perdonato*] *Cam*[1]; *Me pardonato* F; *Mi pardinato* Q; *Mi perdonate* /
*Capell*    32 checks] ethicks *Rann (Blackstone)*

161

Balk logic with acquaintance that you have
And practise rhetoric in your common talk;                          35
Music and poesy use to quicken you;
The mathematics and the metaphysics,
Fall to them as you find your stomach serves you.
No profit grows where is no pleasure ta'en:
In brief, sir, study what you most affect.                          40

LUCENTIO

Gramercies, Tranio, well dost thou advise.
If, Biondello, thou wert come ashore,
We could at once put us in readiness
And take a lodging fit to entertain
Such friends as time in Padua shall beget.                          45
But stay awhile, what company is this?

TRANIO

Master, some show to welcome us to town.

---

34 **Balk logic** chop logic, bandy words
(*OED* balk $v.^1$ 6)
36 **quicken** enliven
38 'study them according to your appetite';
punning on *Fall to* = begin to eat
39 a commonplace of Renaissance
criticism. Ard$^2$ cites Horace, *Ars
Poetica*, 343–4, and translates: 'He has
won every vote who has blended profit
and pleasure, at once delighting and
instructing the reader'.
**ta'en** taken. F regularly spells as
'tane'; always monosyllabic. Although
modernizing spelling clarifies meaning,
it encourages mistaken disyllabic
pronunciation.
40 **affect** like, prefer
41 **Gramercies** many thanks (Old French
*grant merci*)
42 **Biondello** Lucentio's absent boy-
servant, who enters at 219. Ard$^1$
observes that Lucentio has two
servants (Tranio and Biondello),
as in Gascoigne's *Supposes* (1566),
where the real Dulipo and Lytio are

Philogano's servants.
**come ashore** in this context, idiomatic
for 'arrived', although, as Ard$^1$ and Ard$^2$
note, at this time a network of canals and
waterways threaded through northern
Italy and was much used by travellers,
who could go from Padua to Venice by
boat. Cam$^2$ suggests the influence of
Gascoigne's *Supposes*, where Philogano
(Vincentio's equivalent) describes
travelling 'to Ancona, from thence by
water to Ravenna, and from Ravenna
hither, continually against the tide'
(4.3.12–14); *TS* also may be following
Roman comedy convention, in which
the harbour or port was assumed to be
just offstage.
47 **show** pageant or spectacle. Elaborate
civic shows welcomed foreign dignitaries to London (Manley, *Literature*).
47.1–3 Presumably offstage noise prompts
Lucentio's question at 46. Some editors
place the SD to follow 45; again, entry
placement will depend on a particular
performance space. If Sly, his 'wife'

34 Balk] Talk *Rowe; Chop (Capell);* Hack *(anon., Ard$^1$)*    39 ta'en] *(tane)*    42 thou wert] now were
*Dyce (Collier)*    47.1–3] *after* 45 *Cam$^2$*

*Enter* BAPTISTA *with his two daughters,* KATHERINA
*and* BIANCA; GREMIO, *a pantaloon;* HORTENSIO, *suitor*
*to Bianca. Lucentio and Tranio stand by.*

BAPTISTA

Gentlemen, importune me no farther,
For how I firmly am resolved you know:
That is, not to bestow my youngest daughter          50
Before I have a husband for the elder.
If either of you both love Katherina,
Because I know you well and love you well,
Leave shall you have to court her at your pleasure.

GREMIO

To cart her, rather. She's too rough for me.          55
There, there, Hortensio, will you any wife?

KATHERINA

I pray you, sir, is it your will
To make a stale of me amongst these mates?

and the Lord remain on stage, with
Lucentio and Tranio *stand[ing]* *by* to
watch (together with the audience),
the moment stretches the limits of
the frame. As Katherina and Bianca
enter, the play introduces two of its
'real' women, performed originally, of
course, by boy actors.

47.1 KATHERINA On various spellings of
Katherina's name, see LR, 9n.
BIANCA See LR, 10n.

47.2 *pantaloon* lean and foolish old
man, a stock Venetian figure in Italian
*commedia dell'arte*, often serving as an
obstacle to young lovers and as the butt
of jokes

47.3 *stand by* stand aside (to watch the
entering procession). On *TS*'s onstage
spectators and layers of performance,
see Shapiro.

50 **bestow** give in marriage. The practice
of not marrying younger daughters

until older daughters were married was
common and (if she wished to marry)
would work to Katherina's advantage.
**youngest** The superlative occurs often
when only two objects are compared
(Abbott, 10).

55 **cart her** draw her through the streets
either in or behind an open cart,
with pun on *court* (54). Carting was
a common punishment for scolds,
convicted prostitutes and witches
(Boose, 'Scolding', 185–90).
**rough** difficult to manage, not properly
broken in, as a horse (*OED a.* 7c)

58 Katherina plays on several levels of
meaning: *stale* as decoy, lower-class
prostitute, laughing-stock and stalemate
in chess; *mate* as the final position in a
game of chess, a habitual companion
or one of a pair, especially husband or
wife. The last of these is Hortensio's
meaning at 59.

47.1 KATHERINA] *F2; Katerina F*    47.2 *pantaloon*] *(Pantelowne)*    HORTENSIO] *F2;* Hortentio *F*    suitor] *F3;*
sister *F; shuiter F2*    57 SP] *Rowe (Kath.); Kate. F*    will] will and pleasure *Hanmer*    58 these] those *F3*

HORTENSIO

    'Mates', maid? How mean you that? No mates for you

    Unless you were of gentler, milder mould.　　　　　　　　60

KATHERINA

    I'faith, sir, you shall never need to fear.

    Iwis it is not half-way to her heart:

    But if it were, doubt not her care should be

    To comb your noddle with a three-legged stool

    And paint your face and use you like a fool.　　　　　　65

HORTENSIO

    From all such devils, good Lord deliver us!

GREMIO

    And me too, good Lord.

TRANIO

    Husht, master, here's some good pastime toward;

    That wench is stark mad or wonderful froward.

LUCENTIO

    But in the other's silence do I see　　　　　　　　　　70

    Maids' mild behaviour and sobriety.

62 'Certainly it (marriage) is not even her half-hearted desire'. By speaking of herself in the third person, Katherina further distances herself from the idea of marriage.

64–5 On rhyming couplets here and at 70–1, 160–1 and 235–6, see Oliver, 61–2.

64 **comb your noddle** hit you on the head (*noddle*), thrash you; proverbial: 'To comb one's head with a three-legged stool' (Dent, H270)

65 **paint** bloody (i.e. scratch with fingernails)
    **use** treat

66 Hortensio quotes from the Litany in the *BCP* (1559), where the priest prays for deliverance from the deceits of the world, the flesh and the devil, and the congregation responds, 'Good Lord deliver us' (ll. 68–9).

68–73 Theobald's indication '*aside*' for this exchange has often been adopted by modern editors. On '*aside*' in this edition, see pp. 340–1.

68–9 On doggerel couplets in *TS*, see pp. 333–4.

68 **Husht** 'be still'. A 16th- and 17th-century dialect form; cf. 'Even as the wind is husht before it raineth' (*VA* 458, 1593 Quarto) and 'Husht, here comes the lords of Tyre' (*Per* 1.3.8–9).
    **toward** about to occur

69 **wonderful froward** remarkably or incredibly obstinate, wilful, ungovernable

70 **silence** one of the virtues of the (masculine) ideal of femininity; proverbial: 'Silence is the best ornament of a woman' (Dent, S447)

59] *Pope; F lines* that? / you, /　66 us] me *Hanmer*　68 Husht] hush'd *F3*　71 Maids'] *(Maids); Maid's Rowe*

Peace, Tranio.

TRANIO

Well said, master. Mum, and gaze your fill.

BAPTISTA

Gentlemen, that I may soon make good
What I have said – Bianca, get you in;                                    75
And let it not displease thee, good Bianca,
For I will love thee ne'er the less, my girl.

KATHERINA     A pretty peat. It is best put finger in the eye,
an she knew why.

BIANCA

Sister, content you in my discontent.                                    80
– Sir, to your pleasure humbly I subscribe:
My books and instruments shall be my company,
On them to look and practise by myself.

LUCENTIO

Hark, Tranio, thou mayst hear Minerva speak.

HORTENSIO

Signor Baptista, will you be so strange?                                 85
Sorry am I that our good will effects
Bianca's grief.

GREMIO               Why will you mew her up,
Signor Baptista, for this fiend of hell,

---

73 **Mum** 'keep quiet'
**gaze your fill** proverbial: 'To look
one's fill' (Dent, FF2)
78 **peat** pet, spoilt child
78–9 **It . . . why** 'She should make
herself cry, if she had an excuse',
echoing *commanded tears* as *a woman's
gift* (Ind.1.123–4). Proverbial: 'To put
the finger in the eye' (Dent, F229);
the phrase also occurs at *CE* 2.2.04.
Omitting 'to' is common (Abbott,
351).
81 **subscribe** submit
84 **Minerva** Roman goddess of wisdom

and some of the arts; she was supposed
to have invented the flute (Oxf[1]).
85 **Signor** Sir (Italian). Some editors retain
F's 'Signior', presumably to reflect the
play's conflation of Italian and Spanish.
Oxf reads 'Signior' not as 'authentic
Italian' but as 'Shakespearian-ese'.
**will . . . strange** 'do you wish to be so
distant (or reserved)'
87 **mew** coop up, confine; a hawk was
caged in a 'mew' at moulting time. On
hawking terms as taming metaphors,
see 4.1.177–200n. and pp. 56–8.
88 **for** because of

---

75 said – Bianca] *Capell;* said, Bianca *F*   78–9] *Rowe lines* eye, / why. /; *Capell lines* best /
why. /   79 an] *(and)*   85 Signor] *Ard²;* Signior *F*

And make her bear the penance of her tongue?

BAPTISTA

Gentlemen, content ye: I am resolved.　　　　　　　90

Go in, Bianca.　　　　　　　　　　　　*[Exit Bianca.]*

And for I know she taketh most delight

In music, instruments and poetry,

Schoolmasters will I keep within my house

Fit to instruct her youth. If you, Hortensio,　　　95

Or, Signor Gremio, you know any such,

Prefer them hither; for to cunning men

I will be very kind, and liberal

To mine own children in good bringing up.

And so farewell. – Katherina, you may stay,　　　100

For I have more to commune with Bianca.　　　　*Exit.*

KATHERINA

Why, and I trust I may go too, may I not?

What, shall I be appointed hours, as though, belike,

I knew not what to take and what to leave? Ha!　　*Exit.*

GREMIO　　You may go to the devil's dam! Your gifts are so　105

good here's none will hold you. Their love is not so

---

89 'and make *her* (Bianca) atone for *her*
(Katherina's) shrewish tongue'. On the
tongue as a woman's 'unruly member'
and an analogue for the male penis, see
Boose, 'Scolding'.

91 SD F has no SD for Bianca's exit;
equally, she might delay, leaving with
Baptista at 101.

97 **Prefer** recommend
**cunning** skilful, learned, as at 186
(*OED a.* 1, 2)

101 **commune** discuss; accented on first
syllable

103 **appointed hours** given a schedule
**belike** perhaps, 'like'

105 **dam** mother; *devil's dam* was a term
for a threatening woman.

105–6 **Your . . . you** 'You are such a trial
that no one wants you'; proverbial: 'No
man holds you' (Dent, M328).

106–44 On the play's proverbial language,
which grounds this conversation, see
pp. 61–2.

106 **Their love** the love of women (?).
Some editors emend to 'There! Love'
on the grounds that 'there' and 'their'
were spelled interchangeably (and often
appeared as 'ther' in copy) and that
Gremio's *There, there* at 56 suggests a
speech mannerism.

---

91 SD] *Theobald*　98 kind, and liberal] *(*kind and liberall*)*; kind; and liberal *Theobald*　103–4]
*Capell; F lines* though / take, / Ha. / ; *Bevington lines* hours, / take, / Ha! /　106 you. Their love]
*(*you: Their love*)*; you. There love *Q;* you. Our love *F3;* you. Your love *Rowe (Malone);* you. There!
Love *Collier subst.*

166

great, Hortensio, but we may blow our nails together
and fast it fairly out. Our cake's dough on both sides.
Farewell. Yet for the love I bear my sweet Bianca, if I
can by any means light on a fit man to teach her that      110
wherein she delights, I will wish him to her father.

HORTENSIO    So will I, Signor Gremio. But a word, I pray:
though the nature of our quarrel yet never brooked
parle, know now, upon advice, it toucheth us both – that
we may yet again have access to our fair mistress and be   115
happy rivals in Bianca's love – to labour and effect one
thing specially.

GREMIO    What's that, I pray?

HORTENSIO    Marry, sir, to get a husband for her sister.

GREMIO    A husband? A devil.                               120

HORTENSIO    I say a husband.

GREMIO    I say a devil. Think'st thou, Hortensio, though
her father be very rich, any man is so very a fool to be
married to hell?

HORTENSIO    Tush, Gremio: though it pass your patience     125
and mine to endure her loud alarums, why, man, there
be good fellows in the world, an a man could light
on them, would take her with all faults, and money
enough.

---

107 **but we may** that we cannot
**blow our nails** to warm them; perhaps
meaning 'pass the time'; proverbial
(Dent, N10.1)

108 **fast . . . out** 'still manage to wait
(without quarrelling)'; *fast out*
= observe abstinence (*OED v.* 2d);
*fairly* = peaceably (*OED adv.* 5). Both
meanings are obsolete.
**Our . . . sides** 'We're both out of luck';
proverbial: 'His cake is dough', i.e. his
cake has failed to rise (Dent, C12).
Gremio echoes the phrase ('My cake is
dough') at 5.1.130.

110 **light on** meet with, chance upon
(*OED* light *v.*[1] 10c)

111 **wish** commend

113–14 **brooked parle** allowed negotiations; *parle* is a shortened form of
'parley' (*OED n.* 1).

114 **advice** reflection

123 **so . . . fool** 'such a complete fool as'

126 **alarums** disturbances, outcries
(metaphor from the military 'calls to
arms')

127 **an** if (Abbott, 101, 103)

128 **with all faults** a phrase from the
cattle-market; still used ('WAF') in
the second-hand book market (RP).
*TS* consistently compares women (as
prospective wives) to animals, as when
Petruccio refers to his new wife as 'My
horse, my ox, my ass, my anything'
(3.2.233; see 3.2.231–3n.).

---

108 cake's] *(cakes)*   126 loud] *(lowd)*; lewd *F2*   127 an] *(and)*   128 all faults] all her faults *F4*

GREMIO    I cannot tell, but I had as lief take her dowry    130
with this condition: to be whipped at the high cross
every morning.

HORTENSIO    Faith, as you say, there's small choice in
rotten apples. But come, since this bar in law makes us
friends, it shall be so far forth friendly maintained till    135
by helping Baptista's eldest daughter to a husband we
set his youngest free for a husband – and then have
to't afresh. Sweet Bianca! Happy man be his dole. He
that runs fastest gets the ring. How say you, Signor
Gremio?    140

GREMIO    I am agreed, and would I had given him the
best horse in Padua to begin his wooing that would
thoroughly woo her, wed her, and bed her, and rid the
house of her. Come on.      *Exeunt [Gremio and Hortensio].*

TRANIO

I pray, sir, tell me, is it possible    145
That love should of a sudden take such hold?

LUCENTIO

O Tranio, till I found it to be true
I never thought it possible or likely.
But see, while idly I stood looking on,

---

130 **had as lief** would gladly
131 **whipped . . . cross** Whippings
(usually for minor offences) took place
at the market cross, often located at a
town's centre.
133–4 **small . . . apples** proverbial
(Dent, C358)
134 **bar in law** legal impediment,
presumably, Baptista's refusal to let
them woo Bianca. Ard² observes that
this refusal does not represent a *legal*
impediment.
137–8 **have to't afresh** renew combat

138 **Happy . . . dole** proverbial: 'May his
lot be happy' (Dent, M158)
138–9 **He . . . ring** proverbial (Dent, R130),
with a sexually explicit implication, as at
*MV* 5.1.306–7: 'I'll fear no other thing /
So sore, as keeping safe Nerissa's ring'
(Partridge, 175). The phrase alludes to
jousting, where combatants 'rode at the
ring', attempting to drive a lance-point
through it and win the bout.
143 **woo . . . bed her** Gremio adds 'rid
the house of her' to a proverbial cliché
(Dent, W731).

143 woo] *(woe)*    144 SD] *Capell; Exeunt ambo. Manet Tranio and Lucentio F*

I found the effect of love-in-idleness, 150
And now in plainness do confess to thee
That art to me as secret and as dear
As Anna to the Queen of Carthage was:
Tranio, I burn, I pine; I perish, Tranio,
If I achieve not this young modest girl. 155
Counsel me, Tranio, for I know thou canst;
Assist me, Tranio, for I know thou wilt.

TRANIO

Master, it is no time to chide you now;
Affection is not rated from the heart.
If love have touched you, naught remains but so: 160
*Redime te captum quam queas minimo.*

LUCENTIO

Gramercies, lad. Go forward, this contents;
The rest will comfort, for thy counsel's sound.

TRANIO

Master, you looked so longly on the maid,
Perhaps you marked not what's the pith of all. 165

---

150 **love-in-idleness** popular name for heartsease or *Viola tricolor*, thought to have aphrodisiac powers, as when Oberon claims its juice 'Will make or man or woman madly dote / Upon the next live creature that it sees' (*MND* 2.1.171–2); proverbial: 'Love is the fruit of idleness' (Dent, L513.1)
151 **in plainness** frankly
152 **secret** intimately trusted
153 **Anna** sister and confidante to Dido, Queen of Carthage and beloved of Aeneas (see *Aeneid*, 4.8–75)
154 '**I . . . perish** Standard lovers' rhetoric; cf. 'I burne, I freese, I sinke, I swim' from 'The Lover Wounded

with his Lady's Beauty Craveth Mercy' (*Gorgeous*, 40).
159 **rated** scolded (*OED v.²* 1a). Tranio claims that chiding does not drive away affection.
161 'Ransom yourself from captivity as cheaply as you can'; the quotation comes from Lyly's *Latin Grammar* (1542), used in Elizabethan schools, and derives from Terence's *Eunuch* 1.1.28–9; F's '*captam*' is incorrect (Oxf¹).
162 **Go . . . contents** 'proceed: your advice satisfies me'
164 **so longly** for such a long time; so longingly
165 **marked** observed
**pith of all** central issue

---

150 love-in-idleness] *(*Loue in idlenesse*)*   151 do] to *F3*   161 *captum*] *F2*; *captam F*   163 counsel's] *(*counsels*)*

LUCENTIO

    O yes, I saw sweet beauty in her face,
    Such as the daughter of Agenor had
    That made great Jove to humble him to her hand
    When with his knees he kissed the Cretan strand.

TRANIO

    Saw you no more? Marked you not how her sister    170
    Began to scold and raise up such a storm
    That mortal ears might hardly endure the din?

LUCENTIO

    Tranio, I saw her coral lips to move,
    And with her breath she did perfume the air;
    Sacred and sweet was all I saw in her.    175

TRANIO

    Nay, then 'tis time to stir him from his trance.
    – I pray, awake, sir. If you love the maid,
    Bend thoughts and wits to achieve her. Thus it stands:
    Her elder sister is so curst and shrewd
    That till the father rid his hands of her,    180
    Master, your love must live a maid at home,
    And therefore has he closely mewed her up
    Because she will not be annoyed with suitors.

---

166–9, 173–5 Lucentio's praise of Bianca is the first of several short blazons, or recitals of virtues; others occur at 2.1.169–75 and 4.5.30–3; see also 3.2.43–68, where Biondello gives a type of reverse blazon of Petruccio and his horse.

167 **daughter of Agenor** Europa, beloved of Jove, who transformed himself into a bull, wooed her and abducted her from Sidon to Crete on his back (Ovid, *Met.*, 2.1043–96). Lucentio reinterprets the myth as an instance of male humility rather than Jovian deceit. Cf. *2H4* 2.2.167–8: 'From a god to a bull? A heavy descension! It was Jove's case'.

170 **Saw . . . more** In Roman comedy, from which Shakespeare borrows, servants regularly explain the plot to lovesick masters; see 185–96, 4.2.64–72 and 4.4.80–95, and cf. *TGV* 2.1.131–62, where Speed explains the significance of Silvia's 'letter' to Valentine.

176 Some editors mark this line as an aside, but since Lucentio is in a trance, speaking *aside* seems optional. Bell directs '*Shaking him*' at 177.

179 **curst and shrewd** bad-tempered and sharp

182 **mewed her up** confined her; see 87n.

183 **Because** so that; although F makes sense, Dyce's emendation to 'Because he' also is persuasive, since Baptista may not wish to be troubled by suitors.

169 strand] *(strond)*    178 achieve] *(atcheeue)*    183 she] he *Dyce (Singer)*

LUCENTIO

Ah, Tranio, what a cruel father's he.

But art thou not advised he took some care                          185

To get her cunning schoolmasters to instruct her?

TRANIO

Ay, marry am I, sir – and now 'tis plotted.

LUCENTIO

I have it, Tranio.

TRANIO                          Master, for my hand,

Both our inventions meet and jump in one.

LUCENTIO

Tell me thine first.

TRANIO                          You will be schoolmaster               190

And undertake the teaching of the maid:

That's your device.

LUCENTIO                          It is. May it be done?

TRANIO

Not possible: for who shall bear your part

And be in Padua here Vincentio's son,

Keep house and ply his book, welcome his friends,              195

Visit his countrymen and banquet them?

LUCENTIO

*Basta*, content thee, for I have it full.

We have not yet been seen in any house,

Nor can we be distinguished by our faces

For man or master. Then it follows thus:                          200

Thou shalt be master, Tranio, in my stead,

Keep house and port and servants as I should;

---

185 **art . . . advised** 'do you not realize'
188 **for my hand** for my part
189 **inventions . . . one** plans coincide perfectly; cf. *TN* 5.1.248: 'cohere and jump'. Proverbial: 'Good wits jump' (Dent, W578).
192 **device** plot, scheme (*OED* 6)
    **It is** 'It is?' is equally possible, but just as much comic mileage results

from Lucentio pretending that he had devised the exchange of roles, an echo of the Lord's 'practice' on Sly.
195 **Keep house** receive and entertain guests
    **ply his book** study
197 *Basta* enough (Italian)
    **I . . . full** 'I have it completely plotted.'
202 **port** style of living, social station

I will some other be – some Florentine,
Some Neapolitan, or meaner man of Pisa.
'Tis hatched, and shall be so. Tranio, at once                    205
Uncase thee; take my coloured hat and cloak.
[*They exchange outer clothing.*]
When Biondello comes, he waits on thee,
But I will charm him first to keep his tongue.

TRANIO

So had you need.
In brief, sir, sith it your pleasure is,                          210
And I am tied to be obedient –
For so your father charged me at our parting:
'Be serviceable to my son,' quoth he,
Although I think 'twas in another sense –
I am content to be Lucentio,                                      215

204 **Some** the third use of *some* in two
lines; metrically unnecessary
**Neapolitan . . . Pisa** Oxf¹ notes: 'If
Lucentio is not to pretend to be from
some other city, he must disguise himself
as from a lower rank of society than the
one he really belongs to in Pisa.'

206 **Uncase thee** 'take off your outer
garments'. Although hat and cloak are
enough to signify a complete change of
clothes, in performance, exactly what
(and how much) clothing gets exchanged
here varies, as does the timing of the
exchange, which must be complete by
the time Biondello enters at 219. In
Bogdanov (1978), the two stripped down
to their underwear (prompting the quick
exit of a waiter bringing an aperitif).
'*Enter* TRANIO *brave*' (1.2.216.1)
suggests additional finery.
**coloured** Early modern sumptuary
laws prescribed dress codes for each
social level (see Harrison, *Description*,
145–8). The original statute decreeing
servingmen's attire dates from 1585:
at *TS*'s first performances, Tranio

would probably have worn a servant's
blue livery (mentioned at 4.1.81) and
Lucentio a finer cloak, hat and doublet
marking his superior station; some
modern Elizabethan-dress productions
have conformed to these dress codes.
*TS* consistently keys the performance
of identity, gender and social status to
clothing.

207 **waits on** is to serve
208 **charm . . . tongue** 'persuade him to
be quiet'; proverbial: 'to charm the
tongue' (Dent, CC9)
209 Some editors read the short line as
evidence of a cut or of missing text.
However, it underlines Tranio's reply:
as Oxf¹ points out, 'money is something
the Biondellos of the world understand'.
210 **sith** since
211 proverbial: 'They that are bound must
obey' (Dent, B354)
213 **serviceable** devoted (in your duty) as
a servant; faithful, loyal
215 Audiences hear the name Lucentio
just at the moment when he and Tranio
exchange clothes and identities.

204 meaner] mean *Capell*   206 coloured] *F2* (Coulord); Conlord *F*   SD] *this edn; They . . . clothes.
*Theobald subst.; after 209 Oxf; after 216 Oxf¹*   210 sir] (Sir); good sir *Pope*   sith it] sithence it *Dyce²*

Because so well I love Lucentio.

LUCENTIO

Tranio, be so, because Lucentio loves,
And let me be a slave to achieve that maid
Whose sudden sight hath thralled my wounded eye.

*Enter* BIONDELLO.

Here comes the rogue. Sirrah, where have you been?     220

BIONDELLO     Where have I been? Nay, how now, where are
you? Master, has my fellow Tranio stolen your clothes,
or you stolen his, or both? Pray, what's the news?

LUCENTIO

Sirrah, come hither. 'Tis no time to jest,
And therefore frame your manners to the time.     225
Your fellow Tranio here, to save my life,
Puts my apparel and my countenance on,
And I for my escape have put on his;
For in a quarrel since I came ashore
I killed a man, and fear I was descried.     230
Wait you on him, I charge you, as becomes,
While I make way from hence to save my life.
You understand me?

---

218–19 **slave . . . thralled . . . eye**
a Petrarchan conceit familiar in
Elizabethan love poetry: the sight of
the beloved was thought to enslave or
bewitch the lover.

222 **you** Oxf italicizes, emphasizing
Biondello's confusion.
**fellow** fellow-servant, also at 226.
References to servants and masters
from here to 243 clarify, for Biondello
and audiences, the changed identities.

225 **frame** adapt

226–30 Lucentio fantasizes Tranio and
himself as hero-villains of a romantic
adventure; Valentine also claims to have

killed a man to justify himself to the
Outlaws (*TGV* 4.1.26–9). Petruccio
invents a similar back-story at 1.2.199–
205.

227 i.e. puts on my clothes and imitates
my manner, thus assuming my identity

229 **ashore** See 42n. on *come ashore*.

231 **as becomes** as is suitable; i.e. 'as if
he were me'

233 **I, sir?** Since 'I' is F's habitual spelling
of the affirmative 'Ay', some editors
emend to 'Ay, sir'. If that choice is
played, *Ne'er a whit* might be spoken
as an aside.
**Ne'er a whit** not at all

---

218 to achieve] *(*t'atchieue*)*    221–3] *Cam¹ lines* been? / you? / clothes, / news? /    222 you?] *you?*
*Oxf*    225 time.] *F2; time F*    227 countenance] *(count'nance)*

BIONDELLO                    I, sir? Ne'er a whit.

LUCENTIO

And not a jot of 'Tranio' in your mouth:

Tranio is changed into Lucentio.                                    235

BIONDELLO

The better for him; would I were so too.

TRANIO

So could I, faith, boy, to have the next wish after:

That Lucentio indeed had Baptista's youngest
    daughter.

But sirrah, not for my sake but your master's, I advise

You use your manners discreetly in all kind of
    companies.                                                     240

When I am alone, why then I am Tranio,

But in all places else, your master Lucentio.

LUCENTIO

Tranio, let's go.

One thing more rests that thyself execute:

To make one among these wooers. If thou ask me why,     245

Sufficeth my reasons are both good and weighty.          *Exeunt.*

*The Presenters above speak.*

234 **not a jot** proverbial (Dent, JJ1)
237–42 F prints as prose; editors vary in accepting Capell's lineation as stress-based rhyming doggerel verse (as here). See pp. 333–5.
237–8 The couplet suggests Tranio's own attraction to Bianca; see Gilbert, 323–8.
237 **faith** in all (good) faith
**boy** The relationship between Tranio and Biondello – adult servant and boy – resembles that between Launce and Speed (*TGV*, esp. 3.1.275–371).
244–6 These three lines emblematize the stylistic shifts in this scene (as well as

elsewhere): one line of regular blank verse, one of stress-based rhyming doggerel, one which might scan as either.
244 **rests . . . execute** remains for you to do
246 **Sufficeth** it suffices that (Abbott, 297)
246 SD2 *Presenters* The presenter, a familiar figure in Elizabethan drama (*Spanish Tragedy*; *Every Man Out of His Humour*), might be either allegorical or human; responsible for 'presenting' or putting on the play, he often explained or commented on the action.

233 I, sir?] *(I sir,)*; Ay, sir, *Rowe*    237–42] *Capell; prose* F    237 could] would F3    242 your] *F2;* you
F    243–6] *prose Pope*    246 SD2 speak] *Rowe; speakes* F

SERVANT

My lord, you nod; you do not mind the play.

SLY    Yes, by Saint Anne do I – a good matter, surely.

Comes there any more of it?

BARTHOLOMEW

My lord, 'tis but begun.                                                                 250

SLY    'Tis a very excellent piece of work, madam lady.

Would 'twere done. *They sit and mark.*


[1.2]        *Enter* PETRUCCIO *and his man* GRUMIO.


PETRUCCIO

Verona, for a while I take my leave

To see my friends in Padua, but of all

My best-beloved and approved friend

Hortensio – and I trow this is his house.

Here, sirrah Grumio, knock, I say.                                              5

GRUMIO    Knock, sir? Whom should I knock? Is there any

man has rebused your worship?


247 SP Hibbard's '*Lord*' assumes that the Lord is 'disguised' (at least to Sly) as a servant.
247 **mind** pay attention to
248 **Saint Anne** mother of the Virgin Mary; also invoked at *TN* 2.3.115
250 SP the Lord's page, disguised as Sly's wife (Ind.2.96.1)
252 SD The Presenters remain onstage, watching; F does not mention them again. At this point, the 'frame' disappears and what had been a play within a play metamorphoses into the play proper, transforming its identity. In *AS*, however, Sly intervenes at four other points in the action and appears in a final scene; modern performances of *TS* have introduced these moments selectively (see e.g. Barton, 1960; Alexander, 1992). Pope moved 247–52 to follow 1.2, thus securing a strong act-closure. Editors

from Pope to Malone omitted this SD, indicating 18th-century performance practice; Rowe concluded Act 1 here.
1.2 Cam² observes that, given the Presenters' dialogue and the repetition in the entry SD noted below, spectators may sense that the play is beginning again, especially since Petruccio's first speech, like Lucentio's (though more briefly), explains his origins and why he has come to Padua.
0.1 The opening SD echoes 1.1.0: '*Enter* LUCENTIO *and his man* TRANIO.'
2 **of all** most important of all
3 **beloved** belovèd
  **approved** approvèd; tried and tested
4 **I trow** 'I am pretty sure'
5–17 The play on *here* and 'ear' behind this exchange between Grumio and Petruccio appears again at 4.1.53–4.
7 **rebused** malapropism for 'abused'

247 SP] *(1. Man.) F; Lord / Hibbard*    1.2] *Capell*    3 best-beloved] *(best beloued)*

PETRUCCIO    Villain, I say, knock me here soundly.

GRUMIO    Knock you here, sir? Why, sir, what am I, sir,
that I should knock you here, sir?                                    10

PETRUCCIO

Villain, I say, knock me at this gate,

And rap me well or I'll knock your knave's pate.

GRUMIO

My master is grown quarrelsome. I should knock you
first,

And then I know after who comes by the worst.

PETRUCCIO

Will it not be?                                                      15

Faith, sirrah, an you'll not knock, I'll ring it.

I'll try how you can *sol-fa* and sing it.

*He wrings him by the ears.*

GRUMIO    Help, masters, help! My master is mad.

PETRUCCIO

Now knock when I bid you, sirrah villain.

*Enter* HORTENSIO.

HORTENSIO    How now, what's the matter? My old friend    20

---

8    **knock me here** Petruccio uses *me*
to mean 'knock for me' (an archaic
dative, Abbott, 220), but Grumio
(9–10) understands *me* as the object of
*knock*, meaning 'hit me'.

12    **knave's pate** male servant's (deceitful
rogue's) head

13–14    **I should ... worst** 'If I were to
hit you first, I know who would then
get the worst of it'. Retaining F's
lineation emphasizes the rhymes here
and at 16–17 in passages of irregular
verse.

16    **ring it** use the ring fastened to the
door as a knocker (?); punning on

'*wrings*' at 17 SD).

17    *sol-fa* ... **it** sing a scale. Some editors
(e.g. Oxf), following 18th-century
stage business, direct Grumio to kneel
here.

18    **masters** Most editors assume that
F's 'mistris' represents erroneous
compositorial expansion of the MS
reading 'Mrs', also at 5.1.5 and 48. But
if the Presenters remain on the stage,
'mistress' might reflect Grumio's
appeal to Sly's 'wife', and in a theatre
of gender confusions, either 'mistress'
or 'masters' might be directed to the
offstage audience.

13] *Theobald; F lines* quarrelsome: / first, / master] (M') 16 an] (and) 17 SD *wrings*]
(*rings*)  18 masters] *Theobald;* mistris *F*

Grumio and my good friend Petruccio? How do you all
at Verona?

PETRUCCIO

Signor Hortensio, come you to part the fray?
*Con tutto il cuore ben trovato*, may I say.

HORTENSIO    *Alla nostra casa ben venuto, molto honorato*     25
*signor mio Petruccio.*

Rise, Grumio, rise; we will compound this quarrel.

GRUMIO    Nay, 'tis no matter, sir, what he 'lleges in Latin.
If this be not a lawful cause for me to leave his service
– look you, sir: he bid me knock him and rap him     30
soundly, sir. Well, was it fit for a servant to use his master so, being perhaps, for aught I see, two-and-thirty, a
pip out?
Whom would to God I had well knocked at first,
Then had not Grumio come by the worst.     35

PETRUCCIO

A senseless villain. Good Hortensio,
I bade the rascal knock upon your gate,
And could not get him for my heart to do it.

21–2 **How . . . Verona?** 'How are you and
your family?'

23 **part the fray** stop the fight

24 *Con . . . trovato* 'With all my heart,
well met.'

25–6 'Welcome to our house, much
honoured Signor Petruccio.'

27 **compound** settle

28 **'lleges** alleges. Like *compound* (27) and
*pledge* (44), a legal term.
  **in Latin** Apparently Grumio, that most
English of 'Italian' servants, hears the
preceding exchange not as vernacular
but as Latin, an educated (and 'foreign')
language.

32–3 **two-and-thirty . . . out** 'not quite

right in the head', alluding to a card
game called 'one-and-thirty' (also
referred to at 4.2.58). According to
Grumio, Petruccio is one *pip* – one
mark on the card – over the goal
of the game; proverbial: 'He is one-
and-thirty' (Dent, O64). Ard[1] cites
John Taylor's *Divers Crabtree Lectures*
(1639), 'or he's pot-shaken, or out,
two and thirty', a cant term for being
drunk.

34–5 a forceful rhetorical finish to
Grumio's explanation

38 **for my heart** for my life. Cf. *Cym*
2.1.54, 'Cannot take two from twenty,
for his heart'.

24 *Con . . . trovato*] Theobald (Rowe); Contutti le core bene trobatto F    25–6] Capell lines venuto, /
Petruchio. /    25 *ben*] (bene)    molto] Theobald; multo F    honorato] F2; honorata F    26 Petruccio]
Oxf; Petruchio F    28 'lleges] (leges); be leges Rann (Tyrwhitt); ledges Cam[2]    29–30 service – look]
(seruice, looke); service! Look Oxf[1]    33 pip] Rowe[3]; peepe F    34–5] Rowe[3]; prose F    34 knocked]
(knockt)

GRUMIO    Knock at the gate? O heavens, spake you not
    these words plain: 'Sirrah, knock me here, rap me here,          40
    knock me well and knock me soundly'?
    And come you now with knocking at the gate?
PETRUCCIO
    Sirrah, be gone, or talk not, I advise you.
HORTENSIO
    Petruccio, patience, I am Grumio's pledge.
    Why this' a heavy chance 'twixt him and you –          45
    Your ancient, trusty, pleasant servant Grumio.
    And tell me now, sweet friend, what happy gale
    Blows you to Padua here from old Verona?
PETRUCCIO
    Such wind as scatters young men through the world
    To seek their fortunes farther than at home,          50
    Where small experience grows. But in a few,
    Signor Hortensio, thus it stands with me:
    Antonio my father is deceased,
    And I have thrust myself into this maze,
    Haply to wive and thrive as best I may;          55

42 **come . . . with** 'do you now claim that
you said'
44 **pledge** guarantor
45 **this'** this is (Abbott, 461)
    **heavy chance** sad, regrettable
    happening
46 **ancient** long-time; not necessarily a
reference to Grumio's age
47 **what happy gale** proverbial: 'What
wind blows you hither?' (Dent, W441)
50–1 **home . . . grows** proverbial: 'He
who still keeps home knows nothing'
(Dent, N274). It was common for
young men to seek their fortunes away
from home; a similar sentiment occurs
at *TGV* 1.1.56–60. Salingar observes
that these lines may reflect 'something
of [Shakespeare's own] inner struggle

for adjustment, as a young provincial
trying his fortunes in London' (243).
51 **in a few** briefly; in few words (*OED*
few *a.* 1g)
54 **maze** confusing labyrinth; also, the
sense that the world away from home
'amazes'
55 **Haply** with luck; perhaps. Some
editors emend to 'happily', as at 75;
the words were interchangeable in the
period (*OED* happily *adv.* 1).
    **to . . . thrive** alludes to several
common proverbs: 'First thrive and
then wive' (Dent, T264), 'Who weds
ere he be wise shall die ere he thrive'
(Tilley, W229) and 'It is hard to wive
and thrive both in a year' (Tilley,
Y12).

45 this'] *Dyce;* this *F;* this is *Rowe;* this's *Cam¹* 49 young men] *(yongmen)* 51 grows. But]
*Theobald subst.;* growes but *F* few] mew *Pope* 55 Haply] *Rowe²* (Happly); Happily *F*

Crowns in my purse I have and goods at home,
And so am come abroad to see the world.

HORTENSIO

Petruccio, shall I then come roundly to thee
And wish thee to a shrewd, ill-favoured wife?
Thou'dst thank me but a little for my counsel:                     60
And yet I'll promise thee she shall be rich,
And very rich. But thou'rt too much my friend,
And I'll not wish thee to her.

PETRUCCIO

Signor Hortensio, 'twixt such friends as we
Few words suffice; and therefore, if thou know                     65
One rich enough to be Petruccio's wife –
As wealth is burden of my wooing dance –
Be she as foul as was Florentius' love,
As old as Sibyl, and as curst and shrewd
As Socrates' Xanthippe or a worse,                     70
She moves me not – or not removes at least
Affection's edge in me – were she as rough

---

56 **Crowns** coins, variously minted in both silver and gold and having a denomination of five shillings (or a quarter of a sovereign). See Harrison, *Description*, 298–9.
58 **come roundly** speak bluntly
59 **shrewd** shrewish
   **ill-favoured** usually meaning 'unattractive' or 'ugly'; but since Hortensio refers to Katherina as *beauteous* at 85, the word functions to intensify *shrewd*.
60 **counsel** advice
64–5 **'twixt . . . suffice** proverbial: 'Few words among friends are best' (Dent, W796)
67 **burden** musical undersong, bass line of a song; refrain. Cf. *TGV* 1.2.85: 'Belike it hath some burden then?'

68 **Florentius'** In John Gower's *Confessio Amantis* (1, fols 16–18), Florent, in order to save his life, agrees to marry an old hag, later transformed into a young beauty. Chaucer's *Wife of Bath's Tale* also tells the story.
69 **Sibyl** the Sibyl of Cumae, an aged prophetess granted as many years of life as there are grains in a handful of sand (Ovid, *Met.*, 14.120–81)
70 **Xanthippe** Socrates' notoriously bad-tempered wife
71 **moves . . . removes** Katherina repeats this word-play at 2.1.194–5.
72 **Affection's . . . me** 'the sharpness of my desire'; proverbial: 'To take off love's edge' (Dent, E57.1)
72–3 **rough . . . seas** translates Horace, *Odes*, 3.9.23 ('*iracundior Hadria*')

62 thou'rt] *(th'art)*   67 wooing] *(woing)*   dance] song *(Johnson)*   68 Florentius'] Florentio's *(Warburton)*   69 Sibyl] *(Sibell)*   shrewd] *(shrow'd)*; shrew'd *F3*   70 Xanthippe] *(Zentippe)*; Zantippe *F2*   72 me] time *F3*   me . . . as] *this edn (RP)*; me. Were she is as *F*; me, were she as *Q*; me. Whe'er she is as *Riv¹*

As are the swelling Adriatic seas.
I come to wive it wealthily in Padua;
If wealthily, then happily in Padua.                                        75

GRUMIO    Nay, look you, sir, he tells you flatly what his
    mind is. Why, give him gold enough and marry him to
    a puppet or an aglet-baby, or an old trot with ne'er a
    tooth in her head, though she have as many diseases as
    two and fifty horses, why, nothing comes amiss – so      80
    money comes withal.

HORTENSIO
Petruccio, since we are stepped thus far in,
I will continue that I broached in jest.
I can, Petruccio, help thee to a wife
With wealth enough, and young and beauteous,                  85
Brought up as best becomes a gentlewoman.
Her only fault – and that is faults enough –
Is that she is intolerable curst,
And shrewd and froward so beyond all measure
That, were my state far worser than it is,                           90
I would not wed her for a mine of gold.

PETRUCCIO
Hortensio, peace; thou knowst not gold's effect.

---

74 **wive it** The use of *it* makes the noun function as a verb; cf. the modern 'lord it (over somebody)'.

78 **puppet** small figure moved by strings or wires; contemptuous term for a person (usually a woman) who is easily manipulated; *aglet-baby* continues the idea.
**aglet-baby** unclear meaning; perhaps a doll-shaped figure forming the tag of a lace or worn as a tag-like ornament on a dress (*OED* aglet 6)
**old trot** hag (*OED* trot *n.*²)

79–80 **she . . . horses** again comparing wives to livestock (see 1.1.128n.); Biondello catalogues equine diseases

at 3.2.48–55.

80–1 **nothing . . . withal** proverbial: 'If money go before all ways lie open' (Dent, M1050); *withal* = in addition (*OED adv.* 1)

82 **are . . . in** have gone so far (in considering this possibility); cf. *Mac* 3.4.135–6: 'I am in blood / Stepp'd in so far'.

83 **that** that which
**broached** opened

88 **intolerable** adjective used adverbially

89 **shrewd and froward** shrewish and ill-tempered, refractory

90 **state** estate; financial status

73 seas.] Seas, *Rowe*³    82 far] *(*farre)    89 shrewd] *(*shrow'd)

Tell me her father's name and 'tis enough,
For I will board her though she chide as loud
As thunder when the clouds in autumn crack.                        95

HORTENSIO

Her father is Baptista Minola,
An affable and courteous gentleman;
Her name is Katherina Minola,
Renowned in Padua for her scolding tongue.

PETRUCCIO

I know her father, though I know not her,                          100
And he knew my deceased father well.
I will not sleep, Hortensio, till I see her,
And therefore let me be thus bold with you
To give you over at this first encounter –
Unless you will accompany me thither.                              105

GRUMIO    I pray you, sir, let him go while the humour lasts.
O'my word, an she knew him as well as I do, she would
think scolding would do little good upon him. She may
perhaps call him half a score knaves or so – why, that's
nothing; an he begin once, he'll rail in his rope-tricks.         110

---

94 **board her** address, woo; naval
metaphor for going aboard a hostile
enemy vessel, with sexual implication.
Cf. *TN* 1.3.55–6: '"Accost" is front her,
board her, woo her, assail her', and *MA*
2.1.130: 'I would he had boarded me'.

95 **crack** split, make a sharp noise, as in
thunder (*OED v.* 1a)

99 **scolding tongue** Scolding wives were
publicly shamed by having their heads
encased with a 'scold's bridle', a metal
harness with a device (sometimes
pronged) which depressed the tongue.
See Boose, 'Scolding', 205, and Fig. 2.

101 **deceased** deceasèd

103–4 'even though we've just met, let
me take the liberty of leaving you
immediately (to see Baptista and

Katherina)'

106 **humour** whim

107 **O'** on
**an** if (Abbott, 101, 103)

110–12 **rail . . . rope-tricks . . . disfigure her** 'Rail in his rope-tricks' is
obscure, possibly meaning 'scold outrageously' or 'use abusive language that
deserves hanging'. Reed glosses as 'such
language as parrots are taught to speak'.
Since Grumio repeatedly invents or
adapts terms and confuses meanings, he may refer to 'rope-rhetorics'
(Thomas Nashe, in *Have With You
to Saffron-Walden* (1596), speaks of
Gabriel Harvey's 'Paracelsian rope-
rethorique'). Ard[2] observes that *figure*
(112) supports the idea of rhetoric (see

---

105 thither.] thither? *Cam²*    107 O'my] *(A my) Rowe*    an] *(and)*    110 an] *(and)*    rope-tricks]
*(rope trickes); rhetorick Hanmer; rhetricks Sisson (Mason)*

I'll tell you what, sir, an she stand him but a little, he
will throw a figure in her face and so disfigure her with
it that she shall have no more eyes to see withal than a
cat. You know him not, sir.

HORTENSIO

Tarry, Petruccio, I must go with thee,                           115
For in Baptista's keep my treasure is.
He hath the jewel of my life in hold,
His youngest daughter, beautiful Bianca,
And her withholds from me and other more –
Suitors to her and rivals in my love –                          120
Supposing it a thing impossible,
For those defects I have before rehearsed,
That ever Katherina will be wooed.
Therefore this order hath Baptista ta'en:
That none shall have access unto Bianca                         125
Till Katherine the Curst have got a husband.

also Levin). In an extended note on
Grumio's 'corruptions', Sisson's emendation, 'rhetricks', makes the malapropism obvious; *stand him* (111) and 'throw
a figure in her face' suggest sexual
innuendo. In the encounters between
Petruccio and Katherina, the two con-
spicuously throw around 'figures of
speech' (2.1.194–269; 4.5.1–26); generally, Petruccio will overcome Katherina
with rhetorical tricks. Garrick's
*Catharine and Petruchio* (1754) includes
'throw a figure in her face', suggesting
that the phrase was still idiomatic.
111 **I'll . . . what** proverbial (Dent,
    W280.1)
    **stand** stand up to, confront, withstand
    (*OED v.* B 52)
113–14 **no . . . cat** Although this may
    be an allusion to the proverbial 'Well
    might the cat wink when both her eyes
    were out' (Tilley, C174), the meaning
    is obscure: the phrase barely, if at all,
    sustains a pun (*cat*/Kate). Grumio may

mean that Petruccio will *disfigure* (112)
Kate by scratching her eyes out, but it's
difficult to see a blind cat wink. Again,
Garrick includes the phrase.
116 **keep** keeping; figurative reference:
    *keep* = heavily fortified tower of a
    castle, appropriate for storing treasure
117 **in hold** in keeping and in prison,
    continuing the pun in 116. Cf. *R3* 4.5.3:
    'My son George Stanley is franked up
    in hold').
119 **other more** others; the singular form
    for the plural was common (Abbott,
    12).
122 **For** because of
    **rehearsed** narrated, reported, listed
124 **this order** these measures
125 **access** possible stress on second
    syllable
126 **Katherine the Curst** F's 'Curst'
    suggests a mock-heroic title which
    Grumio repeats at 127 and Petruccio
    echoes at 2.1.185; cf. *Kate of Kate Hall*
    at 2.1.187.

111 an] *(and)*   119 And her] Her he *Rann*   me and other] *Hanmer;* me. Other *F;* me, and others
*Theobald (Thirlby)*   124 ta'en] *(tane)*   126 Curst] curst *Ard¹*

GRUMIO

   'Katherine the Curst' –

   A title for a maid of all titles the worst.

HORTENSIO

   Now shall my friend Petruccio do me grace

   And offer me disguised in sober robes          130

   To old Baptista as a schoolmaster

   Well seen in music, to instruct Bianca,

   That so I may by this device at least

   Have leave and leisure to make love to her

   And unsuspected court her by herself.          135

*Enter* GREMIO [*with a paper*] *and* LUCENTIO *disguised*
[*as Cambio, a schoolmaster*].

GRUMIO   Here's no knavery. See, to beguile the old folks,
how the young folks lay their heads together. Master,
master, look about you. Who goes there, ha?

HORTENSIO

   Peace, Grumio, it is the rival of my love.

   Petruccio, stand by awhile.          140

GRUMIO

   A proper stripling and an amorous.

     [*Petruccio, Hortensio and Grumio stand aside.*]

GREMIO

   O, very well; I have perused the note.

---

129 **do me grace** do me a favour
132 **Well seen** well qualified
134 **make ... her** court; pay amorous attention to, not the modern meaning of copulate (*OED* love *n.*[1] P3a)
136 **beguile** delude, hoodwink
137 **lay ... together** proverbial (Dent, H280)
138 **look about you** keep your eyes open;

be alert; proverbial (Dent, 427.1)
139 **the rival ... love** my rival for Bianca
141 i.e. a handsome youth (sarcastically, of Gremio) and an amorous one, which might refer either to Gremio or to Lucentio
142 **note** bill, account – presumably, for Lucentio's purchase of books

---

133 least] last *Hosley*  135.1–2] *after* together.  *137 Ard¹*  135.1 *with a paper*] *Oxf*  135.2
*as ... schoolmaster*] *Capell subst.*  140 stand by awhile] stand we by a little while *Capell*  141 SD]
*Capell (They stand aside.)*

Hark you, sir, I'll have them very fairly bound
(All books of love, see that at any hand)
And see you read no other lectures to her:                                        145
You understand me. Over and beside
Signor Baptista's liberality,
I'll mend it with a largess. Take your paper too,
And let me have them very well perfumed,
For she is sweeter than perfume itself                                            150
To whom they go to. What will you read to her?

LUCENTIO

Whate'er I read to her I'll plead for you
As for my patron, stand you so assured,
As firmly as yourself were still in place;
Yea, and perhaps with more successful words                                      155
Than you – unless you were a scholar, sir.

GREMIO

O, this learning, what a thing it is!

GRUMIO

O, this woodcock, what an ass it is!

PETRUCCIO     Peace, sirrah.

HORTENSIO     Grumio, mum. – God save you, Signor          160
Gremio.

GREMIO

And you're well met, Signor Hortensio.

---

143 **fairly bound** handsomely bound (books were sold unbound)
144 **All . . . love** According to Humanist handbooks like Vives' *Instruction of a Christian Woman* (1523), such books (especially popular erotica such as *Venus and Adonis*) were improper reading for young women.
**at any hand** in any case
145 **lectures** personal instruction, not a public presentation
147 **liberality** generosity; here, 'what Baptista pays you'
148 **mend . . . largess** add to it with a gift of money

**paper** the *note* mentioned at 142
149 **them** the books
**perfumed** a customary practice; cf. *AW* 5.2.1–17, where the Clown jokes about a foul-smelling paper.
151 **read to her** teach her (as in a university readership)
153 **stand** rest
154 **still in place** constantly present
158–60 Some editors mark these lines as asides; see pp. 340–1.
158 **woodcock** dupe, simpleton; the woodcock (a small game bird) was considered stupid because so easily caught.

148 paper] papers *Pope*    162–9] *prose Pope*

Trow you whither I am going? To Baptista Minola.
I promised to inquire carefully
About a schoolmaster for the fair Bianca,                165
And by good fortune I have lighted well
On this young man, for learning and behaviour
Fit for her turn, well read in poetry
And other books – good ones, I warrant ye.

HORTENSIO
'Tis well, and I have met a gentleman                170
Hath promised me to help me to another,
A fine musician to instruct our mistress.
So shall I no whit be behind in duty
To fair Bianca, so beloved of me.

GREMIO
Beloved of me, and that my deeds shall prove.                175

GRUMIO    And that his bags shall prove.

HORTENSIO
Gremio, 'tis now no time to vent our love.
Listen to me, and if you speak me fair,
I'll tell you news indifferent good for either.
Here is a gentleman whom by chance I met,                180
Upon agreement from us to his liking
Will undertake to woo curst Katherine,
Yea, and to marry her, if her dowry please.

---

163 **Trow you** do you know
166 **lighted** met by chance
168 **Fit . . . turn** Perfect for her, with sexual play on *turn*. Cf. *AC* 2.5.59: 'For the best turn i'th' bed'.
176 **bags** money-bags, with possible play on testicles, suggesting that Gremio cannot 'do the deed' – i.e. perform sexually. The *commedia dell'arte* figure on which Gremio is based was traditionally a miserly old man, consistently duped by a young woman or cuckolded by his wife.
177 **vent** express
178 **speak me fair** speak courteously to me; proverbial: 'to speak one fair' (Dent, SS16)
179 **indifferent** equally (*OED a.*[1] 1)
181 'if we agree to his financial terms'; Hortensio refers to these again at 213–14.

164 promised] (promist)    165 the fair] fair *Steevens*    171 help me] *Rowe;* helpe one *F*

GREMIO

So said, so done, is well.

Hortensio, have you told him all her faults?                    185

PETRUCCIO

I know she is an irksome brawling scold.

If that be all, masters, I hear no harm.

GREMIO

No, sayst me so, friend? What countryman?

PETRUCCIO

Born in Verona, old Antonio's son.

My father dead, my fortune lives for me,                    190

And I do hope good days and long to see.

GREMIO

O sir, such a life with such a wife were strange.

But if you have a stomach, to't o'God's name;

You shall have me assisting you in all.

But will you woo this wildcat?

PETRUCCIO                                Will I live?                    195

GRUMIO   Will he woo her? Ay, or I'll hang her.

PETRUCCIO

Why came I hither but to that intent?

Think you a little din can daunt mine ears?

---

184  proverbial: 'No sooner said than done' (Dent, S116, S117)
186  **irksome** loathsome, annoyingly offensive
188  **sayst me so** equivalent to 'you don't say' (Abbott, 201)
**What countryman?** 'Where do you come from?'
190  **my fortune . . . me** Oxf's reading 'his fortune' seems more consistent, but *my fortune* is equally playable as a character point. The first-born son customarily inherited both his father's wealth and his title; at 5.1.60–2, Vincentio complains that

his son and servant 'spend all at the university'.
193  **stomach** inclination; cf. *MA*, 1.3.14: 'eat when I have stomach'.
**to't** to the test
195  **Will I live?** 'Yes, certainly'; proverbial (Dent, I.374.1). The question mark emphasizes assent, as at *2H4* 2.1.159–61, where the Hostess asks, 'You'll pay me all together?', and Falstaff responds, 'Will I live?'
196  Grumio's remark draws on two proverbs: 'Better be half hanged than ill wed' (Dent, H130) and 'Wedding and hanging go by destiny' (Dent, W232).

---

188 No, sayst] No? Say'st *Cam²*   189 Antonio's] *Rowe; Butonios F*   190 father] father's *Rowe*   my] his *Oxf*   193 stomach, to't o'] *(stomacke, too 't a)*   196 I'll] (Ile); he'll *Hosley*

Have I not in my time heard lions roar?
Have I not heard the sea, puffed up with winds,                    200
Rage like an angry boar chafed with sweat?
Have I not heard great ordnance in the field,
And heaven's artillery thunder in the skies?
Have I not in a pitched battle heard
Loud 'larums, neighing steeds and trumpets' clang?                    205
And do you tell me of a woman's tongue,
That gives not half so great a blow to hear
As will a chestnut in a farmer's fire?
Tush, tush, fear boys with bugs.

GRUMIO                                    For he fears none.

GREMIO

Hortensio, hark:                    210
This gentleman is happily arrived,
My mind presumes, for his own good and yours.

HORTENSIO

I promised we would be contributors
And bear his charge of wooing, whatsoe'er.

GREMIO

And so we will – provided that he win her.                    215

---

199–205 Petruccio's account of his military career may (or may not) be fictional; it sounds like boasting; cf. Lucentio's imagined adventures (1.1.226–30).

201 **chafed** chafèd; irritated

202 **ordnance** artillery, cannon

204 **pitched** pitchèd

205 **'larums** alarms, calls to arms made with drum and trumpet

206–9 Petruccio's catalogue of fearsome noises deflates into comparing a woman's chatter to a chestnut fizzling in the fire, and frightening children with imaginary creatures.

209 **fear . . . bugs** proverbial: 'Bugbears to scare babes' (Dent, B703)

212 **yours** Many editors follow Theobald's emendation to 'ours', but F's reading stresses Gremio's attempt to shift the costs of Petruccio's wooing expenses onto Hortensio; Hortensio's *we* at 213 and Gremio's comeback ('And so we will') at 215 emphasize the point. Hortensio again mentions sharing the costs at 272; the matter does not come up again. Zeffirelli's 1967 film makes explicit what it might cost to entertain a Petruccio who smashes tableware, spills quantities of wine, disturbs the furniture and requires rose-scented water for washing.

214 **charge** expenses

205 trumpets'] *Capell;* trumpets *F*     207 to hear] to th' ear *Hanmer*     208 chestnut] *(*Chesse-nut*)*
212 yours] ours *Theobald (Thirlby)*

GRUMIO

I would I were as sure of a good dinner.

*Enter* TRANIO *brave* [*as Lucentio*], *and* BIONDELLO.

TRANIO     Gentlemen, God save you. If I may be bold,
tell me, I beseech you, which is the readiest way to the
house of Signor Baptista Minola?

BIONDELLO     He that has the two fair daughters – is't he        220
you mean?

TRANIO     Even he, Biondello.

GREMIO

Hark you, sir, you mean not her to –

TRANIO

Perhaps him and her, sir: what have you to do?

PETRUCCIO

Not her that chides, sir, at any hand, I pray.                          225

TRANIO

I love no chiders, sir: Biondello, let's away.

LUCENTIO [*aside*]

Well begun, Tranio.

HORTENSIO                        Sir, a word ere you go:
Are you a suitor to the maid you talk of – yea or no?

216.1 **brave** finely dressed (*OED a*. 2)
218 **readiest** shortest
220 **He . . . daughters** Oxf conjectures
(but does not emend to) 'He, Bianca's
father, Biondello', on the grounds
that Bianca's name seems necessary
to account for Gremio's *her* at 223
and that the compositor's eye could
easily have skipped from 'Bianca' to
'Biondello'. Capell assigns to Gremio,
emending Tranio's response at 222 to
'Even he, sir'. Biondello seems to be
prompting Tranio to make sure he
mentions the two daughters and thus
presents himself as a wooer.

223 **her to –** Gremio presumably asks,
'you mean not her to woo?' though
some editors, following Tyrwhitt,
modernize as 'her too?', which would
make the dash unnecessary and fit with
Tranio's response at 224. 'To' and 'too'
were spelled interchangeably in the
period. However spoken, either *to* or
*woo* rhymes with *do* at 224.
224 **what . . . do?** 'What business is it of
yours?'; proverbial (Dent, DD14)
225 **at any hand** in any case; see 144n.
227 **Well begun, Tranio** a clear reminder
to the audience of Lucentio's 'real'
identity

216.1 *as Lucentio*] Rowe² *subst. (disguised as Lucentio)*     217–19] Pope; F *lines* bold / way / Minola? /
223 her to –] her to woo? *Halliwell (Malone)*; her too? *Hibbard (Tyrrwhit)*

TRANIO

And if I be, sir, is it any offence?

GREMIO

No, if without more words you will get you hence.              230

TRANIO

Why, sir, I pray, are not the streets as free

For me as for you?

GREMIO                              But so is not she.

TRANIO

For what reason, I beseech you?

GREMIO

For this reason, if you'll know:

That she's the choice love of Signor Gremio.              235

HORTENSIO

That she's the chosen of Signor Hortensio.

TRANIO

Softly, my masters. If you be gentlemen,

Do me this right: hear me with patience.

Baptista is a noble gentleman

To whom my father is not all unknown,              240

And were his daughter fairer than she is

She may more suitors have, and me for one.

Fair Leda's daughter had a thousand wooers,

Then well one more may fair Bianca have.

And so she shall: Lucentio shall make one,              245

Though Paris came in hope to speed alone.

---

229 **be** should be; conditional (Hope, 2.1.2)
237 **Softly** gently (*OED adv.* 8); 'not so fast'
240 **all** entirely
243 **Leda's daughter** the legendary beauty Helen of Troy, daughter of the god Jove and Leda. Marlowe's celebrated line from *Doctor Faustus* (*c.* 1590–2): 'Was this the face that launched a thousand ships' (5.1.97), may have suggested the *thousand wooers*.
245 **make one** be one (among the wooers); proverbial: 'To make one' (Dent, MM2)
246 **Though Paris came** 'even if Paris, Helen's lover (who stole her from her husband Menelaus), were to come' **speed alone** be the only winner

243 Leda's] *(Laedaes)*    244 one more may] may one more *F3*    246 came in] *Singer;* came, in *F*

GREMIO
    What, this gentleman will out-talk us all.
LUCENTIO
    Sir, give him head, I know he'll prove a jade.
PETRUCCIO
    Hortensio, to what end are all these words?
HORTENSIO
    Sir, let me be so bold as ask you,                                   250
    Did you yet ever see Baptista's daughter?
TRANIO
    No, sir, but hear I do that he hath two;
    The one as famous for a scolding tongue
    As is the other for beauteous modesty.
PETRUCCIO
    Sir, sir, the first's for me; let her go by.                         255
GREMIO
    Yea, leave that labour to great Hercules,
    And let it be more than Alcides' twelve.
PETRUCCIO
    Sir, understand you this of me in sooth:
    The youngest daughter whom you hearken for
    Her father keeps from all access of suitors,                         260
    And will not promise her to any man
    Until the elder sister first be wed.
    The younger then is free, and not before.
TRANIO
    If it be so, sir, that you are the man

248 **prove a jade** proverbial (Dent, J29.2);
   a *jade* is a worn-out horse – who, if
   given his head, will soon tire.
250 Some editors emend, following F2's
   'let me be so bold as to ask you', but
   the expansion is not strictly necessary;
   the short line is neither unusual nor
   ineffective.
255 **let . . . by** leave her alone
257 **And . . . be** 'even if it should prove

to be'
   **Alcides' twelve** Hercules (Alcides)
   performed twelve tasks or labours;
   Gremio suggests that wooing Katherina
   will entail even greater labour.
258 **sooth** truth
259 **hearken for** ask for (*OED* hearken *v.*
   6); be attracted to. Ard¹ glosses as 'lie in
   wait' (*OED v.* 7).
260, 268 **access** stress on second syllable

250 as ask] as to ask *F2*

Must stead us all, and me amongst the rest,     265
An if you break the ice and do this feat –
Achieve the elder, set the younger free
For our access – whose hap shall be to have her
Will not so graceless be to be ingrate.

HORTENSIO

Sir, you say well, and well you do conceive;     270
And since you do profess to be a suitor
You must, as we do, gratify this gentleman,
To whom we all rest generally beholding.

TRANIO

Sir, I shall not be slack; in sign whereof,
Please ye we may contrive this afternoon     275
And quaff carouses to our mistress' health,
And do as adversaries do in law,
Strive mightily, but eat and drink as friends.

GRUMIO, BIONDELLO

O excellent motion! Fellows, let's be gone.

HORTENSIO

The motion's good indeed, and be it so.     280
Petruccio, I shall be your *ben venuto*.     *Exeunt.*

---

265 **stead** help (*OED v.* 1c)
266 **break the ice** proverbial (Dent, I3)
    \***do this feat** *feat* = sexual act; Tranio means 'bed her'. All modern editors follow Rowe and emend F's 'seeke' to 'feat', correcting a presumed compositorial misreading of *f* as long *s* and *t* as *k*.
268–9 Cam² reads Tranio as imitating affected upper-class speech and sounding like Polonius (*Ham* 2.2.96–107).
268 **whose hap** he whose good luck
269 **ingrate** ungrateful (*OED a.* 3)
270 **conceive** understand
272 **gratify** reward, pay
273 **beholding** obliged, indebted
275 **contrive** spend, wear away (*OED v.²*).

Shakespeare's only use of *contrive* in this obsolete sense (*OED v.²* records it as the latest example). Theobald conjectured 'convive', matching *quaff carouses* and *eat and drink as friends*.
276 **quaff carouses** drink toasts; *carouses* implies drinking deep, with no restraint.
277 **adversaries . . . law** The legal reference emphasizes this contract 'between men'; cf. the wager at 5.2.
279–80 **motion . . . motion's** plays on *motion* as 'proposal' (continuing the chain of legal references) and, given *let's be gone*, as 'movement'.
281 **be . . . *venuto*** 'introduce you and thus ensure your welcome'; *ben venuto* (Italian) = welcome. Ard¹ glosses: 'your entertainment will be at my charge'.

---

265 stead] *(steed)*   266 An] *(And)*   feat] *Rowe;* seeke F   273 beholding] beholden *Rowe*   275 contrive] convive *Theobald*   281 ben] F2; Been F; bene Oxf¹

[2.1]          *Enter* KATHERINA *and* BIANCA.

BIANCA

    Good sister, wrong me not, nor wrong yourself
    To make a bondmaid and a slave of me –
    That I disdain; but for these other goods,
    Unbind my hands, I'll pull them off myself,
    Yea, all my raiment to my petticoat,          5
    Or what you will command me will I do,
    So well I know my duty to my elders.

KATHERINA

    Of all thy suitors here I charge thee tell
    Whom thou lov'st best. See thou dissemble not.

BIANCA

    Believe me, sister, of all the men alive        10
    I never yet beheld that special face
    Which I could fancy more than any other.

KATHERINA

    Minion, thou liest. Is't not Hortensio?

BIANCA

    If you affect him, sister, here I swear

---

2.1 Early editors imagine 'A Room in Baptista's House' (Pope). Baptista's 'Bianca, get thee in' (30) alludes to an offstage theatrical space; the mass entry at 38.1–3 suggests a public rather than a private space. The scene begins with Katherina binding Bianca and ends with Katherina bound to Petruccio (Rutter, *Clamorous*, 9).

2 **bondmaid** slave girl; Bell's edition, which starts the scene with the mass entry at 38.1–3, attempts to protect Bianca from 'being seen in such an awkward, disagreeable situation'.

3 **goods** possessions; purchased items or objects; a more neutral term than Theobald's emendation, the slightly contemptuous 'gauds' ('plaything',

'trinket', *OED n.²* 2), which suggests that Bianca is a decorated creature. Cf. *MND* 1.1.33: 'bracelets of thy hair, rings, gauds, conceits'.

4 Either 'If you unbind my hands, then I will pull them off myself' or 'Please unbind my hands, and then I will be able or willing to pull them off myself'.

5 **petticoat** underskirt of calico or flannel (*OED n.* 2c)

8 *\*I . . . tell* Most modern editors accept F2's addition of 'thee' and assume that *the* at 10 represents a misplaced compositorial attempt at a correction of 8.

13 **Minion** hussy (*OED n.¹* 1c); spoilt darling

14 **affect** fancy, like, love (*OED v.¹* 4a)

2.1 *Pope* 0.1 BIANCA] *Bianca, her Hands bound. / Capell* 3 goods] gawds *Theobald;* gards *Collier* 8 charge thee] *F2;* charge *F* 10 all the] all *Pope*

I'll plead for you myself but you shall have him.        15
KATHERINA

O then, belike you fancy riches more:
You will have Gremio to keep you fair.
BIANCA

Is it for him you do envy me so?
Nay then, you jest, and now I well perceive
You have but jested with me all this while.        20
I prithee, sister Kate, untie my hands.
KATHERINA

If that be jest, then all the rest was so.    *Strikes her.*

*Enter* BAPTISTA.

BAPTISTA

Why, how now, dame, whence grows this insolence?
Bianca, stand aside. Poor girl, she weeps.
Go ply thy needle, meddle not with her.        25
For shame, thou hilding of a devilish spirit,
Why dost thou wrong her that did ne'er wrong thee?
When did she cross thee with a bitter word?
KATHERINA

Her silence flouts me, and I'll be revenged.    *Flies after Bianca.*

---

15 'I'll plead for you myself so as to ensure that you win him', or 'I'll even plead for myself if that is what it takes to make sure you gain him'.
16 **belike** probably; possibly (*OED adv.* A)
17 **fair** beautifully dressed, with possible innuendo: 'even when your good looks decay, his money will give you means to keep your beauty'.
18 **envy** hate; accented on the second syllable well into the 17th century (Abbott, 490)
19 **Nay . . . jest** F has no punctuation; the phrase may be heard equally idiomatically as punctuated here or as 'Nay, then you jest'.

22 SD Despite F's (marginal) placement, the more logical place for '*Strikes her*' is either before or accompanying 'If that be jest'; it is, however, crucial that Baptista see the gesture.
24–5 Kittredge adds '*He unties her hands*' following 24; the next line might address Bianca or Kate, though 'plying a needle' (sewing or embroidering) seems more appropriate to the (supposedly) domesticated Bianca.
26 **hilding** baggage, good-for-nothing (*OED* reports 'obscure etymology')
28 **cross** contradict (*OED v.* 14c; noted as obsolete)
29 **flouts** mocks, insults

22 SD] *opp. 22 F; after 21 Cam²*

BAPTISTA

    What, in my sight? – Bianca, get thee in.    *Exit [Bianca].*

KATHERINA

    What, will you not suffer me? Nay, now I see    31

    She is your treasure, she must have a husband,

    I must dance barefoot on her wedding day

    And, for your love to her, lead apes in hell.

    Talk not to me, I will go sit and weep    35

    Till I can find occasion of revenge.    *[Exit.]*

BAPTISTA

    Was ever gentleman thus grieved as I?

    But who comes here?

*Enter* GREMIO, LUCENTIO *[as Cambio], in the habit of a*
*mean man,* PETRUCCIO *with* [HORTENSIO *as Licio,*]
    TRANIO *[as Lucentio], with his boy* [BIONDELLO]
    *bearing a lute and books.*

GREMIO    Good morrow, neighbour Baptista.

BAPTISTA    Good morrow, neighbour Gremio. God save    40
    you, gentlemen.

PETRUCCIO

    And you, good sir. Pray, have you not a daughter

    Called Katherina, fair and virtuous?

---

31 **suffer** allow

33–4 traditional (and proverbial) notions about the role of an older, unmarried sister. Katherina combines two proverbs: 'To dance barefoot' (Dent, D22) and 'Old maids lead apes in hell' (Dent, M37) – they were said to do so because they had no children to lead them into heaven. Custom decreed that an elder, unmarried sister of a bride must dance in yellow stockings at her wedding to avert bad luck and catch a husband (Linthicum, 48). Does this custom suggest that Malvolio's yellow stockings (*TN* 3.4.15.1) mark him as an unmarried elder male who attempts to avert bad luck and catch a wife?

36 **occasion of** opportunity for

37 **grieved** vexed, ill-used (*OED ppl.a.* 4)

38.1–2 **habit . . . man** attire characteristic of a lower-class person

38.2 *Licio* On variant spellings and meanings, see LR, 13n.

42–3 as verse, following Rowe, though F's lineation as prose seems equally acceptable

30 SD *Bianca*] *Rowe*  36 SD] *Rowe*  38.1 *as Cambio*] *Rowe subst.*  38.2 HORTENSIO *as Licio*] *Rowe subst.*  38.3 *as Lucentio*] *Rowe subst.*  BIONDELLO] *Rowe, his boy* F  42–3] *Rowe²; prose* F

BAPTISTA

    I have a daughter, sir, called Katherina.

GREMIO

    You are too blunt; go to it orderly.                                    45

PETRUCCIO

    You wrong me, Signor Gremio, give me leave.

    – I am a gentleman of Verona, sir,

    That hearing of her beauty and her wit,

    Her affability and bashful modesty,

    Her wondrous qualities and mild behaviour,                              50

    Am bold to show myself a forward guest

    Within your house to make mine eye the witness

    Of that report which I so oft have heard,

    And for an entrance to my entertainment

    I do present you with a man of mine,                                    55

    Cunning in music and the mathematics,

    To instruct her fully in those sciences,

    Whereof I know she is not ignorant.

    Accept of him or else you do me wrong.

    His name is Licio, born in Mantua.                                      60

BAPTISTA

    You're welcome, sir, and he for your good sake.

    But for my daughter Katherine, this I know:

    She is not for your turn – the more my grief.

PETRUCCIO

    I see you do not mean to part with her,

    Or else you like not of my company.                                    65

---

45 **orderly** properly, in due order (*OED* *adv*. 2)

51, 73 **forward** eager, ardent (*OED a*. 6c)

54 **for . . . entertainment** 'as a way of ensuring a favourable reception'

56 **Cunning** learned, skilful (*OED a*. 2a)

57 **sciences** branches of knowledge

63 **She . . . turn** 'she is not right for you'; *OED n.* V 30 defines *turn* as 'purpose, use, convenience'; the sexual meaning, which Petruccio makes explicit at 274 (see n.), also hovers here.

60 Licio] *F2*; Litio *F*    61 You're] *(Y'arc)*

**BAPTISTA**

   Mistake me not, I speak but as I find.

   Whence are you, sir? What may I call your name?

**PETRUCCIO**

   Petruccio is my name, Antonio's son,

   A man well known throughout all Italy.

**BAPTISTA**

   I know him well. You are welcome for his sake.        70

GREMIO    Saving your tale, Petruccio, I pray let us that
are poor petitioners speak too. *Baccare*, you are
marvellous forward.

**PETRUCCIO**

   O, pardon me, Signor Gremio, I would fain be doing.

**GREMIO**

   I doubt it not, sir. But you will curse your wooing.    75

   Neighbour, this is a gift very grateful, I am sure of it.

   To express the like kindness, myself, that have been

   more kindly beholding to you than any, freely give unto

   you this young scholar that hath been long studying

---

66 **I speak . . . find** proverbial (Dent, S724)
71 **Saving** with all respect to
72 **poor petitioners** a conventionally polite courtship formula; both Gremio and Hortensio are rich men.
*Baccare* corrupt Latin for 'stand back' (*OED* Backare, baccare), with play on Petruccio's *forward* (51), which Gremio repeats (73). Following Warburton, Theobald emends to '*Baccalare*, thou arrogant presumptuous man!' Proverbial: '*Backare*, quoth Mortimer to his sow' (Heywood, *Proverbs*; Dent, M1183). Ard[2] cites Lyly's *Midas*: 'The

Masculin gender is more worthy then the feminine, therefore *Licio*, backare' (1.2.3). Ferguson suggests that this is one of several schoolboy jokes, centring on Shakespeare's Licio, having to do with holes and backsides; see 3.1.9n.
74 **I . . . doing** *fain* = willingly, eagerly, gladly (*OED adv*.); the phrase suggests 'I am eager to get to work' – on everything from wooing to having sex.
75 Adopting Theobald's emendation stresses the rhyme with 74.
76 **Neighbour** polite honorific, addressed to Baptista
**grateful** acceptable

66 as] what *F2*   71–3] *Capell lines* let / too. / forward. /   72 *Baccare*] *F2*; *Bacare F*; Backare *Collier*   75–86] *prose* Pope; *F lines* curse / guift / expresse / beene. / any: / hath / cunning / Languages, / Mathematickes: / seruice. / *Gremio*: / sir, / stranger, / comming? /   75–6 wooing. Neighbour, this] *Theobald*; wooing neighbours: this *F*; wooing, neighbours. This *Rowe*   77 kindness, myself,] *Cam[1]*; kindness my selfe, *F*   78 beholding] beholden *Oxf*   78–9 unto you] *Capell (Tyrwhitt)*; vnto this *F*

at Rheims, as cunning in Greek, Latin and other     80
languages as the other in music and mathematics. His
name is Cambio. Pray accept his service.

BAPTISTA     A thousand thanks, Signor Gremio. Welcome,
good Cambio. [*to Tranio*] But, gentle sir, methinks you
walk like a stranger. May I be so bold to know the cause     85
of your coming?

TRANIO
Pardon me, sir, the boldness is mine own
That, being a stranger in this city here,
Do make myself a suitor to your daughter,
Unto Bianca, fair and virtuous;     90
Nor is your firm resolve unknown to me
In the preferment of the eldest sister.
This liberty is all that I request:
That upon knowledge of my parentage
I may have welcome 'mongst the rest that woo,     95
And free access and favour as the rest.
And toward the education of your daughters
I here bestow a simple instrument
And this small packet of Greek and Latin books;
If you accept them, then their worth is great.     100

BAPTISTA
Lucentio is your name – of whence, I pray?

80 **Rheims** site of a famous university, founded in 1547; Ard² notes that in Shakespeare's day Rheims would have been 'recognized as the most important source of Catholic activity in England'; the English college at Douai transferred there between 1578 and 1593.
82 **Cambio** aptly, 'exchange' in Italian
85 **walk . . . stranger** 'hang back' (rather than pressing forward like Petruccio)
90 **fair and virtuous** echoing Petruccio's description of Katherina at 43
94 **upon knowledge of** 'once you know'

96 **access** with possible stress on second syllable
98 **simple** serviceable, unadorned. Tranio politely diminishes the worth of his gift.
99 **Greek . . . books** reading material appropriate for young women (see Hackel)
101 **Lucentio . . . name** To explain how Baptista knows Lucentio's name, Theobald added '*They greet privately*' following 99; Hibbard adds '*opening one of the books*', assuming that Baptista

80 Rheims] (*Rhemes*)     84 SD] *Rowe*

TRANIO

Of Pisa, sir, son to Vincentio.

BAPTISTA

A mighty man of Pisa – by report

I know him well. You are very welcome, sir.

[*to Hortensio*] Take you the lute [*to Lucentio*] and you

    the set of books;                                                       105

You shall go see your pupils presently.

Holla, within!

*Enter a Servant.*

Sirrah, lead these gentlemen

To my daughters and tell them both

These are their tutors. Bid them use them well.

[*Exeunt Servant, Lucentio and Hortensio, Biondello following.*]

We will go walk a little in the orchard,                              110

And then to dinner. You are passing welcome,

And so I pray you all to think yourselves.

PETRUCCIO

Signor Baptista, my business asketh haste,

And every day I cannot come to woo.

---

sees Lucentio's name on the flyleaf. Performance solves the problem variously: in Ball (1973), Baptista read Lucentio's name from one of the books; in Bogdanov (1978), Tranio handed Baptista a visiting card; in Sothern and Marlowe (1905), Lucentio stepped forward when he heard his name, and Tranio nudged Biondello to drop the books, covering his slip (Schafer, 130–1).

102–3 *Pisa . . . I F reads 'Pisa by report, / I'; since the Merchant's 'disguise' as Vincentio in 4.4 and 5.1 implies that Baptista knows of Vincentio but has not met him, most editors follow or, as here, adapt Rowe's emended punctuation.

107 **Holla** a call for attention, from hunting (*OED int.* 2)
**Sirrah** a socially coded vocative, addressed to an underling

108 F2 adds 'two' before 'daughters' to make a pentameter line. Citing Walker, Ard[1] assumes that *daughters* is sometimes trisyllabic.

109 SD *Biondello following* Alternatively, Biondello might remain, exiting with the rest at 167.

111 **passing** surpassingly, extremely

114 'I cannot come every day to woo' was the refrain of a 16th-century ballad, 'The Wooing of John and Joan' (Baskervill, 93–4).

103 Pisa – by report] *Rowe subst.; Pisa by report, F*    104 know] knew *Rann (Capell)*    105 SD1, 2] *Theobald*    108 my] my two *F2*    109 SD *Exeunt . . . Hortensio*] *Theobald    Biondello following*] *Capell*

| | |
|---|---|
| You knew my father well, and in him me, | 115 |
| Left solely heir to all his lands and goods, | |
| Which I have bettered rather than decreased. | |
| Then tell me, if I get your daughter's love, | |
| What dowry shall I have with her to wife? | |

BAPTISTA

After my death, the one half of my lands,                    120
And in possession twenty thousand crowns.

PETRUCCIO

And for that dowry I'll assure her of
Her widowhood, be it that she survive me,
In all my lands and leases whatsoever.
Let specialties be therefore drawn between us,              125
That covenants may be kept on either hand.

BAPTISTA

Ay, when the special thing is well obtained –
That is, her love, for that is all in all.

115–26 In conventional wedding arrangements, a father was obligated to provide assets (often including land) to his daughter's husband; by contrast, a widow had only a partial claim on her husband's estate, the bulk of which passed to his lineal or collateral heirs. Petruccio's offer of all his lands and leases is an unusually generous response to Baptista's guarantee of 20,000 crowns (£5,000 in 16th-century values), which is itself a great deal of money – one wonders about murmurs in the early modern playhouse. Or laughter? Is it worth this much to be rid of Katherina? A 1587 proclamation regulating London wages puts the amount in context: besides food and drink allowances, the best shoemakers, tailors and hosiers could expect to earn £4 a year; the best clothworkers, £5; alebrewers, blacksmiths, butchers and cooks, £6. Baptista, Tranio and Gremio discuss dowries further at 330–400. On marriage customs, see Jeaffreson.

121 **in possession** at the time of the marriage

125 **specialties** explicit contracts: 'a special contract, obligation, or bond, expressed in an instrument under seal' (*OED* 7)

126 **covenants** formal financial agreements or compacts; cf. *Cym* 1.5.165–6: 'Your hand, a covenant: we will have these things set down by lawful counsel'.

128 **her love** Insisting that Petruccio obtain Katherina's love (not required of Bianca's suitors at 345–8) seems formulaic and/or self-protective, but also reveals Baptista's care.

122 of] for *Hanmer;* on *(Steevens)*

PETRUCCIO

   Why, that is nothing, for I tell you, father,

   I am as peremptory as she proud-minded,          130

   And where two raging fires meet together

   They do consume the thing that feeds their fury.

   Though little fire grows great with little wind,

   Yet extreme gusts will blow out fire and all:

   So I to her, and so she yields to me,          135

   For I am rough and woo not like a babe.

BAPTISTA

   Well mayst thou woo, and happy be thy speed.

   But be thou armed for some unhappy words.

PETRUCCIO

   Ay, to the proof, as mountains are for winds,

   That shakes not though they blow perpetually.          140

*Enter* HORTENSIO [*as Licio*] *with his head broke.*

BAPTISTA

   How now, my friend, why dost thou look so pale?

HORTENSIO

   For fear, I promise you, if I look pale.

---

129  **father** father-in-law; the familiar term suggests Petruccio's self-confidence.

130  **peremptory** determined, resolved, absolutely decided. A loaded term in Petruccio's self-description: the word shares a Latin root (*emptor*) with the act of purchasing; in Roman law, used in the sense that precludes all debate, question or delay. Accented on first and third syllables in (obsolescent) UK pronunciation; eliding 'I am' to 'I'm' aids scansion only if pronounced 'perèmptory', as in US and more recent UK usage.

133–4  proverbial: 'A little wind kindles, much puts out the fire' (Dent, W424)

134  **extreme** with stress on initial syllable or level stress on both syllables; cf. *LLL* 5.2.734.

137  **speed** fortune, profit (*OED n.* 3a), perhaps picking up the idea of Petruccio as a fortune-hunter

138  **unhappy** objectionable, harsh, intemperate

139  **to the proof** 'to the point of invulnerability' (Ard²). 'Armour of proof' is armour which has been tested and will withstand attack; *prove a soldier* (144) continues the metaphor.

140  **shakes** F2 reads 'shake'; the third person plural in *s* is common usage (Abbott, 333).

140.1  *broke* injured, bleeding

142  **promise** assure (*OED v.* 1)

---

130 proud-minded] *(proud minded)*   140 shakes] shake *F2*

BAPTISTA

What, will my daughter prove a good musician?

HORTENSIO

I think she'll sooner prove a soldier;

Iron may hold with her, but never lutes.                          145

BAPTISTA

Why then, thou canst not break her to the lute?

HORTENSIO

Why no, for she hath broke the lute to me.

I did but tell her she mistook her frets

And bowed her hand to teach her fingering

When, with a most impatient devilish spirit,                      150

'Frets call you these?' quoth she, 'I'll fume with them,'

And with that word she struck me on the head,

And through the instrument my pate made way,

And there I stood amazed for a while,

As on a pillory, looking through the lute,                        155

While she did call me 'rascal', 'fiddler',

And 'twangling Jack', with twenty such vile terms,

---

145  **hold with her** stand up to her
**lutes** musical instruments; also, clay used to cement an orifice or joint (*OED n.²* 1)

146–58 What begins with a metaphor from breaking a horse to the bit (and so taming it) quickly encompasses a series of sexual connotations. Hortensio 'bow[s Kate's] hand to teach her fingering' and winds up with his head (*pate*) encased in the lute, an instrument equated with women and also with prostitutes; cf. Middleton's *Your Five Gallants* (1606), where a music school fronts a brothel (Maguire, 'Cultural').

146  **break** discipline (*OED v.* 14); metaphor from breaking a horse to the bit

147  **to me** on me

148  **frets** ridges on the lute's neck, to regulate fingering

149  **bowed** curved, bent (*OED ppl.a.¹* 1)

151  **Frets . . . fume** 'fret' (n.) = vexation; thus, a near-proverbial pairing

153  **pate** head

154  **amazed** amazèd

155  **As . . . pillory** 'As my head appeared through the (new) hole in the lute, so the head of the victim (of minor offences) appears through the pillory's hole'; a *pillory* consisted of a pair of movable boards raised on a post; like the stocks, it was used for minor punishments. For a range of played options, see Schafer, 133.

156  **rascal** common, lower-class rabble
**fiddler** trifler, violator of chastity; see also 3.1.1.

157  **Jack** ill-bred, ill-mannered fellow

---

147 to] on *Hanmer*    150 most] moist *Q*    156 'rascal', 'fiddler'] *(*Rascall, Fidler*)*; rascal fidler *Capell*

As had she studied to misuse me so.

PETRUCCIO

    Now, by the world, it is a lusty wench;

    I love her ten times more than e'er I did.           160

    O, how I long to have some chat with her!

BAPTISTA [*to Hortensio*]

    Well, go with me, and be not so discomfited.

    Proceed in practice with my younger daughter;

    She's apt to learn and thankful for good turns.

    Signor Petruccio, will you go with us,           165

    Or shall I send my daughter Kate to you?

PETRUCCIO

    I pray you, do.           *Exeunt all but Petruccio.*

                    I'll attend her here,

    And woo her with some spirit when she comes.

    Say that she rail, why then I'll tell her plain

    She sings as sweetly as a nightingale;           170

    Say that she frown, I'll say she looks as clear

    As morning roses newly washed with dew;

    Say she be mute and will not speak a word,

    Then I'll commend her volubility

    And say she uttereth piercing eloquence.           175

---

158 **As had she** as if she had

162 **be . . . discomfited** cheer up

163 **Proceed in practice** continue your lessons, but also 'carry on with your plot to win my daughter', playing on *practice* as in Ind.1. Baptista then follows this 'slip' with another at 164 (see 63n.).

167 **I . . . do** 'Please do so.'
**attend** await (*OED v.* 13)

167 SD F places after 167, Cam² after 'I'll attend her here'. The potential mobility of this SD invites several performance possibilities (see Cordner, 'Scripts').

168–79 Ovid, in *The Remedy of Love*, recommends that men follow such conversions as a means of avoiding or exorcising love: 'If she be fat, that she is swollen say: / If browne, than tawny like the Affrike Moor: / If slender, leane, meger, and worne away, / If courtly, wanton, worst of worst before: / If modest, strange, as fitteth woman-head, / Say she is rusticke, clownishe, and ill-bred' (sig. D1ᵛ), paraphrased in Lyly, *Euphues: The Anatomy of Wit*. In revealing his strategy (and at 4.1.177–98), Petruccio resembles stage Machiavels such as Richard III, Iago and *KL*'s Edmund.

171 **clear** pure, faultless; also serene, cheerful (*OED a.* 2d)

175 **piercing** moving, touching, poignant

167 SD] *Ard²*; *after 166 F (Exit. Manet Petruchio.)*

If she do bid me pack, I'll give her thanks
As though she bid me stay by her a week;
If she deny to wed, I'll crave the day
When I shall ask the banns, and when be married.

*Enter* KATHERINA.

But here she comes, and now, Petruccio, speak.　　　180
Good morrow, Kate, for that's your name, I hear.
KATHERINA
Well have you heard, but something hard of hearing:
They call me Katherine that do talk of me.
PETRUCCIO
You lie, in faith, for you are called plain Kate,
And bonny Kate, and sometimes 'Kate the Curst';　　　185
But Kate, the prettiest Kate in Christendom,
Kate of Kate Hall, my super-dainty Kate –

176 **pack** leave
179 **banns** notice of intended marriage posted in church or a public place. Banns are never posted for Katherina's wedding, and Bianca elopes: neither conforms to customary practices.
**married** Petruccio's solo meditation ends on a mid-line half-rhyme (*wed/ married*), as it began (*rail/nightingale*).
179.1 In F, the entry SD follows 180; but Cam²'s placement lets Petruccio register her presence.
182 **heard . . . hard** Both were pronounced 'hard', a homophonic pun (Kökeritz, 112, 250). Yet, despite the pun, how can he have heard well if he has heard wrongly?
185 **\*bonny** F reads 'bony'; editors regularly adopt F4's 'bonny'. Yet 'bony', available in the period and meaning 'big-boned' (*OED a.* 2a), might be possible: if so, then the rhetoric of 185–7 lines up three uncomplimentary terms for Kate (*plain, bony, 'Kate the Curst'*) followed by a sequence of complimentary ones

(*prettiest, Kate of Kate Hall, super-dainty*). *Bonny* shifts that to uncomplimentary, complimentary, uncomplimentary in the first trio – certainly playable, if disorienting for Kate.
**'Kate the Curst'** See 1.2.126n.
187 **Kate Hall** Cam¹ refers to Stopes, *Life of Southampton*: '1 Aug. 1591 the queen's harbinger was allowed payment "for making ready a dining-house at Katherine Hall", one of the places in the South of England at which Elizabeth stopped on a summer progress to Cowdray, the house of Southampton's grandfather, and Tichfield, the house of Southampton himself' (45). Given the known links between Shakespeare and Southampton, Ard² mentions the coincidence but dismisses the evidence as not helpful in understanding the line. Like many topical references, the connection has lost its urgency.
**super-dainty** extremely beautiful or fine

179.1] *Cam²; after 176* F　　185 bonny] *F4;* bony *F*

For dainties are all cates, and therefore 'Kate' –
Take this of me, Kate of my consolation:
Hearing thy mildness praised in every town,      190
Thy virtues spoke of and thy beauty sounded –
Yet not so deeply as to thee belongs –
Myself am moved to woo thee for my wife.

KATHERINA

'Moved'. In good time, let him that moved you hither
Re-move you hence. I knew you at the first      195
You were a movable.

PETRUCCIO      Why, what's a movable?

KATHERINA      A joint-stool.

---

188 **dainties ... cates** punning on *cates* as delicacies and on the adjectival meaning of 'dainty' = excessively fastidious

189 **consolation** comfort, contentment; but also with religious resonances, as in the Psalms

191 **sounded** favorably reported or voiced (in relation to *spoke of*); measured (*OED v.²* 5) – a nautical metaphor for ascertaining the sea's depth which extends to *deeply* at 192

194–268 This passage, containing doggerel, rhymes and off-rhymes, fast word-play and bawdy innuendo, with one speaker building on the words of the other, creates a sense of intimacy between the pair as they try on various verbal styles. As lineated here, short bursts of prose suggest moments where the game is up for grabs; the speaker who re-establishes a full verse line has the opportunity to take control of the exchange (see pp. 334–5). Cf. the 'keen encounter' of wit between Richard III and Lady Anne (*R3* 1.2.49–206).

194–5 **'Moved' ... hence** F reads 'Mou'd, in good time, let him that mou'd you hether / Remoue you hence'. Identical word-play occurs at 1.2.71. Modern editors add one or several exclamation points, yet F's punctuation leaves open whether 'in good time' – (i.e. immediately) – belongs with 'Mou'd' or with the following clause. Several other meanings current in the 1590s offer performance options: '(1) after the lapse of a suitable interval; in due course or process of time; at a proper time, when it seems good; (2) soon or early; quickly; (3) at a right or a seasonable moment; luckily' (*OED* time *n.* 46c). Oxf¹ glosses *in good time* as equivalent to *à la bonne heure*: an exclamation 'used either to express acquiescence, or astonishment and indignation' and claims that Katherine, punning on *moved*, is expressing all three. Such a gloss, however, shuts down the range of playable choices (see Cordner, 'Actors', 191–2).

195–6 **I ... movable** 'I knew from the moment I first saw you that you were a movable' – literally, a portable item of furniture, thus, a changeable person.

198 **joint-stool** low three- or four-legged stool made by a joiner rather than a carpenter, often used at meals; proverbially, someone easily overlooked, as at *KL* 3.6.51: 'Cry you mercy, I took you for a joint-stool.'

---

188 cates] *Pope; Kates F*     198 joint] *Capell; joyn'd F*

PETRUCCIO    Thou hast hit it: come, sit on me.

KATHERINA

Asses are made to bear, and so are you.                    200

PETRUCCIO

Women are made to bear, and so are you.

KATHERINA

No such jade as you, if me you mean.

PETRUCCIO

Alas, good Kate, I will not burden thee,

For, knowing thee to be but young and light –

KATHERINA

Too light for such a swain as you to catch,              205

And yet as heavy as my weight should be.

PETRUCCIO

'Should be'? Should – buzz.

KATHERINA                                    Well ta'en, and like a buzzard.

199 **hit it** 'hit the target'; 'got that right'
**come . . . me** In early modern English, 'come', combined with another verb in this way, forms a continuous imperative.
200, 201 **bear** evoking a range of meanings, including the proverbial 'Asses are born to bear' (Dent, A371.1). Cam² hears a pun on 'bear children', but *bear* also means to suffer, endure, tolerate (*OED v.*¹ 15b, 15c). Cordner suggests that a reference to the 'woman on top' also comes into play here ('Actors', 193–4); Katherina, a self-aware punster, also invokes the sexual meaning of *bear*, and Petruccio's retort (201) reasserts male sexual dominance.
202 **jade** worn-out horse, soon tired
203 **I . . . thee** 'I will take care, when lying on top of you, not to make you bear my full weight'; a *burden* is also a bass undersong or refrain (*OED n.* 9, 10); further musical references – *light, catch, heavy, buzz* – occur at 205–7.

204 *__light__ light in weight; also wanton (*OED a.* 14b). F's full stop after 'light' also suggests a playable option, especially in relation to the previous line: 'I will not burden thee / Because I know you are but young and light' – that is, 'inexperienced and not especially strong'.
206 **as heavy . . . be** Shifting the metaphor to coinage, Katherina refers to 'clipped' coins (below legal weight and thus *Too light*) and by extension to women who are no longer virgins, to claim that she is not *light* in that sense either.
207 ¹**Should . . . buzz** Katherina's comment may catch Petruccio off guard. He puns on *be* as 'bee', leading to *buzz* ('rumour' or 'scandal'), implying that he has heard of Kate's reputation. Reed defines *buzz* as 'a common exclamation (of impatience or contempt) when anyone was telling

202 jade] Jade Sir *F2*; jack, sir *(Farmer)*; load, sir *Singer*   203 burden] *(*burthen*)*   204 light – ] *Rowe*; light. *F*   207 'Should . . . buzz.] *Capell*; Should be, should: buzze. *F*; Should be! should! buz. *Rowe*; Should be; – should buz. – *Theobald*; Should! Bee! Should! – buz. *Hanmer*; Should be? Should buz. *Capell*

**PETRUCCIO**

O slow-winged turtle, shall a buzzard take thee?

**KATHERINA**

Ay, for a turtle, as he takes a buzzard.

**PETRUCCIO**

Come, come, you wasp, i'faith you are too angry.      210

**KATHERINA**

If I be waspish, best beware my sting.

**PETRUCCIO**

My remedy is then to pluck it out.

**KATHERINA**

Ay, if the fool could find it where it lies.

**PETRUCCIO**

Who knows not where a wasp does wear his sting?
In his tail.      215

**KATHERINA**      In his tongue.

**PETRUCCIO**      Whose tongue?

**KATHERINA**

Yours, if you talk of tails, and so farewell.

a well-known story', and also lists *buzz* as 'a sound to command silence', as at *Ham* 2.2.391. The singer of a drone bass part is said to 'buzz the burden', which continues the play on musical terms (Waldo & Herbert, 194; see also Maguire, 'Cultural').

**ta'en** taken; caught in flight – from falconry, sustaining the hawking analogy

**buzzard** an inferior kind of hawk, useless for falconry; figuratively, a worthless or senseless person; proverbial: 'He is a blind buzzard' (Dent, U792)

208 **turtle** turtle-dove; a symbol of constancy and faithful love
**take** win by conquest, with sexual reference

209 Hibbard cites Dover Wilson's

paraphrase: 'the fool will take me for a faithful wife, as the turtle-dove swallows the cock-chafer [another meaning of *buzzard*: May bug, UK; June bug, US]'. The beetle's buzzing noise leads on to *wasp* (210, 211).

210 **wasp** proverbial: 'As angry as a wasp' (Dent, W76); continuing the string of bird/insect references: *wasp* = 'irritating person' (*OED n.*[1] 2a)

218 **tails** with a play on 'genitalia' but also a homonymic pun on 'tales' (F's reading, both readable and playable), and thus, rumours; mischievous gossip. 'Bees that have honey in their mouths have stings in their tails' (or tongues) was proverbial (Dent, B211). A similar run of puns on tongue/tail occurs between Pantino and Lance (*TGV* 2.3.42–7).

209 he] she *Ard*[1]   214–15] *Rowe; prose* F   218 tails] *Q;* tales *F*

PETRUCCIO    What, with my tongue in your tail?
   Nay, come again, good Kate, I am a gentleman –                    220
KATHERINA    That I'll try. *She strikes him.*
PETRUCCIO
   I swear I'll cuff you if you strike again.
KATHERINA
   So may you lose your arms.
   If you strike me you are no gentleman,
   And if no gentleman, why then, no arms.                    225
PETRUCCIO
   A herald, Kate? O, put me in thy books.
KATHERINA    What is your crest – a coxcomb?
PETRUCCIO
   A combless cock, so Kate will be my hen.
KATHERINA
   No cock of mine: you crow too like a craven.

220 F's comma after 'gentleman' suggests punctuating with a dash.
221 Some editors follow this line with a SD such as *'holding her'*. Cordner suggests that F's SD is cued too late: placing it after Petruccio's 'What, with my tongue in your tail?' would give more point to 'I swear I'll cuff you if you strike again' ('Scripts', 222), as Petruccio (perhaps) wards off another blow. Alternatively, Petruccio's *come again* (220) suggests that he calls Kate back from an attempted exit, invites another response, or both.
   **try** test
223 **lose your arms** Neither early modern spelling nor punctuation distinguishes between 'loose' (F's spelling here) and *lose*; identical pronunciation would permit a double meaning: 'So may you lose your (coat of) arms' (your claim to gentlemanly status) and 'So may you let me go' (loose me). Yet the syntax works against the double meaning being heard, since the link to the previous line makes focusing the second option difficult.
226 'To be in the herald's books was to be registered as a gentleman' (Hibbard);

to be 'in someone's books' was to be in their favour, as in current British 'in your good books'; proverbial (Dent, B534). Cf. *MA* 1.1.73–4: 'I see, lady, the gentleman is not in your books'.
227 **crest . . . coxcomb** *crest* = heraldic device set above the shield and helmet in a coat of arms; a 'comb' or crest on a bird's or animal's head (*OED n.*[1] 3a; 1a); *coxcomb* = professional fool's cap; here, one resembling a cock's crest. Fools' coxcombs were often bird- or animal-like as well as sexually suggestive (Wiles). Spectators in the 1590s probably heard 'cock's comb', which combines the two.
228–9 **A combless cock . . . craven** unaggressive cock. Hibbard cites the idiomatic 'cutting down another's comb' = 'taking the conceit out of him', which suggests, 'If you consent to marry me, I won't be the conceited strutter you may fear', so triggering Katherina's reply at 229. *Craven* = a cock that 'is not game', a coward (*OED n.* 2), thus, 'Such a modest, feeble man doesn't attract me'.

220 come . . . gentleman] *Pope lines* again. / gentleman – /    223 lose] *Rowe;* loose *F*

PETRUCCIO

    Nay, come, Kate, come; you must not look so sour.      230

KATHERINA

    It is my fashion when I see a crab.

PETRUCCIO

    Why, here's no crab, and therefore look not sour.

KATHERINA    There is, there is.

PETRUCCIO    Then show it me.

KATHERINA    Had I a glass, I would.      235

PETRUCCIO    What, you mean my face?

KATHERINA    Well aimed of such a young one.

PETRUCCIO

    Now, by Saint George, I am too young for you.

KATHERINA    Yet you are withered.

PETRUCCIO    'Tis with cares.      240

KATHERINA    I care not.

PETRUCCIO

    Nay, hear you, Kate. In sooth, you scape not so.

KATHERINA

    I chafe you if I tarry. Let me go.

PETRUCCIO

    No, not a whit; I find you passing gentle.

    'Twas told me you were rough and coy and sullen,      245

    And now I find report a very liar,

    For thou art pleasant, gamesome, passing courteous,

---

231 **crab** crab apple, fruit with 'sour, harsh, tart, astringent quality' (*OED n.*[2] 1); metaphorically, a 'sour or cross-grained person'

235 **glass** looking-glass

237 The metaphor comes from archery. **young** inexperienced; see 238n.

238 **Saint George** England's patron saint and patron of the Order of the Garter, the highest order of knighthood **young** strong; 'having the freshness and vigour of youth' (*OED a.* 3)

242 **In sooth** a phrase 'used expletively or parenthetically to strengthen or emphasize an assertion' (*OED n.* 4a) **scape** escape (*OED v.*[1] 1a)

243 **chafe you** excite you, irritate you (*OED v.* 2, 5)

244, 247 **passing** surpassing, extremely

245 **coy** disdainful, distant (*OED a.* 3).

246 **report . . . liar** proverbial: 'Report has a blister on her tongue' (Dent, R84)

247 **pleasant** humorous, merry, gay (*OED a.* 4a) **gamesome** playful

But slow in speech, yet sweet as springtime flowers;
Thou canst not frown, thou canst not look askance,
Nor bite the lip, as angry wenches will,                    250
Nor hast thou pleasure to be cross in talk;
But thou with mildness entertain'st thy wooers
With gentle conference, soft and affable.
Why does the world report that Kate doth limp?
O slanderous world! Kate like the hazel twig              255
Is straight and slender, and as brown in hue
As hazelnuts, and sweeter than the kernels.
O, let me see thee walk. Thou dost not halt.

KATHERINA
Go, fool, and whom thou keep'st command.

PETRUCCIO
Did ever Dian so become a grove                           260
As Kate this chamber with her princely gait?
O, be thou Dian, and let her be Kate,
And then let Kate be chaste and Dian sportful.

KATHERINA
Where did you study all this goodly speech?

---

248 **slow in speech** 'not a bit sharp-tongued'
**sweet . . . flowers** proverbial (Dent, F389)
249 **askance** scornfully (*OED adv.* 2); stressed on the second syllable
250 **wenches** 'Wench' can mean working-class girl and/or wanton woman (*OED* 1b, 2); *angry* here favours the former sense, while the latter continues the play on *light* at 204–5. The term is also an endearing form of address (*OED* 1c), as at 5.2.186.
251 **cross** contradictory
252 **entertain'st** engage, hold the attention of (*OED v.* 9)
253 **conference** conversation (*OED n.* 4a)
256 **brown in hue** dark-complexioned. Since the ideal 'sonnet lady' was fair, a dark complexion was less desirable,

though Shakespeare's 'dark lady of the sonnets' is an ironic exception.
258 **halt** limp
259 **whom . . . command** 'give your servants orders, but not me'; proverbial: 'Thou dost not bear my charges that thou shouldst command me' (Dent, C245); *keep'st* = maintain, employ, look after financially
260 **Dian** Diana, Roman goddess of hunting and chastity
**become** suit; adorn
261 **gait** manner of walking, bearing while moving (*OED n.*[1] a)
263 **sportful** playful (*OED a.* 2); given the reference to Diana (260), sexually amorous
264 **study** learn by heart (*OED v.* 9b)
**goodly** admirable, proper; frequently ironical (*OED a.* 3, 3b)

249 askance] *Rowe* (a scance); a sconce F

PETRUCCIO

It is extempore, from my mother-wit.                    265

KATHERINA

A witty mother, witless else her son.

PETRUCCIO    Am I not wise?

KATHERINA    Yes, keep you warm.

PETRUCCIO

Marry, so I mean, sweet Katherine, in thy bed.

And therefore, setting all this chat aside,             270

Thus in plain terms: your father hath consented

That you shall be my wife, your dowry 'greed on,

And will you, nill you, I will marry you.

Now, Kate, I am a husband for your turn,

For, by this light whereby I see thy beauty –           275

Thy beauty that doth make me like thee well –

Thou must be married to no man but me,

*Enter* BAPTISTA, GREMIO [*and*] TRANIO [*as Lucentio*].

---

265 **mother-wit** natural intelligence; proverbial (Dent, M1208.2)

267–8 proverbial: 'He is wise enough that can keep himself warm' (Dent, K10)

269–82 Petruccio's final speech is unusually *plain* talk which indeed sets 'all this chat aside' (270).

269–70 In another outrageous 'chat', Richard III tells Anne that he is fit, not for 'some dungeon' (as she says) but for 'your bedchamber' (*R3* 1.2.113–14).

269 **Marry** simply, to be sure (*OED int.* 2a)

273 'and whether or not you disapprove, your marriage to me will happen'; proverbial: 'will he nill he' (Dent, W401), the modern 'willy-nilly'. Marriage in Protestant England emphasized compatibility and mutuality, even love; the anonymous

*Tell-Troth's New Year's Gift* (1593) denounces constrained marriages as against God's word, especially when such marriages functioned as a business deal (A3ʳ–A4ᵛ). Nonetheless, marriages among gentry often were arranged.

274 **for your turn** perhaps recalling Baptista's comment that Katherina is 'not for your turn' (63); also, continuing the sexual *double entendre*, as in *AC* 2.5.58–9: 'He's bound unto Octavia . . . / For the best turn i'th' bed.'

277.1 F's placement suggests that Petruccio may put on his taming behaviour for the benefit of Baptista and the others (Cohen, 275–7). However, most modern editors, perhaps following *H5* 5.2.266–77.1, place this entry to follow 280.

265 mother-wit] *(mother wit)*  266 witless] witness *Capell*  277.1] *after 282 Pope: after 280 Capell*  TRANIO] *Q; Trayno F  as Lucentio] Oxf¹*

For I am he am born to tame you, Kate,
And bring you from a wild Kate to a Kate
Conformable as other household Kates.                              280
Here comes your father. Never make denial:
I must and will have Katherine to my wife.
BAPTISTA    Now, Signor Petruccio, how speed you with
my daughter?
PETRUCCIO    How but well, sir? How but well?                     285
It were impossible I should speed amiss.
BAPTISTA
Why, how now, daughter Katherine, in your dumps?
KATHERINA
Call you me daughter? Now I promise you
You have showed a tender fatherly regard
To wish me wed to one half lunatic,                               290
A madcap ruffian and a swearing Jack
That thinks with oaths to face the matter out.
PETRUCCIO
Father, 'tis thus: yourself and all the world
That talked of her have talked amiss of her.
If she be curst, it is for policy,                                295
For she's not froward, but modest as the dove;

279  **wild Kate** punning on 'wildcat'
280  **Conformable** compliant, submissive (*OED a.* 3b); the only other occurrence in Shakespeare, spoken by another Katherine (this time a queen), is at *H8* 2.4.21–2: 'I have been to you a true and humble wife, / At all times to your will conformable' (RP).
283  **how speed you** how are you getting on
287  **in your dumps** 'are you as depressed as you usually are?' A 'dump' was a mournful song (*OED n.*¹ 3).
288  **promise** assure
290  **lunatic** Lunacy was a type of recurring madness dependent on the waxing and waning of the moon (*OED a.* 1). Given her exchange with Petruccio, Katherina's use of *lunatic* may thus be suggestive; however, madness affected both men and women and was 'not a distinctively female malady during the early modern period' (Neely, 1).
291  **madcap** reckless, impulsive (*OED n.* b)
292  **face . . . out** get his way; brazen it out
295  **for policy** as a deliberate, advantageous strategy
296  **froward** refractory, wayward
      **modest . . . dove** proverbial (Dent, D573)

279 wild Kate] *(wilde Kate);* wild *Kat F2;* wild Cat *Rowe;* wild cat *Pope*

She is not hot, but temperate as the morn;
For patience she will prove a second Grissel,
And Roman Lucrece for her chastity;
And to conclude, we have 'greed so well together          300
That upon Sunday is the wedding day.

KATHERINA    I'll see thee hanged on Sunday first.

GREMIO    Hark, Petruccio, she says she'll see thee hanged
first.

TRANIO

Is this your speeding? Nay, then, goodnight our part.          305

PETRUCCIO

Be patient, gentlemen. I choose her for myself;
If she and I be pleased, what's that to you?
'Tis bargained 'twixt us twain, being alone,
That she shall still be curst in company.
I tell you, 'tis incredible to believe          310
How much she loves me. O, the kindest Kate,
She hung about my neck, and kiss on kiss
She vied so fast, protesting oath on oath,

297 **hot** angry; also, given the preceding innuendo, sexually passionate
298 **Grissel** Griselda, a model of wifely patience and obedience, a shrew's precise opposite; proverbial: 'As patient as Grissel' (Dent, G456). Her story appears in Boccaccio's *Decameron* (10.10), in ballads and tracts, and in Chaucer's *Clerk's Tale*. See Brown, 178–217.
299 **Lucrece** famous model of wifely chastity who, after being raped by Tarquin, killed herself. Her story appears in Livy's *History of Rome* (Bk 1), in William Painter's *Palace of Pleasure* (1566) and in Shakespeare's narrative poem *The Rape of Lucrece* (1594). Stress falls on the first syllable.
300 **'greed** agreed
302 **I'll ... Sunday** proverbial: 'He that hangs himself on Sunday shall hang still uncut down on Monday' (Dent, S993)

305 **speeding** success (*OED vbl.n.* 1a)
    **goodnight our part** 'goodbye to our hopes (to wed Bianca)'; 'that cancels our debt for Petruccio's wooing expenses'
306–17 Petruccio's canny distinction between public and private behaviour has a pay-off at 5.1.134–40 and again at 5.2.125–85.
308 **twain** two; a pair, couple (*OED n.* 2)
309 **still** always
313 **vied** increased by addition or repetition (*OED v.* 6). In card games, to make a 'vie' was to stake money on the strength of one's hand (*OED v.* 2); 'vie' and 'revie' were terms from Primero, a card game fashionable between 1530 and 1640, described in Sir John Harington's *Epigram* 'The Story of Marcus's Life at Primero' (1615).
    **protesting** proclaiming, affirming (*OED v.* 3a)

313 vied] *(vi'd); ply'd (Johnson)*

212

That in a twink she won me to her love.
O, you are novices! 'Tis a world to see                    315
How tame, when men and women are alone,
A meacock wretch can make the curstest shrew.
– Give my thy hand, Kate, I will unto Venice
To buy apparel 'gainst the wedding day;
– Provide the feast, father, and bid the guests.          320
I will be sure my Katherine shall be fine.

BAPTISTA

I know not what to say, but give me your hands.
God send you joy, Petruccio, 'tis a match.

GREMIO, TRANIO

Amen, say we. We will be witnesses.

PETRUCCIO

Father, and wife, and gentlemen, adieu.                   325
I will to Venice. Sunday comes apace.
We will have rings, and things, and fine array,
And kiss me, Kate, 'We will be married o'Sunday.'

*Exeunt Petruccio and Katherina.*

---

314 **in a twink** proverbial: 'In the twinkling of an eye' (Dent, T635)
315 **'Tis a world** 'it's worth a world'; proverbial: 'It is a world to see' (Dent, W878)
317 **meacock** tame; 'effeminate; cowardly; weak' (*OED a.*); possibly punning on 'me-cock', continuing the play on *cockscomb* and *cock* (227–9). Pope explained as 'mew-cock', one that has been shut up.
319 **'gainst** in preparation for
320 **bid** invite (*OED v.* 8)
321 **fine** highly ornate, showy, thus, smartly dressed (*OED a.* 16)
322–3 **give . . . match** Performed before witnesses, the giving of hands constituted a 'pre-contract', part of an Elizabethan marriage, after which neither party might marry

another person (Hibbard). Ard[2], however, notes that such a pre-contract required the presence and verbal consent of both parties; since Katherina remains silent, the contract is not binding. On marriage customs, see pp. 60–1, and 5.2.183n.
323 **God . . . joy** proverbial (Dent, JJ2); also, a catch-phrase from the cattle-market
326 **apace** quickly, fast (*OED adv.* a)
328 **'We . . . o'Sunday'** Ard[1] notes that this is the refrain of several ballads; one ('I mun be married a Sunday') occurs in Nicholas Udall's *Ralph Roister Doister* (*c.* 1550).
328 SD Some modern editors, following Theobald, add '*severally*', thus prescribing Petruccio's and Katherina's separation at this point.

328 o'] *Hanmer*; a' *F*   SD *Exeunt*] *Exit   Katherina*] *Katherina, severally / Theobald*

GREMIO

    Was ever match clapped up so suddenly?

BAPTISTA

    Faith, gentlemen, now I play a merchant's part        330

    And venture madly on a desperate mart.

TRANIO

    'Twas a commodity lay fretting by you;

    'Twill bring you gain, or perish on the seas.

BAPTISTA

    The gain I seek is quiet in the match.

GREMIO

    No doubt but he hath got a quiet catch.        335

    But now, Baptista, to your younger daughter:

    Now is the day we long have looked for.

    I am your neighbour, and was suitor first.

TRANIO

    And I am one that love Bianca more

    Than words can witness, or your thoughts can guess.    340

GREMIO

    Youngling, thou canst not love so dear as I.

TRANIO

    Greybeard, thy love doth freeze.

GREMIO                        But thine doth fry.

    Skipper, stand back. 'Tis age that nourisheth.

---

329 **clapped up** quickly agreed; initiating a chain of financial metaphors (330–87)

330–401 No mention is made, as it is for Katherina (120–1), of what Baptista will provide for Bianca's dowry; presumably, she is her own dowry.

331 **a desperate mart** a risky business, likely to incur loss (*OED* mart *n.*³ 4)

332 **commodity** tradable article (*OED* 6); woman as sexual convenience, prostitute (Partridge, 82–3)

    **fretting** rotting, decaying (*OED* vbl.n.¹ 1a); irritating (*OED* vbl. n.¹ 3)

334 ***in** F's 'me' is probably a minim error; the same mistake occurs at 4.2.72.

337 **long . . . for** proverbial: 'Long looked for comes at last' (Dent, L423)

341 **Youngling** novice (*OED* 2)

    **dear** deeply; also, expensively

343 **Skipper** light-brained fellow, irresponsible youth (*OED* *n.*¹ 1b)

    **nourisheth** provides sustenance, i.e. has the financial resources to permit a wife to live in luxury

334 in] *Rowe*²; me *F*

TRANIO

But youth in ladies' eyes that flourisheth.

BAPTISTA

Content you, gentlemen, I will compound this strife.     345
'Tis deeds must win the prize, and he of both
That can assure my daughter greatest dower
Shall have my Bianca's love.
Say, Signor Gremio, what can you assure her?

GREMIO

First, as you know, my house within the city     350
Is richly furnished with plate and gold,
Basins and ewers to lave her dainty hands;
My hangings all of Tyrian tapestry;
In ivory coffers I have stuffed my crowns,
In cypress chests my arras counterpoints,     355
Costly apparel, tents and canopies,
Fine linen, Turkey cushions bossed with pearl,

---

345–401 The bride-bartering between a virile youth and an old fool takes an early modern social practice to an extreme.

345 **Content you** calm down; be satisfied (*OED a.* 1b)

**compound** settle, resolve

346 **deeds** actions; punning on legal deeds or documents

**he of both** the one of you two (Abbott, 12)

347 **assure** guarantee, secure, ensure (*OED v.* 1c, 5); legally convey or assign to (*OED v.* 3)

**dower** money or value given by the man to the bride's relatives (*OED n.*[2] 2b)

348 Some editors emend to F2's 'Shall have Bianca's love'.

351 **furnished** furnishèd

**plate** table settings, originally silver or gold (*OED n.* 2)

352 **lave** wash, bathe (*OED v.*[1] 1)

353 **hangings** tapestries or curtains hung

on walls as decoration and for warmth

**Tyrian tapestry** The city of Tyre (in modern Lebanon) was famous for a scarlet or purple dye extracted from shellfish.

354 **crowns** See 1.2.56n.

355 **cypress** a durable wood

**arras counterpoints** counterpanes (bedcovers) of Arras tapestry, a rich fabric woven with figures and scenes, commonly used as wall-hangings. As Gremio lists these domestic items (355–60) as part of his ownings, he appropriates female property (and identity) – yet another instance of the play's shifting gender markers and its masculinist bent.

356 **tents** frameworks for supporting bed-canopies

357 **Turkey cushions** pillows covered in richly coloured Turkish fabric; for *Turkey* and *Venice* (358) as adjectives, see Abbott, 22.

**bossed** studded, ornamented

---

348 my Bianca's] Biancas *F2*     355 cypress] *(*Cypres*)*

Valance of Venice gold in needlework,
Pewter and brass, and all things that belongs
To house or housekeeping; then at my farm                    360
I have a hundred milch-kine to the pail,
Six score fat oxen standing in my stalls,
And all things answerable to this portion.
Myself am struck in years, I must confess,
And if I die tomorrow this is hers,                          365
If whilst I live she will be only mine.

TRANIO

That 'only' came well in. Sir, list to me:
I am my father's heir and only son;
If I may have your daughter to my wife,
I'll leave her houses three or four as good                  370
Within rich Pisa walls as any one
Old Signor Gremio has in Padua,
Besides two thousand ducats by the year
Of fruitful land, all which shall be her jointure.
– What, have I pinched you, Signor Gremio?                   375

GREMIO

Two thousand ducats by the year of land?
[*aside*] My land amounts not to so much in all.

358 **Valance** drapery border hanging around a bed-canopy (*OED* n.[1] 2a)

359 **things that belongs** The relative frequently takes a singular verb, even though the antecedent is plural (Abbott, 247).

361 **milch-kine . . . pail** *milch-kine* = dairy cows, 'in milk'; *to the pail* = milk for sale at a dairy, not kept for calves

363 **answerable . . . portion** 'corresponding to the wedding-settlement I am proposing'

364 **struck** advanced

373 **ducats** Venetian gold coins worth,

at the time, four shillings and eight pence

374 **Of fruitful land** Tranio specifies the amount of annual income *from* the land.
**jointure** estate settled on a woman at marriage as provision for her widowhood (*OED* n. 4a, 4b)

375 **pinched** troubled or distressed, as though by a pinch (*OED* v. 12a); also, pinned down in an argument (*OED* v. 14a)

377 SD Arguably, Gremio's line might be heard by Tranio but not by Baptista.

358 Valance] *Pope;* Vallens *F*   359 belongs] belong *Rowe*   361 pail] *F2;* pale *F*   362 Six score] *(Sixe-score)*   363 portion] proportion *(Theobald)*   377 SD] *Neilson (Warburton)*   not] but *Theobald*

    – That she shall have, besides an argosy
    That now is lying in Marsellis' road.
    – What, have I choked you with an argosy?       380
TRANIO
    Gremio, 'tis known my father hath no less
    Than three great argosies, besides two galliasses
    And twelve tight galleys. These I will assure her,
    And twice as much whate'er thou offer'st next.
GREMIO
    Nay, I have offered all. I have no more,      385
    And she can have no more than all I have.
    If you like me, she shall have me and mine.
TRANIO
    Why, then the maid is mine from all the world
    By your firm promise; Gremio is out-vied.
BAPTISTA
    I must confess your offer is the best,      390
    And, let your father make her the assurance,
    She is your own; else – you must pardon me –
    If you should die before him, where's her dower?
TRANIO
    That's but a cavil: he is old, I young.
GREMIO
    And may not young men die as well as old?      395

---

378 **argosy** largest merchant vessel, originally one from Ragusa (now Dubrovnik), hence the name (*OED*)

379 **Marsellis' road** the safe anchorage at Marseilles harbour. F's reading, 'Marcellus roade' suggests 16th-century (trisyllabic) pronunciation (Kökeritz, 270).

382 **galliasses** A galliass was a heavy, low-built vessel, larger than a galley and using both sail and oars (*OED*).

383 **tight** water-tight, therefore extremely seaworthy

384 **twice as much** 'twice as much as', i.e. double

389 **out-vied** outbid. The card-playing metaphors continue with *gamester* (403) and 'I have faced it with a card of ten' (408). Since Tranio is making it all up, he is sure to win.

391 **assurance** formal pledge; legal evidence of conveyance of property. Baptista repeats the term at 399.

395 proverbial: 'As soon dies a young man as an old' (Dent, M73.1)

379 Marsellis'] *F2*; Marcellus *F*; Marsellies *Rowe*; Marceilles's *Pope*; Marseilles' *Ard¹*

BAPTISTA

Well, gentlemen, I am thus resolved: on Sunday next
You know, my daughter Katherine is to be married.
– Now, on the Sunday following shall Bianca
Be bride to you, if you make this assurance;
If not, to Signor Gremio. 400
And so I take my leave, and thank you both. *Exit.*

GREMIO

Adieu, good neighbour. – Now I fear thee not.
Sirrah, young gamester, your father were a fool
To give thee all and in his waning age
Set foot under thy table. Tut, a toy, 405
An old Italian fox is not so kind, my boy. *Exit.*

TRANIO

A vengeance on your crafty withered hide!
Yet I have faced it with a card of ten.
'Tis in my head to do my master good:
I see no reason but supposed Lucentio 410
Must get a father called supposed Vincentio;
And that's a wonder – fathers commonly
Do get their children, but in this case of wooing
A child shall get a sire, if I fail not of my cunning. *Exit.*

---

403 **gamester** one addicted to amorous sport; a merry person (*OED n.* 4, 5)
405 **Set . . . table** live on your charity; proverbial: 'To thrust one's feet under another man's table' (Dent, F572)
**toy** fantastic, trifling speech; foolish tale (*OED n.* 3a)
406 proverbial: 'An old fox cannot be taken by a snare' (Tilley, F647)
407 **A vengeance** proverbial: 'A vengeance take (on) him' (Dent, VV2)
408 **I . . . ten** 'I have called Gremio's bluff even though I held a low card'; proverbial: 'To outface with a card of ten' (Dent, C75). 'Face' is a term from

the game Primero (see 313n.).
410–11 **supposed . . . supposed** false, substitute. Apart from *counterfeit supposes* at 5.1.108, this is *TS*'s most explicit allusion to Gascoigne's *Supposes* (see pp. 63–6).
411 **get** beget, obtain
413 **case** perhaps punning on 'disguise'
414 **A . . . sire** an absurd inversion; cf. Grumio's 'the oats have eaten the horses' (3.2.206–7).
**if . . . cunning** at least two possible meanings: (1) 'if I do not fail in my plots'; (2) 'if I do not fail to be sufficiently ingenious'

---

396–7] *this edn (RP); F lines* resolu'd, / know /; *Capell lines* gentlemen, / know / 401 SD] *after* neighbour. *402 Ard¹* 413 wooing] *(woing);* winning *(Capell)* 414 cunning] doing *(Steevens)*

[3.1]          *Enter* LUCENTIO *[as Cambio],* HORTENSIO
                    *[as Licio] and* BIANCA.

LUCENTIO

Fiddler, forbear – you grow too forward, sir;
Have you so soon forgot the entertainment
Her sister Katherine welcomed you withal?

HORTENSIO

But, wrangling pedant, this is
The patroness of heavenly harmony.                          5
Then give me leave to have prerogative,
And when in music we have spent an hour,
Your lecture shall have leisure for as much.

LUCENTIO

Preposterous ass, that never read so far
To know the cause why music was ordained!                   10
Was it not to refresh the mind of man

---

3.1 F's heading, '*Actus Tertia.*', is the first
such marker since the play's opening.
Whatever action prompts Lucentio's
first line frames the scene as a music
lesson (Schafer, 150).
1 **forbear** desist, give way (*OED v.* 5)
4 Editors have expanded this short line
variously, from Theobald's proposal to
insert 'She is a shrew' at the beginning
of the line to Tillyard's 'But, wrangling
pedant, this Urania is' (Oxf¹). F,
however, invites *physical* language to
flesh out the short line.
5 **heavenly harmony** Neoplatonism
viewed music as the foundation of the
world; Thomas Elyot, in *The Book
Named the Governor* (1531), considered
that music 'only serveth for recreation
after tedious or laborious affairs'; he
also associated music with turning men
'womanish' (1.7, 20–3).
6 **prerogative** precedence (*OED n.* 1b)

8, 23 **lecture** lesson; see 1.2.151n.
9 **Preposterous** literally, placing first
that which should come last – in this
case, music before philosophy (*OED
a.* 1a; Abbott, 14). Parker (*Margins*,
33) discerns a pun on *ars musica* + *ass*,
citing Lyly's *Endymion*, which rhymes
'I am all *Mars* and *Ars*' with 'Nay, you
are all Masse and Asse' (1.3.91–2); this
is one of several schoolboy jokes having
to do with holes of various kinds (as
at 'Spit in the hole, man' at 39) and
backsides (see 2.1.72n.).
10 Ard² glosses *To know* = 'as to know',
and suggests an allusion to 'duly
considering the causes for the which
matrimony was ordained' (*BCP*, 290);
Ard² also notes that R.W.'s *The Three
Lords and Three Ladies of London* (1590)
has a music lesson, but no direct debt
seems feasible.

---

3.1] *Rowe; Actus Tertia.* F   0.1 *as Cambio*] *Kittredge*   0.2 *as Licio*] *Kittredge*   4] She is a shrew, but,
wrangling pedant, this is *Theobald;* But, wrangling pedant, know this lady is *Hanmer;* But, wrangling
pedant, this Urania is *(Tillyard conj.);* But, wrangling pedant, this Bianca is *Oxf*

After his studies or his usual pain?
Then give me leave to read philosophy
And, while I pause, serve in your harmony.

HORTENSIO

Sirrah, I will not bear these braves of thine.          15

BIANCA

Why, gentlemen, you do me double wrong
To strive for that which resteth in my choice.
I am no breeching scholar in the schools:
I'll not be tied to hours nor 'pointed times
But learn my lessons as I please myself;          20
And to cut off all strife, here sit we down.
– Take you your instrument, play you the whiles;
His lecture will be done ere you have tuned.

HORTENSIO

You'll leave his lecture when I am in tune?

LUCENTIO

That will be never. Tune your instrument.          25

BIANCA    Where left we last?

LUCENTIO    Here, Madam:

[*Reads.*]    *Hic ibat Simois, hic est Sigeia tellus,*
                *Hic steterat Priami regia celsa senis.*

12 **usual pain** daily labour; Ard[1] suggests, for F's 'his vsuall', either 'unusual' or 'his manual'.

14 **serve in** serve up; the modern idiom 'dish out' captures Lucentio's sense.

15 **braves** defiances; also suggesting scornful bravado (*OED n.* 2)

17 **resteth . . . choice** 'is for me to decide'

18 **breeching scholar** youngster still subject to whipping (*OED vbl.n.* 2b); Ard[1] glosses as 'of an age to assume breeches'.

19–20 Bianca echoes Katherina's 'What, shall I be appointed hours' at 1.1.103; in declining to be ruled by either of

her rival masters, she echoes Kate's behaviour.

22 **the whiles** for a while

28–9 'Here flowed the Simois; this is the Sigeian land [Troy]; here stood the lofty palace of ancient Priam' (Ovid, *Heroides*, 1.33–4). Surrounded by unwelcome suitors, Penelope, Ulysses' faithful wife, writes this to her husband; like Penelope, Bianca copes with the amorous attentions of several men. The lines come from a passage that served as a school exercise in demonstrative adverbs; more to the point, they highlight Penelope's

19 'pointed] *Theobald;* pointed *F*    28–9] *Rowe; prose F*    28, 32, 41 *Sigeia*] *F2; sigeria F*

BIANCA   Conster them.                                           30

LUCENTIO   *Hic ibat*, as I told you before; *Simois*, I am
Lucentio; *hic est*, son unto Vincentio of Pisa; *Sigeia
tellus*, disguised thus to get your love; *hic steterat*, and
that Lucentio that comes a-wooing; *Priami*, is my man
Tranio; *regia*, bearing my port; *celsa senis*, that we      35
might beguile the old pantaloon.

HORTENSIO   Madam, my instrument's in tune.

BIANCA   Let's hear. O fie, the treble jars.

LUCENTIO   Spit in the hole, man, and tune again.

BIANCA   Now let me see if I can conster it. *Hic ibat Simois*,   40
I know you not; *hic est Sigeia tellus*, I trust you not; *hic
steterat Priami*, take heed he hear us not; *regia*, presume
not; *celsa senis*, despair not.

HORTENSIO
Madam, 'tis now in tune.

LUCENTIO                                    All but the bass.

HORTENSIO
The bass is right; 'tis the base knave that jars.              45
How fiery and forward our pedant is!

clever evasiveness (Maurer, 244–5).
Lucentio's 'translation' (31–6) is
somewhat idiosyncratic; in returning
the translation exercise like a model
pupil (40–3), Bianca at least keeps the
Latin clauses logically together (Barkan,
39); nicely modulated, her response
both withholds (*presume not*) and gives
(*despair not*), anticipating Beatrice and
Cressida. Ard² notes that all editions of
Ovid read '*Hac ibat*' ('there flowed').

30, 40 **Conster, conster** construe,
translate a passage from an ancient
author (*OED* construe *v.* 3); accented
on the first syllable

34–5 *Priami . . . Tranio* 'Translating'
King Priam as the servant Tranio may
allude to disrupting social roles (Bate,
127).

35 **bearing my port** Ard¹ glosses:
'carrying himself as me'; Oxf¹

paraphrases as 'living in the gentlemanly
style appropriate to me'.

36 **pantaloon** Gremio; see 1.1.47.2n.

39 Spitting in the sound-hole would not
help to tune the lute; the reference is
to the treble peg-hole: the pegs can get
excessively shiny and liable to slip, and
spitting in the peg-hole counters that
tendency (CG, JA).

46–56 The distribution of F's SPs
(see t.nn.) is clearly incorrect. One
explanation is that the compositor was
confused by the forms *Luc.*, *Lit.* and
*Bia.* in MS copy; however, l. 46 would
not have had a SP in the manuscript
'unless it were an afterthought or,
perhaps, began a new page' (Oxf¹).
Maurer argues that F's speech
assignments are playable and that they
have implications for Bianca's character
that editorial emendation has occluded.

30 Conster] Construe *F4*    46 SP] *Hortensio / Rowe*    forward] froward *F3*

221

[*aside*] Now, for my life, the knave doth court my love.
*Pedascule*, I'll watch you better yet.

BIANCA

In time I may believe, yet I mistrust.

LUCENTIO

Mistrust it not, for sure Aeacides                              50
Was Ajax, called so from his grandfather.

BIANCA

I must believe my master; else, I promise you,
I should be arguing still upon that doubt.
But let it rest. – Now, Licio, to you:
Good master, take it not unkindly, pray,                        55
That I have been thus pleasant with you both.

HORTENSIO

You may go walk, and give me leave awhile;
My lessons make no music in three parts.

LUCENTIO

Are you so formal, sir? Well, I must wait –
And watch withal, for, but I be deceived,                       60

48 *Pedascule* little pedant; a diminutive nonce-word (four syllables)
50–1 **Aeacides . . . Ajax** Ajax, Telamon's son, was called Aeacides after his grandfather Aeacus. Ard² suggests that Shakespeare remembers Ovid, *Met.* 13.25, but the line to which Lucentio refers, '*illic Aeacides, illic tendebat Ulixes*', is from *Heroides* (1.35); Nuttall (389–90, n. 47) offers further explanation. Lucentio's reference is a pointed misconstruction: Aeacides refers not to Ajax but Achilles, for whom Aeacides is also a patronymic. Possibly pronounced 'ay-ass-I-des' and 'a-jakes' (see Maurer, 262–3).
53 **still** incessantly
55–6 Editors from Rowe to Bond emend F's 'master' to 'masters', but Bianca addresses Hortensio/Licio (who

most needs apology) before including Lucentio.
56 **pleasant** facetious, joking
57 **give me leave** 'allow me to work alone'; 'you can rely on me (to do the business properly)'
58 **three parts** Some songs were composed in three harmonizing melodies; songbooks displayed all three parts on one page, enabling singers to read from the same book. Hortensio, however, is punning: where courtship is concerned, two is company, three is a crowd.
59 **formal** unduly precise (*OED a.* 8); 'punctilious, concerned for your professional rights' (Hibbard)
59–61 **Well . . . amorous** Some editors, following Johnson, mark these lines '*Aside*'.
60 **but** unless

49 SP] *Pope² (Theobald); Luc. F; continued to Luc. / Rowe*   50 SP] *Pope² (Theobald); Bian. F*
52 SP] *Pope²; Hort. F; continued to Bianca / Rowe*   55 master] masters *Rowe³*   57 awhile] *(a while)*

Our fine musician groweth amorous.

HORTENSIO

Madam, before you touch the instrument,
To learn the order of my fingering,
I must begin with rudiments of art,
To teach you gamut in a briefer sort, 65
More pleasant, pithy and effectual
Than hath been taught by any of my trade;
And there it is in writing fairly drawn.

BIANCA

Why, I am past my gamut long ago.

HORTENSIO

Yet read the gamut of Hortensio. 70

BIANCA [*Reads.*]

*Gamut* I am, the ground of all accord:
*A re*, to plead Hortensio's passion;
*B mi*, Bianca, take him for thy lord;
*C fa, ut*, that loves with all affection;
*D sol, re*, one clef, two notes have I; 75
*E la, mi*, show pity, or I die.

Call you this gamut? Tut, I like it not.
Old fashions please me best; I am not so nice

63 **order** logic, method, pattern
65 **gamut** The medieval hexachordal musical scale, systematized by Guido d'Arezzo (*c*. 1024) and called after 'Gamma ut', the first note (G) on the lowest line of the bass staff (JA). The prevailing method of teaching sight-singing was the 'Guidonian hand': pupils learned to associate parts of the hand and fingers with musical notes which they could then sing back to the teacher as he pointed to those areas. That association may suggest that 'hand play', implicit in the scene, also figures in 'the gamut of Hortensio' (70) (Weiss).

**briefer sort** quicker fashion
66 **effectual** conclusive (*OED a.* 5)
68 **drawn** set down, notated
71 **ground . . . accord** foundation of all harmony; *ground* = lowest note or beginning. The named notes (72–6) continue the gamut upwards.
75 **one . . . notes** Ard[1] notes that lute music requires only the treble (G) clef and that *one clef*, 'that of Love, limits the scale of Hortensio's efforts, his "two notes" being his dual personality as Hortensio and Licio'.
78 **nice** whimsical, capricious, temperamental (Crystal & Crystal*)*

65 gamut] *(gamoth), Rowe* 69, 70, 77 gamut] *(gamouth), Rowe* 71 SD] *Pope Gamut*] *(Gamouth), Rowe* 72 *A re*] *(Are); Q* 73 *B mi*] *(Beeme); Pope* 74 *C fa, ut*] *(cfavt); Q* 75 clef] *(Cliffe); Ard[1]* 76 *E la, mi*] *(Ela, mi); Johnson*

To change true rules for odd inventions.

*Enter a* Servant.

SERVANT

Mistress, your father prays you leave your books 80
And help to dress your sister's chamber up;
You know tomorrow is the wedding day.

BIANCA

Farewell, sweet masters both, I must be gone.

*[Exeunt Bianca and Servant.]*

LUCENTIO

Faith, mistress, then I have no cause to stay. *[Exit.]*

HORTENSIO

But I have cause to pry into this pedant: 85
Methinks he looks as though he were in love.
Yet if thy thoughts, Bianca, be so humble
To cast thy wandering eyes on every stale,
Seize thee that list; if once I find thee ranging, 89
Hortensio will be quit with thee by changing. *Exit.*

79 *odd F reads 'old', presumably repeated from 78; modern editors accept Theobald's emendation.
80 SP F reads '*Nicke*', identified as Nicholas Tooley (Steevens), whose name appears in F's list of the King's Men's principal actors; Cam¹ suggests, on slim evidence, that Tooley played Biondello and one of Petruccio's servants (see pp. 28–9).
81 dress . . . up On marriage customs, see Hodgdon, 'Bride-ing'.
83, 84 SDD F cues no exits until the scene's end. Although the exit at 83 for Bianca would permit a costume

change before her re-entry six lines later, neither costume change nor exit is strictly necessary, though serial exits here repeat a pattern occurring elsewhere (e.g. at 4.4.65, 67).
88 stale decoy or lure (from falconry); figuratively, a person who lures another deceptively (*OED n.*³ 2)
89 Seize . . . list 'Let anyone who wants you have you'; *list* = wish, please (*OED v.* 2a)
ranging straying (of a hawk); inconstant (*OED v.*¹ 7a; 8)
90 be quit with be rid of; requite (*OED quit v.* 6b; 4)

79 change] *F2;* charge *F* odd] *Theobald;* old *F;* new *Rowe²* 79.1 Servant] *Rowe; Messenger F*
80 SP] *Rowe; Nicke. F* 83 SD] *Capell* 84 SD] *Rowe*

**[3.2]**   *Enter* BAPTISTA, GREMIO, TRANIO [*as Lucentio*],
    KATHERINA, BIANCA [, LUCENTIO *as Cambio*]
       *and others, Attendants.*

BAPTISTA

  Signor Lucentio, this is the 'pointed day
  That Katherine and Petruccio should be married,
  And yet we hear not of our son-in-law.
  What will be said? What mockery will it be
  To want the bridegroom when the priest attends          5
  To speak the ceremonial rites of marriage?
  What says Lucentio to this shame of ours?

KATHERINA

  No shame but mine. I must forsooth be forced
  To give my hand opposed against my heart
  Unto a mad-brain rudesby full of spleen                  10
  Who wooed in haste and means to wed at leisure.
  I told you, I, he was a frantic fool,
  Hiding his bitter jests in blunt behaviour,
  And to be noted for a merry man,
  He'll woo a thousand, 'point the day of marriage,         15
  Make feast, invite friends, and proclaim the banns,
  Yet never means to wed where he hath wooed.

---

3.2.0.2 *LUCENTIO as Cambio* F
omits Lucentio/Cambio, probably
because he does not speak. Since
Lucentio is needed when Tranio
addresses him at 127, most editors
(and performances) follow Rowe
and include him in this entry. See
127n.
1, 15 **'pointed, 'point** appointed, appoint
5 **want** lack
7–8 Baptista addresses 'Lucentio', but
Katherina answers.
8 **forsooth** in truth, certainly (sarcastic?)
10 **mad-brain rudesby** hot-headed,

unmannerly fellow (*OED* rudesby)
**spleen** caprice, changeable temper. In
early modern physiology, the spleen
was the seat of melancholy (see
Ind.1.136n.).
11 playing on the proverbial: 'Marry in
haste and repent at leisure' (Dent,
H196)
12 **frantic** lunatic
14 **noted for** celebrated as (*OED a.* 1b)
16 *Most editors follow Dyce's
emendation, which not only aligns with
2.1.320, 'Provide the feast, father, and
bid the guests', but improves sense.

3.2] *Pope*   0.1 *as Lucentio*] *Rowe*   3 son-in-law] *(sonne in Law)*   4 said? . . . be] *Ard¹;* said, . . . be?
*F*   8 forced] *(forst)*   14 man,] *Rowe;* man; *F*   15 'point] *Pope;* point *F*   16 friends, and] *Dyce;*

Now must the world point at poor Katherine
And say, 'Lo, there is mad Petruccio's wife,
If it would please him come and marry her.'　　　　　20
TRANIO
Patience, good Katherine, and Baptista too.
Upon my life, Petruccio means but well;
Whatever fortune stays him from his word,
Though he be blunt, I know him passing wise;
Though he be merry, yet withal he's honest.　　　　　25
KATHERINA
Would Katherine had never seen him though.

*Exit weeping* [*, Bianca following*].

BAPTISTA
Go, girl, I cannot blame thee now to weep,
For such an injury would vex a very saint,
Much more a shrew of impatient humour.


*Enter* BIONDELLO.

BIONDELLO　　Master, master, news – old news, and such　　30
news as you never heard of!
BAPTISTA　　Is it new and old too? How may that be?

---

21–5 Tranio's familiarity with Petruccio's
　　eccentricities has invited editors to
　　conjecture that these lines were written
　　for Hortensio, Petruccio's 'best-beloved
　　and approved friend' (1.2.3).
23 **stays** prevents; delays
24 **passing** See Ind.1.66n.
25 **merry** humorous, facetious (*OED a.*
　　4d)
26 SD Cueing Bianca to exit with
　　Katherina means that only the men
　　remain onstage.
27 **to weep** for weeping (Abbott, 356)

28 **vex . . . saint** Some modern editors
　　prefer F2's 'vex a saint'; proverbial:
　　'Enough to make a saint swear' (Dent,
　　S28); *very* = absolute.
30–1 **\*old . . . news** F contains only
　　'such newes'; editors generally accept
　　Capell's emendation, aligning with
　　Baptista's response at 32. Ard² notes:
　　'Biondello offers the word "old" in its
　　sense of "plentiful, abundant" (*OED
　　a.* 6); Baptista takes it up in its modern
　　sense'.

friends, invite, and proclaim *F;* friends, invite, yes and *F2;* feasts, invite them, and *Malone;* make
friends invited, and *Grant White*　24 know] knew *Q*　26 SD *Bianca following*] *(follow'd by Bianca,
Gremio, Hortensio, and Others* / *Capell*　28 a very saint] a saint *F2*　29 impatient] thy impatient
*F2*　30–1 news – . . . such news] *Capell subst.;* newes, and such newes *F;* news! And such old news
*Collier;* news, new news, old news, and such news *Ridley*

BIONDELLO    Why, is it not news to hear of Petruccio's
coming?

BAPTISTA    Is he come?                                      35

BIONDELLO    Why no, sir.

BAPTISTA    What then?

BIONDELLO    He is coming.

BAPTISTA    When will he be here?

BIONDELLO    When he stands where I am and sees you    40
there.

TRANIO    But say, what to thine old news?

BIONDELLO    Why, Petruccio is coming in a new hat and
an old jerkin, a pair of old breeches thrice-turned; a
pair of boots that have been candle-cases, one buckled,    45
another laced with two broken points; an old rusty
sword ta'en out of the town armoury with a broken hilt
and chapeless; his horse hipped – with an old mothy
saddle and stirrups of no kindred – besides, possessed
with the glanders and like to mose in the chine; troubled    50

---

42 **what to** what of, what about

43–68 As Hibbard notes, this description
of Petruccio and his horse, Gremio's
account of the wedding at 148–81
and Petruccio's abuse of the Tailor
in 4.3 are all 'bravura pieces,
conscious displays of the rhetorical
arts of grotesque description, farcical
narrative and inventive vituperation'.
Ard[1] and Ard[2] give detailed accounts
of the sources behind Biondello's set
piece, a type of reverse blazon: rather
than describing the excellent qualities
of the horse, he marks its defects.

44 **jerkin** close-fitting short jacket
**thrice-turned** turned inside out,
reversed three times for further wear

45 **boots . . . candle-cases**  worn-out
boots used for storing candles

46 ***with . . . points** Laces that fastened

hose to doublet had 'aiglets' or
points. In F, this phrase, enclosed by
colons, applies to the sword at 47; the
emendation here follows Johnson.

48 **chapeless** without a sheath
**his horse** Gervase Markham's
*A Discourse of Horsemanship* (1593)
explains most of the diseases in
Biondello's catalogue.
**hipped** lame in the hips

49 **of no kindred** not matching

50 **glanders** disease that causes swellings
beneath the jaw and nasal discharge
(*OED* 2)
**mose . . . chine** Perhaps an error for
'mourn of the chine', which refers to
the terminal stages of glanders, but
whether the text or Biondello is at fault
hardly matters, for *OED* cites both
terms as obscure.

33 hear] *Q;* heard *F*    44 thrice-turned] *(thrice turn'd)*    46 with . . . points] *Malone (Johnson); after*
chapeless *48 F*    48 hipped – ] *(hip'd)*

227

with the lampass, infected with the fashions, full of
windgalls, sped with spavins, rayed with the yellows,
past cure of the fives, stark spoiled with the staggers,
begnawn with the bots, weighed in the back and
shoulder-shotten, near-legged before and with a half-          55
cheeked bit and a headstall of sheep's leather which,
being restrained to keep him from stumbling, hath
been often burst and now repaired with knots; one
girth six times pieced, and a woman's crupper of velour
which hath two letters for her name fairly set down          60
in studs, and here and there pieced with packthread.

BAPTISTA    Who comes with him?

BIONDELLO    O sir, his lackey, for all the world caparisoned

---

51 **lampass . . . fashions** swellings and
cankerous sores in the mouth (*OED*
lampas *n.*[1])

52 **windgalls** soft tumours on the legs
above the fetlocks
**sped with spavins** terminally afflicted
with bony tumours on the leg-joints;
*sped with* = wrecked, rendered useless
by
**rayed** form of 'berayed', sometimes
spelled 'bewrayed' = disfigured, defiled
**yellows** discolouration; jaundice

53 **fives** malapropism for 'avives' or
'vives', swelling of salivary glands ('the
strangles')
**stark spoiled** utterly ruined
**staggers** disease causing vertigo and
loss of balance

54 **bots** intestinal worms
**weighed . . . back**   sway-backed.
F's 'Waid' may mean overloaded to
the point of permanent damage or
distortion. Some editors, following
Hanmer, emend to 'swayed' = strained
(*OED ppl.a.* 1).

55 **shoulder-shotten** with a dislocated
shoulder

**near-legged before** knock-kneed in
the forelegs (Libbard)

55–6 **half-cheeked bit** having the bit's
'cheeks' or side-pieces broken or badly
adjusted

56 **headstall** part of bridle or halter that
fits round the head
**sheep's leather** rather than the
stronger, more common, pigskin or
cowhide

57 **restrained** drawn tightly (*OED v.*[1] 6)

58 **now repaired** Walker's reading, 'new-
repaired', also makes sense; *o* and *e* are
similar in secretary hand.

59 **girth** band placed around the horse's
belly to keep the saddle in place

59, 61 **pieced** patched, mended

59 **crupper** strap passed under the horse's
tail to hold the saddle steady
**velour** velvet-like fabric

60–1 **two . . . studs** initials marked in
brass or silver

61 **packthread** twine

63 **lackey** footman, valet
**for . . . world** proverbial (Dent,
WW27)
**caparisoned** fitted out

---

51 fashions] farcin *Hanmer*   52 rayed] *(*raied*)*   54 weighed] *(*Waid*)*: sway'd *Hanmer*   55 near-
legged] *(*neere leg'd*)*   55–6 half-cheeked] *Hanmer (*half-check'd*)*: halfe-chekt *F*   58 now repaired]
new-repaired *Dyce*[2] *(Walker)*

like the horse: with a linen stock on one leg and a kersey
boot-hose on the other, gartered with a red and blue                    65
list; an old hat, and the humour of forty fancies pricked
in't for a feather – a monster, a very monster in apparel,
and not like a Christian footboy or a gentleman's lackey.

TRANIO
'Tis some odd humour pricks him to this fashion,
Yet oftentimes he goes but mean-apparelled.                             70

BAPTISTA     I am glad he's come, howsoe'er he comes.

BIONDELLO     Why sir, he comes not.

BAPTISTA     Didst thou not say he comes?

BIONDELLO     Who? That Petruccio came?

BAPTISTA     Ay, that Petruccio came.                                   75

BIONDELLO     No sir, I say his horse comes with him on
his back.

BAPTISTA     Why, that's all one.

BIONDELLO

Nay, by Saint Jamy,
I hold you a penny,                                                     80
A horse and a man

---

64 **stock** stocking, distinct from trunk-
  hose or breeches
64–5 **kersey boot-hose** coarse woollen
  overstocking
66 **list** strip of cloth (*OED n.*[3] 3a)
66–7 **humour . . . feather**     obscure,
  implying some elaborate decoration;
  Stockdale suggests the reference is to
  a ballad. Halliwell suggests 'a parcel
  of forty ribbons tied together [*pricked*
  = pinned] instead of a feather'; the
  combination suggests parody of a
  heraldic device worn in a helmet.
68 **footboy** page-boy, under-servant.
  Cam[2] observes that Biondello may
  be distinguishing between himself
  ('a Christian footboy') and Tranio ('a

gentleman's lackey').
69 **odd humour pricks** strange whim
  that incites (*OED* prick *v.* 9a)
71–8 Biondello's cross-talk with Baptista
  resembles Grumio's exchanges with
  Petruccio and Curtis (1.2.6–17, 4.1.46–
  56).
78 **all one** the same thing
79–83 *F prints as prose, early and
  modern editors as verse. Ard[1]
  assumes the lines are a fragment of a
  lost ballad. *Saint Jamy* (79) probably
  refers to St James of Compostella
  (the apostle, patron saint of Spain),
  whose shrine was the destination of
  medieval pilgrimages.
80 **hold you** bet you

69 odd] *(*od*); old *Q*     70 mean-apparelled] *(*meane apparel'd*)     79–83 Nay . . . many] *Collier; prose
F; Rowe*[3] *lines penny, / many. /*

Is more than one,
And yet not many.

*Enter* PETRUCCIO *and* GRUMIO.

PETRUCCIO    Come, where be these gallants? Who's at
home?                                                                                              85
BAPTISTA    You are welcome, sir.
PETRUCCIO    And yet I come not well.
BAPTISTA    And yet you halt not.
TRANIO    Not so well apparelled as I wish you were.
PETRUCCIO
Were it better I should rush in thus?                                          90
But where is Kate? Where is my lovely bride?
How does my father? Gentles, methinks you frown,
And wherefore gaze this goodly company
As if they saw some wondrous monument,
Some comet or unusual prodigy?                                                   95
BAPTISTA
Why sir, you know this is your wedding day.

---

83 **many** Cam[1] hears a pun on 'meiny' =
'combination (of people) with a single
object'.
87–8 Petruccio plays on *welcome* (86) as
'well come', presumably referring to
his strange attire; Baptista takes *come
not well* to mean that Petruccio does
not limp (*halt* = limp). Alternative
punctuation – 'And yet I come not
well?' – is also possible.
90 *F reads 'Were it better, I should rush
in thus', which Ard[1] retains. Some
modern editors emend to 'Were it
not better', assuming that Petruccio's
ardour makes him a hasty bridegroom;
Riv adds '*Pretends great excitement*' (at
91); Oxf interprets 'I should rush in
thus' as an unfinished sentence which

Petruccio himself interrupts. Cam[2]
glosses 'even if I were better dressed'.
Treating the line as a question opens
the possibility that Petruccio comments
on Tranio's finery, suggesting that he
is either more suitably dressed or even
overdressed.
92 **Gentles** term of polite address
to persons of rank or 'gentle' birth;
perhaps ironic
94 **monument** Oxf[1] suggests that
Elizabethans might understand this as
'an ornamental figure on a tomb (likely
to be "better" than life, or allegorical)'.
95 **comet . . . prodigy** Comets were
thought to anticipate significant events
(usually disasters); *prodigy* = omen
(*OED n*. 1).

---

83.1] *Grumio, fantastically habited. / Rowe*    89] *Capell lines* apparelled / were. /    90 Were it better]
Why, were it better *Hanmer;* Tut! were it better *Capell;* Were it not better *Cam[1] (Keightley)*    thus?]
*Rann;* thus: *F;* thus: [*Pretends great excitement.*] *Riv;* thus – *Oxf*

First were we sad, fearing you would not come,
Now sadder that you come so unprovided.
Fie, doff this habit, shame to your estate,
An eyesore to our solemn festival.                    100

TRANIO

And tell us what occasion of import
Hath all so long detained you from your wife
And sent you hither so unlike yourself?

PETRUCCIO

Tedious it were to tell, and harsh to hear.
Sufficeth I am come to keep my word,                    105
Though in some part enforced to digress,
Which at more leisure I will so excuse
As you shall well be satisfied with all.
But where is Kate? I stay too long from her,
The morning wears, 'tis time we were at church.                    110

TRANIO

See not your bride in these unreverent robes;
Go to my chamber; put on clothes of mine.

PETRUCCIO

Not I, believe me; thus I'll visit her.

BAPTISTA

But thus, I trust, you will not marry her.

PETRUCCIO

Good sooth, even thus. Therefore ha' done with words:                    115

---

98 **unprovided** improperly dressed for a wedding
99 **estate** rank, social status
100 **solemn festival** ceremonious occasion
101 **occasion of import** significant matter (perhaps ironic)
102 **all** an intensive (Abbott, 28)
105 **Sufficeth** it is enough that (Abbott, 297)
106 **enforced** enforcèd
   **digress** go out of my way; deviate from my strategy

108 **with all** The contrast with *in some part* (106) supports retaining F's reading (= 'with everything') rather than emending to 'withal' = 'with my explanation' (Oxf¹).
110 **wears** is passing (*OED v.*¹ 19a)
111 **unreverent** disrespectful
115 **Good sooth** 'yes indeed'; a mild oath. Cf. Hotspur's 'Swear me, Kate, like a lady as thou art, / A good mouth-filling oath, and leave "in sooth"' (*1H4* 3.1.249–50).
   **ha'** have

108 with all] withall *Q*

To me she's married, not unto my clothes.
Could I repair what she will wear in me
As I can change these poor accoutrements,
'Twere well for Kate and better for myself.
But what a fool am I to chat with you                    120
When I should bid good morrow to my bride
And seal the title with a lovely kiss.          *Exit [with Grumio].*

TRANIO

He hath some meaning in his mad attire;
We will persuade him, be it possible,
To put on better ere he go to church.                   125

BAPTISTA

I'll after him, and see th'event of this.
                    *Exit [with Gremio, Biondello and Attendants].*

TRANIO

But sir, to love concerneth us to add

---

116 proverbial: 'Silk and satin make not a gentleman' (Dent, S451); in modern idiom, 'Clothes make (or do not make) the man'. Petruccio speaks like a quintessential essentialist.

117 **wear** possess and enjoy, with sexual pun. Cf. *MA* 5.1.82: 'Win me and wear me'. In possessing and enjoying him, she will also *wear* him down or out through use, a bodily process that cannot be repaired.

118 **accoutrements** apparel

122 **seal** ratify
   **lovely** loving, amorous

122 SD Bell includes Biondello in this exit, the first in what some editions mark as three exits, taking Tranio off with Gremio at 125 and leaving Baptista to exit, either alone or with any remaining 'attendants', at 126. Three successive exits offer a playable comic option, generating an illusion of speedy necessity.

123–5 For the third time, Tranio offers reassurances.

123 **meaning** motive, objective

126 **after** go after
   **event** outcome

127 Oxf begins a new scene here, in an attempt to iron out a bit of dramaturgy that appears more awkward on the page than in performance: Tranio has promised to persuade Petruccio to change his clothes (124), yet he stays behind to speak with Lucentio. Cam[1] conjectures a missing scene, since the conversation between Tranio and Lucentio allows 20 lines of stage time for Petruccio to find Katherina, take her to church and marry her. Cam[2] suggests omitting Tranio and Lucentio altogether until their entry at 127, and assigning Tranio's lines to Hortensio, to whom they seem more appropriate. Yet what seems awkward on the page disappears in theatrical practice: Tranio and Lucentio simply pick up an earlier conversation *in medias res*, a common Shakespearean strategy. See pp. 317–19.

---

122 lovely] loving *Collier*   SD *with Grumio*] *Dyce; Exit. F*   126 th'event] *(the event)*   SD *with . . . Attendants*] *Capell subst.*   127] *3.3 Oxf*   127 But . . . love] *Sisson;* But sir, Loue *F*

Her father's liking, which to bring to pass,
As I before imparted to your worship,
I am to get a man, whate'er he be —                              130
It skills not much, we'll fit him to our turn —
And he shall be 'Vincentio of Pisa',
And make assurance here in Padua
Of greater sums than I have promised.
So shall you quietly enjoy your hope                             135
And marry sweet Bianca with consent.

LUCENTIO
Were it not that my fellow schoolmaster
Doth watch Bianca's steps so narrowly,
'Twere good, methinks, to steal our marriage,
Which once performed, let all the world say no,                  140
I'll keep mine own, despite of all the world.

TRANIO
That by degrees we mean to look into
And watch our vantage in this business:
We'll overreach the greybeard Gremio,
The narrow-prying father Minola,                                 145
The quaint musician, amorous Licio,

---

**\*But . . . love** Editors have variously emended F's 'But, sir, Loue'; Capell's suggestion, 'But to her love', makes sense but combines an omission and a misreading; since omissions are common in this form, Ard² assumes that the word 'to' has been omitted. Knight observes that Tranio is reminding Lucentio that 'to love' is not enough: Baptista must also approve Lucentio's suit to Bianca.
**concerneth** it concerns (impersonal use, see Abbott, 297)
129 **\*As I before** F reads 'As before', which makes sense (and scans); modern editors, however, assuming an omitted word, accept Pope's emendation.

131 **skills not** does not matter (*OED v.*[1] 2b)
**turn** purpose, convenience
134 **promised** promisèd
138 **narrowly** closely, with such attention
139 **steal our marriage** elope; marry secretly; cf. *RJ* 5.3.232: 'their stol'n marriage day'. Scansion invites pronouncing *marriage* as trisyllabic (RP).
143 **watch . . . business** look out for a favourable (to us) opportunity; scansion invites pronouncing *business* as trisyllabic (RP).
144 **overreach** outdo (*OED v.* 6a), suggesting 'out-scheme' the others
145 **narrow-prying** overly watchful, suspicious
146 **quaint** ingenious, cunning (*OED a.* 1)

129 As I before] *Pope;* As before *F;* As before I *F2*     145 narrow-prying] *Pope;* narrow prying *F*

All for my master's sake, Lucentio.

*Enter* GREMIO.

Signor Gremio, came you from the church?
GREMIO
As willingly as e'er I came from school.
TRANIO
And is the bride and bridegroom coming home?                    150
GREMIO
A bridegroom, say you? 'Tis a groom indeed –
A grumbling groom, and that the girl shall find.
TRANIO
Curster than she? Why, 'tis impossible.
GREMIO
Why, he's a devil, a devil, a very fiend.
TRANIO
Why, she's a devil, a devil, the devil's dam.                    155
GREMIO
Tut, she's a lamb, a dove, a fool, to him.
I'll tell you, Sir Lucentio: when the priest
Should ask if Katherine should be his wife,
'Ay, by gog's wounds,' quoth he, and swore so loud

149 proverbial: 'With as good a will as ever I came from school' (Dent, W398)
150 **is** another instance of a singular verb with a plural subject (Abbott, 333–9)
152 **grumbling groom** rough, lower-class fellow. F's 'grumlling' may reflect pronunciation.
153 **Curster** more bad-tempered, quarrelsome
155 **a devil . . . dam** proverbial: 'The devil and his dam' (Dent, D225); cf. 1.1.105.
156–81 Gremio's description of the wedding ceremony suggests its *mad* or parodic nature; 5.2 stages a second 'marriage'.

156 Gremio draws on two proverbial phrases: 'as innocent as a lamb' and 'as harmless as a dove' (Dent, L34.1, D572); 'she's a fool to him' = 'Katherina's behaviour is nothing compared to Petruccio's'.
157 **Sir Lucentio** 'Sir' was widely applied in Shakespeare's age; here, it signifies courtesy rather than aristocratic status.
157–8 **when . . . ask** at the point in the marriage service where the priest asks
159 **by gog's wounds** euphemistic form of 'by God's wounds', a common oath (elsewhere in Shakespeare only as 'zounds'); inappropriate to a church ceremony

152 grumbling] *(grumlling)*

That, all amazed, the priest let fall the book,                160
And as he stooped again to take it up,
This mad-brained bridegroom took him such a cuff
That down fell priest and book, and book and priest.
'Now take them up,' quoth he, 'if any list.'

TRANIO

What said the wench when he rose up again?                165

GREMIO

Trembled and shook; for why he stamped and swore
As if the vicar meant to cozen him.
But after many ceremonies done
He calls for wine: 'A health,' quoth he, as if
He had been aboard, carousing to his mates                170
After a storm; quaffed off the muscadel
And threw the sops all in the sexton's face,
Having no other reason
But that his beard grew thin and hungerly
And seemed to ask him sops as he was drinking.                175
This done, he took the bride about the neck

---

164 Ard² suggests that Petruccio is inviting anyone who wishes to do so to pick up both priest and book; Ard¹ observes that he suspects the priest of 'taking up' the bride's dress; Gremio is horrified at a similar 'taking up' of a dress at 4.3.156–8. Hibbard mentions the Elizabethan marriage custom during which, following the ceremony, 'the young men rushed forward to pull the ribbons off the bride's dress and to remove her garter ribbons'. On bridal customs and dress, see Hodgdon, 'Bride-ing'.

166–82 *F lines as prose. A possible explanation is that the lines had been cast off as prose and F didn't have room to reline them; theatrically, the slip from

verse (156–64) to prose might suggest Gremio's heightened excitement or lack of control (see also 2.1.75–82).

166 **for why** wherefore, for what purpose (*OED* why *adv.* (*n.*, *int.*) 8)

167 **cozen** cheat (*OED v.* 1)

170 **aboard** on board ship
   **carousing to** drinking toasts to and with; see 1.2.276n.

171 **muscadel** strong, sweet wine, traditional at weddings. Rann observes that the bowl was called the knitting, or nuptial cup.

172 **sops** pieces of cake soaked in wine, traditionally shared with wedding guests

174 **hungerly** sparsely (as if ill-fed)

175 **ask him sops** ask him for the sops

---

165 wench] vicar *Oxf*   rose up] *F2*; rose *F*; arose *Reed*   166–73] *Reed*; *prose F*   171 muscadel] *(Muscadell)*; muscatel *Oxf*   174–82] *Reed*; *F2 lines* beard, / aske, / tooke, / lips, / parting, / this, / me, / marryage, / play. /

And kissed her lips with such a clamorous smack
That at the parting all the church did echo.
And I seeing this came thence for very shame,
And after me, I know, the rout is coming.                    180
Such a mad marriage never was before.            *Music plays.*
Hark, hark, I hear the minstrels play.

*Enter* PETRUCCIO, KATHERINA, BIANCA, HORTENSIO
    [*as Licio*], BAPTISTA [, GRUMIO *and others*].

PETRUCCIO
    Gentlemen and friends, I thank you for your pains.
    I know you think to dine with me today
    And have prepared great store of wedding cheer,          185
    But so it is my haste doth call me hence
    And therefore here I mean to take my leave.
BAPTISTA
    Is't possible you will away tonight?
PETRUCCIO
    I must away today before night come.
    Make it no wonder: if you knew my business               190
    You would entreat me rather go than stay.
    And, honest company, I thank you all
    That have beheld me give away myself
    To this most patient, sweet and virtuous wife.
    Dine with my father, drink a health to me,               195
    For I must hence, and farewell to you all.
TRANIO
    Let us entreat you stay till after dinner.
PETRUCCIO    It may not be.
GREMIO    Let me entreat you.

---

180 **rout** crowd (of wedding-guests)
184 **think** expect
185 **cheer** food, drink, entertainment

186 **so it is** the situation is that
190 **Make . . . wonder** 'Do not think it
    unusual or extraordinary.'

181 SD] *Cam²; opp. 56 F*    182.2 *as Licio*] *Hosley (Litio)*    GRUMIO *and others*] *Capell subst. (Grumio and Train)*    199 SP] *F2 (Gre.); Gra. F*    you] you, sir *Hanmer*

PETRUCCIO     It cannot be.                                      200
KATHERINA     Let me entreat you.
PETRUCCIO
   I am content.
KATHERINA                    Are you content to stay?
PETRUCCIO
   I am content you shall entreat me stay –
   But yet not stay, entreat me how you can.
KATHERINA
   Now, if you love me, stay.
PETRUCCIO                         Grumio, my horse.             205
GRUMIO    Ay, sir, they be ready: the oats have eaten the
   horses.
KATHERINA
   Nay then –
   Do what thou canst, I will not go today,
   No, nor tomorrow – not till I please myself.         210
   The door is open, sir, there lies your way;
   You may be jogging whiles your boots are green:
   For me, I'll not be gone till I please myself.
   'Tis like you'll prove a jolly surly groom
   That take it on you at the first so roundly.          215
PETRUCCIO
   O Kate, content thee; prithee be not angry.

---

205–6 **horse . . . they** The plural *horse*
was in general use down to the 17th
century (*OED n.* 1b).

206–7 **oats . . . horses** deliberately
inverted nonsense talk; making sense
of it requires reversing subject and
object – i.e. the horses have eaten
the oats and thus are ready to travel.
Cam[1] suggests that *oats* may have been
pronounced 'aits' (a 16th-century
variant), thus producing assonance:
'the aits have aten the horses'.

211 proverbial: 'Here is the door and there
is your way' (Dent, D556)

212 proverbial: 'Be jogging while your
boots are green' (Dent, B536), said to
encourage an unwelcome guest to leave;
*green* = new, unmarked

214 **jolly** intensifier (ironic) for *surly* (*OED
adv.* 2b); equally possible is adjectival
usage, meaning self-confident, arrogant
(*OED a.* 6).

215 **roundly** bluntly, rudely

---

201 you] you stay *Steevens*     206–7] *one line Oxf*[1]     210 tomorrow – not] *(*tomorrow, not*)*; tomorrow,
nor *F4;* to-morrow *Cam*[1]

**KATHERINA**

    I will be angry; what hast thou to do?

    – Father, be quiet; he shall stay my leisure.

**GREMIO**

    Ay, marry, sir, now it begins to work.

**KATHERINA**

    Gentlemen, forward to the bridal dinner.           220

    I see a woman may be made a fool

    If she had not a spirit to resist.

**PETRUCCIO**

    They shall go forward, Kate, at thy command.

    – Obey the bride, you that attend on her.

    Go to the feast, revel and domineer,           225

    Carouse full measure to her maidenhead,

    Be mad and merry, or go hang yourselves;

    But for my bonny Kate, she must with me.

    – Nay, look not big, nor stamp, nor stare, nor fret,

    I will be master of what is mine own.          230

    She is my goods, my chattels; she is my house,

    My household-stuff, my field, my barn,

217 **what . . . do?** 'what has it to do with you?'; proverbial (Dent, DD14): 'What right have you to interfere?'

218 **stay my leisure** 'wait until I am ready'

219 **marry** originally the name of the Virgin Mary, used as a mild oath; Ard² notes that it eventually came to mean 'indeed, to be sure', and comments: 'As Gremio uses the word here it is subtly ironic'.

    **work** seethe, rage, a metaphor from liquor fermenting or the sea becoming stormy (*OED v.* 32, 34)

225 **domineer** revel, feast riotously (*OED v.* 2)

227 proverbial: 'Farewell and be hanged' (Dent, H130.1)

228 **for** as for

229 Petruccio combines three proverbs:

'To look (talk) big' (Dent, BB10), 'to stamp and stare' (Dent, SS19) and 'to fret and fume' (Dent, F672.1). The line makes equally good sense whether spoken to Katherina, to the assembled guests or even to all of them.

231–3 Petruccio warns off anyone who would intervene to defend Katherina, since by marriage law she now belongs to him. Petruccio's identification of her as his property also echoes the language of the tenth commandment: 'Thou shalt not couet thy neyghbours house, neyther shalt thou couet thy neighbours wife, nor his man seruant, nor his mayde, nor his oxe, nor his asse, nor any thing that is thy neyghbours' (Exodus, 20.17).

232 **household-stuff** collectively, household goods, contents (*OED*)

232 barn] barn, my stable *Capell;* barn, my grange *(W.S. Walker)*

My horse, my ox, my ass, my anything,
And here she stands. Touch her whoever dare,
I'll bring mine action on the proudest he                      235
That stops my way in Padua. – Grumio,
Draw forth thy weapon, we are beset with thieves;
Rescue thy mistress, if thou be a man.
– Fear not, sweet wench, they shall not touch thee,
    Kate;
I'll buckler thee against a million.                           240

*Exeunt Petruccio, Katherina [and Grumio].*

BAPTISTA
Nay, let them go – a couple of quiet ones.

GREMIO
Went they not quickly, I should die with laughing.

TRANIO
Of all mad matches never was the like.

LUCENTIO
Mistress, what's your opinion of your sister?

BIANCA
That being mad herself, she's madly mated.                     245

GREMIO
I warrant him, Petruccio is Kated.

---

235–40 This passage begins with legal references ('bring mine action on' = bring a lawsuit against, though, given 237, the *action* threatened could also be physical) that grow out of 231–3 and its preoccupation with Katherina as property; this then leads to branding those who would part a husband from the wife he 'owns' as *thieves* (237) from whom she must be defended.

235 **he** common usage for 'man' (Abbott, 224)

240 **buckler** shield, defend

242 **Went they not** if they had not left
**die with laughing** proverbial (Dent, L94.1)

246 **Kated** afflicted with 'the Kate', as if with a disease. Ard[2] compares to Beatrice's 'God help the noble Claudio! If he have caught the Benedick' (*MA* 1.1.83–4). 'Catching the Benedick' is close but not strictly analogous; 'it out-Herods Herod' (*Ham* 3.2.13–14) offers an equally suggestive parallel. An echo of '[check]mated' seems even more pointed (JA).

240 SD *and Grumio*] Capell *subst.*; *Exeunt P. Ka.* F

BAPTISTA

> Neighbours and friends, though bride and bridegroom wants
>
> For to supply the places at the table,
>
> You know there wants no junkets at the feast.
>
> Lucentio, you shall supply the bridegroom's place,                250
>
> And let Bianca take her sister's room.

TRANIO

> Shall sweet Bianca practise how to bride it?

BAPTISTA

> She shall, Lucentio. Come gentlemen, let's go.          *Exeunt.*

**[4.1]**                          *Enter* GRUMIO.

GRUMIO     Fie, fie on all tired jades, on all mad masters, and
all foul ways! Was ever man so beaten? Was ever man
so rayed? Was ever man so weary? I am sent before to
make a fire, and they are coming after to warm them.
Now were not I a little pot and soon hot, my very lips        5
might freeze to my teeth, my tongue to the roof of my
mouth, my heart in my belly, ere I should come by a

---

247 **wants** are lacking; singular verb with plural subject (Abbott, 336)
249 **junkets** sweetmeats, delicacies (*OED* n. 3)
251 **room** place at the table
252 **bride it** play the bride. Cf. 'queen it', *WT* 4.4.451. Here, Bianca plays bride with a 'play groom'; later, Katherina upstages Bianca at her wedding feast (5.2).
4.1 Pope was the first editor to locate this action in '*Petruchio's Country House*', a setting that echoes other Shakespearean comedies, which typically move from city or court to country or forest, where transformations often occur. Since Petruccio is a landed gentleman, this 'country house' is a manor house,

reminiscent of the Lord's house in Ind.1 and 2. The location has an analogue in Goldsmith's *She Stoops to Conquer* (1773), where a scheme of imposture and dislocation also occurs and where Hardcastle's attempts to instruct his servants in 'table exercise' echo Petruccio's dialogue with his servants (Harris, 162–4).
1 **jades** worn-out horses
3 **rayed** dirtied, bespattered (with mud); see 3.2.52n.
5 **little . . . hot** proverbial: 'A little pot is soon hot' (Dent, P497), referring to a small person who angers quickly
6–7 **my tongue . . . mouth** Oxf[1] notes Psalms, 137.6: 'let my tongue cleaue to the roofe of my mouth'.

4.1] *Pope*   3 rayed] *(raide)*; wray'd *Capell*

fire to thaw me; but I with blowing the fire shall warm
myself, for considering the weather, a taller man than I
will take cold. Holla, ho, Curtis!                                    10

*Enter* CURTIS.

CURTIS    Who is that calls so coldly?

GRUMIO    A piece of ice. If thou doubt it, thou mayst slide
from my shoulder to my heel with no greater a run but
my head and my neck. A fire, good Curtis.

CURTIS    Is my master and his wife coming, Grumio?          15

GRUMIO    O ay, Curtis, ay – and therefore fire, fire, cast on
no water.

CURTIS    Is she so hot a shrew as she's reported?

GRUMIO    She was, good Curtis, before this frost; but thou
knowst winter tames man, woman and beast, for it hath        20
tamed my old master, and my new mistress, and myself,
fellow Curtis.

CURTIS    Away, you three-inch fool, I am no beast.

GRUMIO    Am I but three inches? Why, thy horn is a foot,

---

8  **blowing the fire** proverbial: 'Let
them that be acold blow at the Coal'
(Tilley, C460)

9  **taller** stronger, more capable; also
referring to the small stature of the
actor playing Grumio, as at 5 and 23–5

10  **Holla, ho** a hunting call, to excite
attention

11  **is** is it
**so coldly** numbed with cold; in an
unfriendly manner

13  **run** running start

15  **Is** For the singular verb, see 3.2.150
and n.

16–17  **fire . . . water** Grumio misquotes
a familiar catch, 'Scotland's burning,
/ See yonder! See yonder! / Fire,
fire! Fire, fire! / Cast on water! Cast
on water!'; it occurs *c*. 1580 in a MS
in King's College, Cambridge, which

also contains 'Jack boy, how boy, news'
(Ard[2]); see 36n.

18  **hot** passionate, intemperate

20  **winter . . . beast** proverbial:
'Winter and wedlock tame both man
and beast' (Dent, A64). Grumio
omits 'wedlock' and adds *woman*;
*man . . . woman . . . beast* leads to
*master . . . mistress . . . myself* which,
by including *fellow Curtis*, prompts
Curtis's response.

23–5  In one scenario, Curtis begins with
a jibe at Grumio's height (*three-inch
fool*), which Grumio then chooses
to interpret as a phallic slur on his
own genital endowment (24–5); *horn*
= cuckold's horn, penis. Earlier
editors attempt to avoid indecency:
Warburton glosses *three-inch fool* as
'i.e. with a scull three inches thick, a

---

11 is that] is that's *Q;* is it that *F2*    16 ay – ] *(*I,*)*    21 myself] thyself *Hanmer (Warburton)*    23 SP]
*Q; Gru. F*    three-inch] *(*three inch*)*    24 thy] my *Theobald*

and so long am I at the least. But wilt thou make a fire,          25
or shall I complain on thee to our mistress, whose hand
– she being now at hand – thou shalt soon feel, to thy
cold comfort, for being slow in thy hot office?

CURTIS     I prithee, good Grumio, tell me, how goes the
world?                                                            30

GRUMIO     A cold world, Curtis, in every office but thine –
and therefore fire. Do thy duty, and have thy duty, for
my master and mistress are almost frozen to death.

CURTIS     There's fire ready, and therefore, good Grumio,
the news.                                                         35

GRUMIO     Why, 'Jack boy, ho boy!' and as much news as
wilt thou.

CURTIS     Come, you are so full of cony-catching.

GRUMIO     Why, therefore, fire, for I have caught extreme
cold. Where's the cook, is supper ready, the house              40
trimmed,   rushes   strewed,   cobwebs   swept,   the

phrase taken from the thicker sort of
planks'.
28 **cold comfort** satisfaction that is far
from encouraging; proverbial – Dent
(C542) cites Golding (1571), *Psalms*,
10.14: 'We receive but cold comfort
of whatsoever the scripture speaketh
concerning Gods power and justice'
(Ard²). Cf. *KJ* 5.7.40–2, where a dying
King John, burning hot from poison,
entreats the north wind to 'kiss my
parched lips / And comfort me with
cold. I do not ask you much, / I beg
cold comfort'.
  **hot office** literal: the task of making a
  fire
29–30 **how . . . world** proverbial (Dent,
W884.1)
32 **Do . . . ²duty** Grumio changes the
saying, 'Do thy duty and take thy due';
*duty* can also mean 'due' (*OED* 2), i.e.
reward.

36 **'Jack . . . boy!'** Grumio's reference
to a catch suggests that there is no
news, or none that he is yet ready
to divulge (Oxf¹); see 16–17n. The
words and music of the catch appear
in Ravenscroft's *Pammelia*. *Music's
Miscellany* (1609), the first printed book
of English catches (Ard²).
37 F2's 'thou wilt' offers a playable
alternative.
38 **cony-catching** literally, rabbit-
hunting; more generally, swindling or
thievery, as in Robert Greene's popular
*Defence of Cony-Catching* (1593); also a
pun on 'catch': Grumio has just quoted
two catches, and at 39 turns 'catch' to
*caught*.
41 **trimmed** put in order, made trim
(*OED* v. 2)
  **rushes strewed** Fresh rushes were
  strewed on floors in preparation for a
  ceremony or occasion.

37 wilt thou] thou wilt *F2*     38 cony-catching] *(conicatching)*

servingmen in their new fustian, their white stockings,
and every officer his wedding garment on? Be the Jacks
fair within, the Jills fair without, the carpets laid, and
everything in order?                                                    45

CURTIS    All ready, and therefore, I pray thee, news.

GRUMIO    First, know my horse is tired, my master and
mistress fallen out.

CURTIS    How?

GRUMIO    Out of their saddles into the dirt, and thereby    50
hangs a tale.

CURTIS    Let's ha't, good Grumio.

GRUMIO    Lend thine ear.

CURTIS    Here.

GRUMIO [*Cuffs him.*]    There.                                         55

CURTIS    This 'tis to feel a tale, not to hear a tale.

GRUMIO    And therefore 'tis called a sensible tale; and this
cuff was but to knock at your ear and beseech listening.
Now I begin: *Inprimis*, we came down a foul hill, my
master riding behind my mistress —                                      60

CURTIS    Both of one horse?

GRUMIO    What's that to thee?

---

42 **fustian** coarse, cheap cotton and linen
  cloth, appropriate for servants' clothes
  **white stockings** worn for special
  occasions
43 **officer** servant with assigned
  responsibilities
43–4 **Jacks . . . Jills** male and female
  servants. *Jacks* were leather containers
  for liquor. *Jills* ('gills') were measures
  containing half a pint (about a quarter
  of a litre) or less, often made of metal,
  which would need polishing to make
  them *fair without*.
44 **carpets** used as table-coverings (*OED*
  *n.* 1a) rather than floor-coverings
48 **fallen out** interpreted literally at 50,

but also = at odds, fighting
50–1 **thereby . . . tale** proverbial (Dent,
  T48)
52 **ha't** have it
53–4 **Lend . . . Here** proverbial: 'Lend
  me your ears' (Dent, E18). Grumio
  repeats the play on 'here'/'ear' at 1.2.5–
  17, turning Petruccio's joke on him
  towards Curtis.
57 **sensible** making sense; capable of
  being felt (like a knock on the ear)
58 **beseech listening** beg (you to)
  listen
59 *Inprimis* first (Latin legal jargon); also
  at 4.3.133
61 **of** on (Abbott, 175)

42 their white] *F3;* the white *F*    46 news] what newes *F2*    55 SD] *Oxf¹ (Cuffing him.): Strikes him.
/ Rowe; He boxes Curtis's ear. Cam¹*    56 'tis] is *Rowe*    57 'tis] is *Rowe*    59 Inprimis] *(*Inprimis*):
Imprimis *F4*

CURTIS   Why, a horse.

GRUMIO   Tell thou the tale. But hadst thou not crossed
me, thou shouldst have heard how her horse fell, and     65
she under her horse; thou shouldst have heard in how
miry a place, how she was bemoiled, how he left her
with the horse upon her, how he beat me because her
horse stumbled, how she waded through the dirt to
pluck him off me, how he swore, how she prayed that     70
never prayed before, how I cried, how the horses ran
away, how her bridle was burst, how I lost my crupper
– with many things of worthy memory which now shall
die in oblivion, and thou return unexperienced to thy
grave.     75

CURTIS   By this reckoning he is more shrew than she.

GRUMIO   Ay, and that thou and the proudest of you all
shall find when he comes home. But what talk I of this?
Call forth Nathaniel, Joseph, Nicholas, Philip, Walter,

---

64–75 The post-wedding journey described here features prominently in folklore taming stories.

64 **crossed** thwarted, interrupted

67 **bemoiled** mud-spattered; the earliest occurrence noted in *OED*, and the only one in Shakespeare

70–1 **she . . . before** The phrase occurs, though in a different context, in *The Chronicle History of King Leir* (1605) where Leir, Cordilla and the King of Gallia kneel to ask for forgiveness; the moment ends comically as Lord Mumford also kneels – 'Let me pray to, that never pray'd before' – asking for sexual gratification (Bullough, 7.278–83).

72 **burst** broken
**crupper** leather saddle-strap on a horse (see 3.2.59n.)

76 **shrew** *OED* shrew *n.*[2] lists 'a wicked, evil-disposed or malignant man; a mischievous or vexatious person; a rascal, villain' (1a); 'the Devil' (1b); 'a

thing of evil nature or influence' (2); 'a person, *esp.* (now only) a woman given to railing or scolding or other perverse or malignant behaviour; freq. a scolding or turbulent wife' (3a). Although Katherina has been called *shrewd* (at 1.1.179, 1.2.59, 1.2.89) and *froward* (at 1.1.69, 1.2.89, 2.1.296), this is the first time she is called *shrew*.

77 **proudest . . . all** proverbial (Dent, P614.1)

78 **what** why (Abbott, 253)

79–80 **Nathaniel . . . rest** '*Nat.*', '*Phil.*', '*Ios.*' and '*Nick.*' appear in F's SPs at 95–9; including Grumio, Curtis, Gabriel, Peter, Adam, Rafe and Gregory (119–22), Petruccio has 13 servants – a large number, even if roles are doubled. Mahood suggests that a contrast with Baptista's household is more striking if the same players appear in both (46–8). A 'sugarsop' = slices of white bread, sweetened, spiced and steeped in wine; see 3.2.172n.

76 reckoning] *(reckning)*

Sugarsop and the rest. Let their heads be sleekly     80
combed, their blue coats brushed, and their garters of
an indifferent knit; let them curtsy with their left legs,
and not presume to touch a hair of my master's horse-
tail till they kiss their hands. Are they all ready?

CURTIS   They are.     85

GRUMIO   Call them forth.

CURTIS   Do you hear, ho? You must meet my master to
countenance my mistress.

GRUMIO   Why, she hath a face of her own.

CURTIS   Who knows not that?     90

GRUMIO   Thou, it seems, that calls for company to countenance her.

CURTIS   I call them forth to credit her.

*Enter four or five* Servants.

GRUMIO   Why, she comes to borrow nothing of them.

NATHANIEL   Welcome home, Grumio.     95

PHILIP   How now, Grumio.

JOSEPH   What, Grumio.

NICHOLAS   Fellow Grumio.

NATHANIEL   How now, old lad.

GRUMIO   Welcome you; how now you; what you; fellow     100

---

80 **sleekly** smoothly

81 **blue coats** usual colour for servants' liveries (see 1.1.206n. on *coloured*)

82 **indifferent** Several meanings are possible: (1) plain, moderate; (2) uniform, not different; (3) immaterial (it doesn't matter what kind of knit).
**curtsy . . . legs** gesture of deference used by men and women; to curtsy with the right leg implied defiance.

84 **kiss their hands** Kissing one's own hands indicated respect.

88 **countenance** pay your respects to; Grumio takes *countenance* as *face* (89), wilfully and arbitrarily turning verb to noun.

93 **credit** do credit to (*OED v.* 5), which Grumio (94) understands as provide credit for (*OED v.* 3a)

93.1 **four or five** See 79–80n. Although only four speak, there would be distinct advantages to recruiting available players to heighten the busy-ness (and business) of the scene.

80 sleekly] *Rowe²*; slickely *F*   91 calls] call'st *Rowe*   93.1] *after 94 Capell*   98 SP] *(Nick.)*

you; and thus much for greeting. Now, my spruce companions, is all ready, and all things neat?

NATHANIEL    All things is ready. How near is our master?

GRUMIO    E'en at hand, alighted by this; and therefore be
not – Cock's passion, silence, I hear my master.                    105

*Enter* PETRUCCIO *and* KATHERINA.

PETRUCCIO

Where be these knaves? What, no man at door
To hold my stirrup nor to take my horse?
Where is Nathaniel, Gregory, Philip?

ALL SERVANTS    Here, here sir, here sir.

PETRUCCIO    'Here sir, here sir, here sir, here sir'!                    110
You logger-headed and unpolished grooms.
What, no attendance? No regard? No duty?
Where is the foolish knave I sent before?

GRUMIO

Here sir, as foolish as I was before.

PETRUCCIO

You peasant swain, you whoreson malthorse drudge,                    115
Did I not bid thee meet me in the park
And bring along these rascal knaves with thee?

GRUMIO

Nathaniel's coat, sir, was not fully made,

---

103 **All . . . ready** another instance of a
plural subject taking a singular verb
(Abbott, 333). Nathaniel's answer
echoes the syntax of Grumio's
question.
105 **Cock's passion** God's passion; a
common euphemistic oath
111 **logger-headed** blockheaded, stupid
(*OED a.* 1)
115 **peasant swain** rustic; male servant.
This is the first in a string of abusive

terms.
**whoreson** wretched, vile (literally, son
of a whore); using noun as abusive
intensifier
**malthorse drudge** heavy horse used
to power a mill for grinding malt
118–24 Grumio, usually a prose or
doggerel speaker, shifts into blank
verse, his excuses for the servants'
unreadiness performed, perhaps, for
Petruccio's benefit.

104 SP] *F3 (Gru.)*; *Gre. F*    105.1 KATHERINA] *Rowe*; *Kate. F*

And Gabriel's pumps were all unpinked i'th' heel;
There was no link to colour Peter's hat,                    120
And Walter's dagger was not come from sheathing;
There were none fine but Adam, Rafe and Gregory,
The rest were ragged, old and beggarly.
Yet, as they are, here are they come to meet you.           124

PETRUCCIO

Go, rascals, go, and fetch my supper in.     *Exeunt Servants.*
   [*Sings.*]     Where is the life that late I led?
   Where are those – ?
Sit down, Kate, and welcome. Soud, soud, soud, soud.

*Enter* Servants *with supper.*

Why, when, I say? – Nay, good sweet Kate, be merry.
– Off with my boots, you rogues, you villains: when?       130
   [*Sings.*]     It was the friar of orders grey,

---

119 **pumps** light shoes
   **all unpinked** not ornamented, i.e. not
   pierced with eyelet holes (*OED* pink
   *v.*[1] 3)
120 **link** blacking made from burnt torches
   of tow and pitch; used to restore old,
   worn hats
121 **sheathing** fitting with a scabbard
122 **fine** well-presented, elegant
126–7 first lines of a now-lost ballad;
   reinvented in Cole Porter's *Kiss
   Me, Kate* (1948), this is perhaps
   Shakespeare's most familiar legacy to
   the Broadway musical. Also quoted
   by Pistol (*2H4* 5.3.140), the original
   ballad turned on the newly married
   man's loss of freedom. Ard[2] notes that
   a song sung to this tune occurs in *A
   Gorgeous Gallery of Gallant Inventions*
   (1578); Oxf[1] conjectures a second line
   beginning 'Where are those pleasant
   days?' and suggests that Petruccio

'leaves [it] unfinished as he turns, in
pretended deference, to Kate'.
128 **Soud . . . soud** Cam[1] emends
to 'Food . . . food', citing the easy
confusion of *f* and long *s* in secretary
hand. Although this makes good
sense in the context, Hanmer's SD,
'*Humming*' (adopted by Ard[1] and Oxf[1]),
seems equally reasonable. *OED* records
*soud* as a variant spelling of 'sold' (*v.*[1],
*v.*[2]) and as a Scottish variant of 'should'.
129, 130 **when** literal: Petruccio is
sarcastically asking the servants
whether they are finally about to serve
them with food.
131–2 fragment of a ballad, apparently
one of many bawdy variations on the
popular theme of the Friar seducing the
Nun (Oxf[1]); *friar grey* refers to a friar
of the Franciscan order. Oxf[1] notes that
'in the full form of the carol, the Friar's
seducing of the nun under the pretence

---

119 Gabriel's] *F2 (Gabriels); Gabrels F*     122 Rafe] Ralph *Oxf*[1]     126 SD] *Theobald (Singing.)*     126–8
Where . . . soud.] *Theobald; F lines* led? / Kate, / soud. / ; *127 only as song Capell*     127 those] those
villains *Capell*     128 Soud . . . soud.] Food . . . food! *Cam*[1]*; (Humming)* Soud . . . soud. *Hanmer*
131–2] *F italicizes*     131 SD] *Rowe*

As he forth walked on his way –
Out, you rogue, you pluck my foot awry.
Take that, and mend the plucking off the other.
– Be merry, Kate. – Some water here. What ho!          135

*Enter one with water.*

Where's my spaniel Troilus? Sirrah, get you hence
And bid my cousin Ferdinand come hither –
One, Kate, that you must kiss and be acquainted with.
– Where are my slippers? Shall I have some water?
Come, Kate, and wash, and welcome heartily.          140
– You whoreson villain, will you let it fall?

KATHERINA
Patience, I pray you, 'twas a fault unwilling.

of teaching her the gamut, the singing
of Latin hymns, and other devotional
exercises' parallels the wooing of
Bianca by Hortensio and Lucentio in
the music and Latin 'lessons' of 3.1.
See also Croft.
132  **walked** walkèd
133–56 Most modern editions, following
Rowe, introduce SDs at 134 ('*Strikes
him*'), 141 ('*Strikes Servant*') and 154
('*He throws the food and dishes at them*');
performances often incorporate such
stage business, implied by the language.
Yet the scene has also been played
without some or all of the traditional
physical action, an option that suggests
Petruccio's strategy is a performance
(Cohen, 270–3).
133  **you pluck . . . awry** 'you are twisting
my foot the wrong way (in pulling off
the boot)'
134  **Take that** perhaps a blow or a kick;
perhaps 'take that boot (off)'
**mend** improve; i.e. 'take better care
with the other boot'
135  **Some water here** Hand-washing
before meals was done at the table.
135.1  Ard[1] postpones this SD until

after Petruccio calls for water again
(139). Ard[2] argues that the service in
Petruccio's household is prompt; it is
Petruccio himself who refuses to accept
it as satisfactory.
136  **spaniel Troilus** The dog's name
ironically invokes the faithful, tragic
lover of medieval Troy legends. A
real dog sometimes appears on stage;
more often, either *spaniel Troilus* is
heard barking offstage or servants call
and whistle for him (Schafer, 177).
At Shakespeare's Globe (Lloyd, 2003),
Sonia Ritter, playing Troilus, defended
the beef from Kate's attempt to
recover it; Kate also imitated the dog's
behaviour (Shand, 'Guying', 556–7).
137  **cousin Ferdinand** Like Mercutio's
brother    Valentine    (*RJ*  1.2.68),
Ferdinand is a marginal character who
never appears.
141  **it** presumably, the basin of water
142  In urging Petruccio to be patient,
Katherina evokes a virtue attributed to
Griselda, the pattern of a patient wife
and polar opposite of the scold or shrew
(Brown, 200–17).
**unwilling** unintentional

134 off] *Rowe;* of *F*    135.1] *after 139 Ard[1]*

PETRUCCIO

    A whoreson beetle-headed, flap-eared knave.

    Come, Kate, sit down, I know you have a stomach.

    Will you give thanks, sweet Kate, or else shall I?     145

    – What's this – mutton?

1 SERVANT    Ay.

PETRUCCIO    Who brought it?

PETER    I.

PETRUCCIO

    'Tis burnt, and so is all the meat.     150

    What dogs are these? Where is the rascal cook?

    How durst you villains bring it from the dresser

    And serve it thus to me that love it not?

    There, take it to you, trenchers, cups and all;

    You heedless jolt-heads and unmannered slaves.     155

    What, do you grumble? I'll be with you straight.

                  *[Exeunt Grumio and Servants.]*

KATHERINA

    I pray you, husband, be not so disquiet.

    The meat was well, if you were so contented.

PETRUCCIO

    I tell thee, Kate, 'twas burnt and dried away,

---

143 **beetle-headed** thick-headed (from 'beetle', a wooden mallet with a heavy head); proverbial: 'to have a beetle-head or to be beetle-headed' (Dent, BB5)
    **flap-eared** having pendulous, floppy ears (*OED* flap *n.* 10), like e.g. a spaniel (perhaps an echo of 136; JA)

144 **stomach** appetite; proud spirit or temper (as at 5.2.182)

145 **give thanks** say grace

150 **meat** food, nourishment

152 **dresser** either the serving-table or the person who prepared the meat

154 **trenchers** wood, metal or earthenware plates

155 **jolt-heads** blockheads, fools; cf. 'Fie on thee, jolt-head' (*TGV* 3.1.284).

156 **I'll . . . straight** 'I'll attend to you (to discipline you) immediately.'

156 SD F has no SD, but Petruccio's 'I'll be with you straight' and F's '*Enter Servants severally*' at 167 suggest an exit, including Grumio, which momentarily leaves Kate and Petruccio alone. Grumio might, however, remain to hear Petruccio's advice on avoiding choleric foods (160–4); he later rehearses and enforces these restrictions to Kate (4.3.19–30).

157 **disquiet** restless, disturbed; impatient

156 SD] *this edn*; *Exeunt Servants.* / *Dyce*

And I expressly am forbid to touch it;　　　　　　　160
For it engenders choler, planteth anger,
And better 'twere that both of us did fast,
Since, of ourselves, ourselves are choleric,
Than feed it with such over-roasted flesh.
Be patient, tomorrow't shall be mended,　　　　　165
And for this night we'll fast for company.
Come, I will bring thee to thy bridal chamber.　　　*Exeunt.*

*Enter* [GRUMIO *and*] Servants *severally.*

NATHANIEL　Peter, didst ever see the like?
PETER　He kills her in her own humour.

*Enter* CURTIS, *a Servant.*

GRUMIO　Where is he?　　　　　　　　　　　170
CURTIS　In her chamber,
　Making a sermon of continency to her;
　And rails, and swears, and rates, that she, poor soul,
　Knows not which way to stand, to look, to speak,
　And sits as one new risen from a dream.　　　　175
　Away, away, for he is coming hither.
　　　　　　　　　[*Exeunt Grumio and Servants.*]

---

161 **engenders choler** In Elizabethan humours theory, overcooked meat was thought to produce an excess of bile which, in turn, caused anger.

163 **of ourselves** in ourselves; by our makeup

166 **for company** together. Some Petruccios counter this promise by eating before or during the set speech when he returns at 177 (Schafer, 179–81).

167.1 *severally* one at a time and/or perhaps from several directions

169 i.e. he over-masters her, overtopping her anger and arbitrary bad temper. For 'kill' in the sense of suppress, see *OED v.* 4a.

172 **continency** self-control – in general, not just in sexual behaviour

173 **rates** chides, provokes (*OED v.*² 1)
　**that** so that

175 **one . . . dream** Kate's situation parallels that of Sly (Ind.2), whose 'wife', like Petruccio, advises sexual continency; if Sly remains onstage, the line gains additional resonance (Ard²).

169.1] *Cam²; after* he? *170 F*　171-6] *Pope; prose F*　176 SD] *Exeunt. / Pope*

*Enter* PETRUCCIO.

PETRUCCIO
Thus have I politicly begun my reign,
And 'tis my hope to end successfully.
My falcon now is sharp and passing empty,
And till she stoop she must not be full-gorged,                    180
For then she never looks upon her lure.
Another way I have to man my haggard,
To make her come and know her keeper's call:

177–200 At 2.1.167–79, Petruccio divulges his wooing strategy; here, his plan to *man* Kate (182) exactly parallels how a falconer 'mans' a hawk. Such strategies were a means not just of dominating a wild, rebellious creature (invariably identified as feminine) but also of distinguishing oneself from other men (Dolan, 305). Elaborately detailed instructions in early modern falconry manuals, such as *Latham's Falconry* (1614), advise letting the bird rest, hooding and unhooding her to 'drawe her loue vnto the hood and your selfe . . . all the while she is a feeding . . . [that] she may learne to know that when she heareth your voice, she shall bee fed'; '[H]old this order, vntill you shall finde her familiar, and her stomacke perfect; for it is that onely that guides and rules her, it is the curbe and bridle that holds and keepes her in subiection to the man, & it is the spurre that pricketh her forwarde to perform the duty she oweth to her keeper . . . and without that one only thing bee preserued and carefully kept ripe, perfect, sharpe, and truely edged, there is no subiection to be gained; nor no content to be receiued: but scornefull disobedience, and alltogether offensiuenesse' (Latham, 1.9–11). In Doran (2003), Petruccio sat before the crape-hung portrait of his father, who had posed with a falcon on

his wrist; acknowledging the genesis of his hawking metaphors, Petruccio saluted the portrait on the soliloquy's final line.

177 **politicly** prudently, diplomatically (*OED adv.* 2). Michael Siberry's Petruccio (Edwards, 1995) spoke this as 'po–lit–i–cal–ly'; so emending the word resonates with *reign* and also links to Kate's evocation of politics at 5.2.161–6.

179 **sharp** famished (*OED a.* 4f); *passing empty* intensifies the idea of extreme hunger.
   **passing** See Ind.1.66n.

180–1 proverbial: 'Gorged hawks do not esteem the lure' (Dent, H228.1)

180 **stoop** Latham defines stooping as 'when a Hawke being vpon her wings at the height of her pitch, bendeth violentlie downe to strike the fowle or an other pray'; or, if tame, flies straight to the lure, made of feathers and containing food.
   **full-gorged** completely fed (*OED* full *a.* 12b)

182 **man my haggard** tame my hawk. Latham describes the haggard falcon: 'such is the greatnesse of her spirit, she wil not admit of any society, vntill such time as nature worketh in her an inclination to put that in practise which all Hawkes are subiect vnto at the spring time' (1.5).

180 full-gorged] *(*full gorg'd*)*

251

That is, to watch her, as we watch these kites
That bate, and beat, and will not be obedient.          185
She ate no meat today, nor none shall eat;
Last night she slept not, nor tonight she shall not.
As with the meat, some undeserved fault
I'll find about the making of the bed,
And here I'll fling the pillow, there the bolster,          190
This way the coverlet, another way the sheets.
Ay, and amid this hurly I intend
That all is done in reverend care of her;
And in conclusion she shall watch all night,
And if she chance to nod I'll rail and brawl          195
And with the clamour keep her still awake.
This is a way to kill a wife with kindness,
And thus I'll curb her mad and headstrong humour.
He that knows better how to tame a shrew,          199
Now let him speak; 'tis charity to show.          *Exit.*

[4.2]     *Enter* TRANIO [*as Lucentio*] *and* HORTENSIO
[*as Licio*].

184  **watch her** keep her awake
     **kites** a general term for falcons (*OED*
     *n.* 1a); also, a possible pun on kite/Kate
     (JA)
185  **bate, and beat** flutter and flap the
     wings away from the lure
188  **undeserved** undeservèd
192  **hurly** commotion, strife (*OED* hurly[1])
     **intend** mean or propose; pretend
     (*OED v.* 22)
196  **still** all the time
197  **kill . . . kindness** proverbial: 'To kill
     with kindness' (Dent, K51) = spoil or
     ruin through mistaken care, indulgence;
     here, apparently ironic
199–200  **shrew . . . show** 'Shrew' was
     pronounced, as often spelled, 'shrow'
     (Kökeritz, 211); Elizabethans would
     have heard a true rhyme on the *o* sound,
     here and also in the play's final couplet.

200  **Now . . . speak** 'Therefore, if any
     man can show any just cause why they
     may not lawfully be joined together,
     let him now speak, or else hereafter
     forever hold his peace' (*BCP*, 291).
     Adopting the language of the marriage
     service anticipates Katherina's later
     allusions to the ceremony at 5.2.152–70.
     For an actor to address the audience
     directly in the middle of the play is
     unusual in Shakespeare; cf. Pandarus
     at *TC* 3.2.205–6; unlike Pandarus,
     Petruccio invites audience response. If
     Sly remains onstage, the line might be
     directed to him.
     **charity** public benevolence, Christian
     charity
4.2  F does not indicate act or scene
     division. Assuming that Hortensio's
     visit to Petruccio should precede

185 bate] *(baite):* bait *Rowe*     4.2] *Steevens*     0.1 *as Lucentio*] *Kittredge*     0.2 *as Licio*] *Kittredge (Litio)*

TRANIO

    Is't possible, friend Licio, that mistress Bianca
    Doth fancy any other but Lucentio?
    I tell you, sir, she bears me fair in hand.

HORTENSIO

    Sir, to satisfy you in what I have said,
    Stand by, and mark the manner of his teaching.    5

*Enter* BIANCA [*and* LUCENTIO *as Cambio*].

LUCENTIO

    Now, mistress, profit you in what you read?

BIANCA

    What master read you? First resolve me that.

LUCENTIO

    I read that I profess, *The Art to Love*.

BIANCA

    And may you prove, sir, master of your art.

his renunciation of Bianca, Pope transposed this scene with the next and began Act 5 here.

3 **bears . . . hand** is leading me on with (false) expectations; proverbial: 'to bear one in hand' (Dent, H94). The context suggests that Bianca is deceiving Tranio (as Lucentio); but the deception is double, for Tranio also is leading Hortensio on.

4–8 *F assigns 4–5 to Lucentio, 6 to Hortensio, 7 to Bianca and 8 to Hortensio, perhaps as a result of confusing '*Luc.*' (for Lucentio) with '*Lic.*' or '*Lit.*' (for Hortensio in disguise) in manuscript SPs. F2 sorts out the confusion as well as that caused by omitting Lucentio from the entry at 5. See Maurer, 247–50, and pp. 313–16.

4 **satisfy you in** convince you of (*OED* v. 7)

6–10 **mistress . . . master . . . mistress**

a string of word-play, bandying the two terms. Another series, *Art . . . dear . . . heart* (8–10), playing on 'deer' and 'hart' and rhyming *Art/ heart*, intensifies Lucentio and Bianca's verbal coupling, which anticipates that of Beatrice and Benedick; screwball comedy offers a modern analogue for such flights of wit.

6, 7, 8 **read** study; teach; also (perhaps) interpret

7 'What is your text? First answer that for me.' Here, *master* = author. Following Theobald, most modern editions punctuate: 'What, master, read you?'

8 **that I profess** what I study; also, play on *profess* as in 'professor' of an academic discipline
    *The Art to Love* Ovid's *Ars Amatoria*, a poetic compendium, popular (and notorious) in Elizabeth's age, that represents love as a science

1+ Licio] *(Lisio) F2; Luc. F*    4 SP] *F2; Luc. F*    5.1 *and* LUCENTIO] *Rowe  as Cambio] Kittredge*    6, 8 SP] *F2; Hor. F*    7 What . . . First?] *this edn;* What master reade you first, *F;* What, master, read you? First *Theobald*    8 The . . . Love] *Rowe subst.;* the Art to loue *F*

LUCENTIO

    While you, sweet dear, prove mistress of my heart.      10

HORTENSIO

    Quick proceeders, marry! Now tell me, I pray,

    You that durst swear that your mistress Bianca

    Loved none in the world so well as Lucentio –

TRANIO

    O despiteful love, unconstant womankind!

    I tell thee, Licio, this is wonderful.      15

HORTENSIO

    Mistake no more, I am not Licio,

    Nor a musician, as I seem to be,

    But one that scorn to live in this disguise

    For such a one as leaves a gentleman

    And makes a god of such a cullion.      20

    Know, sir, that I am called Hortensio.

TRANIO

    Signor Hortensio, I have often heard

    Of your entire affection to Bianca;

    And since mine eyes are witness of her lightness

    I will with you, if you be so contented,      25

    Forswear Bianca and her love forever.

---

10 Following Capell, Oxf¹ adds a SD, '*They move away. Tranio and Hortensio come forward*', thus turning the Hortensio–Tranio exchange (11–43) into a lengthy aside.

11, 14 Modern editions often mark the first half of 11 and 14 as asides, a playable though not necessary option (see pp. 340–1).

11 **proceeders** Not only does the Bianca–Lucentio courtship 'proceed quickly', but Hortensio puns on 'to proceed Master of Arts', moving from a Bachelor of Arts to a Master of Arts degree.

14 **despiteful** cruel, malicious

15 **wonderful** amazing; to be wondered at

18 **scorn** singular verb form 'attached' to *I* at 17 or the regular plural, i.e. 'one |of those| that scorn'

20 **cullion** base fellow, rascal (literally, 'testicle')

21 Hortensio seems to be insisting on his status as a gentleman, yet this appears in a context where he (disguised as a servant) tells Tranio (a servant disguised as a gentleman) that Bianca is being wooed by a servant who is actually Lucentio, another gentleman in disguise.

23 **entire** sincere, unfeigned (*OED a.* 10)

24 **lightness** unfaithfulness

11–13 Quick . . . Lucentio| *prose F3*    13 none| *Rowe;* me *F*    18 scorn| scorns *Collier*

HORTENSIO

See how they kiss and court. Signor Lucentio,
Here is my hand, and here I firmly vow
Never to woo her more, but do forswear her
As one unworthy all the former favours          30
That I have fondly flattered her withal.

TRANIO

And here I take the like unfeigned oath
Never to marry with her though she would entreat.
Fie on her! See how beastly she doth court him.

HORTENSIO

Would all the world but he had quite forsworn.     35
For me, that I may surely keep mine oath,
I will be married to a wealthy widow
Ere three days pass, which hath as long loved me
As I have loved this proud disdainful haggard.
And so farewell, Signor Lucentio.                40
Kindness in women, not their beauteous looks,
Shall win my love; and so I take my leave,
In resolution as I swore before.        [*Exit.*]

TRANIO

Mistress Bianca, bless you with such grace
As 'longeth to a lover's blessed case.             45

---

31 **fondly** foolishly, madly
32 **unfeigned** unfeignèd
34 **beastly** like an animal
35 i.e. I wish all Bianca's suitors but he had sworn to leave her.
37 **a wealthy widow** The widow (who appears only in 5.2) not only provides Hortensio with a partner but also makes up the traditional number of three women in taming stories. After a husband's death, a woman could have a considerable inheritance, including the jointure that came from her family and whatever lands and wealth her

husband's will might have bestowed on her. On her remarriage, this would pass to her second husband – unless it had been entailed to her dead husband's estate or to the children of the marriage. Like Petruccio, Hortensio decides to *wive it wealthily* (1.2.74). **haggard** wild hawk; see 4.1.182 and n.
43 Following Capell, Oxf[1] adds a SD, '*Lucentio and Bianca come forward again*'.
45 **'longeth to** belongs to, is appropriate to
**blessed** blessèd

31 her] *F3;* them *F*     35 forsworn] forsworn her *Rowe[2]*     43 SD] *Rowe*

Nay, I have ta'en you napping, gentle love,
And have forsworn you with Hortensio.

BIANCA

Tranio, you jest – but have you both forsworn me?

TRANIO

Mistress, we have.

LUCENTIO                    Then we are rid of Licio.

TRANIO

I'faith, he'll have a lusty widow now                          50
That shall be wooed and wedded in a day.

BIANCA    God give him joy.

TRANIO    Ay, and he'll tame her.

BIANCA    He says so, Tranio?

TRANIO

Faith, he is gone unto the taming school.                     55

BIANCA

The taming school? What, is there such a place?

TRANIO

Ay, mistress, and Petruccio is the master
That teacheth tricks eleven-and-twenty long
To tame a shrew and charm her chattering tongue.

---

46 **ta'en you napping** caught you unawares; proverbial: 'to take one napping' (Dent, N36–7)
   **gentle love** That Tranio has attempted to claim Bianca's love for himself is a playable option, though here his words are more probably ironic. See the exchange at 5.2.50–4 (Gilbert).

50 **lusty widow** Widows (especially as represented in drama and popular pamphlets) were linked with sexual appetite and thought apt for quick courtship and marriage. Thomas Becon (1560) advises remarriage to prevent unchaste behaviour, 'For how light, vain, trifling, unhonest, unhousewife-like, young widows have been in all ages and are also at this present day, experience doth

sufficiently declare' (365). However, *lusty* also meant 'healthy, strong, vigorous' (*OED a.* 5a).

52 **God . . . joy** proverbial: 'God give you joy' (Dent, JJ2), as at 2.1.323; the standard early modern formula for offering congratulations on a marriage

54 *Riverside adds a question mark; F has none; either option is playable.

55 How Tranio knows Hortensio's plans (never mentioned) may cause readers to wonder but does not stop the theatrical action.

58 **eleven-and-twenty long** just right; a reference to the card game Thirty-one (*Trente-et-un*), where the goal was to get a hand of 31 points

59 **charm . . . tongue** reduce her to silence; proverbial (Dent, CC9)

---

46 ta'en] (tane)    54 Tranio?] *Riv.; Tranio. F*

*Enter* BIONDELLO.

BIONDELLO
    O, master, master, I have watched so long                    60
    That I am dog-weary, but at last I spied
    An ancient angel coming down the hill
    Will serve the turn.

TRANIO                         What is he, Biondello?

BIONDELLO
    Master, a marcantant or a pedant,
    I know not what, but formal in apparel,                    65
    In gait and countenance surely like a father.

LUCENTIO    And what of him, Tranio?

TRANIO
    If he be credulous and trust my tale,
    I'll make him glad to seem Vincentio
    And give assurance to Baptista Minola                    70
    As if he were the right Vincentio.
    Take in your love, and then let me alone.

                              [*Exeunt Lucentio and Bianca.*]

61 **dog-weary** tired out; proverbial: 'as
    weary as a dog' (Dent, D441)
62 **ancient angel** worthy old man;
    combines 'guardian angel' with the
    name of a gold coin
63 **serve the turn** suffice for our purposes;
    proverbial: 'to serve one's turn' (Dent,
    TT25)
64   **marcantant** merchant; the only use
    recorded in *OED*; perhaps stressed on
    second syllable. Oxf¹ argues that this
    is Biondello's version of 'mercatante'
    (some editors' emendation) 'on the false
    analogy (probably deliberately so) of
    "pedant"'.
    **pedant** schoolmaster, tutor
66 **countenance** appearance, demeanour
    (*OED n.* 1, 2)
72 ***Take in** F reads 'Take me' and gives
    the SP '*Par.*' Cam¹ conjectures that

'*Par.*' indicates a player's name written
in the prompt copy's margin opposite
the SD for the Merchant/Pedant entry,
and mistaken for a SP to the previous
line by compositors, proposing William
Parr, an actor with the Admiral's Men
in 1602 (see pp. 27–8).

72.1 ***Merchant** F reads '*Pedant*' here and
in all subsequent SDs and SPs, but
Hosley points out that, like his analogues
in Ariosto's *Suppositi* and Gascoigne's
*Supposes*, he is a merchant, carrying
'bills for money by exchange' (90) from
Florence, Italy's financial centre (289–
308); Cam² cites the itinerary at 75–7 as
further confirmation. Oxf¹ suggests that
schoolmasters also might carry bills of
exchange; 'Pedant' is a stock character-
type, and even Biondello seems uncertain
about this figure's identity.

61 I am] I'm *Pope*    64 marcantant] mercantant *Pope; mercatantè / Capell*    66 surely] surly *F2*    72 Take]
*F2; Par.* Take *F*    in] *Theobald;* me *F*    SD] *Rowe*    72 SD] *Cam² (Hosley)*    72.1+ Merchant] *Pedant F*

*Enter a* Merchant.

MERCHANT
God save you, sir.

TRANIO    And you, sir. You are welcome.
Travel you far on, or are you at the farthest?

MERCHANT
Sir, at the farthest for a week or two,      75
But then up farther, and as far as Rome,
And so to Tripoli, if God lend me life.

TRANIO
What countryman, I pray?

MERCHANT      Of Mantua.

TRANIO
Of Mantua, sir? Marry, God forbid!
And come to Padua, careless of your life?    80

MERCHANT
My life, sir? How, I pray? For that goes hard.

TRANIO
'Tis death for anyone in Mantua
To come to Padua. Know you not the cause?
Your ships are stayed at Venice, and the Duke,
For private quarrel 'twixt your Duke and him,   85
Hath published and proclaimed it openly.
'Tis marvel, but that you are but newly come,
You might have heard it else proclaimed about.

---

74 **far** F reads 'farre', an obsolete comparative for 'farther'; found in that sense in *WT* 4.4.433: 'Farre than Deucalion off'. Throughout *TS*, 'far' is regularly spelled 'farre' by different compositors.

81 **goes hard** is serious

82–3 **'Tis . . . Padua** This piece of plot from Gascoigne's *Supposes* (2.1) is also used by Shakespeare in *CE* 1.1; here,

it is a joke; there, it is a serious life or death matter.

84 **Your . . . stayed** ships sailing under the Mantuan flag; *stayed* = held

87 **but that . . . newly** Some editors omit the second *but* as a careless repetition; Cam² suggests that both make sense if the first means 'except that' and the second is an intensive meaning 'only'.

---

73+ SP1] *Cam²* (*Hosley*); *Ped. F* (*throughout*)  74 far] (farre) *Rowe*; farrer *Hibbard*  87 you . . . newly] you're but newly *Pope*; you are newly *Collier*

MERCHANT

    Alas, sir, it is worse for me than so,

    For I have bills for money by exchange         90

    From Florence, and must here deliver them.

TRANIO

    Well, sir, to do you courtesy,

    This will I do, and this I will advise you –

    First tell me, have you ever been at Pisa?

MERCHANT

    Ay, sir, in Pisa have I often been,         95

    Pisa renowned for grave citizens.

TRANIO

    Among them know you one Vincentio?

MERCHANT

    I know him not, but I have heard of him,

    A merchant of incomparable wealth.

TRANIO

    He is my father, sir, and sooth to say,         100

    In countenance somewhat doth resemble you.

BIONDELLO    As much as an apple doth an oyster, and all

    one.

TRANIO

    To save your life in this extremity,

    This favour will I do you for his sake –        105

    And think it not the worst of all your fortunes

    That you are like to Sir Vincentio.

    His name and credit shall you undertake,

---

90 **bills . . . exchange** promissory notes to exchange for cash

92, 113 **courtesy** a favour

96 repeats 1.1.10; see n.
   **renowned** renownèd

100 **sooth** truth

102 **apple . . . oyster** proverbial: 'As like as an apple is to an oyster' (Dent, A291).

Most editions adopt Rowe's '*aside*', but the line, characteristic of Biondello's tendency to interrupt or say what he thinks, might be heard by Tranio, though not, perhaps, by the Merchant.

102–3 **all one** no matter

108 **credit** standing, reputation (*OED n.* 5)
   **undertake** assume, take on (*OED v.* 4)

102 and] (&); but *Hosley*

And in my house you shall be friendly lodged.
Look that you take upon you as you should –　　　　110
You understand me, sir? So shall you stay
Till you have done your business in the city.
If this be courtesy, sir, accept of it.

MERCHANT

O sir, I do, and will repute you ever
The patron of my life and liberty.　　　　115

TRANIO

Then go with me to make the matter good.
This, by the way, I let you understand:
My father is here looked for every day
To pass assurance of a dower in marriage
'Twixt me and one Baptista's daughter here.　　　　120
In all these circumstances I'll instruct you.
Go with me to clothe you as becomes you.　　　　*Exeunt.*

[4.3]　　　　　　*Enter* KATHERINA *and* GRUMIO.

GRUMIO

No, no, forsooth, I dare not for my life.

KATHERINA

The more my wrong, the more his spite appears.

---

110 **take upon you** play your role
114 **repute** think of, value (*OED v.* 4)
116 **make . . . good** carry out the plan
117 **by the way** as we go along
118 **looked for** expected, as in the modern usage, but also playing on looking for/ expecting duplicate fathers
119 **pass . . . dower** make a formal legal agreement of marriage; *dower* can be monosyllabic.
121 **circumstances** details, particulars
122 F2 expands by printing 'Go with me sir' and some modern editions follow.
　　**to clothe . . . you** Presumably this

means to change into clothes more appropriate to his (and Vincentio's) status – a further instance of the play's obsession with exchanging clothes, with proprieties and improprieties of attire and with (theatrical) disguise; 4.4.0.2's SD makes the disguise more precise: he is *'dressed like Vincentio'*.
4.3 *F's 'Actus Quartus. Scena Prima.'* is the first division since *'Actus Tertia.'* at the beginning of 3.1; both mark literary not theatrical divisions.
1 **forsooth** in truth
2 **The . . . wrong** 'the more wrong that is done to me'

119 dower] *(dowre)*　　122 me to] me sir to *F2*　　4.3] *Actus Quartus. Scena Prima.*

What, did he marry me to famish me?
Beggars that come unto my father's door
Upon entreaty have a present alms;                                    5
If not, elsewhere they meet with charity.
But I, who never knew how to entreat,
Nor never needed that I should entreat,
Am starved for meat, giddy for lack of sleep,
With oaths kept waking and with brawling fed;                         10
And that which spites me more than all these wants,
He does it under name of perfect love,
As who should say, if I should sleep or eat
'Twere deadly sickness or else present death.
I prithee, go and get me some repast –                               15
I care not what, so it be wholesome food.

GRUMIO
What say you to a neat's foot?

KATHERINA
'Tis passing good; I prithee, let me have it.

GRUMIO
I fear it is too choleric a meat.
How say you to a fat tripe finely broiled?                           20

KATHERINA
I like it well; good Grumio, fetch it me.

GRUMIO
I cannot tell, I fear 'tis choleric.
What say you to a piece of beef and mustard?

---

5 'are given charity or assistance when they ask'
present immediate, as at 14
9 meat food of any kind (*OED n.* 1a)
11 spites irritates (*OED v.* 3)
13 As who should as if to
16 so it be as long as it is
17 neat's calf's or ox's; a *neat* was 'a bovine animal' (*OED n.* 1)
19 choleric causing bile, thus anger. Choler 'is hot and drie, wherein the

fire hath dominion' (Elyot, *Castle*, sig. C1ʳ).
23 beef and mustard 'in a cholerike stomake biefe is better dygested than a chykens legge, forasmoche as in a hotte stomacke, fyne meates be shortly aduste and corrupted' (Elyot, *Castle*, sig. D3ᵛ). Elyot also advised choleric persons to avoid garlic, onions, rocket, leeks, mustard, pepper, honey, wine and sweetmeats.

19 choleric] *(chollericke)*: phlegmaticke *F2*

KATHERINA

A dish that I do love to feed upon.

GRUMIO

Ay, but the mustard is too hot a little.                                    25

KATHERINA

Why then, the beef, and let the mustard rest.

GRUMIO

Nay then, I will not: you shall have the mustard

Or else you get no beef of Grumio.

KATHERINA

Then both, or one, or anything thou wilt.

GRUMIO

Why then, the mustard without the beef.                                    30

KATHERINA

Go, get thee gone, thou false deluding slave    *Beats him.*

That feed'st me with the very name of meat.

Sorrow on thee and all the pack of you

That triumph thus upon my misery.

Go, get thee gone, I say.                                                    35

*Enter* PETRUCCIO *and* HORTENSIO *with meat.*

PETRUCCIO

How fares my Kate? What, sweeting, all amort?

HORTENSIO     Mistress, what cheer?

KATHERINA     Faith, as cold as can be.

PETRUCCIO

Pluck up thy spirits, look cheerfully upon me.

---

26 **let . . . rest** do without the mustard
32 **very name** only the name (*OED a.* 9b)
35 F gives no exit for Grumio; he does not speak again until 120.
36 **sweeting** sweetheart, darling (*OED n.*[1] 1)
**amort** sick to death, dispirited, from French *à la mort* (*OED* alamort *pred.a.*

2); proverbial (Dent, AA6)
37 **what cheer?** how are you? Ard[2] notes that *cheer* meant 'face, expression, countenance' (*OED n.* 1, 2a) and suggests that Kate's reply at 38 understands *cheer* as 'provisions, viands, food' (*OED* 6a).
39 **Pluck . . . spirits** proverbial: 'Pluck up your heart' (Dent, H323)

Here, love, thou seest how diligent I am                              40
To dress thy meat myself and bring it thee.
I am sure, sweet Kate, this kindness merits thanks.
What, not a word? Nay then, thou lov'st it not,
And all my pains is sorted to no proof.
Here, take away this dish.                                           45
KATHERINA     I pray you, let it stand.
PETRUCCIO
The poorest service is repaid with thanks,
And so shall mine before you touch the meat.
KATHERINA     I thank you, sir.
HORTENSIO
Signor Petruccio, fie, you are to blame.                             50
Come, Mistress Kate, I'll bear you company.
PETRUCCIO [*to Hortensio*]
Eat it up all, Hortensio, if thou lovest me.
– Much good do it unto thy gentle heart.
Kate, eat apace; and now, my honey love,
Will we return unto thy father's house                               55
And revel it as bravely as the best,
With silken coats and caps, and golden rings,
With ruffs and cuffs, and farthingales and things,
With scarves and fans, and double change of bravery,
With amber bracelets, beads and all this knavery.                    60

---

41 **dress** prepare
44 'All my labour comes to nothing'; *pains* is treated as singular.
48 **mine before** Although grammar requires 'shall mine be', Shakespeare regularly omits the verb 'be'.
50 **to blame** F reads 'too blame' ('too blameworthy'), perfectly idiomatic in early modern English.
52 In Bogdanov (1978), Hortensio wolfed down an entire chicken in what seemed like three seconds.
53 proverbial: 'Much good do it your good heart' (Dent, MM23). Petruccio

might address either Katherina or Hortensio (Schafer, 192).
54 **apace** quickly
56 **bravely** splendidly (*OED adv.* 2)
58 **ruffs** starched linen or muslin neck ruffs; more generally, frills, ruffles
   **cuffs** bands, sometimes of lace, on sleeves
   **farthingales** wide hooped petticoats which made skirts stand out from the body
59 **double . . . bravery** more than one outfit of fine clothes
60 **knavery** tricks of dress (*OED* 2b)

50 to blame] *Q;* too blame *F*     52 SD] *Theobald*

What, hast thou dined? The tailor stays thy leisure,
To deck thy body with his ruffling treasure.

*Enter* Tailor.

Come, tailor, let us see these ornaments.
Lay forth the gown.

*Enter* Haberdasher.

What news with you, sir?

HABERDASHER
Here is the cap your worship did bespeak.                65
PETRUCCIO
Why, this was moulded on a porringer –
A velvet dish. Fie, fie, 'tis lewd and filthy.
Why, 'tis a cockle, or a walnut-shell,
A knack, a toy, a trick, a baby's cap.
Away with it; come, let me have a bigger.                70
KATHERINA
I'll have no bigger: this doth fit the time,
And gentlewomen wear such caps as these.

---

61 **stays thy leisure** awaits your
   convenience
62 **ruffling** ornate, elaborately ruffled
   (*OED ppl.a.*[1] 1, 'forming, or rising in,
   ruffles'); Ard[1] and Hibbard gloss as
   'embellishing, gay' (*OED* ruffle *v.*[2] 2).
62.1 **Tailor** see LR, 27n.
63 **ornaments** articles of dress
65 SP *F*'s '*Fel.*' probably refers to
   'Fellow'; Cam[1] implausibly suggests a
   reference to William Felle, mentioned
   in Henslowe's *Diary* for 1599 as William
   Bird's 'man'.
   **bespeak** order
66 **porringer** small basin or dish
67 **lewd and filthy** vulgar, worthless
   (*OED* lewd *a.* 3, 6); Hibbard glosses
   as 'Elizabethan equivalent of "cheap

and nasty"'. Petruccio's taunts about
the cap resonate in Jonson's *Every
Man in His Humour*: Kitely, fearful
of being cuckolded, remarks, 'Our
great heads, / . . . never were in safety,
/ Since our wives wore these little
caps . . . Mine shall no more / Wear
three-piled acorns, to make my horns
ache' (3.3.34–8). If Petruccio alludes
to the idea that the 'curtailed cap',
no longer covering the head, makes a
woman sexually available, that nuance
(like many others) has been lost.
68 **cockle** i.e. cockleshell (boat-shaped); a
   *cockle* is a small edible mollusc.
69 **knack . . . toy . . . trick** trinket . . .
   worthless toy . . . bauble, trifle
71 **doth . . . time** suits the current fashion

---

64.1] *Ard[1]; after* ornaments. *63 F*   65 SP] *Rowe (Hab.); Fel. F*

PETRUCCIO

> When you are gentle you shall have one too,
> And not till then.

HORTENSIO                    That will not be in haste.

KATHERINA

> Why, sir, I trust I may have leave to speak,                    75
> And speak I will. I am no child, no babe;
> Your betters have endured me say my mind,
> And if you cannot, best you stop your ears.
> My tongue will tell the anger of my heart,
> Or else my heart concealing it will break,                    80
> And, rather than it shall, I will be free
> Even to the uttermost, as I please, in words.

PETRUCCIO

> Why, thou sayst true – it is a paltry cap,
> A custard-coffin, a bauble, a silken pie;
> I love thee well in that thou lik'st it not.                    85

KATHERINA

> Love me or love me not, I like the cap,
> And it I will have, or I will have none.

PETRUCCIO

> Thy gown? Why, ay: come, tailor, let us see't.

                              [*Exit Haberdasher.*]

---

79–80 proverbial: 'Grief pent up will break the heart' (Dent, G449). Ard[2] identifies this as 'one of the great commonplaces of the age'; frequent in early modern drama (cf. *Mac* 4.3.209–10) and deriving from Seneca's *Hippolytus*, 2.3.607: '*Curae leves loquuntur, ingentes stupent*', translated by John Studely as 'Light cares haue wordes at will. But great doe make vs sore agast' (K1ᵛ) and appearing in Thomas Newton's *Seneca's Tragedies* (1581).

84 **custard-coffin** pastry crust in which a custard could be baked; perhaps with play on 'costard' (literally, 'apple' but slang for 'head')

88 **Thy gown** Ard[2] suggests that Petruccio 'deliberately mishears "have none" [87] as "my gown", though "none" was usually pronounced . . . "known" (Kökeritz, 121)'. Equally possible is that Petruccio, ignoring Katherina, addresses the Tailor.

88 SD *F cues no exit for the Haberdasher; although this is a convenient moment for his exit, there is potential comic mileage in leaving him onstage to observe his fellow-tradesman's treatment.

83 a paltry] *Q*; paltrie *F*    88 gown?] *Rowe*; gowne, *F*    SD] *after 87 Cam¹*

O mercy, God, what masking stuff is here?
What's this? A sleeve? 'Tis like a demi-cannon.                    90
What, up and down carved like an apple tart?
Here's snip, and nip, and cut, and slish and slash,
Like to a cithern in a barber's shop.
Why, what i'devil's name, tailor, call'st thou this?

HORTENSIO

I see she's like to have neither cap nor gown.                     95

TAILOR

You bid me make it orderly and well,
According to the fashion and the time.

PETRUCCIO

Marry, and did; but if you be remembered,
I did not bid you mar it to the time.
Go, hop me over every kennel home,                               100
For you shall hop without my custom, sir:

89 **masking stuff** material suitable for masques, noted for their extravagant, symbolic costumes, or for masquerades
90 **demi-cannon** literally, half-cannon, though still fairly large, with a six-and-a-half-inch (16.5 cm) bore
91 Petruccio compares the slashing on the sleeve (revealing another fabric layer beneath) to the slits in the top crust of an apple tart; this reference and those at 66 (*porringer*) and 84 (*custard-coffin*) align withholding clothes with withholding food, so central to the taming process.
93 **cithern** a type of lute with grotesque carvings (gargoyle-like heads or clowns) on the neck. Cithern-playing in barbershops was common; the tailor's elaborate pinking resembles the cithern's grotesqueries (Maguire, 'Petruccio', 120).
95 Most modern editions follow Theobald's '*aside*', a playable though not necessary option.
96 **orderly** as you prescribed

98 **Marry, and did** 'Indeed, I did'; 'Marry' ('by the Virgin Mary') was a common oath. On the subject's ellipsis, see Abbott, 400.
   **be remembered** recall; common in the period (*OED v.*[1] 6c), now archaic; comparable to the present-day expression, 'if I might remind you'.
99 **mar . . . time** ruin it by following 'the fashion and the time' (97); proverbial: 'to make or (and) mar' (Dent, M48). Philip Stubbes (1583) rails against changing fashions: 'when they haue all these goodly robes vppon them, women seeme to be the smallest part of themselues, not naturall women, but artificiall Women, not Women of flesh & blod, but rather puppits, or mawmets of rags & clowtes compact together' (1.75).
100 **hop . . . kennel** 'hop over every gutter'. For the dative *me*, see Abbott, 220. A *kennel* was an open drain in a street (*OED n.*[2]).
101 **custom** patronage

89 masking] masquing *Ard¹*  90 like a] *Q;* like *F*  93 cithern] *(Maguire);* Censor *F;* censer *Rowe²;*
scissor *Oxf*  94 i'] *(a')*  95 neither] nor *Oxf*

I'll none of it. Hence, make your best of it.

KATHERINA

    I never saw a better-fashioned gown,

    More quaint, more pleasing, nor more commendable.

    Belike you mean to make a puppet of me. 105

PETRUCCIO

    Why true, he means to make a puppet of thee.

TAILOR    She says your worship means to make a puppet
of her.

PETRUCCIO

    O monstrous arrogance. Thou liest, thou thread, thou
      thimble,

    Thou yard, three-quarters, half-yard, quarter, nail, 110

    Thou flea, thou nit, thou winter-cricket, thou!

    Braved in mine own house with a skein of thread?

    Away, thou rag, thou quantity, thou remnant,

    Or I shall so bemete thee with thy yard

102 **make . . . it** make the best use of it
you can

104 **quaint** skilfully made (*OED a.* 3b)

106 **puppet** The term catches up
several ideas: a stringed mechanism
whose movements are controlled by a
puppet-master, who pulls the strings;
a child's doll; a derogatory term, used
especially of women (*OED n.* 2 A;
1b; 3).

109–11 *F prints as four lines; however
arranged, Petruccio's railing at 109
strains metre.

109 **arrogance.** Most editions punctuate
with an exclamation mark.

110 **nail** one-sixteenth of a yard (two-
and-a-quarter inches or 5.7 cm), a
cloth measure (*OED n.* 8)

111 **nit** egg of a louse, gnat or small fly
(*OED n.*[1] 1)

    **winter-cricket** cricket that appears in
winter. Cam[1] reads the references to

small size as suggesting a boy player
or to the appearance of John Sincklo
(see Ind.1.81n.). Hibbard connects the
diminutive references to the phrase,
'Nine tailors make a man'.

112 **Braved** defied (*OED v.* 3). Oxf[1] notes
that one would expect to be *Braved* in
the sense of 'fitted out' or 'decked out'
by a tailor; the pun is explicit at 126–7.
    **with** by (Abbott, 193)

113 **rag . . . quantity . . . remnant** scrap
. . . fragment . . . leftover: all references
to cloth

114 **bemete . . . yard** literally, 'measure
you with your own yard-rule', punning
on 'beat' and 'mete out' (punishment);
*yard* is the 'mete-yard', a cloth-
measure used by tailors, perhaps
punning on 'penis', as (more plausibly)
at 151. 'Mete' and 'meat' were spelled
interchangeably in the early modern
period.

103 better-fashioned] (*better fashion'd*) 107–8] *Pope lines* means / her. / 109] *Capell; F lines*
arrogance: / thimble, / 110 three-quarters] (*three quarters*) half-yard] (*halfe yard*) 111 winter-
cricket] (*winter cricket*)

As thou shalt think on prating whilst thou liv'st.                115
I tell thee, I, that thou hast marred her gown.
TAILOR
    Your worship is deceived; the gown is made
    Just as my master had direction.
    Grumio gave order how it should be done.
GRUMIO    I gave him no order; I gave him the stuff.            120
TAILOR
    But how did you desire it should be made?
GRUMIO    Marry, sir, with needle and thread.
TAILOR
    But did you not request to have it cut?
GRUMIO    Thou hast faced many things.
TAILOR    I have.                                                125
GRUMIO    Face not me. Thou has braved many men; brave
    not me. I will neither be faced nor braved. I say unto
    thee, I bid thy master cut out the gown, but I did not bid
    him cut it to pieces. *Ergo*, thou liest.
TAILOR    Why, here is the note of the fashion to testify.       130
PETRUCCIO    Read it.
GRUMIO    The note lies in's throat if he say I said so.
TAILOR    '*Inprimis*, a loose-bodied gown.'
GRUMIO    Master, if ever I said 'loose-bodied gown', sew
    me in the skirts of it and beat me to death with a          135

---

115 'so that you will remember your idle
    talk for the rest of your life'
120 **stuff** material
124 **faced** trimmed, often with braid
    or velvet; **braved**; brazened out
    (*OED v.* 12; 2a; 3b). Grumio puns
    on *face* = 'confront impudently' at
    126–7.
126, 127 **braved** challenged, defied (*OED
    v.* 1)
129 *Ergo* therefore (Latin); logical term
130 **note ... fashion** written order for
    the style

132 **lies in's throat** lies utterly; proverbial
    (Dent, T268). Grumio's phrase can
    mean 'the note lies', 'the tailor's words
    are a lie', or both.
133 *Inprimis* first (Latin)
    **loose-bodied** loose-fitting; but
    Grumio puns (134) on 'loose body's
    gown', the kind of (loose) dress worn
    by a prostitute. An Italian spectator at
    Jonson's *The Vision of Delight* (1617)
    remarks, 'There are no folds, so that
    any deformity, however monstrous,
    remains hidden' (*Calendar*, 112).

133 *Inprimis*] *(*Inprimis*); Imprimis / Rowe*    loose-bodied] *(loose bodied)*

bottom of brown thread. I said 'a gown'.

PETRUCCIO    Proceed.

TAILOR    'With a small-compassed cape.'

GRUMIO    I confess the cape.

TAILOR    'With a trunk sleeve.'                                                     140

GRUMIO    I confess two sleeves.

TAILOR    'The sleeves curiously cut.'

PETRUCCIO    Ay, there's the villainy.

GRUMIO    Error i'th' bill, sir, error i'th' bill! I commanded
the sleeves should be cut out and sewed up again, and    145
that I'll prove upon thee though thy little finger be
armed in a thimble.

TAILOR    This is true that I say; an I had thee in place
where, thou shouldst know it.

GRUMIO    I am for thee straight. Take thou the bill, give me    150
thy mete-yard and spare not me.

136 **bottom** elongated wooden bobbin on which thread was wound (*OED n.* 15a); shaped like a phallus, the weaver's *bottom* (which also evokes 'backside') is sexually suggestive (Parker, *Margins*, 95). Cf. the sexual connotation to spinning flax on a distaff at *TGV* 3.1.307–8 and at *TN* 1.3.98–100: 'I hope to see a huswife take thee between her legs and spin it off'; at *TGV* 3.2.51–3, *bottom* figures in a metaphor for winding and rewinding love as a thread.

138 **small-compassed cape** a short cape; *compassed* = cut on the bias to form a circle (*OED* compass *n.*[1] 5). Speaking of excessive fashions, Stubbes writes: 'Some haue Capes reaching downe to the middest of their backs, faced with Veluet, or els with some fine wrought silk Taffatie, at the least, and fringed about very brauely' (1.74).

140 **trunk sleeve** large wide sleeve tapering from shoulder to wrist, held in place by wire, reed or whalebone; see *demi-cannon*, 90. Slashed, puffed, padded,

embroidered and bejewelled sleeves were high fashion in the late 16th century.

141 Ard[2] notes Hulme's suggestion that emphasizing *two* alludes to the proverbial 'The Tailor must cut three sleeves for every woman's gown' (Dent, T18).

142 **curiously** carefully, elaborately

144 **bill** the *note* or order mentioned at 130; a bill of indictment (*OED n.*[3] 4a)

146 **prove upon thee** prove by defeating you in combat; demonstrate against you

148–9 **an ... where** 'if I had you in a place where we could fight it out'; throughout, the Tailor–Grumio cross-talk slips between legal and trial-by-combat vocabularies.

150 **for thee straight** ready to fight you at once
**bill** the note at 130, 144; a kind of pike used by soldiers and watchmen (*OED n.*[1] 2; 3)

151 **mete-yard** tailor's measuring stick; F's 'meat-yard' makes a pun on 'penis' explicit (see 114n.), at least to modern ears.

138 small-compassed] *(small compast)* 148 an] *(and) Pope* 149 where, thou] *Q; where thou F* 151 mete-yard] *F2; meat-yard F; meet-yard Pope*

HORTENSIO    God-a-mercy, Grumio, then he shall have no
odds.

PETRUCCIO

Well sir, in brief, the gown is not for me.

GRUMIO    You are i'th' right, sir, 'tis for my mistress.        155

PETRUCCIO

Go, take it up unto thy master's use.

GRUMIO    Villain, not for thy life! Take up my mistress'
gown for thy master's use?

PETRUCCIO    Why sir, what's your conceit in that?

GRUMIO    O sir, the conceit is deeper than you think for.    160
'Take up my mistress' gown to his master's use'? O fie,
fie, fie!

PETRUCCIO [*aside to Hortensio*]

Hortensio, say thou wilt see the tailor paid.
– Go, take it hence; be gone, and say no more.

HORTENSIO

Tailor, I'll pay thee for thy gown tomorrow –                165
Take no unkindness of his hasty words.
Away, I say, commend me to thy master.            *Exit Tailor.*

---

152 **God-a-mercy** corruption of 'may
God have mercy'
152–3 **he ... odds** 'he will not have an
advantage', perhaps punning on 'odds
and ends' as leftover scraps of material,
which a tailor would have considered
his (*OED n.* 7)
156–8 **take it up ... master's use?**
Petruccio means 'let your master
make what use of it he can'; Grumio
understands *take ... up* as 'lift ... up',
i.e. preparing to 'use' Kate sexually.
158 **gown** The word's vulgar form,
'gownd', might be heard, as in *H5*
3.4.51, as a homophonic pun on 'count'

or 'cunt' (PP); the pronunciation is
closer than it seems to modern ears.
159 **conceit** meaning, innuendo; possible
(strained) pun on 'cunt'
160 **deeper** more serious or devious
(*deeper* into Kate?)
**think for** imagine, expect (*OED v.*[2]
12d)
161–2 **fie, fie, fie** expression of strong
disgust or disapproval
163 an instance of what might be called a
'split *aside*', since all except Katherina
might hear the line; see p. 341.
166 **no unkindness of** no offence at
**hasty** angry

155 mistress] *(mistris)*    157 mistress'] *(Mistresse)*    160–1 O . . . use'?] *Oxf'; F lines* for: / vse. /
161 mistress'] *(Mistris)*    163 SD] *Rowe*

PETRUCCIO
  Well, come, my Kate, we will unto your father's,
  Even in these honest mean habiliments:
  Our purses shall be proud, our garments poor,                    170
  For 'tis the mind that makes the body rich,
  And as the sun breaks through the darkest clouds,
  So honour peereth in the meanest habit.
  What is the jay more precious than the lark
  Because his feathers are more beautiful?                          175
  Or is the adder better than the eel
  Because his painted skin contents the eye?
  O no, good Kate; neither art thou the worse
  For this poor furniture and mean array.
  If thou account'st it shame, lay it on me,                        180
  And therefore frolic: we will hence forthwith
  To feast and sport us at thy father's house.
  – Go call my men, and let us straight to him,
  And bring our horses unto Long-lane end.
  There will we mount, and thither walk on foot.                    185

169–80 Petruccio again preaches against fine dress; *BCP* contrasts outward apparel and the inner man and offers instruction to wives in relation to clothing (298–9); see also 3.2.116–19 and Hodgdon, 'Bride-ing'.

169 **honest mean habiliments** respectable, perhaps inferior everyday clothes; *mean* = humble, poor

172–3 Ard[1] cites the prose tract *The History of Patient Grissel* (1619, probably first printed before 1590): 'sit downe till the dinner is done, and bid the company welcome in this poore attire; for the sun will break through slender clouds, and vertue shine in base array'. The idea also appears, much extended, at *1H4* 1.2.187–205.

173 **peereth** appears; to cause to appear or peep out (*OED v.* 6 *trans.*)

174 **What . . . jay** F has no comma here; Ard[1] glosses *What* as 'How' (see Abbott, 253). Noting the grammatical form of 174–7, Ard[2] reads *What* as an interrogative exclamation. In *Knack, Honesty* remarks: 'The Courtier resembleth the Iay, that decketh her self with the feathers of other birds, to make her self glorious' (sig. E1[r]).

177 **painted** 'Brightly coloured or variegated, as if painted' (*OED a.* 3)

179 **furniture** equipment, dress (*OED n.* 2a)
  **mean array** humble attire

180 **lay** 'blame'

181 **frolic** be merry

184 **Long-lane end** In early modern London, Long Lane was 'A Place of Note for the sale of Apparel, Linnen, and Upholsters Goods, both Second-hand and New, but chiefly for Old, for which it is of note' (Stow, 1.122).

174 What is] What, is *Pope*    180 account'st] *Rowe;* accountedst *F*    me,] me. *F4*

Let's see, I think 'tis now some seven o'clock,
And well we may come there by dinner-time.

KATHERINA

I dare assure you, sir, 'tis almost two,
And 'twill be supper-time ere you come there.

PETRUCCIO

It shall be seven ere I go to horse.                                    190
Look what I speak, or do, or think to do,
You are still crossing it. Sirs, let't alone.
I will not go today, and ere I do,
It shall be what o'clock I say it is.                                   194

HORTENSIO

Why so, this gallant will command the sun.                    [*Exeunt.*]

[**4.4**]        *Enter* TRANIO [*as Lucentio*] *and the* Merchant
              [*, booted and*] *dressed like Vincentio.*

TRANIO

Sir, this is the house; please it you that I call?

MERCHANT

Ay, what else? And but I be deceived,
Signor Baptista may remember me.
Near twenty years ago in Genoa –

187 **dinner-time** between 11 and noon
189 **supper-time** about six or seven in the evening
191 **Look what** whatever
192 **crossing** opposing, contradicting
195 **Why so,** Exactly where the comma goes ('Why so,' or 'Why, so' depends on editorial taste and a performer's choice; *so* = at this rate. Most editions (unnecessarily) mark the line '*aside*'.
4.4.0.1–2 *This combines F's opening SD with part of that at 18.1. See pp. 319–20.

0.2 *booted . . . Vincentio*  presumably in his travelling boots (see Dessen & Thomson, 39) but otherwise resembling Vincentio, who first appears as he is travelling to Padua (4.5.26); the boots are a reminder that the Merchant impersonates Vincentio.
1 **please it** The subjunctive 'represents our modern "may it please?" and expresses a modest doubt' (Abbott, 361).
2 **what else** certainly, of course
  **but I be** 'unless I am' (see Abbott, 120)

187 dinner-time] *(dinner time)*  189 supper-time] *(supper time)*  195 Why so, this] *Ard¹* ; Why so this *F*; Why so! This *Malone*  SD] *Rowe*  4.4] *Steevens*  0.1 *as Lucentio*] *Kittredge*  Merchant] Pedant *F*  0.2 *booted*] *at 18.1 F*  1 Sir] *Theobald*; Sirs *F*

TRANIO

    Where we were lodgers at the Pegasus. 5

    'Tis well, and hold your own, in any case,

    With such austerity as 'longeth to a father.

*Enter* BIONDELLO.

MERCHANT

    I warrant you. But, sir, here comes your boy;

    'Twere good he were schooled.

TRANIO

    Fear you not him. Sirrah Biondello, 10

    Now do your duty throughly, I advise you.

    Imagine 'twere the right Vincentio.

BIONDELLO

    Tut, fear not me.

TRANIO

    But hast thou done thy errand to Baptista?

BIONDELLO

    I told him that your father was at Venice, 15

    And that you looked for him this day in Padua.

TRANIO

    Thou'rt a tall fellow; hold thee that to drink.

    – Here comes Baptista. Set your countenance, sir.

---

5 **Pegasus** Pegasus, a winged horse in classical mythology, featured on the arms of the Middle Temple and was also a popular inn sign. Theobald assigned this line to the Merchant, as do Ard[2] and Oxf[1], but the Merchant may be rehearsing his story (3–4), which Tranio interrupts and completes.

6 **hold your own** play your part; sustain your role

7 **austerity** gravity (*OED* austere *a.* 5)
   **'longeth** belongs

9 **schooled** instructed in his part (*OED* $v.^1$ 5)

11 **throughly** fully, perfectly
   **advise** tell you for your own good (Oxf[1])

16 **looked for** expected

17 **tall** capable; proverbial: 'To be a tall man (or fellow)' (Dent, TT3)
   **hold . . . drink** 'take this to buy yourself a drink'

18 **Set your countenance** 'assume an appropriately grave demeanour'

---

5] *Theobald assigns to Merchant (Pedant)* 7 'longeth] *Hanmer;* longeth F 7.1] *after* you. 8 Ard[1]

*Enter* BAPTISTA *and* LUCENTIO [*as* Cambio].
Merchant [*stands*] bare-headed.

TRANIO

Signor Baptista, you are happily met.
– Sir, this is the gentleman I told you of.                    20
I pray you stand good father to me now:
Give me Bianca for my patrimony.

MERCHANT

Soft, son. – Sir, by your leave, having come to Padua
To gather in some debts, my son Lucentio
Made me acquainted with a weighty cause                    25
Of love between your daughter and himself;
And for the good report I hear of you,
And for the love he beareth to your daughter –
And she to him – to stay him not too long,
I am content, in a good father's care,                    30
To have him matched; and if you please to like
No worse than I, upon some agreement
Me shall you find ready and willing
With one consent to have her so bestowed;

18.2 *bare-headed* out of respect to
Baptista. Ard² conjectures that the
scene originally opened with this
SD, only partially corrected by
excluding Tranio. Cf. the mass entry
at *CE* 5.1.129, where the Merchant
of Syracuse appears '*barehead*', and
*STM* 1159–60: 'doing courtesy to
each other, Clerk of the Council
waiting barecheaded' (Dessen &
Thomson, 20).
19, 53 **happily** haply, by chance; see
1.2.55n. on *Haply*
20 The line might be addressed to Baptista
or the Merchant, though probably the
latter, since 21–2 are clearly addressed
to the Merchant.

21 **stand good father** act the part of a
good father (*OED v.* 15b)
22 **patrimony** property, estate,
inheritance
23–36 Content and syntax suggest that
the Merchant is not just deferential
but straining to please.
23 **Soft** steady
**having come** 'I having come'; the
subject is the Merchant, not Lucentio;
on omitting the noun or pronoun in a
participial phrase, see Abbott, 378.
25 **weighty cause** important matter
29 **stay** delay
34 **With one consent** in unanimity
**bestowed** given in marriage (*OED
v.* 4)

18.1–2] *after 16 Cam²*   18.1 *as Cambio*] *Kittredge*   18.2 *stands*] *Oxf¹; at 4.4.0.2 F*   23] *Hanmer lines*
son. / Padua /   32 I, upon] I sir upon *F2*   agreement] agreement, sir *Keightley;* sure agreement
*(Oxf)*   33 ready and willing] most ready and most willing *F2*

For curious I cannot be with you,                              35
Signor Baptista, of whom I hear so well.
BAPTISTA
   Sir, pardon me in what I have to say;
   Your plainness and your shortness please me well.
   Right true it is your son Lucentio here
   Doth love my daughter, and she loveth him –        40
   Or both dissemble deeply their affections –
   And therefore if you say no more than this,
   That like a father you will deal with him
   And pass my daughter a sufficient dower,
   The match is made and all is done:                 45
   Your son shall have my daughter with consent.
TRANIO
   I thank you, sir. Where, then, do you know best
   We be affied and such assurance ta'en
   As shall with either part's agreement stand?
BAPTISTA
   Not in my house, Lucentio, for you know           50
   Pitchers have ears, and I have many servants;
   Besides, old Gremio is hearkening still,
   And happily we might be interrupted.
TRANIO
   Then at my lodging, an it like you;

---

35 **curious** over-particular (*OED a.* 10). In the context of potential negotiations over dowries, the Merchant is saying that he won't be too demanding or insistent on gaining all that might be gained.

44 **pass** settle upon, pledge (*OED v.* 46)

45 The short line, made up of monosyllables, stresses the conclusion.

48 **affied** formally betrothed before witnesses, a ceremony nearly as binding as marriage; together with the legal settlement referred to, known as an *assurance* (*OED* 2), a term occurring more frequently in *TS* than in any other Shakespearean play (Ard²).

49 'as shall have the agreements of both parties to support it'

51 **Pitchers have ears** proverbial: 'Small pitchers have wide ears' (Dent, P363); literally, the *ears* or handles of water-jugs

52 **hearkening still** constantly watchful

54 **an . . . you** 'if that idea pleases you'

---

47 know best] trow is best *Hanmer;* trow best *(Johnson)*   48 ta'en] *(tane)*   52 hearkening] *(harkning)*   54 an] *(and) Oxf¹* you] you, sir *F2*

There doth my father lie, and there this night                    55
We'll pass the business privately and well.
Send for your daughter by your servant here;
My boy shall fetch the scrivener presently.
The worst is this, that at so slender warning
You are like to have a thin and slender pittance.               60

BAPTISTA

It likes me well. Cambio, hie you home,
And bid Bianca make her ready straight;
And if you will, tell what hath happened:
Lucentio's father is arrived in Padua,                          64
And how she's like to be Lucentio's wife.        [*Exit Lucentio.*]

BIONDELLO

I pray the gods she may, with all my heart.

TRANIO

Dally not with the gods, but get thee gone.      *Exit* [*Biondello*].
– Signor Baptista, shall I lead the way?
Welcome: one mess is like to be your cheer.
Come, sir, we will better it in Pisa.                           70

---

55 **lie** stay, punning on 'deceive'(?)
56 **pass** transact (*OED v.* 45)
57 **your servant** i.e. Lucentio as Cambio; observing the spoken cue at 74, Cam[1] and Hibbard direct Tranio to wink at Lucentio.
58 **My boy** i.e. Biondello
   **scrivener** notary, person authorized to draw up legal contracts
60 **pittance** allowance of food and drink; rations (*OED n.* 2)
61 **It . . . well** it pleases me; impersonal use of 'like' (Abbott, 297)
   **hie** hurry
62 **make . . . straight** make herself ready immediately
63 **happened** happenèd
65–71 SDD *This patterning of exits

– Lucentio at 65 and Biondello at 67 – and the re-entry at 71 combines a number of editorial options. Rowe assigned 66 to Lucentio (whose primary interest is marrying Bianca), then had him exit instead of Biondello; Pope, Hanmer and Warburton began a new scene at 71, as does Oxf, marking a literary, not theatrical division (there is no change of location).
67 *F reads '*Enter Peter.*'; Theobald established the tradition that omits him, though he survives as 'Pedro' in Garrick's *Catharine and Petruchio*.
69 **one . . . cheer** 'one dish is all you're likely to get'

61–2] *Steevens; F lines* well: / straight: /   63 happened] *Capell subst.;* hapned *F*   65 SD] *Rowe (after 66)*   66 SP] *Luc. / Rowe*   67 gone.] gone. Enter Peter. *F*   SD] *Cam[1]; (Exit) F, after 66; Bion. moves off. Ard[1] subst.*

BAPTISTA    I follow you.                                *Exeunt.*

*Enter* LUCENTIO [*as Cambio*] *and* BIONDELLO.

BIONDELLO    Cambio.
LUCENTIO    What sayst thou, Biondello?
BIONDELLO    You saw my master wink and laugh upon
you?                                                              75
LUCENTIO    Biondello, what of that?
BIONDELLO    Faith, nothing, but h'as left me here behind
to expound the meaning or moral of his signs and
tokens.
LUCENTIO    I pray thee moralize them.                       80
BIONDELLO    Then thus: Baptista is safe, talking with the
deceiving father of a deceitful son.
LUCENTIO    And what of him?
BIONDELLO    His daughter is to be brought by you to the
supper.                                                          85
LUCENTIO    And then?
BIONDELLO    The old priest at Saint Luke's church is at
your command at all hours.
LUCENTIO    And what of all this?
BIONDELLO    I cannot tell, except they are busied about a     90
counterfeit assurance. Take you assurance of her, *cum
privilegio ad imprimendum solum*: to th' church take the

---

72 In Daly's 1887 production, Biondello
doffed his hat to Lucentio, reminding
spectators of the 'real' master's identity
(Schafer, 204).
74 **my master** i.e. Tranio
80 **moralize** interpret, explain (*OED v.* 1)
81 **safe** safely taken care of, out of the
way
91 **counterfeit assurance** legal contract
mentioned at 48; *counterfeit* because

invalid: the Merchant is not who he
claims to be.
91–2 *cum . . . solum* (Latin): 'with the sole
right to print', a formula denoting a
monopoly of publication. Oxf[1] notes:
'the bridegroom's right to the bride
is similarly a monopoly'. Hibbard
suggests 'a pun on printing in the sense
of "stamping one's own image on [a
woman] by getting her with child"'.

71 SD] *Exeunt Tranio, Pedant, and Baptista. Ard[1]; Exeunt all except Biondello Oxf[1]*   71.1] *Re-enter
Lucentio. Ard[1] subst. after 72*   72–106] as [4.5] *Oxf*   72 Cambio.] Cambio. *calling Luc. back /
Capell*   77 h'as] *Hanmer subst.;* has *F;* he's *Oxf*   81 safe, talking] *Cam[2];* safe talking *F*   90 except]
*F2;* expect *F*   92 privilegio . . . solum] *F2; preuilegio ad Impremendum solem F*   church take] church!
Take *Rann (Tyrrwhitt)*

277

priest, clerk and some sufficient honest witnesses.
If this be not that you look for, I have no more to say,
But bid Bianca farewell for ever and a day.                    95

LUCENTIO    Hear'st thou, Biondello?

BIONDELLO    I cannot tarry. I knew a wench married in
an afternoon as she went to the garden for parsley to
stuff a rabbit; and so may you, sir; and so adieu, sir. My
master hath appointed me to go to Saint Luke's to bid    100
the priest be ready to come against you come with your
appendix.                                                   *Exit.*

LUCENTIO

I may and will, if she be so contented.
She will be pleased, then wherefore should I doubt?
Hap what hap may, I'll roundly go about her:               105
It shall go hard if Cambio go without her.                  *Exit.*

[4.5]    *Enter* PETRUCCIO, KATHERINA, HORTENSIO
[*and* GRUMIO].

PETRUCCIO

Come on, i'God's name, once more toward our father's.
Good Lord, how bright and goodly shines the moon!

93 **sufficient** substantial, well-to-do (*OED* a. 4)
95 **for . . . day** proverbial (Dent, D74)
97–8 **wench . . . afternoon** Early modern England equated such an elopement with abduction, property theft against the woman's father.
101 **against you come** in anticipation of your coming
102 **appendix** appendage, referring to Bianca; *appendix* also caps the reference at 91–2 to printing and legal documents.
105 **Hap . . . may** 'whatever may happen'; proverbial (Dent, C529)
**roundly . . . her** 'demand her definite answer'

106 **go hard** 'be hard luck'; proverbial (Dent, H117)
4.5.0.2 *F has neither Grumio (who does not speak) nor servants; adding the latter is usual in modern editions. Although playing the scene with Hortensio doing duty as a servant is workable, theatrical practice regularly includes Grumio. Another option would be to recruit Kate as a servant.
1–26 This dialogue reprises 4.3.186–94, where Kate and Petruccio argue about the time; in addition, verbal repetitions and parallelisms echo the patterned language of their initial encounter in 2.1.

KATHERINA

The moon? The sun; it is not moonlight now.

PETRUCCIO

I say it is the moon that shines so bright.

KATHERINA

I know it is the sun that shines so bright.                    5

PETRUCCIO

Now by my mother's son – and that's myself –

It shall be moon or star or what I list

Or e'er I journey to your father's house.

[*to Grumio*] Go on and fetch our horses back again.

– Evermore crossed and crossed, nothing but crossed.       10

HORTENSIO [*to Katherina*]

Say as he says, or we shall never go.

KATHERINA

Forward, I pray, since we have come so far,

And be it moon or sun or what you please,

And if you please to call it a rush-candle,

Henceforth I vow it shall be so for me.                      15

PETRUCCIO     I say it is the moon.

KATHERINA     I know it is the moon.

PETRUCCIO

Nay then, you lie; it is the blessed sun.

KATHERINA

Then God be blest, it is the blessed sun,

But sun it is not, when you say it is not,                   20

---

5 In Miller (1987), Fiona Shaw's
Katherina took off her wedding ring,
held it up like a telescope and gazed
at the *sun* through it, occasioning a
pause that grew longer as the run
continued.
6 **mother's son** In such matters, it
is the mother, not the father or the
son, who is the authority – a familiar
trope in Shakespeare (cf. 5.1.31–2); *son*

puns on *sun* (see also the 'reverse' pun
(*sun*/'son') at 47).
7 **list** please, choose
8 **Or . . . journey** 'before ever I'll
consider making the journey'
10 **crossed** thwarted, contradicted
14 **rush-candle** candle of poor quality
made from dipping a rush in grease or
tallow
18, 19 **blessed** blessèd

9 SD] *this edn; To Servants Cam²*  Go on] Go one *Rann*     11 SD] *Oxf¹*   14 And if] An if *Collier*   rush-
candle] *(rush Candle)*     19 is] *Q;* in *F*

And the moon changes even as your mind.
What you will have it named, even that it is,
And so it shall be so for Katherine.

HORTENSIO

Petruccio, go thy ways, the field is won.

PETRUCCIO

Well, forward, forward, thus the bowl should run, 25
And not unluckily against the bias.

*Enter* VINCENTIO.

But soft, what company is coming here?
Good morrow, gentle mistress, where away?
– Tell me, sweet Kate, and tell me truly too,
Hast thou beheld a fresher gentlewoman, 30
Such war of white and red within her cheeks?
What stars do spangle heaven with such beauty
As those two eyes become that heavenly face?
– Fair lovely maid, once more good day to thee.
– Sweet Kate, embrace her for her beauty's sake. 35

HORTENSIO   'A will make the man mad, to make the
woman of him.

---

21 **moon . . . mind**  proverbial: 'As
changeful as the moon' (Dent, M1111)
23 Early editors, Ard[1] included, add a
comma after *he*; Capell changed *so* to
'sir'.
24 **go thy ways** well done, carry on
**field** battle (from 'battlefield')
25–6 **bowl . . . bias** a metaphor from
lawn-bowls; proverbial: 'To run against
(out of) the bias' (Dent, B339). The *bias*
refers to weighting one side of the bowl
(ball) so that it takes a curving path;
*unluckily* – unfortunately, i.e. against
the grain.
26.1 F places this SD at 27. Placement of
entries varies according to particular

performance spaces.
29–50 This exchange marks a new-found
comic collaboration, analogous to a
modern vaudeville act, as Petruccio
and Kate take turns feeding each other
lines.
30 **fresher** more youthful, blooming
(*OED* fresh *a*.[1] 9b)
31–3 a recital of sonneteers' commonplaces
36 'A he (common colloquial form)
36–7 **the woman** F2 emends to 'a
woman'; Hibbard argues that F jokes on
theatrical practice, where boys played
women's parts: Petruccio is assigning
the old man the woman's role in the
play he is staging.

---

23 be so] be, so, *Rowe*; be, sir *Capell*  26.1] *after 26 Cam*[2]  27 soft, what company] *Steevens*; soft,
company *F*; soft, some company *Pope*  36–7 the woman] a woman *F2*

KATHERINA

Young budding virgin, fair, and fresh, and sweet,
Whither away, or where is thy abode?
Happy the parents of so fair a child; 40
Happier the man whom favourable stars
Allots thee for his lovely bedfellow.

PETRUCCIO

Why, how now, Kate, I hope thou art not mad.
This is a man – old, wrinkled, faded, withered –
And not a maiden, as thou sayst he is. 45

KATHERINA

Pardon, old father, my mistaking eyes
That have been so bedazzled with the sun
That everything I look on seemeth green.
Now I perceive thou art a reverend father.
Pardon, I pray thee, for my mad mistaking. 50

PETRUCCIO

Do, good old grandsire, and withal make known
Which way thou travell'st – if along with us,

---

39 ***where** F2's emendation seems preferable to F's 'whether', which may have resulted either from repeating *whither* or from the compositor's auditory error, since 'whether' could be pronounced *where* (RP). In either case, the line hints that Katherina may be correcting Petruccio at 28.

40–2 Steevens locates the source of these lines as Golding's Ovid, *Met.* 4.396–7: 'far more blest than these is she / Whom thou vouchsafest for thy wife and bedfellow for to be'; Ard[1] notes that Ovid took the passage from *Odyssey*, 6.165–71. The incident offers a compressed imitation of Salmacis addressing the reluctant Hermaphroditus (a sort of male shrew), a classic instance of sexual role-reversal as well as of taming. Bate notes: 'Kate switches the gender back to that of

convention, changing lucky wife into a lucky husband, but the switch is ironically turned again when one remembers that, like Salmacis, she is in fact addressing a man. In a sense, she goes one up on Petruccio . . . by bringing their relationship into play, Kate inverts the roles which Petruccio has so painstakingly set up. This small linguistic victory may be seen as a first sign that Kate can give as well as take a taming' (123–4).

41–2 *****stars** / **Allots** a third person plural in *s* (Abbott, 333)

48 **green** green in colour, punning on fresh, youthful (*OED a.* 7)

49, 61 **reverend** to be revered. F's spelling, 'reverent', and 'reverend' were not clearly distinguished in the early modern period.

39 Whither] *(whether)* where] *F2;* whether *F* 42 Allots] *(A lots);* Allot *Pope*

We shall be joyful of thy company.

VINCENTIO

Fair sir, and you, my merry mistress,

That with your strange encounter much amazed me,          55

My name is called Vincentio, my dwelling Pisa,

And bound I am to Padua, there to visit

A son of mine which long I have not seen.

PETRUCCIO

What is his name?

VINCENTIO                    Lucentio, gentle sir.

PETRUCCIO

Happily met – the happier for thy son.                    60

And now by law, as well as reverend age,

I may entitle thee my loving father.

The sister to my wife, this gentlewoman,

Thy son by this hath married. Wonder not,

Nor be not grieved: she is of good esteem,                65

Her dowry wealthy, and of worthy birth;

Beside, so qualified as may beseem

The spouse of any noble gentleman.

Let me embrace with old Vincentio,

And wander we to see thy honest son,                      70

Who will of thy arrival be full joyous.

VINCENTIO

But is this true, or is it else your pleasure,

---

55 **encounter** greeting, mode of address
(*OED n.* 3)
**amazed** amazèd
62 **father** The term includes 'a father-
in-law, stepfather, or one who adopts
another as his child' (*OED n.* 1e).
63–4 **The        sister . . . married**
Neither Petruccio nor Hortensio
(who concurs with Petruccio at 75,
though see 75n.) can know this, as
it has not yet happened. Apparently
Hortensio does not remember that
he and Tranio-as-Lucentio forswore

Bianca in 4.2. Similar inconsistencies
occur elsewhere in Shakespeare and
often pass unnoticed in the theatre.
However, Bogdanov (1978) replaced
the lines with 'Lucentio, Hey we
know him well' (Schafer, 210). In
Potter (2003) a Pony Express rider
delivered the news to Petruccio; while
he read his mail, Katherina shrugged
at the audience, before Vincentio was
told.
67 **so qualified** of such (good) qualities
**beseem** befit

Like pleasant travellers, to break a jest
Upon the company you overtake?

HORTENSIO

I do assure thee, father, so it is.                          75

PETRUCCIO

Come, go along and see the truth hereof,
For our first merriment hath made thee jealous.

*Exeunt [all but Hortensio].*

HORTENSIO

Well, Petruccio, this has put me in heart.
Have to my widow, and if she be froward,                     79
Then hast thou taught Hortensio to be untoward.    *Exit.*

[5.1]    *Enter* GREMIO; [*then, unseen by him,*] BIONDELLO,
LUCENTIO *and* BIANCA.

BIONDELLO    Softly and swiftly, sir, for the priest is ready.
LUCENTIO    I fly, Biondello; but they may chance to need
thee at home, therefore leave us.

*Exeunt Lucentio [and Bianca].*

---

73 **pleasant** light-hearted, fun-seeking
   **break a jest** play a practical joke
75 This line is reassigned to Katherina
   when, as sometimes occurs, Hortensio
   has been cut from the scene (Schafer,
   211).
77 **jealous** suspicious, mistrustful (*OED*
   *a.* 5a, 5b)
79 **Have to** now for
   **froward** unreasonable, difficult
80 In one performance (Cass, 1935), the
   performers walked around the stage to
   arrive at 'Padua' without any change of
   scene; the first lines of 5.1 were omitted
   (Crosse, *Diaries*).
   **untoward** unruly, perverse (*OED a.*
   2)

5.1 *Theobald. No act or scene division
   in F.
0.1 *then ... him* F's '*Gremio is out
   before*', which follows the others'
   entrance, is unique among Elizabethan
   and Jacobean SDs (Hibbard considers
   it an afterthought); repositioning it,
   and suggesting that he doesn't see the
   others, reflects usual stage practice.
   Gremio's presence recalls the original
   threesome of suitors; he is the last
   remaining obstacle to Bianca's and
   Lucentio's marriage. Cam[2] adds '*as
   himself*' after 'LUCENTIO', but Lucentio
   might remain in disguise, not revealing
   his 'true' identity until his re-entry
   at 97.1.

77 SD *all but Hortensio*] *Warburton subst.; Exeunt. F*   79 *she be froward*] *F2; she froward F*
5.1] *Warburton; Act 5 / Theobald*   0.1 *then, unseen by him,*] *this edn; is out before. F; walking on
one side. Rowe*   3 SD] *Capell; Exit. F*

BIONDELLO    Nay, faith, I'll see the church o'your back,        4
    and then come back to my master's as soon as I can.    [*Exit.*]
GREMIO    I marvel Cambio comes not all this while.

> *Enter* PETRUCCIO, KATHERINA, VINCENTIO,
> GRUMIO *with Attendants.*

PETRUCCIO
    Sir, here's the door, this is Lucentio's house.
    My father's bears more toward the market-place;
    Thither must I, and here I leave you, sir.
VINCENTIO
    You shall not choose but drink before you go:        10
    I think I shall command your welcome here,
    And by all likelihood some cheer is toward.    *Knocks.*
GREMIO    They're busy within; you were best knock
    louder.

> Merchant *looks out of the window.*

MERCHANT    What's he that knocks as he would beat down    15
    the gate?
VINCENTIO    Is Signor Lucentio within, sir?
MERCHANT    He's within, sir, but not to be spoken withal.
VINCENTIO    What if a man bring him a hundred pound or
    two to make merry withal?                        20
MERCHANT    Keep your hundred pounds to yourself; he

---

4 **I'll . . . back** 'I'll see you safely
  married'; *o'your back* = behind you
5 **\*master's** F reads 'mistris', emended
  by Capell; see 1.2.18 and n., and 48.
8 **bears** lies; the sense is nautical (*OED*
  *v.*[1] 39).
10 Combines two proverbial expressions:
  'cannot choose (but)' (Dent, CC11) and
  'drink before you go' (Dent, D605.1).

12 **cheer is toward** hospitality awaits
14 SD This staging derives directly from
  Gascoigne's *Supposes*, 4.4.0.1–2, where
  Dalio, a servant of Erostrato's cook
  (here, Tranio), 'cometh to the window,
  and there maketh them answer' (i.e. to
  the hero's real father).
18, 20 **withal** with

5 master's] *Capell*; mistris *F*; Master *Theobald*    SD] *Capell*    12 SD] *(Knock.)*    14 SD Merchant]
*Cam²*; Pedant *F*

shall need none so long as I live.

PETRUCCIO    Nay, I told you your son was well beloved in
Padua. – Do you hear, sir? To leave frivolous
circumstances, I pray you tell Signor Lucentio that his          25
father is come from Pisa and is here at the door to speak
with him.

MERCHANT    Thou liest. His father is come to Padua and
here looking out at the window.

VINCENTIO    Art thou his father?                                30

MERCHANT    Ay, sir, so his mother says, if I may believe
her.

PETRUCCIO    Why, how now, gentleman! Why, this is flat
knavery, to take upon you another man's name.

MERCHANT    Lay hands on the villain. I believe 'a means to     35
cozen somebody in this city under my countenance.

*Enter* BIONDELLO.

BIONDELLO [*aside*]    I have seen them in the church
together, God send 'em good shipping. But who is
here – mine old master Vincentio? Now we are
undone and brought to nothing.                                  40

---

24–5 **To . . . circumstances** 'to get down
to what really matters'
28 **Padua** As Oxf[1] remarks, 'perhaps not
the best of jokes', but it is better than
giving away the Merchant's Mantuan
'origins'; he can be thought of as
'*recently* from Padua', which is where
he currently is. Theatrical geography is
a slippery business.
28–9 **is** understood with both *come* and
*here*
31 **his mother says** proverbial: 'Ask the
mother if the child be like his father'
(Dent, M1193); cf. *MA* 1.1.100: 'Her
mother hath many times told me so.'
33–4 Capell directs '*To Vincentio*'; it seems

equally possible (and perhaps more
probable, since he has been travelling
with the 'true' Vincentio and has no
reason to suspect that the latter is
not who he says he is) that Petruccio
addresses the Merchant; either option
is playable.
33 **flat** downright (*OED a.* 6a)
36 **cozen** cheat
**under my countenance** whilst
pretending to be me
38 **good shipping** 'a good marriage
voyage'; proverbial: 'God send you
good shipping' (Dent, SS7)
39, 60, 61 **undone** ruined, brought down,
destroyed

28 to Padua] *Pope;* from *Padua F;* from Mantua *Capell*     36] *Capell*    40 brought] *Q;* brough *F*

VINCENTIO    Come hither, crackhemp.

BIONDELLO    I hope I may choose, sir.

VINCENTIO    Come hither, you rogue. What, have you
    forgot me?

BIONDELLO    Forgot you? No, sir. I could not forget you,          45
    for I never saw you before in all my life.

VINCENTIO    What, you notorious villain, didst thou never
    see thy master's father, Vincentio?

BIONDELLO    What, my old worshipful old master? Yes,
    marry, sir, see where he looks out of the window.          50

VINCENTIO    Is't so indeed? *He beats Biondello.*

BIONDELLO    Help, help, help! Here's a madman will
    murder me.                                          [*Exit.*]

MERCHANT    Help, son! Help, Signor Baptista!

                [*Leaves the window.*]

PETRUCCIO    Prithee, Kate, let's stand aside and see the          55
    end of this controversy.

*Enter* Merchant [*below*] *with Servants,* BAPTISTA
*and* TRANIO [*as Lucentio*].

TRANIO    Sir, what are you that offer to beat my servant?

VINCENTIO    What am I, sir? Nay, what are you, sir? O
    immortal gods! O fine villain! A silken doublet, a velvet

41 **crackhemp** one who strains at or
breaks the hangman's rope. Ard[2]
notes the more usual 'crack-halter',
which *OED* cites first in Gascoigne's
*Supposes*, 1.4; *crackhemp* is uniquely
Shakespearean, only in *TS*.

42 **choose** please myself; have some choice
(*OED v.* B 4a, 4b)

47 **notorious** notable, out-and-out,
evident

53 SD *F cues no exit for Biondello; his
'escape' enables him to tell Lucentio
and Bianca what has happened.

54 SD *F has no SD, but the staging is

implied by the Merchant's entrance
at 56.1.

55 Reprises 1.1.47 and the ensuing entrance of the Minola family
with Gremio and Hortensio. There,
Lucentio and Tranio stood aside;
here, it is Kate and Petruccio who
stand apart to watch a different
'show'.

57 **offer** dare, venture

59–60 **velvet hose** pair of loose breeches.
Sumptuary laws prohibited those below
the degree of a knight's eldest son to
wear velvet.

48 master's] *F2;* Mistris *F*    49 old worshipful old] worshipful old *Q*    53 SD] *Capell*    54 SD] *Capell*
*subst.*    56.1 *below*] *Capell*    56.2 *as Lucentio*] *Pelican*

hose, a scarlet cloak and a copatain hat! O, I am undone,     60
I am undone. While I play the good husband at home,
my son and my servant spend all at the university.

TRANIO     How now, what's the matter?

BAPTISTA     What, is the man lunatic?

TRANIO     Sir, you seem a sober ancient gentleman by your     65
habit, but your words show you a madman. Why, sir,
what 'cerns it you if I wear pearl and gold? I thank my
good father, I am able to maintain it.

VINCENTIO     Thy father! O villain, he is a sailmaker in
Bergamo.     70

BAPTISTA     You mistake, sir; you mistake, sir. Pray, what
do you think is his name?

VINCENTIO     His name? As if I knew not his name: I have
brought him up ever since he was three years old, and
his name is Tranio.     75

MERCHANT     Away, away, mad ass. His name is Lucentio,
and he is mine only son, and heir to the lands of me,
Signor Vincentio.

---

60 **scarlet cloak** an expensive, very fine cloth, often of (but not limited to) a bright red colour. The right to wear crimson scarlet cloth was restricted to the royal family, noblemen and civil officials (Linthicum, 88).
**copatain hat** 'a high-crowned hat in the form of a sugar-loaf' (*OED* copataine), the same as 'copintank'; of obscure etymology. The name may derive from 'copped', meaning sharp and high; 'Sometimes they were them sharp on the crowne, pearking vp like a sphere, or shafte of a steeple, standing a quarter of a yard aboue the crowne of their heades' (Stubbes, 1.50). Such hats were trimmed with a band and a small plume or large jewelled ornament, usually placed in front against the turned-up brim (Linthicum, 228).

61 **good husband** thrifty manager
67 **'cerns** short for 'concerns'
68 **maintain** afford (*OED v.* 5c)
70 **Bergamo** an inland town, neither a port nor known for sail-making. Hibbard suggests it might be appropriate as Tranio's birthplace because it was the traditional home of the *commedia dell'arte*'s servant-figure Harlequin.
73–4 **I have ... old** Ard[1] notes a close resemblance to Gascoigne's *Supposes*: 'he whom I brought up of a child, yea and cherished him as if he had been mine own, doth now utterly deny to know me' (4.8.2–5). The echo continues at 79: 'Out and alas, he whom I sent hither with my son to be his servant, and to give attendance on him, hath either cut his throat, or by some evil means made him away' (4.8.31–4).

---

60 copatain] *(copataine);* copintank *Oxf*     67 'cerns] *Collier;* cernes *F;* concerns *Rowe*     75 Tranio] *F2; Tronio F*

VINCENTIO    Lucentio? O, he hath murdered his master!
  Lay hold on him, I charge you, in the Duke's name. O        80
  my son, my son! Tell me, thou villain, where is my son
  Lucentio?

TRANIO    Call forth an officer.

*[Enter an Officer.]*

  Carry this mad knave to the jail. Father Baptista, I
  charge you see that he be forthcoming.                                        85

VINCENTIO    Carry me to the jail?

GREMIO    Stay, officer; he shall not go to prison.

BAPTISTA    Talk not, Signor Gremio; I say he shall go to
  prison.

GREMIO    Take heed, Signor Baptista, lest you be cony-          90
  catched in this business. I dare swear this is the right
  Vincentio.

MERCHANT    Swear, if thou dar'st.

GREMIO    Nay, I dare not swear it.

TRANIO    Then thou wert best say that I am not Lucentio.        95

GREMIO    Yes, I know thee to be Signor Lucentio.

BAPTISTA    Away with the dotard; to the jail with him.

*Enter* BIONDELLO, LUCENTIO *and* BIANCA.

VINCENTIO    Thus strangers may be haled and abused. O
  monstrous villain!

---

83.1 *The Officer does not always
appear: in Alexander's staging (1992),
Grumio handed Petruccio a truncheon
(promptbook).
85 **forthcoming** available for trial
90–1 **cony-catched** deceived, cheated
97 Ard¹ suggests that the first half of the

line refers to Gremio, the second to
Vincentio.
**dotard** one in his dotage or second
childhood; stupid person
98 ***haled** dragged about (by the Officer).
F3 changed F's 'haild', possibly
meaning 'greeted', to 'hal'd'.

83.1] *Capell subst.(Enter one with an officer.); Exit Servant, who returns with an Officer. Riv
(Dyce)    90–1 cony-catched] (conicatcht)    97.1] Enter Lucentio and Bianca. / Rowe; after 99 Capell
BIANCA] F2; Biancu. F    98 haled] F3; haild F

BIONDELLO    O, we are spoiled, and – yonder he is. Deny    100
   him, forswear him, or else we are all undone.
       *Exeunt Biondello, Tranio and Merchant as fast as may be.*
LUCENTIO    Pardon, sweet father. *Kneels.*
VINCENTIO    Lives my sweet son?
BIANCA    Pardon, dear father.
BAPTISTA
   How hast thou offended? Where is Lucentio?                    105
LUCENTIO
   Here's Lucentio, right son to the right Vincentio,
   That have by marriage made thy daughter mine
   While counterfeit supposes bleared thine eyne.
GREMIO    Here's packing, with a witness, to deceive us all.
VINCENTIO
   Where is that damned villain, Tranio,                    110
   That faced and braved me in this matter so?
BAPTISTA
   Why, tell me, is not this my Cambio?
BIANCA
   Cambio is changed into Lucentio.
LUCENTIO
   Love wrought these miracles. Bianca's love
   Made me exchange my state with Tranio                    115
   While he did bear my countenance in the town,

---

100 **spoiled** ruined, undone
101 SD *as fast . . . be* securely bound or restrained; a similar phrase occurs in *CE* 4.4.149 SD.
106 **right son . . . Vincentio** Oxf[1] points out that Shakespeare borrows closely from Gascoigne's *Supposes*, the source for *TS*'s subplot, which reads: 'the right *Philogano* the right father of the right *Erostrato*'. See pp. 63–6.
108 **counterfeit supposes** false assumptions of identity, impersonations; echo-

ing Gascoigne's title (see 106n.)
**bleared thine eyne** 'dimmed your eyes' (with tears); in this context, 'deceived'; *eyne* is an archaic plural.
109 **packing** plotting (*OED* pack *n.*[2])
**with a witness** with clear evidence, with a vengeance (*OED n.* 14); proverbial (Dent, W591)
110 **damned** damnèd
111 **faced and braved** outfaced and defied; cf. 4.3.124–7.
116 **bear my countenance** assume my identity

---

100 and – ] *Capell;* and, F    101 SD *Merchant*] *Cam²; Pedant* F    102 SD] *(Kneele.)*

And happily I have arrived at the last
Unto the wished haven of my bliss.
What Tranio did, myself enforced him to;
Then pardon him, sweet father, for my sake.                    120

VINCENTIO    I'll slit the villain's nose that would have sent
me to the jail.

BAPTISTA    But do you hear, sir? Have you married my
daughter without asking my good will?

VINCENTIO    Fear not, Baptista, we will content you –    125
go to. But I will in to be revenged for this villainy.    *Exit.*

BAPTISTA    And I, to sound the depth of this knavery.    *Exit.*

LUCENTIO    Look not pale, Bianca, thy father will not
frown.                    *Exeunt [Lucentio and Bianca].*

GREMIO

My cake is dough, but I'll in among the rest,    130
Out of hope of all but my share of the feast.    [*Exit.*]

KATHERINA    Husband, let's follow to see the end of this
ado.

---

118 **wished** wishèd
121 **I'll ... nose** Slitting or cutting off
the nose was a recognized form of
revenge. Cf. 'I see that nose of yours,
but not that dog I shall throw it to' (*Oth*
4.1.141–2).
126 **go to** 'don't worry'
130 **My ... dough** 'My project has
failed'; proverbial: 'His cake is dough'
(Dent, C12). See 1.1.108 and n.
131 'with no expectation of anything
except a place at the (wedding) feast'
132–41 This exchange anticipates
Katherina's later behaviour as well
as her speech at 5.2.142–85. Notably,
Katherina refers to Petruccio as
*Husband* at 132 and as *love* at 139;
beginning in prose, the dialogue moves
into doggerel rhyming couplets (138–
41), sealing the relationship with a

verbal flourish. With the taming a
*fait accompli*, that plot, and the play,
might end here, in compliance with
Petruccio's distinction between private
and public behaviour (2.1.308–17). If
the Officer remains onstage (together
with Grumio), this may explain
Katherina's hesitation about kissing
Petruccio in public. Although it is for
different reasons, another Katherine,
the Princess of France, is equally
hesitant to kiss (*H5* 5.2.248–77).
Alternatively, the Officer might leave
with Tranio (101) or with Vincentio or
Baptista, both seeking out villainy and
knavery (126 and 127 respectively).
In one performance (Monette, 1988),
the Officer turned his back, giving
Katherina and Petruccio privacy
(Schafer, 217).

117 at the last] at last *F2*    129 SD] *Capell; Exeunt. F*    131 SD] *Rowe*

PETRUCCIO     First kiss me, Kate, and we will.
KATHERINA     What, in the midst of the street?          135
PETRUCCIO     What, art thou ashamed of me?
KATHERINA     No sir, God forbid – but ashamed to kiss.
PETRUCCIO

Why then, let's home again. – Come, sirrah, let's away.
KATHERINA

Nay, I will give thee a kiss. [*She kisses him.*] Now pray
thee love, stay.

PETRUCCIO

Is not this well? Come, my sweet Kate.                  140
Better once than never, for never too late.      *Exeunt.*

[5.2]     *Enter* BAPTISTA, VINCENTIO, GREMIO, *the*
Merchant, LUCENTIO *and* BIANCA, [PETRUCCIO,
KATHERINA, HORTENSIO] *and* Widow, GRUMIO,
BIONDELLO *and* TRANIO *with Servants bringing in
a banquet.*

134 **kiss me, Kate** The phrase echoes
2.1.328 and anticipates 5.2.186.
139 SD See 132–41n. In this case, a kiss
is not 'just a kiss' (as the song goes):
Elizabeth Taylor's Katherina (Zeffirelli,
1967) gave Petruccio a peck on his
nose; other performances celebrate this
moment: in Edwards (1995), Katherina
and Petruccio turned upstage to walk
towards a glorious sunset (see also
Schafer, 218).
141 Combines two proverbial expressions:
'Better late than never' (Dent, L85) and
'It is never too late to mend' (Dent,
M875).
141 SD If *Exeunt* is obeyed, Kate
and Petruccio must exit and return
immediately, breaking the so-called law
of re-entry (which Shakespeare usually
avoids, although Prospero has a re-entry

between Acts 4 and 5 of *The Tempest*).
In most modern performances, a scene-
break offers time for a costume change,
but if the two scenes overlap, as they
may have done on the Elizabethan stage
and as they sometimes do in present-
day staging, Katherina and Petruccio
might simply join the others (see
pp. 321–2).
5.2   *\*'Actus Quintus.'* in F; all editors since
Theobald consider this scene and 5.1 as
the fifth act. The structure resembles
*MND* and *LLL*, in each of which a
public scene, with a central set piece,
caps the play.
0.1–5   *\*F* does not include either
Katherina and Petruccio or Hortensio
(though his Widow is mentioned).
Despite F's '*Exeunt*' at 5.1.141 for
Katherina and Petruccio, its omission

137 No] *Q*; Mo F   138–9] *Hibbard lines again. / away. / kiss. / stay. /*   139 SD] *Capell*   141 once]
late *Hanmer*   5.2] *Steevens; Actus Quintus. F*   0.2–3 PETRUCCIO . . . HORTENSIO] *Rowe subst.*   0.3–4
Widow . . . Servants] *Rowe subst.; Biondello, Grumio, and Widdow: The Seruingmen with Tranio F*

LUCENTIO

At last, though long, our jarring notes agree,
And time it is when raging war is done
To smile at scapes and perils overblown.
My fair Bianca, bid my father welcome,
While I with selfsame kindness welcome thine.          5
Brother Petruccio, sister Katherina,
And thou, Hortensio, with thy loving widow,
Feast with the best, and welcome to my house.
My banquet is to close our stomachs up
After our great good cheer. Pray you, sit down,          10
For now we sit to chat as well as eat.

PETRUCCIO

Nothing but sit and sit, and eat and eat.

BAPTISTA

Padua affords this kindness, son Petruccio.

PETRUCCIO

Padua affords nothing but what is kind.

of them in this entry may suggest that they remain. Usual theatrical practice, however, has them exit and return, allowing time for a costume change. All editors emend to include Katherina, Petruccio and Hortensio, though with considerable variation of placing. Oxf[1], for instance, directs Katherina and Petruccio to follow Tranio, Biondello and Grumio and precede the Servants bringing in the banquet. Having the Servants enter first to set the banquet offers one solution to editorial dilemmas about the timing of their entry. See pp. 321–2.

0.5 *banquet* sweetmeats, fruit and wine, following the main courses (*OED n.*[1] 3)

1 **long** after a long time
**jarring notes** Although Lucentio speaks to the company, his reference also may recall the *jarring notes* of the music lesson (3.1.38, 45).

2 *done] Rowe;* come *F;* gone *Collier*

2 *done F's 'come' makes sense only if one reads marital relations as a war between the sexes; most editors adopt Rowe's emendation, though Malone suggests 'calm', which edges toward Lucentio's reference to *perils overblown* (3).

3 **scapes** escapes from danger
**overblown** that have blown over, passed as a storm passes (*OED* overblow *v.*[1] 2)

5 **kindness** affection; kinship (*OED* 5; 1)

8 **with** on (Abbott, 193)

9 **close . . . up** provide a finale to the wedding feast; 'put an end to our quarrelling'. Ard[1] notes that 'and cheese to close up the stomach' concludes old lists of dinner dishes.

10 **our . . . cheer** i.e. the preceding wedding feast

12 a sign that Petruccio is bored by conventional manners (?)

14 **affords** provides; the modern (anachronistic) sense also applies.

HORTENSIO
  For both our sakes I would that word were true.          15
PETRUCCIO
  Now, for my life, Hortensio fears his widow.
WIDOW
  Then never trust me if I be afeared.
PETRUCCIO
  You are very sensible, and yet you miss my sense:
  I mean Hortensio is afeard of you.
WIDOW
  He that is giddy thinks the world turns round.          20
PETRUCCIO
  Roundly replied.
KATHERINA
  Mistress, how mean you that?
WIDOW
  Thus I conceive by him.
PETRUCCIO
  Conceives by me – how likes Hortensio that?
HORTENSIO
  My widow says, thus she conceives her tale.            25
PETRUCCIO
  Very well mended. Kiss him for that, good widow.
KATHERINA
  'He that is giddy thinks the world turns round' –

16 **for** upon
   **fears** is afraid of (*OED v.* 5). The
   Widow understands Petruccio to mean
   'frightens' (*OED v.* 1).
17 **never . . . if** proverbial (Dent, T558.1)
18 **sensible** having good sense; reasonable
   (*OED a.* 14); sensitive
20 proverbial (Dent, W870)
21–3 These lines admit of two
   arrangements: 21–2 constitute a blank
   verse line, but, if *Mistress* (22) is
   regarded as an extra-metrical vocative,
   so do 22–3. The present arrangement
   reflects this ambiguity.
21 **Roundly** plainly, frankly; possibly also
   'fluently' (*OED adv.* 3; 6)
23 'I reply because of what I take him
   (Petruccio) to mean, and to be.'
   Petruccio picks up *conceive* as 'to make
   pregnant' (24); Hortensio builds the
   sexual innuendo further (25), punning
   on *tale*/'tail', as at 2.1.218–19.

17 SP] *Hor. F2*    18 You are] You're *(RP)*

I pray you tell me what you meant by that.

WIDOW

Your husband, being troubled with a shrew,

Measures my husband's sorrow by his woe: 30

And now you know my meaning.

KATHERINA

A very mean meaning.

WIDOW Right, I mean you.

KATHERINA

And I am mean indeed, respecting you.

PETRUCCIO To her, Kate!

HORTENSIO To her, widow! 35

PETRUCCIO

A hundred marks my Kate does put her down.

HORTENSIO That's my office.

PETRUCCIO

Spoke like an officer. Ha' to thee, lad.

*Drinks to Hortensio.*

BAPTISTA

How likes Gremio these quick-witted folks?

---

29 **shrew** probably pronounced 'shrow' to rhyme with *woe* at 30 (Kökeritz, 211)

32 **mean** petty; nasty. Ard² suggests several meanings, continuing to the following lines, from 'demean' (*OED a.¹* 2) to 'moderate' (*OED a.²* 7). Thus at 33 Katherina may mean, 'I demean myself in paying attention to you' or 'My behaviour is moderate compared to yours'. *OED* (*a.²* 9) supports the idea of 'living mean' as 'living chastely': Katherina may imply that she is a respectable married woman, in contrast to the remarried Widow, conventionally associated with sexual lust.

34, 35 **To her** A variant of the hunting cry, urging a hound to pursue game; cf. Ind.1 and the hawking allusions at 4.1.179–85.

36 **marks** A mark was worth thirteen shillings and four pence, two-thirds of a pound.
**put her down** defeat her (in argument)

37 Hortensio picks up a second meaning for *put her down* (36): 'have sexual intercourse with her'.

38 **like an officer** like an office-holder fulfilling his duties. The point is that Hortensio will see that his wife's 'legal' duties are performed.
**Ha' to thee** 'here's to you', a toast which cues 38 SD.

38 thee] *Q*; the *F*  39 quick-witted] *(quicke witted)*

GREMIO

   Believe me, sir, they butt together well.                40

BIANCA

   Head and butt? An hasty-witted body

   Would say your head and butt were head and horn.

VINCENTIO

   Ay, mistress bride, hath that awakened you?

BIANCA

   Ay, but not frighted me; therefore I'll sleep again.

PETRUCCIO

   Nay, that you shall not. Since you have begun,                45

   Have at you for a better jest or two.

BIANCA

   Am I your bird? I mean to shift my bush,

   And then pursue me as you draw your bow.

   You are welcome all.

            *Exeunt Bianca* [, *Katherina and Widow*].

PETRUCCIO

   She hath prevented me. Here, Signor Tranio,                50

   This bird you aimed at, though you hit her not;

---

40 **butt** i.e. like cattle; *butt* = 'to strike with the head or horns' (*OED v.* 2g *trans.*). Rowe emended (unnecessarily) to 'butt heads together'.

41 **Head and butt** head and tail, with *butt* meaning 'buttock' (*OED n.*³ 3)
**hasty-witted** quick-witted; F2 reads 'hasty witty'.

42 **your . . . horn** 'your butting head was a horned head'; *horn* is the cuckold's symbol; also a phallus.

46 **Have at you** 'I'm coming to get you'; a warning given by a person about to wield a sword or otherwise attack someone.
**better** Although F's *better* makes good sense, modern editors accept Capell's emendation to 'bitter', meaning

'shrewd' or 'sharp' (*OED a.* 7).

47–8 The reference is to killing birds with a stone-bow or birding-bow resembling a hand-catapult; if the bird moved, the sportsman would need to pursue it (Oxf¹). Bianca's allusion shifts the sense of the previous word-play to archery – flight and butt shooting, where *butt* = the goal or target. Cam² suggests sexual undertones, reading *bush* as 'pubic hair' and (implicitly) 'arrow' as 'penis'.

49 a hostess's polite greeting to assembled guests

50–60 This exchange recalls the previous *supposes* at 5.1.108 (see n.); in addition, 53–4 suggest that Tranio had hoped to win Bianca for himself.

50 **prevented** anticipated; escaped from

---

40 butt] *Theobald;* But *F;* butt Heads *Rowe³*  41 hasty-witted] *(*hastie witted*) Pope;* hasty witty *F2*  45 not. Since] *Pope (*not, since*);* not since *F*  46 better] bitter *Capell (Theobald)* two] *F3;* too *F*  49 SD] *Rowe; Exit Bianca. F*  50 me. Here, Signor] *(*me, here signior*);* me here, Signor *Oxf*

Therefore a health to all that shot and missed.

TRANIO

　O sir, Lucentio slipped me like his greyhound,

　Which runs himself and catches for his master.

PETRUCCIO

　A good swift simile, but something currish.　　　　　55

TRANIO

　'Tis well, sir, that you hunted for yourself –

　'Tis thought your deer does hold you at a bay.

BAPTISTA

　O, O, Petruccio, Tranio hits you now.

LUCENTIO

　I thank thee for that gird, good Tranio.

HORTENSIO

　Confess, confess, hath he not hit you here?　　　　　60

PETRUCCIO

　'A has a little galled me, I confess,

　And as the jest did glance away from me,

　'Tis ten to one it maimed you two outright.

BAPTISTA

　Now in good sadness, son Petruccio,

　I think thou hast the veriest shrew of all.　　　　　65

PETRUCCIO

　Well, I say no: and therefore, Sir Assurance,

---

53 **slipped** unleashed

55 **swift** quick-witted
　**something** **currish** somewhat
　snappish – i.e. having less in common
　with a speedy *greyhound* (53) than with
　a cur

57 A stag is 'at bay' when it turns on
　hounds, defending itself (*OED n.⁴* 4);
　Tranio puns on *deer*/'dear'.

58 **hits** scores against

59 **gird** gibe, sharp remark

61 **galled me** made me sore (*OED v.¹* 1)

62 **did . . . me** 'bounced or ricocheted off
　me'

63 **maimed . . . outright** wounded you
　two instantly

64 **in good sadness** seriously (*OED*
　sadness *n.* 2); proverbial (Dent, SS1)

66–111 *Cym* 1.5 stages a (somewhat
　different) wife-wagering scene; the
　husbands' behaviour in the Argument
　to *Lucrece* offers another broad
　analogue. The wager, though not its
　outcome, also resembles the 'love-trial'

---

58 O, O] *(Oh, oh)*; O ho *Capell*　63 two] *Rowe*; too *F*　66 Sir Assurance] *(sir assurance) Cam²*;
for assurance *F2*

Let's each one send unto his wife,
And he whose wife is most obedient
To come at first when he doth send for her
Shall win the wager which we will propose.                    70

HORTENSIO   Content. What's the wager?

LUCENTIO   Twenty crowns.

PETRUCCIO   Twenty crowns!
I'll venture so much of my hawk or hound,
But twenty times so much upon my wife.                        75

LUCENTIO
A hundred then.

HORTENSIO                   Content.

PETRUCCIO                                   A match – 'tis done.

HORTENSIO   Who shall begin?

LUCENTIO   That will I. Go, Biondello, bid your mistress
   come to me.                                                79

BIONDELLO   I go.                                        *Exit.*

BAPTISTA
Son, I'll be your half Bianca comes.

LUCENTIO
I'll have no halves; I'll bear it all myself.

*Enter* BIONDELLO.

How now, what news?

in *KL* 1.1. Bullough observes that the
tradition of the wife-wager is nearly
as extensive as that for the bed-trick
(8.12–16).

66 **Sir Assurance** ironic form of address;
cf. 'Sir Smile' at *WT* 1.2.196. Most
modern editors prefer F2's 'for
assurance' ('to put the matter to the
test'); 'for' and 'sir' (with a long *s*) could
be easily confused in secretary hand.

67 **Let's . . . send** a short line; suggestions
to regularize it include: 'Let us each one
send one' (RP); 'Let's each one send

command', as at *H8* 2.1.150 (TWC).

69 **To come** in coming; 'gerundive use of
the infinitive' (Abbott, 356)

72 **Twenty crowns** a crown was worth five
shillings, so five pounds (see 1.2.56n.)

74 **of** on

81 **I'll . . . half** 'I'll pay half the risk' – in
certainty of getting half the winnings
(*OED n.* 5).

82 **have no halves** Ard² notes a possible
pun, depending on the pronunciation
of 'half' and *halves*, probably varying
in the period.

67 Let's each one send] Let us each one send one *(RP)*

297

BIONDELLO    Sir, my mistress sends you word that she is
busy, and she cannot come.                                                    85

PETRUCCIO

How? 'She's busy and she cannot come'?
Is that an answer?

GREMIO                              Ay, and a kind one too:
Pray God, sir, your wife send you not a worse.

PETRUCCIO    I hope better.

HORTENSIO    Sirrah Biondello, go and entreat my wife         90
to come to me forthwith.                                *Exit Biondello.*

PETRUCCIO

O ho, 'entreat' her – nay then, she must needs come.

HORTENSIO

I am afraid sir, do what you can,


*Enter* BIONDELLO.


Yours will not be entreated. Now, where's my wife?

BIONDELLO

She says you have some goodly jest in hand.                    95
She will not come; she bids you come to her.

PETRUCCIO

Worse and worse: 'She will not come' – O vile,
Intolerable, not to be endured.
Sirrah Grumio, go to your mistress;                                99

---

86–7  *F prints as prose.
86  **How? 'What?';** elliptical form of 'How
say you?' (*OED adv.* 4a)
89  **I hope better** 'I have higher hopes';
*hope* = believe: Petruccio is almost
certainly displaying considerable
confidence in the outcome.
95  **goodly** excellent (ironic)
97  **Worse and worse** proverbial (Dent,

WW34)
98  Cf. *MA* 3.3.35–6, where Dogberry
remarks: 'to talk is most tolerable, and
not to be endured'. Claire McEachern
(238) suggests the phrase comes
from John Northbrooke's *Treatise
Against . . . Plays* (1577): 'Plays and
Players are not tolerable nor to be
endured'.

86–7] *Capell; prose F*  89 better] a better *Capell*  92] *Capell lines* her! / come. /  93–4] *Capell lines*
sir, / entreated. / wife? /  93.1] *after* entreated. *94 Ard¹*  97–8] *Steevens; F lines* come: / indur'd: /

Say I command her come to me.                    *Exit* [*Grumio*].
HORTENSIO    I know her answer.
PETRUCCIO    What?
HORTENSIO    She will not.
PETRUCCIO
    The fouler fortune mine, and there an end.


*Enter* KATHERINA.


BAPTISTA
    Now, by my halidom, here comes Katherina.                    105
KATHERINA
    What is your will, sir, that you send for me?
PETRUCCIO
    Where is your sister, and Hortensio's wife?
KATHERINA
    They sit conferring by the parlour fire.
PETRUCCIO
    Go fetch them hither; if they deny to come,
    Swinge me them soundly forth unto their husbands.           110
    Away, I say, and bring them hither straight.    [*Exit Katherina.*]
LUCENTIO
    Here is a wonder, if you talk of a wonder.
HORTENSIO
    And so it is. I wonder what it bodes.


104 **fouler** worse
  **there an end** that's the end of the
    matter; there is no more to say;
    proverbial (Dent, E113.1)
105 **by my halidom** 'by all that I hold
    sacred' (*OED* 3b); *halidom* is spelled
    'hollidam' in F, suggesting the popular
    though erroneous etymology 'holy
    dame' = the Virgin Mary.
108 **conferring**    talking    together,

conversing (*OED v.* 6)
110 **Swinge me them** 'whip or thrash
    them for me' (*OED* swinge *v.*¹ 1; ethic
    dative 'for me')
111 **straight** immediately, straightaway
112 **wonder** miracle, referring to the belief
    that preternatural events were omens
    or portents; a *wonder* = an object of
    admiration or astonishment, a prodigy
113 **bodes** portends

100 SD *Grumio*] *Rowe subst.*    105 halidom] *(*hollidam*)*    111 SD] *Rowe*    112 of a wonder] of
wonder *Dyce (Walker);* of wonders *Hudson (Lettsom)*


299

PETRUCCIO

Marry, peace it bodes, and love, and quiet life,
An awful rule and right supremacy                                   115
And, to be short, what not that's sweet and happy.

BAPTISTA

Now fair befall thee, good Petruccio!
The wager thou hast won, and I will add
Unto their losses twenty thousand crowns,
Another dowry to another daughter,                                 120
For she is changed as she had never been.

PETRUCCIO

Nay, I will win my wager better yet
And show more sign of her obedience –
Her new-built virtue and obedience.


*Enter* KATHERINA, BIANCA *and* Widow.

See where she comes, and brings your froward wives       125
As prisoners to her womanly persuasion.
Katherine, that cap of yours becomes you not:
Off with that bauble – throw it underfoot.

WIDOW

Lord, let me never have a cause to sigh

---

115 **awful** commanding awe or respect
  **right** true, appropriate
116 **what not that's** 'all that is'
117 **fair befall thee** 'may good luck be yours'
121 **as . . . been** 'as if she were a different person'
124 **obedience** Editors have suspected dittography, but the repetition from 123 works to intensify the idea (not to say *wonder*); cf. Katherina's further, climactic, repetition at 159.
127 **Katherine** Petruccio's form of address here and at 136 may suggest

that he acknowledges her chosen name ('They call me Katherine that do talk of me', 2.1.183), yet he reverts at 186 and 190 to the diminutive 'Kate', the name he has given her. Maguire observes that here (as cued by 4.5), 'Katherine and Kate compete or coexist' (*Names*, 128). **that cap** probably the cap that Petruccio refused in 4.3 (see 4.3.67n.)
128 **bauble** showy trifle, plaything. Most editors, following Rowe's '*She pulls off her Cap and throws it down*', cue Katherina to obey.

124 new-built] *(*new built*)*   128 underfoot.] underfoot. *She pulls off her Cap and throws it down. / Rowe*

Till I be brought to such a silly pass.                    130

BIANCA

Fie, what a foolish duty call you this?

LUCENTIO

I would your duty were as foolish too:
The wisdom of your duty, fair Bianca,
Hath cost me five hundred crowns since supper time.

BIANCA

The more fool you for laying on my duty.                    135

PETRUCCIO

Katherine, I charge thee tell these headstrong women
What duty they do owe their lords and husbands.

WIDOW

Come, come, you're mocking: we will have no telling.

PETRUCCIO

Come on, I say, and first begin with her.

WIDOW    She shall not.                                     140

PETRUCCIO

I say she shall: 'and first begin with her'.

KATHERINA

Fie, fie, unknit that threatening unkind brow,

---

130 **pass** predicament; critical juncture
134 **five hundred** F's reading, which Capell and most later editors emend to agree with the one-hundred-crown bargain (76). Sisson argues that the compositor misread *a* as *v*, the roman numeral for five, and expanded it (*New*, 1.167); but it is also possible that Lucentio exaggerates his losses.
135 **more fool you** proverbial (Dent, F505.1)
**laying** betting money
136–7 *prose in F
138 **you're mocking** you can't be serious
142–85 Katherina's speech (the longest in the play; the only one nearly

as long is where the Lord sets up the play world – at Ind.1.101–37, some seven lines shorter) contains numerous Elizabethan as well as biblical commonplaces, along with echoes of the marriage service and the *Homily of the State of Matrimony* (*Homilies*, sigs Gg3ᵛ–Hh4ᵛ); cf. *CE* 2.1.10–31, where Luciana 'lectures' Adriana on male rights. On the cultural and theatrical history of this speech, see pp. 118–31.
142 **unkind** unfriendly; unnatural – i.e. not according to the law of nature, in this case, the 'law' requiring Katherina to be submissive.

134 five] an *Rowe*; a *Capell*; one *Collier*    136–7] *Rowe³*; prose *F*    138 you're] *F3*; your *F*    142 threatening] (thretaning); threating *F2*

And dart not scornful glances from those eyes
To wound thy lord, thy king, thy governor.
It blots thy beauty as frosts do bite the meads,                145
Confounds thy fame as whirlwinds shake fair buds
And in no sense is meet or amiable.
A woman moved is like a fountain troubled,
Muddy, ill-seeming, thick, bereft of beauty
And while it is so, none so dry or thirsty          150
Will deign to sip or touch one drop of it.
Thy husband is thy lord, thy life, thy keeper,
Thy head, thy sovereign: one that cares for thee
And for thy maintenance; commits his body
To painful labour both by sea and land,            155
To watch the night in storms, the day in cold,
Whilst thou liest warm at home, secure and safe,
And craves no other tribute at thy hands

143 The darting gaze of the sonnet lady wounded her lover; a commonplace of Elizabethan sonnet discourse. Cf. *VA* 196.

145 **blots** stains, tarnishes (*OED v.*[1] 3a)
**meads** meadows

146 **Confounds thy fame** spoils your reputation
**shake fair buds** 'shake young buds off the trees'; cf. *Son* 18.3: 'Rough winds do shake the darling buds of May'.

148 **moved** stirred to anger, exasperated
**a fountain troubled** Cf. *TC* 3.3.309, 'My mind is troubled, like a fountain stirred'.

149 **ill-seeming** of unpleasant appearance; *OED* records no other example.

150 **none so dry** 'nobody – no matter how dry' (see Abbott, 281)

152 **Thy . . . lord** See Genesis, 3.16; Ephesians, 5.22; 1 Peter, 3.1. See also *An Exhortation, Concerning Good Order and Obedience to Rulers and Magistrates*

(1547) (*Homilies*, sigs R1ʳ–S4ʳ); multiple references intensify the force of Kate's words.

154 **maintenance; commits** F reads 'maintenance. Commits'. Retaining the full stop offers another playable option. 'Thy husband . . . maintenance.' states the traditional relationship between husband and wife; what follows catalogues what a husband must endure to secure his wife's regard: arguably, Katherina's words express her understanding of the rules of the game (Freedman, *Gaze*, 95). Ard[2] notes that Ard[1] reads 'maintenance commits', generating the sense that the husband 'commits his body / to painful labour' in order to maintain his wife, but Sisson suggests that the contrast 'is between the husband facing dangers abroad and the wife's safety at home' (*New*, 1.167).

155 **painful** exacting, exhausting (*OED a.* 1b)

156 **watch** be on watch throughout

145 do bite] bite *F2*  154 maintenance; commits] *Collier;* maintenance. Commits *F;* maintenance, commits *Grant White;* maintenance commits *Cam*[1]

But love, fair looks and true obedience –
Too little payment for so great a debt.          160
Such duty as the subject owes the prince,
Even such a woman oweth to her husband;
And when she is froward, peevish, sullen, sour,
And not obedient to his honest will,
What is she but a foul contending rebel          165
And graceless traitor to her loving lord?
I am ashamed that women are so simple
To offer war where they should kneel for peace,
Or seek for rule, supremacy and sway
When they are bound to serve, love and obey.     170
Why are our bodies soft, and weak, and smooth,
Unapt to toil and trouble in the world,
But that our soft conditions and our hearts
Should well agree with our external parts?
Come, come, you froward and unable worms,        175
My mind hath been as big as one of yours,
My heart as great, my reason haply more,
To bandy word for word and frown for frown.
But now I see our lances are but straws,

---

161–2 another biblical echo: 'as the churche is subject vnto Christe, lykewyse the wyues to their owne husbandes in all thinges' (Ephesians, 5.24)
164 **honest will** honourable inclination or purpose; *will* also = sexual desire (lawful within marriage)
165 **contending** antagonistic
166 **graceless** ungrateful; the word also carries theological overtones: 'not in a state of grace, unregenerate' (*OED a.* 1).
167 **simple** simple-minded
170 **serve . . . obey** 'The Form of Solemnization of Matrimony' from *BCP* reads: 'Wilt thou obey him and serve him, love, honor, and keep him, in sickness, and in health?' (292). At

this point, Kate has accomplished what Petruccio asked of her.
172 **Unapt** unfit
173 **conditions** dispositions, characteristics (*OED n.* 11–13)
175 **unable** weak, impotent
178 **bandy** exchange, send to and fro (as in a tennis game)
179 **lances . . . straws** The metaphor is from tilting; perhaps also playing on *scornful glances* (143). Cf. *KL* 4.6.162–3, 'And the strong lance of justice hurtless breaks; / Arm it in rags, a pigmy's straw does pierce it' (F only). After removing her cap, Paola Dionisotti kept the hatpin, which she threw down on the table, underscoring this line (Bogdanov, 1978).

177 as] is *F2*

Our strength as weak, our weakness past compare,          180
That seeming to be most which we indeed least are.
Then vail your stomachs, for it is no boot,
And place your hands below your husband's foot:
In token of which duty, if he please,
My hand is ready, may it do him ease.                     185

PETRUCCIO
Why, there's a wench. Come on, and kiss me, Kate.

LUCENTIO
Well, go thy ways, old lad, for thou shalt ha't.

VINCENTIO
'Tis a good hearing when children are toward.

LUCENTIO
But a harsh hearing, when women are froward.

181 This is extremely cryptic syntax: *That seeming* elides the *we* that seems to be its subject; subject and object risk conflation; *most* transforms to *least*; comparisons fail altogether. Is it just accidental that *least are* falls outside the iambic pentameter and so would be termed a feminine rhyme? Spoken by the boy actor, these lines say that he is indeed the thing he is not, and they say it twice. Oxf¹'s reading suggests the syntactic complexity: 'Our weakness is greater than anything one can think to compare it with in that we strive hardest to pretend to that very quality – strength – of which we have least.'

182 **vail your stomachs** suppress your pride (*OED v.*² 4a)
**no boot** to no avail

183 Katherina's gesture alludes to 'the script that appears in the Sarum, the York, the (Scottish) Rathen, and the (French) Martène (Ordo IV) manuals for actions that the bride was to perform upon receipt of the wedding ring and her husband's accompanying vow of endowment. Following his pledge of worldly goods, the bride is directed to fall prostrate at the bridegroom's

feet, and . . . the rite then directs that she is to "courtesy" his foot in gratitude before he stoops to raise her up into her new status as wife' (Boose, 'Husbandry', 195). By the 1590s, the custom had been officially prohibited for some 40 years; resurrecting it either 'marks Petruccio and Katherine's union as obviously anachronistic or endows it with the nostalgic prestige of a recently lost custom' (Dolan, 35).

185 **may . . . ease** 'may it give him comfort' or 'if it will give him comfort'

186 As at 5.1.139, the kiss (a playable option) confirms Katherina and Petruccio's partnership.

187 **go thy ways** well done
**old lad** affectionate form of address, meaning roughly 'good old Petruccio'. Cf. 4.1.99, where Grumio is addressed as 'old lad' by his fellow-servant Nathaniel.
**ha't** have it = have the prize, 'be the winner'

188 **good hearing** a good thing to hear; a pleasant sight
**toward** willing, compliant (*OED a.* 4); opposite of *froward* at 189

188 SP] *Bap. (Capell)*

PETRUCCIO

   Come Kate, we'll to bed.                      190

   We three are married, but you two are sped.

   – 'Twas I won the wager, though you hit the white,

   And being a winner, God give you good night.

                                    *Exit Petruccio.*

HORTENSIO

   Now go thy ways; thou hast tamed a curst shrew.     194

LUCENTIO

   'Tis a wonder, by your leave, she will be tamed so.    [*Exeunt.*]

FINIS

191 **sped** defeated, brought to the wrong end (*OED v.* 7b)

192 **hit the white** proverbial (Dent, W314.1): to hit the centre of the target in archery; with pun on Bianca ('white' in Italian) – thus, 'won Bianca'. Also, as at 47–52, playing on shooting and having sex: 'hit it' = 'to attain the sexual target of the pudend' (Partridge, 120); cf. *LLL*'s extended word-play on the term at 4.1.117–29.

193 Ard¹ comments: 'alluding to the natural wish of successful gamesters to leave the table before their luck turns'. Proverbial: 'God give you good night' (Dent, G185.1).

193 SD As in F. In some performances, Petruccio and Katherina exit separately; some performances end the play here (see Schafer, 232). For a discussion

of F's textual indeterminacy at this point and the issues that raises, see LN (pp. 306–8). For a critical and theatrical history of the play's sense of ending, see pp. 118–31.

194 Hortensio's *thy* may refer to the couple (man and wife as one); given the sliding definitions of *shrew*, *thou* might refer to Petruccio, to Kate or to both: have Petruccio *and* Kate 'tamed a curst shrew'? F reads 'Shrow', indicating pronunciation rhyming with the final *so*.

195 **wonder** marvel, prodigy; object of astonishment, implying profound admiration; astonishing event, surprising incident (*OED n.* 1a; 1c; 4a); cf. 112.

195 SD1, 2 F reads 'FINIS' but prints no exit SD. See LN (pp. 306–8).

193 SD] *Exeunt Petruccio and Katherina. / Rowe*   194 shrew] *(Shrow)*   195 SD1] *Rowe*

# LONGER NOTE

5.2.193 SD–195 SD2  At 5.2.193 SD (TLN 2747, sig. V1ʳ), F reads '*Exit Petruchio*'; 'FINIS.' (centred within rules) follows two final lines of dialogue. According to F, only Petruccio exits; all the other players, including Katherina, remain onstage. Observing that 'F1 and Q omit Katherina's exit', Rowe (1709) emended F's '*Exit Petruchio*' to '*Exeunt Petruchio and Katherina.*' and ended the play by directing a final '*Exeunt.*' With the exception of Thompson, who calls attention to F's SD in her commentary and to 'FINIS.' in a textual note, all modern editions follow Rowe's lead, consigning F's '*Exit Petruchio*' to textual notes with no further comment and appending a final '*Exeunt.*'. By so neatening F, that widely accepted choice has belied its genuine difficulty and drawn attention away from the degree of ambiguity that results from the lack of exit directions – an ambiguity that, as in the endings of *Measure for Measure* and *All's Well*, pertains especially to the woman's part. What might account for this puzzling lack of clarity?

Exit SDs, of course, are notoriously irregular: detailed directions by playwrights and playhouse personnel are the exception rather than the rule, and no hard evidence suggests that F's SDs represent 'Shakespearean' dramaturgy (see Long, 'Precious', esp. 417–18; *TxC*, 9–31). Notably, '*Exit Petruchio*' (TLN 2747) lacks a full stop – an omission that occurs twice earlier, at TLN 448 ('*Exeunt ambo. Manet Tranio and Lucentio*') and at TLN 1845 ('*Exit*'), following Petruccio's soliloquy on how he plans to tame Katherina. Moreover, the three sheets containing the final page of *TS* and seven pages of the early acts of *AW* (sheets V1:6 and V2:5) have, in all, nine unpunctuated exits and only one with a final stop – '*Exit Par.*', where the stop seems as likely to mark an abbreviation for Parolles as the end of the SD. On the basis of Hinman's evidence, Compositor B set all these pages and was also responsible for setting *TS*'s other two unpunctuated exits (on sigs S4ʳ and T3ᵛ) mentioned above. The absence of the full stop at TLN 2747 might be explained, then, as a compositorial quirk, the result of B's occasional carelessness about adding full stops or leaving space for them (Hinman, *Printing*, 447, 451–3, 458, 461). On a page set by Compositor D, no direction marks Petruccio's and Katherina's exit as they return to Padua (TLN 2178), nor is there an exit direction for Hortensio, who has the scene's final line (TLN 2179). Katherina is included in F's earlier exits of the couple – '*Exit Petruchio and Katherine.*' (TLN 1205, following the wedding bargain) and '*Exeunt P.Ka.*' (TLN

1625, as they leave the wedding banquet) – but Compositor C set these pages (T1ʳ and T2ᵛ). Yet B had set enough of *TS* (sigs S2ᵛ–S6ᵛ, T3ʳ–T4ᵛ and V1ʳ) to be aware of Katherina's full name as well as its abbreviated form, 'Kate'. It is tempting to argue from context that B may not have known that two earlier joint exit SDs had specified both Katherina and Petruccio and that he saw no need to add the name of a character to a SD that, given a dialogic cue ('Come, Kate, we'll to bed', TLN 2743), included her. But it seems more likely, especially since *TS* was divided among several typesetters, that B set only what he saw in his copy. Rehearsing these bibliographical data raises the question of whether, when setting by formes, B or *any* compositor ever read an entire text, a proposition that goes against arguing from context (RP).

Nonetheless, and regardless of its provenance, F's indeterminacy is suggestive as well as provocative. Like any text, *TS* speaks as powerfully through its formal incoherences (even when those may be attributed to a compositor) as through its coherences. What conditions of possibility result from reconsidering F's choreography of *ending by not ending*? That F's sense of ending has gone unremarked seems easy to explain on the grounds that Rowe's emendation, by obeying Petruccio's dialogic cue and adding a final '*Exeunt.*', bows to conventions of comic closure as a kind of law of the stage (no unravelling permitted) and aligns with the assumption that it is an editor's responsibility to amplify or clarify extant SDs (Wells, 7, citing McKerrow). Moreover, not only does Rowe's emended SD not tell players *how* to perform this (or any other) exit but performance history also provides ample evidence that his emendation has provoked a wide range of enactments (see Schafer 231–2). Re-choreographing these final moments on the evidence of previous performance practice – say, marking an exit for Katherina at 5.2.190 or 191 (TLN 2743 or 2744), following Petruccio's 'Come Kate, we'll to bed', a choice made by Zeffirelli and Leach (in the latter case, giving Petruccio a solo exit) – offers one potential editorial alternative. But as Marco de Marinis observes, 'It is *never* possible to go "backward" from the theatrical transcoding (or performance) of a given stage direction to the stage direction itself . . . the stage directions within a dramatic text do not constitute a "score," since they are not expressed in a notational language' (28–9). Yet Rowe's emendation surely represents just such a transcoding – if not the transcoding of performance as Rowe knew it, then certainly a transcoding that endows *TS* with a sense of ending seen through the lens of his culture. Culture, of course, is an unstable term – constantly produced and reproduced by historical actors, whether readers or players, whose performance and re-performance of coded meanings is unsystematic, changeable (Sewell, 88–93). What was once perceived as a transparently neutral (even timeless?) choice has since been called into question and attracted a variety of meanings, projections of equally time-bound socio-political and ideological investments (Grigely, 106). Nor can the question of ending be explained by appealing to historically specific contexts (say, by invoking early modern debates on marriage), to the supposedly normative endings of 'Shakespeare's early comedies' or to 'original' performances: as Peter Blayney claims, there is 'no uniquely authoritative record of the [early modern] performance text' ('Introduction', xxx).

Since the timing of Katherina's exit is not self-evident from F, does it need to be precisely determined? She might exit before Petruccio or with him (both have been played); she might pause briefly and then exit herself; she might stay, exiting with the others, perhaps even leading them off; she might remain after all the others have left, an enigmatic, silent 'epilogue'. Each – and this list does not necessarily exhaust all potential choices – can be considered within F's 'field of possibility' (Eco, 19); each represents an option, not an obligation. To choose one over another is not only to imagine 'a reader who is an entirely passive spectator to the textual performance' constructed by an editor but also to accept 'the all-too easy assumption that early modern scripts are incomplete until editorially completed' (Kidnie, 'Staging', 175–6; see also Cox). After all, even the questions voiced in *TS*'s final lines of dialogue point away from closure and towards open-endedness. Although both address Petruccio, Katherina is their subject, the body in question. While Hortensio's 'Now go thy ways; thou hast tamed a curst shrew' assumes his success, Lucentio's ''Tis a wonder, by your leave, she will be tamed so' strikes a slightly hesitant note (TLN 2748–50). Ultimately, any answers to those questions rest in the imaginations of its onstage and offstage audiences – including readers. Significantly, F not only offers opportunities that Rowe's emendation precludes but also dispenses with tacking on *AS*'s 'Sly epilogue'. Continuing its final tropes of dialectical exchange, *TS* ends on a 'non-final' note in which, as Margie Burns argues, 'the wish for closure can be exchanged for the pleasures of vitality' (101) – and, I would add, potentially productive ambiguity.

Although reasserting F may risk fetishizing a print document, doing so not only unsettles an emendation that has functioned to tame the textual indeterminacy surrounding Katherina's exit but also assumes that *TS* in print is a work in process, one that always is 'coming-into-performance' (Hodgdon, 'New', 220), looking forward to future critical as well as theatrical re-stagings. On the one hand, in leaving open precisely when Katherina exits, this edition takes a radical editorial position; on the other, in directing a final '*Exeunt.*' to mark the end of the staged event, it acknowledges a print convention that appears in some (though not all) Folio texts.

# APPENDIX 1

## TEXTUAL ANALYSIS

*The Taming of the Shrew* appears as the eleventh play in the Comedies section of the 1623 First Folio, after *As You Like It* and before *All's Well That Ends Well*. Occupying twenty-two pages (208–29; sigs S2ᵛ–V1ʳ), it is titled '*The Taming of the Shrew*' in its head-title (in roman type) and running titles as well as in its listing in the Catalogue. There is no list of *Dramatis Personae*; the final page (sig. V1ʳ) bears 'FINIS.' and a printer's ornament. The Comedies section of the First Folio begins with *The Tempest*, the play whose supposed date of composition is closest to F's publication; four other plays, also apparently transcribed by the professional scrivener Ralph Crane, precede *The Shrew*, which is followed by plays already in print, and finally by the remaining F-only comedies. Alone among the non-Crane plays (like *Merry Wives* in the Crane group), *The Shrew* replaces a putatively 'stolne, and surreptitious' earlier text in need of cure – one that, until recently, has been labelled a 'bad' quarto (Greg, *Folio*, 80–1; Werstine, 'Narratives', 'Quartos'; Maguire, *Suspect*). *The Shrew*'s status thus stands in direct contrast to that of *Love's Labour's Lost*, *A Midsummer Night's Dream*, *The Merchant of Venice* and *Much Ado* (whether or not Heminge and Condell disingenuously meant to imply that all Q texts were seriously unsatisfactory, a proposition they well knew was simply false (RP)).

On the evidence of Hinman and later analysts (*Printing*, 2.446–62, 514–18; see also Howard-Hill; O'Connor), *The Shrew* was set by three compositors. Compositor B, who set most of the volume, set fourteen pages, 1,723 lines of type comprising sigs S2ᵛ–S6ᵛ, T3ʳ–T4ᵛ and V1ʳ (pp. 208–16, 221–4, 229; 1.1.0–2.1.262); C set four pages, sigs T1ʳ⁻ᵛ and T2ʳ⁻ᵛ (pp. 217–20; 2.1.260–4.1.13); and

D set the remaining four pages, sigs T5$^{r-v}$ and T6$^{r-v}$ (pp. 225–8; 4.3.189–5.2.131). All three occasionally set verse as prose (e.g. C, at 3.2.156–82/TLN 1541–64; B, at 4.1.72–6/TLN 1816–20); prose is set as verse once (B, at 2.1.75–82/TLN 937–46). Although these pages lack evidence of strain to compress or expand copy, which would have reflected error in casting off, this does not mean that the copy had not been cast off or that the compositor had licence to depart from the lining on which the counting of that cast-off was based. Accordingly, it is reasonable to assume that F here reproduces the mislining of the copy MS (RP). Hinman identifies an interruption of two or three months during *The Shrew*'s printing, between quires S and T and the final page, sig. V1$^r$, set in the quire that contains the first eleven pages of *All's Well* (*Printing*, 2.446–62). This delay, however, Hinman suggests, has no apparent textual implications beyond the possibility that B was engaged in other work during the ensuing months (see LN, pp. 306–8). Surviving F copies contain no important variant readings: six (sig. S5$^v$) are obvious corrections of typographical errors; sig. V1$^r$ has one variant only. According to Hinman, 'The text was certainly read, and read with some care; but reference to copy is by no means implied' (*Printing*, 1.262–3).

Although *The Shrew*'s textual history is bound up with the anonymous *A Shrew*, the controversy over the relationship of the two plays (see pp. 8–28) has little impact on editing *The Shrew*, which at first sight would seem to be a fairly straightforward process. However, closer examination reveals a text that is far removed either from Heminge's and Condell's claim that F's plays (if previously printed) have been 'cur'd, and [are] perfect of their limbes', and that F adds 'all the rest, absolute in their numbers, as he conceiued them' (a convenient half-truth designed to market the book as commemorating Shakespeare) or from the text of editorial desire: one written in Shakespeare's hand for which he was solely responsible (*TxC*, 145–7). The play exhibits several curious features: among them, incomplete act and scene divisions; irregularities and errors at the text's micro-level; plot inconsistencies; speech prefix errors (some linked to the presence of actors' names); problematic entry and exit SDs; and indications of possible revision. In attempting to account for F's derivation and to create an orderly text, editors have mobilized these features to fit pre-existing, and problematic, categories – foul papers, scribal copy, playbook, literary transcript – without reaching any firm consensus (see Werstine, 'Suggestion', esp. 169; Mowat). Yet although such categories may serve the editorial project, F's *Shrew* is a workable theatrical document that could have served the theatre as it is, even though it need not have done so (see Gurr, 'Maximal'). In reconsidering the evidence and its previous interpretations, how, then, does looking from a theatrical perspective help to reshape the conditions of textual analysis?

## ACT AND SCENE DIVISIONS

Act and scene divisions ('*Actus primus. Scaena Prima.*', TLN 1; '*Actus Tertia.*', TLN 1293; '*Actus Quartus. Scena Prima.*', TLN 1978; '*Actus Quintus.*', TLN 2532) are not systematic, nor is it possible to discern their origin precisely. It cannot, for example, be assumed that some were added by one hand and some by another – say, for the play as acted at Blackfriars, where act breaks allowed for candles to be trimmed (Taylor & Jowett, 4–8). Are these divisions evidence of printing-house sophistication? Greg thought so, arguing that act breaks were added at the printing-house to 'fresh' foul papers (*Folio*, 142, 212–15); Taylor, however, claims that *The Shrew* was set from a late transcript and that the act divisions (at least presumptively) originate in the theatre (Taylor & Jowett, 44–5; but see Massai, *Rise*, 136–58). Currently, debate has swung towards viewing them as of printing-house origin (Massai, 'Shakespeare'), though their incompleteness in *The Shrew* might seem to argue against such a conclusion and be congruous with some history of revision inscribed in the manuscript copy (RP). All that can be claimed is that a non-theatrical agent other than the author has added act breaks incorrectly and incompletely.

## AUTHOR, SCRIBE OR COMPOSITOR?

When turning to textual irregularities, inconsistencies and errors, there seems no clear way of distinguishing between authorial, scribal and compositorial agency, though the latter has seemed most likely to previous editors, who have attributed many of them to Compositor B (Bowers, *Dramatists*, 56; Werstine, 'Compositor'), an assumption that Laurie Maguire's reconsideration of the evidence calls into question ('Petruccio', 122–5). Among these supposed or apparent errors, ten result from simple misreadings (e.g. *'sister'* for *'suitor'*, 1.1.47.2/ TLN 345); one from probable eyeskip (*'Vincentio*'s come' for *'Vincentio*, come', 1.1.13/TLN 312); eight from omitting a word or phrase (e.g. 'I charge [thee] tell', 2.1.8/TLN 863; 'it is [a] paltry cap', 4.3.83/TLN 2066); and two from incorrect expansion.[1] A further ten concern potential errors in pronouns, verb mood and number and adverbs. Of the six occurring in SPs (*'Gru.'*[*mio*] for *Cur.*[*tis*] at 4.1.23/TLN 1664, *'Gre.'* for *Gru.* at 4.1.104/TLN 1744, *'Luc.'* for *Hor.* at 4.2.4/TLN 1850, *'Hor.'* for *Luc.* at 4.2.6/TLN 1853 and 4.2.8/TLN 1855 and *'Par.'* for *Ped.* at 4.2.73/TLN 1924), the last four are considered in more detail below. Excluding corrections to Italian (which vary from edition to edition), modern editors have introduced over fifty substantive emendations, 'indicative more of [their] need for logic and metrical smoothness than of B's carelessness' (Maguire, 'Petruccio', 125). Of the eight supposed errors of omission, only five require correction in order to make sense; and only five of the ten pronoun, verb mood or adverb references invite emendation. Finally, nine miscellaneous

1    Wells and Taylor consider the number of single-word omissions larger than usual (*TxC*, 169).

instances – for example, 'Their love is not so great' (1.1.106–7/ TLN 411–12); 'you mean not her to –' (1.2.223/TLN 793) – do not require emendation: F's text seems satisfactory as it stands (all emendations are tracked in textual notes and commentary).

## PLOT INCONSISTENCIES AND THE 'HORTENSIO PROBLEM'

Most plot inconsistencies or 'loose ends' occur in the subplot, and many concern questions about who knows what at particular points in the action (on timing, see Daniel) – for example, Petruccio tells Vincentio that the latter's son, Lucentio, has married Bianca, but neither he nor Hortensio, who confirms what Petruccio says, can know this yet (4.5.63–4, 75/TLN 2360–1, 2373). Bogdanov (1978) thought this troubling enough to replace most of Petruccio's speech with 'Lucentio, Hey we know him well' (promptbook), and cut all but 'And wander we to see thy honest son, / Who will of thy arrival be full joyous' (4.5.70–1/ TLN 2368–9); Schafer records more fanciful solutions (210– 11). Some have seemed insignificant and are more noticeable at the level of editing than in the theatre. Several – such as the men's agreeing to fund Petruccio's courtship, which is never mentioned again (1.2.213–15/TLN 782–4); although Baptista insists on keeping Bianca's wedding plans secret (4.4.50–3/ TLN 2233–6), Gremio knows of them – can be explained as 'opportunistic dramaturgy' and by assuming, as did Levin L. Schücking, that Shakespeare 'quite naively exchanges the point of view of the speaker for that of the audience' (cited in Wells & Taylor, 365–6).

Perhaps the most curious textual features concern the nexus of peculiarities surrounding Hortensio's role. Like Hortensio himself, the 'Hortensio problem' has two parts, both of which are related to Hortensio's *alter ego* Licio, his schoolmaster-disguise. Once disguised as Licio (2.1.38.2/TLN 898), he gets forgotten in the bride-bartering competition (2.1.330–401/

TLN 1207–81) and more or less dismissed as a serious wooer (3.1). Since he appears as Licio at the opening of 3.1, his presence at the bartering might present a practical problem, but only if his Licio-disguise were too cumbersome to be quickly put on or taken off. By Katherina and Petruccio's wedding (3.2), however, Tranio seems to have taken over Hortensio's role: although he has barely met Petruccio, he suddenly seems familiar with his usual way of dressing, offers to lend him clothes and hopes to persuade him to change into a more suitable outfit. (In a prime example of reading a play as though it were a novel, R.A. Houk argues that Tranio might have known about Petruccio's behaviour and habits.[1]) It would appear that Hortensio's 'character' becomes a casualty – that is, his role not only gets situationally reconceived (see Sinfield, 52–79) but also slips between actors' bodies to meet the demands of the comic action.[2] Textual trouble has invited theatrical revision: from Garrick's *Catharine and Petruchio* on, some theatrical performances have reassigned to Hortensio those lines which seem inappropriate to Tranio. Bogdanov had Baptista address 'Hortensio', not 'Lucentio', at 3.2.1 and 7/TLN 1389 and 1395 (1978, promptbook); twentieth-century stagings have also reassigned other lines in the scene: 21–5/TLN 1409–13; 69–7/TLN 1457–8; 89/TLN 1473; 111–12/TLN 1507–9 (Schafer, 156–62). It would, however, be possible to read Tranio's lines as a character point: the brash, upwardly mobile servant insisting on his say and ingratiating himself with Baptista by attempting to defuse Petruccio's embarrassing appearance. In any case, no costume change occurs: rather than moving offstage with the others, Tranio remains talking with Lucentio.

1  Raymond A. Houk, 'The integrity of Shakespeare's *The Taming of the Shrew*', *Journal of English and Germanic Philology*, 39 (1940), 222–9.
2  Performances tend to confirm that Hortensio's role is necessary to the plot (as is that of the Provost in *Measure for Measure*, who appears in more scenes than anyone save the Duke (RP)), although his character is not conceived in complex psychological terms.

Even more puzzling is a series of speech prefix confusions associated with Hortensio's role, occurring at 3.1.50 and 51/TLN 1345 and 1347, and at 4.2.4, 6 and 8/TLN 1850, 1852 and 1854. Although these suggest some irregularity in the manuscript, traditional emendations have not been disputed and are generally accepted by modern editors. The errors in 4.2 appear to have resulted from someone taking *Li.* or *Lit.* as a prefix for Hortensio's schoolmaster's disguise as *Licio*, and someone else misunderstanding that as *Lu.* or *Luc.* for *Lucentio* (*TxC*, 169). *Litio* and *Licio* are similar enough to be easily interchanged, especially given the ease with which *i/u* and *c/t* can be confused in secretary hand. Yet although it might well have seemed easier to identify Hortensio by his disguise rather than to name him 'as himself', the number of anomalous speech prefixes attached to one role remains difficult to explain with any certainty. Did these irregularities result from 'hasty composition' (that useful catchphrase) and do they thus represent evidence of an authorial hand? Perhaps. Given that *Supposes*, the subplot's acknowledged source, has no equivalent for Hortensio's role, which seems to be Shakespeare's invention, that explanation seems likelier than assuming that these odd 'bumps' or glitches derive either from an earlier version of *The Shrew* or from a lost *ur-Shrew* play (see Honigmann, 'Lost'; Hosley, 'Sources'; Maxwell). Equally likely, however, is that they suggest scribal or compositorial confusion over disguises and supposings – a confusion shared by readers and also, occasionally, by spectators. Or does the Hortensio problem, as Wells and Taylor have argued, represent evidence of internal revision (360–5)? If such revision indeed does figure in *The Shrew*, does this necessarily suggest that F's text *probably* derives from foul papers that have undergone revision and been copied out anew? That would be one story, but no editorial consensus has yet been reached: Thompson, for instance, sees a lack of evidence for major internal revision but nonetheless acknowledges different stages of composition

(181). But even if revision has occurred, the Hortensio problem represents a stage of revision we cannot recover. Nor does what is textually evident enable us to distinguish either the motivating factors or the agency (or agencies) behind any proposed instance: much rests on interpretation, behind which lies the murky territory of authorial intention and of attempting to intuit Shakespeare's compositional practices (see Rasmussen, 'Revision', 451–6).

## STAGE DIRECTIONS

For the most part, *The Shrew*'s stage directions are adequate, even generous, in indicating and managing stage action and, at times, in advising players what to do and/or how to do it – see, for example, F's '*Enter Hortensio with his head broke.*' (2.1.140.1/TLN 1007) or '*Exit Biondello, Tranio and Pedant as fast as may be.*' (5.1.101 SD/TLN 2490). Some – for example '*Enter Baptista with his two daughters, Katerina & Bianca, Gremio a Pantelowne, Hortentio sister [sic] to Bianca. Lucen. Tranio, stand by.*' (1.1.47.1–3/TLN 347–9) – are unusually explicit, providing an order of entry which, in suggesting character relationships, might be explained as a playwright feeling his way towards what is necessary and what is not, as the work of a theatrical annotator, or as that of a non-theatrical scribe constructing a reader's text. Following William Long's assumption that most SDs can be considered authorial unless proved otherwise, *The Shrew*'s directions would seem to be authorial, though Long carefully qualifies his statement by suggesting that William Shakespeare the author/player/shareholder may well have worked in concert with playhouse personnel and that players may regularly have added or deleted SDs according to their needs ('Precious', 417–18). There is no reason, therefore, to conclude that F derives exclusively from foul papers. Even Morris, who assembles evidence pointing to Shakespeare's hand,[1] considers that F represents either 'foul papers, annotated, fairly lightly, by the bookkeeper, or a transcript of those papers, made by their author or by another hand, to which the bookkeeper has made additions' (6–7, 10) – which leaves the question open.[2]

If most existing SDs are more or less unremarkable (however, see LN, pp. 306–8), several omitted SDs raise further questions about the extent of the Hortensio problem. An omitted entry direction for Hortensio (2.1.38.2/TLN 898) seems likely to be related to the other peculiarities surrounding his role and is easily emended: clearly his presence is necessary in order for Petruccio to introduce him (as Licio the schoolmaster) to Baptista (2.1.55/TLN 916). Although F marks no exit for him, editorial tradition adds one (2.1.109 SD/TLN 975); he then re-enters '*with his head broke*' (2.1.140.1/TLN 1007). Omitting Lucentio from the entry at 3.2.0.2/TLN 1388 offers a different nexus of problems. Following Rowe, editors have traditionally included him, yet he is silent for 126 lines until Tranio addresses him ('But sir, to love concerneth us to add / Her father's liking', 3.2.127–8/TLN 1511), explaining his plans to find a false father and reassuring Lucentio that, despite the obstacles presented by Gremio, Baptista and 'the amorous Licio', he will attain Bianca. On the page, the quick gear-shift seems undeniably awkward – so much so that Wilson conjectured a missing scene (158). Tying the abrupt shift to the Hortensio problem, Thompson floats the possibility that *A Shrew*'s scene 8, a conversation between Sander and Polidor's

---

1 Other features Morris views as authorial are the presence of speech prefixes and actors' names and some spellings correlating with those of Hand D in the three pages of *Sir Thomas More* (constituting 2.3.1–159) that some have considered to be in Shakespeare's hand (Morris, 8–9; see also Anthony Munday *et al.*, *Sir Thomas More*, ed. Vittorio Gabrieli and Giorgio Melchiori (Manchester, 1990), 23). On the difficulty of that attribution, see Woudhuysen, 320; Paul Werstine, 'Shakespeare, more or less: A.W. Pollard and twentieth-century editing', *Florilegium*, 16 (1999), 125–45; John Jowett's Arden 3 edition of *Sir Thomas More* (forthcoming) may well provide further arguments concerning attribution.

2 There is, however, a growing presumption that Jaggard preferred to use transcripts as copy, perhaps for tidiness and ease of accurate cast-off (RP).

Boy (equivalent to Grumio and Biondello), might be a reported version of a Shakespearean original (186–8); she also suggests omitting *both* Tranio and Lucentio from the entry at 3.1.0.1, reassigning Tranio's lines to Hortensio (see above) and marking an entry for both Tranio and Lucentio at 3.2, thus creating a new scene (Thompson, 114). Wells and Taylor do just that. Arguing not only that the Tranio–Lucentio conversation has 'no organic relationship with the earlier part of the scene at its earliest composition', but also that Shakespeare 'did not write the episodes in the order in which they were printed', they note that having characters meet to continue a conversation begun offstage is a common Shakespearean strategy (*TxC*, 169; Wells & Taylor, 361–3).

Yet while creating a new scene provides an editorial solution based on intuiting compositional practices and suiting Wells's and Taylor's rationale of 'making editorial sense without actually rewriting' (359), doing so occludes the possibility of inviting readers to imagine potential theatrical solutions, whether on early modern or present-day stages. Long's suggestion that little was done to a playwright's directions 'unless the players found it to be necessary' and his corollary assumption that players made additions or deletions according to their needs provides an alternative rationale for *theatrical* revision ('Precious', 417–19). It seems entirely appropriate to a staging idiom of continuous action or overlapping scenes to assume that Tranio and Lucentio stay behind following the mass exit at 3.2.126 and that their conversation, however short (21 lines) in terms of real time, is not only crucial to the plot but also perfectly adequate for getting Katherina and Petruccio to the church on time and for Gremio to return with an account of the marriage. Moreover, if this is the scene's primary purpose, then all other explanations become rationalizations. Indeed, modern theatrical revisions have spanned a wide range: performances staged in proscenium theatres where drop curtains demarcated one scene from another effectively created a new scene; Jewett's 1915 promptbook, for instance, marks a lowered curtain following the Tranio–Lucentio conversation, further extending the time-lapse before Gremio's report of the wedding (Schafer, 162); Nunn (1967 promptbook) added a speech for Lucentio ('I tell thee Tranio she loves me sure, / And cares not for my name and parentage') to clarify the sense. Bogdanov (1978) covered the moment with a noisy, chaotic spectacle; Miller (1987 promptbook) turned the mass exit into a procession: the wedding party paraded across the stage, Baptista dragging an unwilling Katherina; Tranio and Lucentio then re-entered.

Further confusions over managing entries as well as exits occur in 4.4, beginning with what appears to be a double entry for the Merchant/Pedant, the first of which reads, in F, '*Enter Tranio, and the Pedant drest like Vincentio.*' (4.4.0.1–2/ TLN 2180), followed eighteen lines later by '*Enter Baptista and Lucentio: Pedant booted and bare headed.*' (4.4.18.1–2/TLN 2200–1). Two explanations seem equally possible. Reading the first eighteen lines either as a false start or an afterthought, Wells and Taylor view the scene as originally beginning with 'Signor Baptista, you are happily met' (4.4.19/TLN 2202) and suggest cancelling the second entry for the Merchant/ Pedant (Wells & Taylor, 354–5). While a false start would imply carelessness, an afterthought would suggest revision. Yet the second direction may not mark the Merchant/Pedant's re-entry but instead combine an entry for Baptista and Lucentio with an advisory direction for the Merchant/Pedant, already onstage, to remove his hat as a token of respect or deference to Baptista. Analogues occur in *Comedy of Errors* in the mass entry at 5.1.129, where the Merchant of Syracuse appears '*barehead*', and in *Sir Thomas More* at 4.1.0.2–3: '*doing courtesy to each other, Clerk of Council waiting bareheaded*' (Dessen & Thomson, 20). Since this supposed anomaly has no theatrical or character consequences, and given *The Shrew*'s consistent attention to costume, the simplest solution is to retain both directions, clarifying the notations pertaining to costume by adding '*booted*' to the initial entry direction and retaining '*bare headed*' at 4.4.18.2.

The appearance of '*Peter*' in a later entry direction (4.4.67.1/ TLN 2140) is even more curious. Ever since Theobald omitted him, 'Peter' has been an editorial casualty, but his presence has attracted several inventive, even elaborate explanations. Is he the same 'Peter' who is one of Petruccio's servants and speaks the most lines of all of them? Drawing on Bond's conjecture that 'Peter' has 'come to warn Tranio that his meal is ready', Wilson assumed that 'Peter' refers not to a role but to a player's name, noting that Edward Alleyn sent a letter and a horse to his father-in-law Henslowe by a servant named Peter (Henslowe, 2.302; Wilson, 118–19). Although Wilson's conjecture is tied to his desire to find as many apprentices as possible in the servants' quarters (see pp. 28–9), it is by no means impossible to rule out that 'Peter' may represent a vestigial trace of *The Shrew*'s early modern casting. Wells and Taylor, however, conjecture that '*Enter Peter.*' is 'a misexpansion of an uncancelled remnant of a direction for the entry of *Pet*(ruchio) or *Petr*(uchio) as well as "others," possibly either for what is now 4.5 (the sun/ moon scene) or for the episode which now begins at 5.1.7/ TLN 2266' (*TxC*, 170), and they imagine a scenario in which Shakespeare initially included Petruccio and then abandoned the idea, realizing that 'an expository scene with Lucentio's marriage was needed' (Wells & Taylor, 355–6).

Even though this assumption offers a plausible alternative explanation of a local curiosity, the problem (if it is one) is easily solved by omitting '*Enter Peter.*' altogether. Wells and Taylor also, however, identify problems of logic and sequence in the remainder of the scene: Baptista orders Cambio to 'bid *Bianca* make her ready straight', but the exit at 4.4.67/TLN 2251 is for Biondello. Conjecturing that, as originally written, the scene did not include Biondello, they suggest that Shakespeare 'seems to have been composing episodically, failing (at least in the text as printed) to pull the episodes together'. Since restoring Biondello, they argue, seems contrary to the purpose of Shakespeare's revision (at this point in their argument, what had been a *theory* of internal revision seems to have hardened into fact), they 'prefer to revert to what [they] believe to be Shakespeare's unrevised intention', and reassign Biondello's 'I pray the gods she may, with all my heart' (68/TLN 2250) to Lucentio (Wells & Taylor, 359). Five lines later, F clears the stage with '*Exeunt.*' (4.4.71/TLN 2257), and then directs '*Enter Lucentio and Biondello.*', yet a few lines later Biondello says, '[My master] has left me here behind' (4.4.77/TLN 2264). To ease this supposed textual difficulty, Wells and Taylor mark a new scene at 4.4.71/TLN 2257, justifying their decision by suggesting that a possible time-gap increases the plausibility of the following conversation. To be sure, this represents minimal editorial intervention; yet, once again, what may trouble the editorial eye causes little theatrical difficulty: both Lucentio and Biondello might make false exits or Biondello only might linger behind after Tranio and Baptista leave at 71. If Tranio's 'Dally not with the gods, but get thee gone' (4.4.67/TLN 2252) is not obeyed and Biondello does remain, then '*Enter Lucentio and Biondello*' may constitute the 'real' problem: just as it is possible to imagine that what F marks as an exit may not be observed, either by editors or theatrical practitioners, an entry (as with the so-called Merchant/Pedant double entry) may not be an entry. Indeed, it seems possible to solve this proposed tangle, editorially as well as theatrically, without attempting to intuit Shakespeare's compositional practice or imagining complex instances of revision.

Finally, the entry direction at 5.2.0.1–4/TLN 2534–7, '*Enter Baptista, Vincentio, Gremio, the Pedant, Lucentio, and Bianca. Tranio, Biondello Grumio, and Widdow: The Seruingmen with Tranio bringing in a Banquet.*' (F), not only omits Hortensio, Katherina and Petruccio but also includes other anomalies: Tranio is mentioned twice; the Widow comes after Grumio, and the Servants enter last. Although F's processional order has the older generation precede Lucentio and Bianca, the banquet's host and hostess, with the others following, such omissions and oddities seem curious, especially given the precision of the Minola family's initial entry (1.1.47.1–3/TLN 347–9). When considered side by side, do the two directions suggest different hands? Perhaps; yet, again, that is impossible to determine. Forgetting Hortensio seems most easily explained as one more instance of the inconsistencies affecting speech prefixes and plotting surrounding his role; that also may account for the double mention of Tranio. Wilson read the repetition as evidence of a later addition (which seems feasible), and has Tranio, however briefly, once again 'become' Hortensio before reverting to his own 'person', and to his status as a servant. Omitting Katherina and Petruccio raises a different issue. Despite F's '*Exeunt.*' at the end of the previous scene (5.1.141/TLN 2532), the couple might remain onstage, with the others entering to them, a solution which not only avoids breaking the so-called law of re-entry but is also consonant with a staging idiom of overlapping scenes (see 4.5.80n.). Does imagining such a possibility also suggest that F's '*Exeunt.*' might point to a literary transcript rather than a playbook? Or, as Miller suggests, might it reflect a Blackfriars staging, where act breaks would mask a re-entry (13–15)? Either option seems possible. Traditional theatrical practice, however, observes the end-of-scene exit, primarily to afford Katherina a costume change, though Doran (2003) offers a notable exception (see pp. 129–31).

## SPEECH PREFIXES AND PLAYERS' NAMES

R.B. McKerrow suggested that 'a play in which the names are irregular was printed from the author's original ms' (460), a proposition accepted by Greg, who nonetheless believed that *The Shrew* derived from a manuscript that had been annotated for the stage (*Folio*, 142, 215), surely the most sensible explanation for the presence of an unusual number of speech prefixes that seem to refer to players rather than to parts. Do these traces record evidence of *The Shrew*'s initial performances? Perhaps, but actors' names could also have been added at a later time. Although Wells and Taylor remark that a number of anomalies attached to one role in a single play seems suspicious (*TxC*, 169), many identifications put forward by earlier editors have been explored further in David Kathman's recent studies of players who, at one time or another, were associated with those companies performing Shakespeare's plays (see 'Reconsidering'; 'Grocers'). Some names, especially those J.D. Wilson linked to servants (presumably played by apprentices), are treated in the Introduction (pp. 28–9) or in the commentary on the List of Roles, as is the SP '*Sincklo.*' (TLN 98), referring to John Sincler, whose presence impacts on the questions surrounding *The Shrew*'s date (see pp. 28–35).

In that regard, another instance which may specify a player is of particular interest. '*Par.*', F's prefix for a speech which editors regularly assign to Tranio (4.2.73/TLN 1924), has been linked with William Parr, a comic actor associated with Tarlton in the 1590s (Nungezer, 354) but who first appears in the plot of the lost *1 Tamar Cam* (1602). Although far from certain, this identification, which Wilson attributes to the bookkeeper, could support either an early 1590s or an early seventeenth-century date (115–16). On the other hand, '*Par.*' seems equally understandable simply as referring to the Merchant (or Pedant), who then enters and speaks the next line: Thompson conjectures that the copyist, picking up on Biondello's 'Marcantant' (4.2.64/TLN 1916), originally wrote '*Mar.*' before correcting to '*Ped.*' in the following line without cancelling '*Par.*', so that the compositor set both (165). Although Thompson's explanation of '*Par.*', as well as Wilson's conjectures, which imagine, through a kind of back-formation, a host of early modern players embodying *The Shrew*'s minor roles, depend on interpreting compositorial, authorial or scribal processes – or a combination of all three – it is important not to discount such evidence, especially in the case of manuscripts.

## WHAT KIND OF TEXT IS F?

Scholars' reluctance to subscribe to a single 'origin' for *The Shrew* or to slot it into one textual category suggests its radically uncertain provenance: each and every current assessment inclines towards indeterminacy. Among *The Shrew*'s editors, it would seem that those who adhere to new bibliographical principles aimed at discovering an 'ideal' text, one as close to authorial manuscript or/and perhaps licensed playscript as possible, are more than likely to find evidence of foul papers;[1] that also was the case with Greg (*Folio*, 212–15) and Hinman ('Introduction', xiii, xv). And the desire for the author has persisted. Yet although Morris, Oliver, Thompson and Wells and Taylor all subscribe to the idea that F records *some* traces of foul papers, each suggests that some kind of transcript intervened; Thompson conjectures that *The Shrew* may have been cut at the same time and that there may once have been a 'Sly Ending' (181).

Was *The Shrew*, then, a theatrical transcript? Considering that F exhibits deficiencies, errors and inconsistencies unusual in such a transcript – among them monosyllabic omissions, 'Shakespearean' spellings and speech prefix tangles – Oliver and Thompson question that derivation (see esp. Thompson, 164–6). Yet such a judgement seems to assume that playwrights worked independently of theatrical personnel rather than, as is now widely accepted, that Shakespeare operated in several capacities simultaneously – as author, reviser, player or all three – with the Lord Chamberlain's Men at the time it was formed in 1594. Indeed, as Rasmussen points out, it is difficult

---

1 Bowers defines foul papers as the 'author's last complete draft in a shape satisfactory to him to be transferred to a fair copy', listing various possible states of copy-text (*Editing*, 11–12); Honigmann prefers 'any kind of draft preceding the first fair copy' (*The Stability of Shakespeare's Text* (1965), 18).

to distinguish authorial from theatrical papers: do foul papers constitute a 'complete version' or are they 'merely preliminary to the preparation of the book of the play?' ('Revision', 451–6). Similarly, distinctions between theatrical and literary transcripts are difficult to maintain. Taylor and Jowett conjecture that F was set from what appear to be non-theatrical early texts – probably literary transcripts rather than scribal copy (241–2). Although incomplete and irregular act and scene breaks do suggest that *The Shrew* represents a literary transcript, that fact alone is not sufficient. What can be claimed is that, whoever the agent may have been, he and Nicholas Rowe are the two 'hands' most responsible for our editions of *The Shrew* – the first, for transcribing *The Shrew* in the form in which it appears in F; the second, for additions, alterations and transformations (notably but not exclusively in SDs) that have heavily influenced editorial tradition. Although the notion of 'improving' Shakespeare's texts is traditionally associated with Restoration theatrical practices, it would not be inaccurate to suggest that this anonymous bookkeeper/scribe stands before Rowe as reshaping Shakespeare (see Massai, *Rise*).

Regardless of whether F represents a theatrical or a literary transcript, is it possible to discern when such a transcript may have been made? Citing the occurrence of 'oh' spellings which counter Shakespeare's preference elsewhere, Taylor and Jowett attribute these either to a scribe or to an early date of composition (44–5). Moreover, whereas other comedies had been expurgated, *The Shrew*, apparently, was not: 'God('s)' occurs nineteen times; 'Heaven(s)', twice. Although 'God' was razed out of some of the King's Men's *late* theatrical transcripts, it still survives in manuscripts some consider more 'literary' – that is, profanity appears to have been in some measure acceptable in a text designed for reading, though not on the stage (Taylor & Jowett, 58, 79–80, 85). Although these facts do not offer compelling proof of a literary transcript, they could support the idea of early transcription. Citing the plague's impact on acting companies in the early 1590s, G.R. Hibbard, for one, attributed what he saw as *The Shrew*'s 'unsatisfactory state' to a transcript having been done 'hurriedly and carelessly' (245–8). Yet more than one story is possible here. Convenient as it would be, for those who view *The Shrew*'s date as *c.* 1590–1, to situate the making of that transcript in the early 1590s, Kathman's re-dating of the plot of *2 Seven Deadly Sins* from 1590–1 to 1597–8 and his consequent reassignment of it from Pembroke's Men to the Lord Chamberlain's Men calls that into question ('Reconsidering', 25; see pp. 32–3). All that can be said with confidence is that a foul-paper copy, a playbook or a scribal copy made by a non-theatrical hand of a version of *The Shrew* acted in London (and/or on tour) at some time during the 1590s (or later) was probably lost or shelved, (expediently) surfacing when Heminge and Condell were assembling texts for the Folio.

The question of dating any potential transcript also affects the issue of revision. Those features pointing towards revision – among them the Hortensio problem, the Pedant's so-called double entry, the presence of 'Peter' – represent traces of *possible* revision rather than amounting to strong evidence for it. And there seems no way of knowing whether such proposed revisions may have occurred, as Wells and Taylor believe, at the level of composition or whether, as Oliver suggests, they represent 'changes of mind' occurring not only during composition but after a period of time, over months or years – indeed at any time before F's publication in 1623 (Oliver, 4, 9–10).

Unless and until further evidence becomes available, the question of what sort of manuscript reached compositors eludes certainty. Current opinion, however, suggests that F's copy *probably* derives from a transcript at least once removed from either authorial or scribal copy, and that there is some evidence of theatrical annotation and/or of revision or alterations. *The Shrew* might, then, be construed, not as what Andrew Gurr calls a 'maximal' text – one consisting of everything written – nor as a 'minimal' text – a text prepared for performance

('Maximal', 76) – but as a text that straddles, or falls between, the two categories. Again, it is possible to subscribe to one of two stories. The editorial story invites viewing *The Shrew* as a composite text – one which offers an intriguing example of the pleasures (and dangers) of collaboration, a term that serves as a problematic place-holder within the larger arena of attribution studies (see Werstine, 'Narratives', 85–6). The theatrical story looks at *The Shrew* as a document that affords a satisfactory basis for theatrical enactment as it stands – a document that has been continuously rewritten through the collaborative practices of theatre.[1] That it has produced such a wide variety of 'theatrical revisions' occurring over centuries – for all we know, from its first early modern performances – stands as perhaps the most secure 'evidence' of the viability of this fascinating play.

---

1    Cf. Roland Barthes's idea of a 'writerly' text ('From work to text', in *Image-Music-Text*, trans. Stephen Heath (New York, 1977), 155–64, esp. 161–4.

# APPENDIX 2

## EDITORIAL PRINCIPLES

### ACT AND SCENE DIVISIONS; LOCATIONS

Act and scene divisions occur only at the beginning of *The Shrew* (*'Actus primus. Scaena Prima.'*) and at TLN 1293 (*'Actus Tertia.'*), TLN 1978 (*'Actus Quartus. Scena Prima.'*) and TLN 2532 (*'Actus Quintus.'*); these divisions almost certainly represent printing-house additions, not theatrical markers. Stage historians conjecture that early modern performances by professional companies were continuous: plays were not performed with gaps between acts before c. 1609–10, except in academic and court performances – and there, breaks were largely made either for social reasons or to allow for musical interludes (Taylor & Jowett, 3–50; see also Massai, *Rise*, 136–58, and 'Shakespeare'). Modern performances usually observe one interval, often positioned following 3.2. *The Oxford Shakespeare: The Complete Works* invokes the re-entry rule[1] and creates a new scene at 3.2.126/TLN 1511. Splitting the scene in two, however, imposes a realist logic on a non-illusionistic playscript. Since the action is comprehensible when played continuously, I have observed a flexible pre-realist space/time convention. Although early editors located scenes, and although 'location' has been (more or less) realistically represented on the stage, especially during the era of pictorial scenery, early modern performances took place on non-localized stages; when narrative exigencies demanded otherwise, dialogue could swiftly conjure a sense of place into existence – even, on occasion, reinventing location within a continuous piece of action. As appropriate, this edition refers to 'imagined location'.

1  See Irwin Smith, 'Their exits and reentrances', *SQ*, 18.1 (1967), 7–16.

# MODERNIZING/SOUNDING/ CHOREOGRAPHING *THE SHREW*

Since F's text is both coherent and playable, and since modernizing risks over-writing or occluding cues that may (or may not) have shaped early modern players' and readers' experiences (see Ong, *Orality*; Weimann, 7, 43), I have adopted a conservative position, emending only where F seems erroneous. There are, however, some exceptions. F's 'Petruchio' becomes 'Petruccio' in SPs and dialogue, but elsewhere I have avoided correcting Shakespeare's practice of 'English-ing' Italian dialogue, which Grumio, slipping from his role as an Italian servant to an Englishman, hears, not as 'his' language but as Latin (1.2.28/TLN 596). Q (1631) and F2 (1632) provide occasional readings; textual notes record all substantive changes from F, the most significant among these (e.g. 'change' for 'charge' and 'odd' for 'old', 3.1.79/ TLN 1374; 'except' for 'expect', 4.4.90/TLN 2277), as well as the alteration of 'Pedant' to 'Merchant' in SPs, have been adopted by previous editors. As with any early modern text on which editors impose modern orthographic conventions, this edition is a compromise between two time-bound signifying systems: although old spellings or phonetic variants are usually modernized (thus, 'hoa', 4.1.10/TLN 1649, becomes 'ho'), 'soud' is retained (4.1.128/TLN 1769).

## PUNCTUATION

Punctuation is another matter in which early modern and modern sign systems differ substantially. Early modern punctuation represented a negotiation between two competing and effectively incompatible systems: an old one 'based on the sound-producing capabilities of the human body' and a 'newer one based on the abstract logic of syntax' – the latter of which had begun to take hold at the time F was published. Even F's pointing often resists precise parsing, so that, for instance, colons and commas 'mark pauses without necessarily specifying just what the logical relationship is between what comes before and what comes after'.[1] Shakespeare's contemporary Ben Jonson explained punctuation marks as signalling pauses for breath (cited in Maguire, *Suspect*, 114); more recently, Richard Flatter, Neil Freeman and Patrick Tucker, among others, have argued that F's pointing represents something 'authentic' or 'original' worth preserving (as it is in the many facsimile editions of early modern plays).[2] Yet since, as Bowers argues (*Editing*, 152, 163–4, 177), F's punctuation is compositorial rather than authorial, all that early texts can tell us is how compositors punctuated the texts they set in type, not that F's pointing indicates, as Tucker has argued, how the language was spoken on the early modern stage. Obviously, paying attention to F's system of linguistic (or musical) notation invites readers and players (those specialized readers) to rethink the syntactic flow of language and so encourages differences in sense-making, though not necessarily in ways that are more radically useful than other modern techniques of theatrical preparation. As Dickens's Mr Curdle remarked, 'by altering the received mode of punctuation, any one of Shakespeare's plays could be made quite different, and the sense completely changed'[3] – an offhand observation borne out by comparing the Q/F punctuation of *Hamlet*, *Othello* or *King Lear*. One does not have to go to such extremes to realize that punctuation is interpretation, or that modernizing can often, as Bowers writes, 'support one meaning over another . . . one idiomatic

1   See Bruce R. Smith, 'Prickly characters', in David M. Bergeron (ed.), *Reading and Writing in Shakespeare* (Newark, NJ, and London, 1996), 25–44, esp. 27; Wells, 3.

2   Richard Flatter, *Shakespeare's Producing Hand: A Study of His Marks of Expression to be Found in the First Folio* (New York, 1948); Freeman; Patrick Tucker, *Secrets of Acting Shakespeare: The Original Approach* (2001); see also, Don Weingust, *Acting from Shakespeare's First Folio: Theory, Text and Performance* (London and New York, 2006).

3   Charles Dickens, *Nicholas Nickleby*, ed. Mark Ford (1987), 385.

usage against its contrary' ('Today's', 161).[1] For example, F's 'What master read you first, resolve me that' retains the sense of 'master' as author, whereas modern editions print 'What, master, read you? First resolve me that', where 'master' refers to the 'schoolmaster' Lucentio (4.2.7/TLN 1853). With a view towards providing the clearest and most theatrically suggestive text, I have opted for light punctuation,[2] which maintains, at least to some degree, what Michael Cordner calls the early modern text's 'original indecisiveness' ('Scripts'). In adopting an eclectic practice this edition attempts on the one hand to respect F's rhetorical pointing, thus gesturing towards one probable form of communication within the early modern playhouse; on the other, it aligns with the modern practice of clarifying logical relations between syntactic units.

Several points deserve further mention. In early modern punctuation, both commas and colons serve (with no regularity or systematic usage) to mark the end of a sentence, usually indicated by the modern full stop or period. Few exclamation marks occur, though at times a question mark (which also can signify a full stop) seems to indicate an exclamation. With the caveat that compositors habitually punctuated the beginning of a long sentence before reading to the end of it, generally speaking, early modern pointing represents what one might call 'forward punctuation' – that is, it serves to keep the text moving, kicking the thought on, pausing rather than stopping, as indicated by the modern full stop. Whereas modern punctuation tends to close off what has gone before in preparation for a new or additional thought, early modern pointing works in the opposite way, opening up to continuing thought. Thus a speaker has the option of keeping the rhetorical movement of a speech moving forward, leading towards what comes next rather than completing the grammatical

---

1   Fredson Bowers, 'Today's Shakespeare texts, and tomorrow's', *Studies in Bibliography*, 19 (1966), 39–65.
2   See Bruce R. Smith, *The Acoustic World of Early Modern England: Attending to the O-Factor* (Chicago, 1999), 110–11; see also *TxC*, 465–6.

unit that has come before.[1] Compared to many modern editions, this text contains fewer full stops (and thus fewer interventions in the forward movement of a speech) as well as fewer exclamation marks: perhaps more than any other means of pointing, the latter dictates speaking as well as sense, suggesting that the speaker is in a state of comic frenzy, surprise or rage (Hodgdon, 'Who'). In instances where F's colon connects one line or thought to another, I have retained it, thus avoiding the longer pause signalled by a full stop. In other instances, however, I have 'translated' F's commas and colons as semicolons, the sign in modern systems of pointing that marks a suspensory pause and best seems to render the flexibility and grace of the early modern colon (see, for example, the Lord's instructions to his servants (Ind.1.44–67/TLN 49–72) and Biondello's description of Petruccio and his horse (3.2.43–61/TLN 1431–49). Not incidentally, Biondello's role requires casting an actor with excellent breath control.

More or less consistently, F marks a caesural pause with a comma: when that seems obvious to present-day readers, I have omitted it. And although (in accordance with Arden guidelines) I have omitted some commas within a series, in cases where to do so would elide the relation between comma and breath or block interpretive choices, I have countered modern practice and retained the serial comma. The dash appears in this edition as a mode of parenthesis, as a means of suggesting moments of interruption or as marking changes of address within a speech (thus eliminating internal SDs, which are also interpretive cues); the dash also signifies moments when a speaker pauses for thought (as with Katherina's 'Nay then – ', 3.2.208/TLN 1593) or is caught wrong-footed (as with Petruccio's 'Should be? Should – buzz', 2.1.207/TLN 1080) and pauses to fashion an appropriate response. Although such pointing imposes phrasing, it also can clarify potential ambiguities.

1   See Philip Davis, *Shakespeare Thinking* (2007), 74–5, and M.B. Parkes, *Pause and Effect: An Introduction to the History of Punctuation in the West* (Berkeley, Calif., 1993), 100–11.

## VERSE/PROSE[1]

A similar strategy of minimal interference governs the treatment of verse and prose. Editorial tradition tends to push F's supposedly unruly verse into normative forms, but doing so imposes a medium of control. Since Shakespearean prose (as well as present-day English syntax) often also tends to fall into iambic rhythms, and since *The Shrew* moves fluently between rhymed, unrhymed, regular and irregular patternings, where verse often trembles into prose and vice versa, regularizing verse form represents an editorial standardization that is at odds with historicist critical practice (which tends to ignore all evidence of the habit of regular versification, especially for the period *c.* 1587–95 (RP)) as well as with theatrical practice and theatrical history. In most instances I have opted to preserve F's rhythmic variety and freedom and have resisted omitting and/or substituting words to regularize metre, though the commentary notes those points where lines admit of several arrangements or where an elision, a cut or an addition can render a line metrical, if so desired. Some verse clearly is not doubtful, and in a verse context would be heard as verse; the opposite is true for dubiously metrical lines or for stray single lines of verse in a prose context. Usually, though not always, verse is the default position when verse speakers are gathered together, yet lapses into prosaic rhythms often seem apt in terms of a character's emotive psychology. Christopher Sly's role offers the most obvious example, moving from prose to verse (Ind.2.66–73/ TLN 220–7) when he is convinced he is a lord, but occasionally lapsing into prose or doggerel (Ind.2.122–4/TLN 279–81; Ind.2.133–4/TLN 291–2). However, in some passages – such as Gremio's account of Katherina's and Petruccio's wedding (3.2.166–82/TLN 1551–64) – I have followed editorial tradition and 'versed' what F prints as prose.

1 On metrics, see George T. Wright, *Shakespeare's Metrical Art* (Berkeley, Calif., 1988).

This edition also attempts to credit playable information that may exist at the junctures between verse and prose – information that often is elided on the basis of assumptions that an historical author has tried and failed to make regular verse or that an historical compositor or book-keeper has failed to set the regularity of his manuscript copy-text. Traditional editorial practice tends to regularize without discerning whether textual irregularity or asymmetry might be useful in interpreting a particular moment. In assuming that the points of negotiation between verse and prose or between regularity and irregularity may indeed offer interpretive information, I have tried not to efface F's 'bumps' or warts for the sake of literary smoothness.

One illustration of how this edition treats short lines (printed as shared lines in most modern editions) and movements between verse and prose occurs in the first encounter between Katherina and Petruccio (2.1.214–21/TLN 1089–96):

PETRUCCIO
 Who knows not where a wasp does wear his sting?
 In his tail.
KATHERINA  In his tongue.
PETRUCCIO  Whose tongue?
KATHERINA
 Yours, if you talk of tails, and so farewell.
PETRUCCIO  What, with my tongue in your tail?
 Nay, come again, good Kate, I am a gentleman –
KATHERINA That I'll try. *She strikes him.*

In this (in)famous 'tongue–tail' stretch, there is performative value in the deliberate stichomythic break from verse at 'In his tail' and the ensuing two lines. These three short lines, like a sudden sharp thrust/parry/thrust, interrupt the regular rhythm of Katherina's and Petruccio's 'flyting' or wit contest. Following a stretch where 'winning' seems indeterminate, Katherina then takes control (or so she imagines) with a full verse line – 'Yours, if you talk of tails, and so farewell'. But Petruccio comes back at her – 'What, with my tongue in your tail?' The prose line is doubly functional: not only does he break up the rhythm she has attempted to restore, throwing her off-stride, but his sense also works (potentially) to derail her. Then, having shattered her rhythm, he offers it back to her – 'Nay, come again, good Kate, I am a gentleman' – pacifying her (so to speak) with an iambic line, an invitation which she rejects – with three monosyllables and a blow. A similar strategic pattern occurs later in the scene (232– 42/TLN 1109–19), beginning with Petruccio's 'Why, here's no crab, and therefore look not sour'. Katherina introduces a series of short ripostes (five lines); Petruccio re-establishes the full verse line with 'Now, by Saint George, I am too young for you'; she rejects the gambit; he takes it back, forcing a full verse line on her and (perhaps) also forcing her physically at the same time – 'Nay, hear you, Kate. In sooth, you scape not so'.

As a means of bringing performance into conversation with textual editing, taking the former from the margins into the mainstream, this instance represents a selective, subjective and limited move, one that must be considered in tandem with theatre history, which reveals more about how Shakespeare's dramatic language has been used by well-documented performers (see pp. 79–80, 93, 119, 125–6).

## STAGE DIRECTIONS

With a view to disengaging *The Shrew* from the tangled histories of its passage through several centuries, this edition relegates many SDs first added by eighteenth-century editors and regularly included in modern editions to the commentary. Doing so, as John Cox argues, 'allows the text to function for readers (and for modern actors and directors) in much the same way the Elizabethan stage itself functioned historically: as a place offering maximum scope for interpretation' (183). Since regularization and completeness do not feature in early modern theatrical notation (Long, 'Factor'), I have not attempted to provide answers to an indeterminate textual condition by imposing editorial staging, whether premised explicitly or implicitly on either early or present-day theatrical practices (Kidnie, 'Text', 470). To be sure, editorial SDs may aid readers, but by pointing to one particular enactment, they not only close off other options but also suggest a mistrust of theatre as a medium – perhaps the most obvious instance of how the nature of theatre and the nature of editing produce contrary impulses. In Edward Gordon Craig's 'First Dialogue' between the Stage-Director and the Playgoer, the Playgoer, having been told that Shakespeare's directions were often '*Actus primus. Scaena Prima*' and only that, asks whether some further descriptions of the action also appeared, to which the Stage-Director replies, 'No, not one word. All the stage directions, from the first to the last, are the tame inventions of sundry editors, Mr. Malone, Mr. Capell, Theobald and others, and they have committed an indiscretion in tampering with the play, for which we, the men of the theatre, have to suffer' (153–4). The case is, of course, overstated, but Craig offers a wise caveat against prescribing stage actions that are better left to performers to imagine.

Especially in terms of interpolated SDs, the version of *The Shrew* that appears in most modern editions is a construct of eighteenth-century editors that bears marks of that century's theatrical practices. As such, it represents a print intervention that papers over one performance history with another, creating what Linda Hutcheon calls a palimpsestuous text (21). Not only do these surviving SDs introduce actions that have become fossilized, denying the flexibility that F affords, but they are also often ideologically charged, as with the interpolations in Petruccio's exchanges with his servants (4.1.125–56/TLN 1766–99; see also Fig. 20). In this scene, many SDs appearing in modern editions derive from *A Shrew*, *Sauny* or Garrick's *Catharine and Petruchio* but are routinely credited either to Rowe (1709) or to Capell (1768): for example, *A Shrew*'s Ferando '*throwes downe the table and meate and all, and beates them.*'

(874–5); *Sauny* reads, '*Throws meat at 'em, Sauny gets it*' (D3ᵛ); *Catharine and Petruchio* provides '*Strikes him*', '*Servant lets fall the water*' and '*Throws the meat, etc. about*' (TLN 1765, 1783, 1797). In each case, however, actions that may appear textually necessary (a conservative rationale for editorial SDs that restate cues present in the language) are not theatrically necessary: they represent options rather than obligations. Hamlet's famous advice to the itinerant players to let the word suit the action, the action suit the word, is just that – advice, not prescription. Significantly, these instances of imported eighteenth-century choreography register behaviour that is historically situated, turning Petruccio (irrevocably, one might say) into a farcical figure: at least in this case, editorial intervention might well be held responsible for the play's 'hard opinions'. For a playable (and suggestive) alternative choreography, see Ralph Alan Cohen's description of a staging that counters these directions (270–3; see also Hodgdon, 'Who', 98–102).

Although reproducing such SDs (or variants of them) points to *The Shrew*'s theatrical past, that history may not be especially useful to present-day readers or performers. Furthermore, although amplifying F's SDs has traditionally been considered an editor's responsibility, no theoretical basis shores up that assumption (see Kidnie, 'Text', 457; Long, 'Factor'; Wells, citing McKerrow, 71). In general, I have not added SDs where an action can be inferred from dialogue, preferring to invite readers and players to explore its performative consequences. I have, however, honoured theatrical/editorial tradition, either (in the case of internal SDs) by referencing historical SDs in commentary notes or (in the case of (most) entry and exit directions) by departing from F only when clarification seems necessary. Major changes from F's entry directions include adding persons not mentioned but included in the dialogue, as with Petruccio, Katherina and Hortensio at 5.2.0.2–3/TLN 2534–5. Since neither the 'glancing bookkeeper' nor compositors were attentive to marking exits, these SDs are subject to more

337

greater a run but my head and my necke. A fire good
*Curtis.*

*Cur.* Is my master and his wife comming *Grumio?*

*Gru.* Oh! *Curtis* I, and therefore fire, fire, cast on no
water.

*Cur.* Is she so hot a shrew as she's reported.

*Gru.* She was good *Curtis* before this frost: but thou
know'st winter tames man, woman, and beast: for it
hath tam'd my old master, and my new mistris, and my
selfe fellow *Curtis.*

*Gru.* Away you three inch foole, I am no beast.

*Gru.* Am I but three inches? Why thy horne is a foot
and so long am I at the least. But wilt thou make a fire,
or shall I complaine on thee to our mistris, whose hand
(she being now at hand) thou shalt soone feele, to thy
cold comfort, for being slow in thy hot office.

*Cur.* I prethee good *Grumio,* tell me, how goes the
world?

*Gru.* A cold world *Curtis* in euery office but thine, &
therefore fire: do thy duty, and haue thy duty, for my
Master and mistris are almost frozen to death.

*Cur.* There's fire readie, and therefore good *Grumio*
the newes.

*Gru.* Why lacke boy, ho boy, and as much newes as
wilt thou.

*Cur.* Come, you are so full of coni-catching.

*Gru.* Why therefore fire, for I haue caught extreme
cold. Where's the Cooke, is supper ready, the house
trim'd, rushes strew'd, cobwebs swept, the seruingmen
in their new fustian, the white stockings, and euery officer his wedding garment on? Be the Iackes faire within, the Gils faire without, the Carpets laide, and euerie
thing in order?

*Cur.* All readie: and therefore I pray thee newes.

*Gru.* First know my horse is tired, my master & mistris falne out.   *Cur.* How?

*Gru.* Out of their saddles into the durt; and thereby
hangs a tale.

*Cur.* Let's ha't good *Grumio.*

*Gru.* Lend thine eare.

*Cur.* Heere.

*Gru.* There.

*Cur.* This 'tis to feele a tale, not to heare a tale.

*Gru.* And therefore 'tis cal'd a sensible tale: and this
Cuffe was but to knocke at your eare, and beseech listning: now I begin, Inprimis wee came downe a fowle
hill, my Master riding behinde my Mistris,

*Cur.* Both of one horse?

*Gru.* What's that to thee?

*Cur.* Why a horse.

*Gru.* Tell thou the tale: but hadst thou not crost me,
thou shouldst haue heard how her horse fel, and she vnder her horse: thou shouldst haue heard in how miery a
place, how she was bemoil'd, how hee left her with the
horse vpon her, how he beat me because her horse stumbled, how she waded through the durt to plucke him off
me: how he swore, how she prai'd, that neuer prai'd before: how I cried, how the horses rann away, how her
bridle was burst: how I lost my crupper, with manie
things of worthy memorie, which now shall die in obli-
uion, and thou returne vnexperienc'd to thy graue.

*Cur.* By this reckning hee is more shrew than she.

*Gru.* I, and that thou and the proudest of you all shall
finde when he comes home. But what talke I of this?
Call forth *Nathaniel, Ioseph, Nicholas, Philip, Walter, Su-
gersop* and the rest: let their heads bee slickely comb'd,

their blew coats brush'd, and their garters of an indifferent knit, let them curtsie with their left legges, and not
presume to touch a haire of my Masters horse-taile, till
they kisse their hands. Are they all readie?

*Cur.* They are.

*Gru.* Call them forth.

*Cur.* Do you heare ho? you must meete my maister
to countenance my mistris.

*Gru.* Why she hath a face of her owne.

*Cur.* Who knowes not that?

*Gru.* Thou it seemes, that cals for company to countenance her.

*Cur.* I call them forth to credit her.

*Enter foure or fiue seruingmen.*

*Gru.* Why she comes to borrow nothing of them.

*Nat.* Welcome home *Grumio.*

*Phil.* How now *Grumio.*

*Iof.* What *Grumio.*

*Nick.* Fellow *Grumio.*

*Nat.* How now old lad.

*Gru.* Welcome you: how now you: what you: fellow you: and thus much for greeting. Now my spruce
companions, is all readie, and all things neate?

*Nat.* All things is readie, how neere is our master?

*Gre.* E'ne at hand, alighted by this: and therefore be
not——Cockes passion, silence, I heare my master.

*Enter Petruchio and Kate.*

*Pet.* Where be these knaues? What no man at doore
To hold my stirrop, nor to take my horse?
Where is *Nathaniel, Gregory, Philip.*

*All ser.* Heere, heere sir, heere sir.

*Pet.* Heere sir, heere sir, heere sir, heere sir.
You logger-headed and vnpollisht groomes:
What? no attendance? no regard? no dutie?
Where is the foolish knaue I sent before?

*Gru.* Heere sir, as foolish as I was before.

*Pet.* You pezant swain, you horson malt-horse drudg
Did I not bid thee meete me in the Parke,
And bring along these rascall knaues with thee?

*Grumio.* Nathaniels coate sir was not fully made,
And *Gabrels* pumpes were all vnpinkt i'th heele:
There was no Linke to colour *Peters* hat,
And *Walters* dagger was not come from sheathing:
There were none fine, but *Adam, Rafe,* and *Gregory,*
The rest were ragged, old, and beggerly,
Yet as they are, heere are they come to meete you.

*Pet.* Go rascals, go, and fetch my supper in. *Ex.Ser.*
Where is the life that late I led?
Where are those? Sit downe *Kate,*
And welcome. Soud, soud, soud, soud.

*Enter seruants with supper.*

Why when I say? Nay good sweete *Kate* be merrie.
Off with my boots, you rogues: you villaines, when?
*It was the Friar of Orders gray,
As he forth walked on his way.*
Out you rogue, you plucke my foote awrie,
Take that, and mend the plucking of the other.
Be merrie *Kate:* Some water heere: what hoa.

*Enter one with water.*

Where's my Spaniel *Troilus?* Sirra, get you hence,
And bid my cozen *Ferdinand* come hither:
One *Kate* that you must kisse, and be acquainted with.
Where are my Slippers? Shall I haue some water?
Come *Kate* and wash, & welcome heartily:
you horson villaine, will you let it fall?

T3                                                *Kate*

20    *The Taming of the Shrew*, sigs T3ʳ–T3ᵛ (4.1.14–4.2.64), from the First Folio,
1623

## 222      *The Taming of the Shrew.*

*Kate.* Patience I pray you, 'twas a fault vnwilling.

*Pet.* A horfon beetle-headed flap-ear'd knaue :
Come *Kate* fit downe, I know you haue a ftomacke,
Will you giue thankes, fweete *Kate*, or elfe fhall I ?
What's this, Mutton ?

1. *Ser.* I.

*Pet.* Who brought it ?

*Peter.* I.

*Pet.* 'Tis burnt, and fo is all the meate :
What dogges are thefe ? Where is the rafcall Cooke ?
How durft you villaines bring it from the dreffer
And ferue it thus to me that loue it not ?
There, take it to you, trenchers, cups, and all :
You heedleffe iolt-heads, and vnmanner'd flaues.
What, do you grumble? Ile be with you ftraight.

*Kate.* I pray you husband be not fo difquiet,
The meate was well, if you were fo contented.

*Pet.* I tell thee *Kate*, 'twas burnt and dried away,
And I expreffely am forbid to touch it :
For it engenders choller, planteth anger,
And better 'twere that both of vs did faft,
Since of our felues, our felues are chollericke,
Then feede it with fuch ouer-rofted flefh:
Be patient, to morrow't fhalbe mended,
And for this night wel faft for companie.
Come I wil bring thee to thy Bridall chamber. *Exeunt.*

*Enter Seruants feuerally.*

*Nath.* Peter didft euer fee the like.

*Peter.* He kils her in her owne humor.

*Grumio.* Where is he?

*Enter Curtis a Seruant.*

*Cur.* In her chamber, making a fermon of continen-
cie to her, and railes, and fweares, and rates, that fhee
(poore foule) knowes not which way to ftand, to looke,
to fpeake, and fits as one new rifen from a dreame. A-
way, away, for he is comming hither.

*Enter Petruchio.*

*Pet.* Thus haue I politickely begun my reigne,
And 'tis my hope to end fucceffefully :
My Faulcon now is fharpe, and paffing emptie,
And til fhe ftoope, fhe muft not be full gorg'd,
For then fhe neuer lookes vpon her lure.
Another way I haue to man my Haggard,
To make her come, and know her Keepers call :
That is, to watch her, as we watch thefe Kites,
That baite, and beate, and will not be obedient :
She eate no meate to day, nor none fhall eate.
Laft night fhe flept not, nor to night fhe fhall not :
As with the meate, fome vndeferued fault
Ile finde about the making of the bed,
And heere Ile fling the pillow, there the boulfter,
This way the Couerlet, another way the fheets :
I, and amid this hurlie I intend,
That all is done in reuerend care of her,
And in conclufion, fhe fhal watch all night,
And if fhe chance to nod, Ile raile and brawle,
And with the clamor keepe her ftil awake :
This is a way to kil a Wife with kindneffe,
And thus Ile curbe her mad and headftrong humor :
He that knowes better how to tame a fhrew,
Now let him fpeake, 'tis charity to fhew.     *Exit*

*Enter Tranio and Hortenfio.*

*Tra.* Is't poffible friend *Lifio*, that miftris *Bianca*
Doth fancie any other but *Lucentio*,
I tel you fir, fhe beares me faire in hand.

*Luc.* Sir, to fatisfie you in what I haue faid,
Stand by, and marke the manner of his teaching.

*Enter Bianca.*

*Hor.* Now Miftris, profit you in what you reade ?

*Bian.* What Mafter reade you firft, refolue me that ?

*Hor.* I reade, that I profeffe the Art to loue.

*Bian.* And may you proue fir Mafter of your Art.

*Luc.* While you fweet deere ptoue Miftreffe of my
heart.

*Hor.* Quicke proceeders marry, now tel me I pray,
you that durft fweare that your miftris *Bianca*
Lou'd me in the World fo wel as *Lucentio.*

*Tra.* Oh defpightful Loue, vnconftant womankind,
I tel thee *Lifio* this is wonderfull.

*Hor.* Miftake no more, I am not *Lifio*,
Nor a Mufitian as I feeme to bee,
But one that fcorne to liue in this difguife,
For fuch a one as leaues a Gentleman,
And makes a God of fuch a Cullion ;
Know fir, that I am cal'd *Hortenfio.*

*Tra.* Signior *Hortenfio*, I haue often heard
Of your entire affection to *Bianca*,
And fince mine eyes are witneffe of her lightneffe,
I wil with you, if you be fo contented,
Forfweare *Bianca*, and her loue for euer.

*Hor.* See how they kiffe and court: Signior *Lucentio*,
Heere is my hand, and heere I firmly vow
Neuer to woo her more, but do forfweare her
As one vnworthie all the former fauours
That I haue fondly flatter'd them withall.

*Tra.* And heere I take the like vnfained oath,
Neuer to marrie with her, though fhe would intreate,
Fie on her, fee how beaftly fhe doth court him.

*Hor.* Would all the world but he had quite forfworn
For me, that I may furely keepe mine oath.
I wil be married to a wealthie Widdow,
Ere three dayes paffe, which hath as long lou'd me,
As I haue lou'd this proud difdainful Haggard,
And fo farewel fignior *Lucentio*,
Kindneffe in women, not their beauteous lookes
Shal win my loue, and fo I take my leaue,
In refolution, as I fwore before.

*Tra.* Miftris *Bianca*, bleffe you with fuch grace,
As longeth to a louers bleffed cafe :
Nay, I haue cane you napping gentle Loue,
And haue forfworne you with *Hortenfio.*

*Bian.* *Tranio* you ieft, but haue you both forfworne
mee ?

*Tra.* Miftris we haue.

*Luc.* Then we are rid of *Lifio.*

*Tra.* I'faith hee'l haue a luftie Widdow now,
That fhalbe woo'd, and wedded in a day.

*Bian.* God giue him ioy.

*Tra.* I, and hee'l tame her.

*Bianca.* He fayes fo *Tranio.*

*Tra.* Faith he is gone vnto the taming fchoole.

*Bian.* The taming fchoole: what is there fuch a place?

*Tra.* I miftris, and *Petruchio* is the mafter,
That teacheth trickes eleuen and twentie long,
To tame a fhrew, and charme her chattering tongue.

*Enter Biondello.*

*Bion.* Oh Mafter, mafter I haue watcht fo long,
That I am dogge-wearie, but at laft I fpied
An ancient Angel comming downe the hill,
Wil ferue the turne.

*Tra.* What is he *Biondello* ?

*Bio.* Mafter, a Marcantant, or a pedant,

339

uncertainty (Cox, esp. 179). Nonetheless, *The Shrew* has more exit directions than one might expect in a supposedly early Shakespearean text. For this edition's treatment of F's final exit SD, which constitutes a special case, see LN, pp. 306–8, and for a history of critical as well as theatrical performances of this moment, see Burns; Schafer, 231–2).

A similarly conservative logic applies to the question of the aside, a convention strongly underpinned by the history of fifteenth- and sixteenth-century drama – Dessen and Thomson note the occurrence of more than 550 asides in the period (15–16) – as well as by some physical features of early modern playhouses. In many modern editions the aside frequently seems to function as a sign of comedy (or duplicity). Introducing an aside assumes a complicitous audience or suggests that the actor plays a character who lives in a world that includes the audience, both of which are fictional assumptions.[1] Yet in *The Shrew*, where performances are framed within other performances and where there are often multiple onstage audiences, introducing asides can over-regiment the flexible 'in and out' of the Elizabethan stage, where rapid shifts occur between private and public stage space. Leah Marcus argues that eliminating asides occludes the possibility of enhancing the prevailing sense of onstage male cliques (LM), but the idea seems slightly suspect, since the play remains relentlessly masculinist – that is, the subject of 'woman' is constantly under surveillance, regardless of whether few, or many, asides are editorially mandated. Since *The Shrew*'s quick switches of address often resist being pinned down, rather than marking particular lines as '*aside*', the commentary notes where a line may be performed as a reply, a choral comment or an aside. In other instances, however, an aside serves to gain the attention of the audience and establish its confidentiality with the speaker, as, for example, Lucentio's 'Well begun, Tranio' (1.2.227/TLN 797), which reminds auditors (who have not heard Tranio's

1 Bert O. States, 'The actor's presence: three phenomenal modes', in Philip B. Zarrilli (ed.), *Acting (Re)Considered: A Theorectical and Practical Guide* (2002), 23–39.

name) that the speaker is the 'real' Lucentio, or with Biondello's 'I have seen them in the church together . . . Now we are undone and brought to nothing' (5.1.37–40/TLN 2420–4), which not only provides, at a crucial juncture, the information that Bianca and Lucentio are married but registers Biondello's fear of the identity switches being discovered. While Bianca and Lucentio might hear Hortensio's 'How fiery and forward our pedant is!' (3.1.46/TLN 1341), two other cases represent what could be called a 'split aside': Gremio's 'My land amounts not to so much in all' (2.1.377/TLN 1255) might be overheard by Tranio but not by Baptista, and Petruccio's 'Hortensio, say thou wilt see the tailor paid' (4.3.163/TLN 2147) might be overheard by others, though not, perhaps, by Katherina. In still other cases, speaking out of turn may work to expand the contours of a role, as with Biondello, who often speaks what he thinks: see, for example, his comment about how little the Merchant resembles Lucentio's father – 'As much as an apple doth an oyster, and all one' (4.2.102–3/TLN 1957). Ultimately, however, whether a line is or is not spoken '*aside*' is best left for performers to work out, for choices will also depend in some measure on the particular space in which the play is staged.

## COMMENTARY

Just as a Shakespeare play is an elaborate memory system that seems to rehearse and rework his reading and lived experience, so too an edition draws on centuries of editorial commentary, critical viewpoints, moments of remembered performance. One problem in writing commentary is that many notes open up gates that lead to a parallel universe of information – potential material for one or several books, not a single edition. Although the Longer Note (see pp. 306–8) represents an exception, I have tended to refer readers to introductory materials for extended discussions of particular points. Commentary is also a construction of one particular editor who, however committed to a (mythical) 'objectivity', inevitably legislates in favour of certain narratives she wishes to promote – a tendency which can narrow the range of options the text makes available. Rather than colonizing the commentary with either/or interpretations, I have tried to indicate a range of choices for readers and players to explore; similarly, I have avoided filling in gaps in what characters know and when they know it or assuming that such information lapses necessarily represent 'textual errors' (see pp. 313–15). Performances, of course, produce their own filters: memories of how an actor spoke a line or performed a particular bit of business function as performative equivalents of critical commentary.

For glosses, I have relied on the *OED Online* and on David Crystal and Ben Crystal, *Shakespeare's Words: A Glossary and Language Companion.* The commentary represents several 'styles', ranging from atomized single definitions to more global comments. In addition, citations from other plays are offered primarily to clarify an idiom or to widen a frame of reference. And at the risk of reading proleptically, I also occasionally bring passages from different scenes into dialogue with one another. All such annotative procedures, of course, inevitably – and desirably – will simplify the challenges a particular passage or passages may pose to present-day readers and players.

# APPENDIX 3

## THE TAMING OF A SHREW

### Reproduced in facsimile by courtesy of the Huntington Library, California (RB 69594)

Line numbering conforms to the Malone Society Reprint facsimile edition, ed. Stephen Roy Miller, with Richard Proudfoot and R.V. Holdsworth (Oxford, 1998).

# A
# Pleaſant Conceited

### Hiſtorie, called The taming
### of a Shrew.

As it was ſundry times acted by the
*Right honorable the Earle of*
Pembrook his ſeruants.

Printed at London by Peter Short and
*are to be ſold by Cutbert Burbie, at his*
ſhop at the Royall Exchange.
1594.

# A Pleaſant conceited Hiſtorie, called *The Taming of a Shrew*.

Enter a Tapſter, beating out of his doores
*Slie Droonken*.

Tapſter.
YOu whorſon droonken ſlaue, you had beſt be gone,
And empty your droonken panch ſome where elſe
For in this houſe thou ſhalt not reſt to night.
*Exit* Tapſter.
*Slie*. *T*illy vally, by criſee Tapſter Ile feſe you anon.
Fils the tother pot and alls paid for, looke you
I doo drinke it of mine owne Inſtegation,    *Omne bene*
Heere Ile lie a while, why Tapſter I ſay,
Fils a freſh cuſhen heere.
Heigh ho, heers good warme lying,
He fals aſleepe.

Enter a Noble man and his men
from hunting.
*Lord*. Now that the gloomie ſhaddow of the night,
Longing to view Orions driſling lookes,
Leapes from th'antarticke World vnto the skie
*A*nd dims the Welkin with her pitchie breath,
*A*nd darkeſome night oreſhades the chriſtall heauens,
Here breake we off our hunting for to night,
                    A 2                    Cuppel

### *The taming of a Shrew.*

Cupple vppe the hounds and let vs hie vs home,
And bid the huntſman ſee them meated well,
For they haue all deſeru'd it well to daie,
But ſoft, what ſleepie fellow is this lies heere?
Or is he dead, ſee one what he dooth lacke?    *(ſleepe,*

*Seruingman.* My lord, tis nothing but a drunken
His head is too heauie for his bodie,
And he hath drunke ſo much that he can go no furder.

   *Lord.* Fie, how the ſlauiſh villaine ſtinkes of drinke.
Ho, ſirha ariſe. What ſo ſound aſleepe?
Go take him vppe and beare him to my houſe,
And beare him eaſilie for feare he wake,
And in my faireſt chamber make a fire,
And ſet a ſumptuous banquet on the boord,
And put my richeſt garmentes on his backe,
Then ſet him at the *T*able in a chaire:
When that is doone againſt he ſhall awake,
Let heauenlie muſicke play about him ſtill,
Go two of you awaie and beare him hence,
And then Ile tell you what I haue deuiſde,
But ſee in any caſe you wake him not.

          *Exeunt* two with *Slie.*

Now take my cloake and giue me one of yours,
Al fellowes now, and ſee you take me ſo,
For we will waite vpon this droonken man,
To ſee his countnance when he dooth awake
And finde himſelfe clothed in ſuch attire,
With heauenlie muſicke ſounding in his eares,
And ſuch a banquet ſet before his eies,
The fellow ſure will thinke he is in heauen,
But we will be about him when he wakes,
And ſee you call him Lord, at euerie word,
And offer thou him his horſe to ride abroad,

                     **And**

A 2

### The taming of a Shrew.

And thou his hawkes and houndes to hunt the deere,
And I will aske what futes he meanes to weare,
And what so ere he saith, fee you doo not laugh,
But still perfwade him that he is a Lord.

Enter one.

*Mef.* And it pleafe your honour your plaiers be com
And doo attend your honours pleafure here.

*Lord.* The fitteft time they could haue chofen out,
Bid one or two of them come hither ftraight,
Now will I fit my felfe accordinglie,
For they fhall play to him when he awakes.

Enter two of the players with packs at their
backs, and a boy.

Now firs, what ftore of plaies haue you?

*San.* Marrie my lord you maie haue a Tragicall
Or a comôditie, or what you will.

*The other.* A Comedie thou fhouldft fay, founs
thout fhame vs all.

*Lord.* And whats the name of your Comedie?

*San.* Marrie my lord tis calde The taming of a fhrew:
Tis a good leffon for vs my lord, for vs ÿ are maried men

*Lord.* The taming of a fhrew, thats excellent fure,
Go fee that you make you readie ftraight,
For you muft play before a lord to night,
Say you are his men and I your fellow,
Hees fomething foolifh, but what fo ere he faies,
See that you be not dafht out of countenance.
And firha go you make you ready ftraight,
And dreffe your felfe like fome louelie ladie,
And when I call fee that you come to me,
For I will fay to him thou art his wife,
Dallie with him and hug him in thine armes,
And if he defire to goe to bed with thee,

A 3　　　　　　　　　Then

347

*The taming of a Shrew.*

Then faine some scufe and say thou wilt anon.
Be gone I say, and see thou doost it well.

  *B y.* Feare not my Lord, Ile dandell him well enough
And make him thinke I loue him mightilie.   *Ex.* boy.

   *Lord.* Now sirs go you and make you ready to,
For you must play assoone as he dooth wake.

   *San.* O braue, sirha Tom, we must play before
A foolish Lord, come lets go make vs ready,
Go get a dishclout to make cleane your shooes,
And Ile speake for the properties, My Lord, we must
Haue a shoulder of mutton for a propertie,
And a little vinegre to make our Diuell rore.

   *Lord.* Very well : sirha see that they want nothing.
                       *Exeunt omnes.*

Enter two with a table and a banquet on it, and two
    other, with *Slie* asleepe in a chaire, richlie
      apparelled,& the musick plaieng.

   *One.* So : sirha now go call my Lord,
And tel him that all things is ready as he wild it.

   *Another.* Set thou some wine vpon the boord
And then Ile go fetch my Lord presentlie.   *Exit.*

Enter the Lord and his men.

   *Lord.* How now, what is all thinges readie ?
   *One.* I my Lord.                ( straight,
   *Lord.* Then sound the musick, and Ile wake him
And see you doo as earst I gaue in charge.
My lord, My lord, he sleepes soundlie : My lord.

   *Slie.* Tapster, gis a little small ale.   Heigh ho,
   *Lord.* Heers wine my lord, the purest of the grape.
   *Slie.* For which Lord?
   *Lord.* For your honour my Lord.

                          *Slie.*

*The taming of a Shrew.*

*Slie.* Who I, am I a Lord? Iesus what fine apparell
haue *I* got.

*Lord.* More richer farre your honour hath to weare,
And if it pleafe you I will fetch them ftraight.

*Wil.* And if your honour pleafe to ride abroad,
Ile fetch you luftie fteedes more fwift of pace
Then winged *Pegafus* in all his pride,
That ran fo fwiftlie ouer the *Perfian* plaines.

*Tom.* And if your honour pleafe to hunt the deere,
Your hounds ftands readie cuppeld at the doore,
Who in running will oretake the Row,
And make the long breathde Tygre broken winded.

*Slie.* By the maffe I thinke I am a Lord indeed,
Whats thy name?

*Lord.* *Simon* and it pleafe your honour.

*Slie.* *Simon*, thats as much to fay *Simion* or *Simon*
Put foorth thy hand and fill the pot.
Giue me thy hand, *Sim.* am I a lord indeed?

*Lord.* I my gratious Lord, and your louelie ladie
Long time hath moorned for your abfence heere,
And now with ioy behold where fhe dooth come
To gratulate your honours fafe returne.

Enter the boy in Womans attire.

*Slie.* *Sim.* Is this fhe?

*Lord.* I my Lord.

*Slie.* Maffe tis a prettie wench, whats her name?

*Boy.* Oh that my louelie Lord would once vouchfafe
To looke on me, and leaue thefe frantike fits,
Or were I now but halfe fo eloquent,
To paint in words what ile performe in deedes,
I know your honour then would pittie me.

*Slie.* Harke you miftreffe, wil you eat a peece of
bread,

                                                    Come

*The taming of a Shrew.*

Come fit downe on my knee, *Sim* drinke to hir *Sim*,
For fhe and I will go to bed anon.

   *Lord.* May it pleafe you, your honors plaiers be come
To offer your honour a plaie.

   *Slie.* A plaie *Sim*, O braue, be they my plaiers?

   *Lord.* I my Lord.

   *Slie.* Is there not a foole in the plaie?

   *Lord.* Yes my lord.

   *Slie.* When wil they plaie *Sim?*

   *Lord.* Euen when it pleafe your honor, they be readie.

   *Boy.* My lord Ile go bid them begin their plaie.

   *Slie.* Doo, but looke that you come againe.

   *Boy.* I warrant you my lord, I wil not leaue you thus.

                  *Exit* boy.

   *Slie.* Come *Sim*, where be the plaiers? *Sim* ftand by
Me and weele flout the plaiers out of their cotes.

   *Lord.* Ile cal them my lord. Hoe where are you there?
                Sound Trumpets.


       Enter two yoong Gentlemen, and a man
               and a boie.

   *Pol.* Welcome to *Athens* my beloued friend,
To *Platoes* fchooles and *Ariftotles* walkes,
Welcome from *Ceftus* famous for the loue
Of good *Leander* and his Tragedie,
For whom the *Helefpont* weepes brinifh teares,
The greateft griefe is I cannot as I would
Giue entertainment to my deereft friend.

   *Aurel.* Thankes noble *Polidor* my fecond felfe,
The faithfull loue which I haue found in thee
Hath made me leaue my fathers princelie court,
The Duke of *Ceftus* thrife renowmed feate,
To come to *Athens* thus to find thee out,

                            Which

## The taming of a Shrew.

Which since I haue so happilie attaind,
My fortune now I doo account as great
As earst did *Cæsar* when he conquered most,
But tell me noble friend where shal we lodge,
For I am vnacquainted in this place.

*Poli.* My Lord if you vouchsafe of schollers fare,
My house, my selfe, and all is yours to vse,
You and your men shall staie and lodge with me.

*Aurel.* With all my hart, I will requite thy loue.

Enter *Simon*, *Alphonsus*, and his
three daughters.

But staie, what dames are these so bright of hew
Whose eies are brighter then the lampes of heauen,
Fairer then rocks of pearle and pretious stone,
More louelie farre then is the morning sunne,
When first she opes hir orientall gates.

*Alfon.* Daughters be gone, and hie you to ý church,
And I will hie me downe vnto the key,
To see what Marchandise is come ashore.

Ex. Omnes.

*Pol.* Why how now my Lord, what in a dumpe,
To see these damsels passe away so soone?

*Aurel.* Trust me my friend I must confesse to thee,
I tooke so much delight in these faire dames,
As I doo wish they had not gone so soone,
But if thou canst, resolue me what they be,
And what old man it was that went with them,
For I doo long to see them once againe.

*Pol.* I cannot blame your honor good my lord,
For they are both louely, wise, faire and yong,
And one of them the yoongest of the three
I long haue lou'd (sweet friend) and she lou'd me,
But neuer yet we could not find a meanes
How we might compasse our desired ioyes.

B                                    *Aurel.*

351

### The taming of a Shrew.

*Aurel.* Why, is not her father willing to the match?

*Pol.* Yes truſt me, but he hath ſolemnlie ſworne,
His eldeſt daughter firſt ſhall be eſpowſde,
Before he grauntes his yoongeſt leaue to loue,
And therefore he that meanes to get their loues,
Muſt firſt proaide for her if he will ſpeed,
And he that hath her ſhall be fettred ſo,
As good be wedded to the diuell himſelfe,
For ſuch a skould as ſhe did neuer liue,
And till that ſhe be ſped none elſe can ſpeed,
Which makes me thinke that all my labours loſt,
And whoſoere can get hir firme good will,
A large dowrie he ſhall be ſure to haue,
For her father is a man of mightie wealth,
And an ancient Cittizen of the towne,
And that was he that went along with them.

  *Aurel.* But he ſhall keepe hir ſtill by my aduiſe,
And yet I needs muſt loue his ſecond daughter
The image of honor and Nobilitie,
In whoſe ſweet perſon is compriſde the ſomme
Of natures skill and heauenlie maieſtie.

  *Pol.* I like your choiſe, and glad you choſe not mine,
Then if you like to follow on your loue,
We muſt deuiſe a meanes and find ſome one
That will attempt to wed this deuiliſh skould,
And I doo know the man. Come hither boy,
Go your waies ſirha to *Ferandoes* houſe,
Deſire him take the paines to come to me,
For I muſt ſpeake with him immediatlie.

  *Boy.* I will ſir, and fetch him preſentlie.

  *Pol.* A man I thinke will fit hir humor right,
As blunt in ſpeech as ſhe is ſharpe of toong,
And he I thinke will match hir euerie waie,
And yet he is a man of wealth ſufficient,

And

## The taming of a Shrew.

And for his person worth as good as she,
And if he compasse hir to be his wife,
Then may we freelie visite both our loues.

*Aurel.* O might I see the center of my soule
Whose sacred beautie hath inchanted me,
More faire then was the Grecian *Helena*
For whose sweet sake so many princes dide,
That came with thousand shippes to *Tenedos,*
But when we come vnto hir fathers house,
Tell him I am a Marchants sonne of *Cestus,*
That comes for traffike vnto *Athens* heere,
And heere sirha I will change with you for once,
And now be thou the Duke of *Cestus* sonne,
Reuell and spend as if thou wert my selfe,
For I will court my loue in this disguise.

*Val.* My lord, how if the Duke your father should
By some meanes come to *Athens* for to see
How you doo profit in these publike schooles,
And find me clothed thus in your attire,
How would he take it then thinke you my lord?

*Aurel.* Tush feare not *Valeria* let me alone,
But staie, heere comes some other companie.

Enter *Ferando* and his man *Saunders*
with a blew coat.

*Pol.* Here comes the man that *I* did tel you of.
*Feran.* Good morrow gentlemen to all at once.
How now *Polidor,* what man still in loue?
Euer wooing and canst thou neuer speed,
God send me better luck when I shall woo.

*San.* I warrant you maister and you take my councell.
*Feran.* Why sirha, are you so cunning?
*San.* Who I, twere better for you by fiue marke
And you could tel how to doo it as well as I.

B 2                                            *Pol.*

### *The taming of a Shrew.*

*Pol.* I would thy maister once were in the vaine,
To trie himselfe how he could woe a wench.

*Feran.* Faith I am euen now a going.

*San.* I faith fir, my maiſters going to this geere now.

*Pol.* Whither in faith *Ferando*, tell me true.

*Feran.* To bonie *Kate*, the patientſt wench aliue
The diuel himſelfe dares ſcarce venter to woo her,
Signior *Alfonſos* eldeſt daughter,
And he hath promiſde me ſix thouſand crownes
If I can win her once to be my wife,
And ſhe and I muſt woo with ſkoulding ſure,
And I will hold hir toot till ſhe be wearie,
Or elſe Ile make her yeeld to graunt me loue.

*Pol.* How like you this *Aurelius*, I thinke he knew
Our mindes before we ſent to him,
But tell me, when doo you meane to ſpeake with her?

*Feran.* Faith preſentlie, doo you but ſtand aſide,
And I will make her father bring hir hither,
And ſhe, and I, and he, will talke alone.

*Pol.* With al our heartes, Come *Aurelius*
Let vs be gone and leaue him heere alone.      *Exit.*

*Feran.* Ho Signiour *Alfonſo*, whoſe within there?

*Alfon.* Signiour *Ferando* your welcome hartilie,
You are a ſtranger ſir vnto my houſe.
Harke you ſir, looke what I did promiſe you
Ile perforine, if you get my daughters loue.

*Feran.* Then when I haue talkt a word or two with hir,
Doo you ſtep in and giue her hand to me,
And tell her when the marriage daie ſhal be,
For I doo know ſhe would be married faine,
And when our nuptiall rites be once performde
Let me alone to tame hir well enough,
Now call her foorth that I may ſpeake with hir.

Enter *Kate.*

*Alfon.*

354

## *The taming of a Shrew.*

*Alfon.* Ha *Kate*, Come hither wench & lift to me,
Vfe this gentleman friendlie as thou canft.

*Feran.* Twentie good morrowes to my louely *Kate.*

*Kate.* You ieft I am fure, is fhe yours alreadie?

*Feran.* I tell thee *Kate* I know thou lou'ft me well.

*Kate.* The deuill you doo, who told you fo?

*Feran.* My mind fweet *Kate* doth fay I am the man,
Muft wed, and bed, and marrie bonnie *Kate.*

*Kate.* Was euer feene fo grofe an affe as this?

*Feran.* I, to ftand fo long and neuer get a kiffe.

*Kate.* Hands off I fay, and get you from this place;
Or I wil fet my ten commandments in your face.

*Feran.* I prethe doo kate; they fay thou art a fhrew,
And I like thee the better for I would haue thee fo.

*Kate.* Let go my hand, for feare it reach your eare.

*Feran.* No kate, this hand is mine and I thy loue.

*Kate.* In faith fir no the woodcock wants his taile.

*Feran.* But yet his bil wil ferue, if the other faile.

*Alfon.* How now *Ferando*, what faies my daughter?

*Feran.* Shees willing fir and loues me as hir life.

*Kate.* Tis for your skin then, but not to be your wife.

*Alfon.* Come hither *Kate* and let me giue thy hand
To him that I haue chofen for thy loue,
And thou to morrow fhalt be wed to him.

*Kate.* Why father, what do you meane to do with me,
To giue me thus vnto this brainfick man,
That in his mood cares not to murder me?

> She turnes afide and fpeakes.

But yet I will confent and marrie him,
For I methinkes haue liude too long a maid,
And match him to, or elfe his manhoods good.

*Alfon.* Giue me thy hand *Ferando* loues thee wel,
And will with wealth and eafe maintaine thy ftate.
Here *Ferando* take her for thy wife,

B 3                                    And

### The taming of a Shrew.

And sunday next shall be your wedding day.

*Feran.* Why so, did I not tell thee I should be the man
Father, I leaue my louelie *Kate* with you,
Prouide your selues against our mariage daie,
For I must hie me to my countrie house
In hast, to see prouision may be made,
To entertaine my *Kate* when she dooth come.

*Alfon.* Doo so, come *Kate*, why doost thou looke
So sad, be merrie wench thy wedding daies at hand.
Sonne fare you well, and see you keepe your promise.

*Exit Alfonso and Kate.*

*Feran.* So, all thus farre goes well. Ho *Saunder*.

*Enter Saunder laughing.*

*San.* Sander, Ifaith your a beast, *I* crie God hartilie
Mercie, my harts readie to run out of my bellie with
Laughing, I stood behind the doore all this while,
And heard what you said to hir.               (wel to hir?

*Feran.* Why didst thou think that I did not speake

*San.* You spoke like an asse to her, Ile tel you what,
And I had been there to haue woode hir, and had this
Cloke on that you haue, chud haue had her before she
Had gone a foot furder, and you talke of Woodcocks
with her, and I cannot tell you what.        (for all this.

*Feran.* Wel sirha, & yet thou seest I haue got her

*San.* I marry twas more by hap then any good cunning
I hope sheele make you one of the head men of the
                         parish shortly.

*Feran.* Wel sirha leaue your iesting and go to *Polidors*
The yong gentleman that was here with me,    (house,
And tell him the circumstance of all thou knowst,
Tell him on sunday next we must be married,
And if he aske thee whither I am gone,
Tell him into the countrie to my house,
And vpon sundaie Ile be heere againe.    *Ex. Ferando,*
                                            *San.*

## *The taming of a Shrew.*

*San.* I warrant you Maister feare not me
For dooing of my businesse.
Now hang him that has not a liuerie cote
To slash it out and swash it out amongst the proudest
On them. Why looke you now Ile scarce put vp
Plaine *Saunder* now at any of their handes, for and any
Bodie haue any thing to doo with my maister, straight
They come crouching vpon me, I beseech you good M.
*Saunder* speake a good word for me, and then am I so
Stout and takes it vpon me, & stands vpon my pantoffles
To them out of all crie, why I haue a life like a giant
Now, but that my maister hath such a pestilent mind
To a woman now a late, and I haue a prettie wench
To my sister, and I had thought to haue preferd my
Maister to her, and that would haue beene a good
Deale in my waie but that hees sped alreadie.

　　　　　　　Enter *Polidors* boie.

*Boy.* Friend, well met.

*San.* Souns, friend well met: I hold my life he sees
Not my maisters liuerie coat,
Plaine friend hop of my thum, kno you who we are.

*Boy.* Trust me sir it is the vse where I was borne,
To salute men after this manner, yet notwithstanding
If you be angrie with me for calling of you friend,
I am the more sorie for it, hoping the itile
Of a foole will make you amends for all.

*San.* The slaue is sorie for his fault, now we cannot be
Angrie, wel whats the matter that you would do with vs.

*Boy.* Marry sir, I heare you pertain to signior
　　　*Ferando.*

*San.* I and thou beest not blind thou maist see,
　　　*Ecce signum,* heere.

*Boy.* Shall I intreat you to doo me a message to your
　　　Maister?

　　　　　　　　　　　　　　　　*San.*

### *The taming of a Shrew.*

*San.* I, it may be, & you tel vs from whence you com.

*Boy.* Marrie sir I serue yong *Polidor* your maisters
      friend.

*San.* Do you serue him, and whats your name?

*Boy.* My name sirha, I tell thee sirha is cald Catapie.

*San.* Cake and pie, O my teeth waters to haue a peece
      of thee.

*Boy.* Why slaue wouldst thou eate me?

*San.* Eate thee, who would not eate Cake and pie?

*Boy.* Why villaine my name is Catapie,
But wilt thou tell me where thy maister is.

*San.* Nay thou must first tell me where thy maister is,
For I haue good newes for him, I can tell thee,

*Boy.* Why see where he comes.

      Enter *Polidor, Aurelius* and *Valeria.*

*Pol.* Come sweet *Aurelius* my faithfull friend,
Now will we go to see those louelie dames
Richer in beawtie then the orient pearle,
Whiter then is the Alpine Christall mould,
And farre more louelie then the terean plant,
That blushing in the aire turnes to a stone.
What *Sander,* what newes with you?

*San.* Marry sir my maister sends you word
That you must come to his wedding to morrow.

*Pol.* What, shall he be married then?

*San.* Faith *I,* you thinke he standes as long about it as
      you doo.

*Pol.* Whither is thy maister gone now?

*San.* Marrie hees gone to our house in the Countrie,
To make all thinges in a readinesse against my new
Mistresse comes thither, but heele come againe to
      morrowe.

*Pol.* This is suddainlie dispatcht belike,
Well, sirha boy, take *Saunder* in with you

                             *And*

*The taming of a Shrew.*

And haue him to the buttrie prefentlie.

 *Boy.* I will fir : come *Saunder*.
    *Exit Saunder and the Boy.*
 *Aurel. Valeria* as erfte we did deuife,
Take thou thy lute and go to *Alfonfos* houfe,
And fay that *Polidor* fent thee thither.

 *Pol.* I *Valeria* for he fpoke to me,
To helpe him to fome cunning Mufition,
To teach his eldeft daughter on the lute,
And thou I know will fit his turne fo well
As thou fhalt get great fauour at his handes,
Begon *Valeria* and fay I fent thee to him.

 *Valer* I will fir and ftay your comming at *Alfonfos*
  houfe.

    *Exit Valeria*

 *Pol.* Now fweete *Aurelius* by this deuife
Shall we haue leifure for to courte our loues,
For whilft that fhe is learning on the lute,
Hir fifters may take time to fteele abrode,
For otherwife fhele keep them both within,
And make them worke whilft fhe hir felfe doth play,
But come lets go vnto *Alfonfos* houfe,
And fee how *Valeria* and *Kate* agreefe,
I doute his Mufick skarfe will pleafe his skoller,
But ftay here comes *Alfonfo*.

    Enter *Alfonfo*

 *Alfonfo.* What M. *Polidor* you are well mett,
I thanke you for the man you fent to me,
A good Mufition I thinke he is,
I haue fet my daughter and him togither,
But is this gentellman a frend of youres?

 *Pol.* He is, I praie you fir bid him welcome,
He's a wealthie Marchants fonne of *Ceftus*.

 *Alfonfo.* Your welcom fir and if my houfe aforde
      C       You

### *The taming of a Shrew.*

You any thing that may content your mind,
I pray you fir make bold with me.

   *Aurel.* I thanke you fir, and if what I haue got,
By marchandife or trauell on the feas,
Sattins or lawnes or azure colloured filke,
Or pretious firie pointed ftones of Indie,
You fhall command both them my felfe and all.

   *Alfon.* Thanks gentle fir, *Polidor* take him in,
And bid him welcome to vnto my houfe,
For thou I thinke muft be my fecond fonne,
*Ferando, Polidor* dooft thou not know
Muft marry *Kate*, and to morrow is the day.

   *Pol.* Such newes I heard, and *I* came now to know.

   *Alfon. Polidor* tis true, goe let me alone,
For I muft fee againft the bridegroome come,
That all thinges be according to his mind,
And fo Ile leaue you for an houre or two.    *Exit.*

   *Pol.* Come then *Aurcleus* come in with me,
And weele go fit a while and chat with them,
And after bring them foorth to take the aire.   *Exit.*

         Then *Slie* fpeakes.

   *Slie.* *Sim*, when will the foole come againe?

   *Lord.* Heele come againe my Lord anon.

   *Slie.* Gis fome more drinke here, founs wheres
The *Tapfter*, here *Sim* eate fome of thefe things.

   *Lord.* So I doo my Lord.

   *Slie.* Here *Sim*, I drinke to thee.

   *Lord.* My Lord heere comes the plaiers againe,

   *Slie.* O braue, heers two fine gentlewomen.


     Enter *Valeria* with a Lute and *Kate*
           with him.

   *Vale.* The fenceleffe trees by mufick haue bin moou'd
And at the found of pleafant tuned ftrings,

                            Haue

## *The taming of a Shrew.*

Haue sauage beastes hung downe their listning heads,
As though they had beene cast into a trance.
Then it may be that she whom nought can please,
With musickes sound in time may be surprisde,
Come louely mistresse will you take your lute,
And play the lesson that I taught you last?

*Kate.* It is no matter whether I doo or no,
For trust me I take no great delight in it.

*Vale.* I would sweet mistresse that it laie in me,
To helpe you to that thing thats your delight.

*Kate.* In you with a pestlence,are you so kind?
Then make a night cap of your fiddles case,
To warme your head, and hide your filthie face.

*Val.* If that sweet mistresse were your harts content,
You should command a greater thing then that,
Although it were ten times to my disgrace.

*Kate.* Your so kind twere pittie you should be
            hang'd,
And yet methinkes the foole dooth looke asquint.

*Val.* Why mistresse doo you mocke me?

*Kate.* No, but I meane to moue thee.

*Val.* Well, will you plaie a little?

*Kate.* I, giue me the Lute.

                    She plaies.

*Val.* That stop was false, play it againe.

*Kate.* Then mend it thou, thou filthy asse.

*Val.* What, doo you bid me kisse your arse?

*Kate.* How now iack sause,your a iollie mate,
Your best be still least I crosse your pate,
And make your musicke flie about your eares,
Ile make it and your foolish coxcombe meet.

            She offers to strike him with the lute.

*Val.* Hold mistresse,souns wil you breake my lute?

*Kate.* I on thy head, and if thou speake to me,
                        C 2                    There

## The taming of a Shrew.

There take it vp and fiddle somewhere else,
      She throwes it downe.
And see you come no more into this place,
Least that I clap your fiddle on your face.    *Ex.Kate.*

  *Val.* Souns, teach hir to play vpon the lute?
The deuill shal teach her first, I am glad shees gone,
For I was neare so fraid in all my life,
But that my lute should flie about mine eares,
My maister shall teach her his selfe for me,
For Ile keepe me far enough without hir reach,
For he and *Polydor* sent me before
To be with her and teach her on the lute,
Whilst they did court the other gentlewomen,
And heere methinkes they come togither.
     Enter *Aurelius, Polidor, Emelia,*
        and *Philena.*

  *Pol.* How now *Valeria*, whears your mistresse?
  *Val.* At the vengeance I thinke and no where else.
  *Aurel.* Why *Valeria*, will she not learne apace?
  *Val.* Yes berlady she has learnt too much already,
And that I had felt had I not spoke hir faire,
But she shall neare be learnt for me againe.
  *Aurel.* Well *Valeria* go to my chamber,
And beare him companie that came to daie
From *Cestus*, where our aged father dwels.  *Ex. Valeria.*
  *Pol.* Come faire *Emelia* my louelie loue,
Brighter then the burnisht pallace of the sunne,
The eie-sight of the glorious firmament,
In whose bright lookes sparkles the radiant fire,
Wilie *Prometheus* slilie stole from *Ioue*,
Infusing breath, life, motion, soule,
To euerie obiect striken by thine eies.
Oh faire *Emelia* I pine for thee,
And either must enioy thy loue, or die.

                    *Emelia.*

## The taming of a Shrew.

*Eme.* Tie man, I know you will not die for loue:
Ah *Polidor* thou needst not to complaine,
Eternall heauen sooner be dissolude,
*And* all that pearseth Phebus siluer eie,
Before such hap befall to *Polidor*.

*Pol.* Thanks faire *Emelia* for these sweet words,
But what saith *Phylena* to hir friend?

*Phyle.* Why I am buying marchandise of him.

*Aurel.* Mistresse you shall not need to buie of me,
For when I crost the bubling Canibey,
And sailde along the Cristall Helispont,
I filde my cofers of the wealthie mines,
Where I did cause Millions of labouring Moores
To vndermine the cauernes of the earth,
To seeke for strange and new found pretious stones,
And diue into the sea to gather pearle,
As faire as *Iuno* offered *Priams* sonne,
*And* you shall take your liberall choice of all.

*Phyle.* I thanke you sir and would *Phylena* might
*In* any curtesie requite you so,
*As* she with willing hart could well bestow.

Enter *Alfonso.*

*Alfon.* How now daughters, is *Ferando* come?

*Eme.* Not yet father, I wonder he staies so long.

*Alfon.* And wheres your sister that she is not heere?

*Phyle.* She is making of hir readie father
To goe to church and if that he were come.

*Pol.* I warrant you heele not be long awaie.

*Alfon.* Go daughters get you in, and bid your
Sister prouide her selfe against that we doo come,
And see you goe to church along with vs.

*Exit Philena* and *Emelia.*

I maruell that *Ferando* comes not away.

C 3                         *Pol.*

*The taming of a Shrew.*

*Pol.* His Tailor it may be hath bin too slacke,
In his apparrell which he meanes to weare,
For no question but some fantasticke sutes
He is determined to weare to day,
And richly powdered with pretious stones,
Spotted with liquid gold, thick set with pearle,
And such he meanes shall be his wedding sutes.

*Alfon.* I carde not I what cost he did bestow,
In gold or silke, so he himselfe were heere,
For I had rather lose a thousand crownes,
Then that he should deceiue vs heere to daie,
But soft I thinke I see him come.

Enter *Ferando* baselie attired, and a
red cap on his head.

*Feran.* Godmorow father, *Polidor* well met,
You wonder I know that I haue staid so long.

*Alfon.* I marrie son, we were almost perswaded,
That we should scarse haue had our bridegroome heere,
But say, why art thou thus basely attired?

*Feran.* Thus richlie father you should haue said,
For when my wife and I am married once,
Shees such a shrew, if we should once fal out,
Sheele pul my costlie sutes ouer mine eares,
And therefore am I thus attired awhile,
For manie thinges I tell you's in my head,
And none must know thereof but *Kate* and *I*,
For we shall liue like lammes and Lions sure,
Nor lammes to Lions neuer was so tame,
If once they lie within the Lions pawes
As *Kate* to me if we were married once,
And therefore come let vs to church presently.

*Pol.* Fie *Ferando* not thus atired for shame,
Come to my Chamber and there sute thy selfe,

Of

## The taming of a Shrew

Of twentie sutes that I did neuer were·

*Feran.* Tush *Polidor* I haue as many sutes
Fantasticke made to fit my humor so
As any in Athens and as richlie wrought
As was the Massie Robe that late adornd,
The stately legate of the Persian King,
And this from them haue I made choise to weare.

*Alfon.* I prethie *Ferando* let me intreat
Before thou goste vnto the church with vs,
To put some other sute vpon thy backe.

*Feran.* Not for the world if I might gaine it so,
And therefore take me thus or not at all,
     Enter *Kate*.
But soft se where my *Kate* doth come,
I must salute hir: how fares my louely *Kate*?
What art thou readie? shall we go to church.?

*Kate.* Not I with one so mad, so basely tirde,
To marrie such a filthie slauish groome,
That as it seemes sometimes is from his wits,
Or else he would not thus haue come to vs.

*Feran.* Tush *Kate* these words addes greater loue in me
And makes me thinke thee fairrer then before,
Sweete *Kate* the louelier then Dianas purple robe,
Whiter then are the snowie Apenis,
Or icie haire that groes on Boreas chin.
Father I sweare by Ibis golden beake,
More faire and Radiente is my bonie *Kate*,
Then siluer Zanthus when he doth imbrace,
The ruddie Simies at Idas feete,
And care not thou swete *Kate* how I be clad,
Thou shalt haue garments wrought of Median silke,
Enchaft with pretious Iewells secht from far,
By Italian Marchants that with Russian stemes,
Plous vp huge sorrowes in the *Terren Maine*,

         And

*The taming of a Shrew.*

*And* better farre my louely *Kate* shall weare,
Then come sweet loue and let vs to the church,
For this I sweare shall be my wedding suite.

                              *Exeunt omnes.*

*Alfon.* Come gentlemen go along with vs,
For thus doo what we can he will be wed.          *Exit.*


                Enter *Polidors* boy and *Sander.*

*Boy.* Come hither sirha boy.

*San.* Boy; oh disgrace to my person, souns boy
Of your face, you haue many boies with such
Pickadeuantes I am sure, souns would you
Not haue a bloudie nose for this?

*Boy.* Come, come, I did but iest, where is that
Same peece of pie that I gaue thee to keepe.

*San.* The pie? I you haue more minde of your bellie
Then to go see what your maister dooes.

*Boy.* Tush tis no matter man I prethe giue it me,
I am verie hungry I promise thee.

*San.* Why you may take it and the deuill burst
You with it, one cannot saue a bit after supper,
But you are alwaies readie to munch it vp.

*Boy.* Why come man, we shall haue good cheere
Anon at the bridehouse, for your maisters gone to
Church to be married alreadie, and thears
Such cheere as passeth.

*San.* O braue, I would I had eate no meat this week,
For I haue neuer a corner left in my bellie
To put a venson pastie in, I thinke I shall burst my selfe
With eating, for Ile so cram me downe the tarts
And the marchpaines, out of all crie.

*Boy.* I, but how wilt thou doo now thy maisters
Married, thy mistresse is such a deuill, as sheele make
Thee forget thy eating quickly, sheele beat thee so.

                                              *San.*


                        366

### *The taming of a Shrew.*

*San.* Let my maifter alone with hir for that, for
Heele make hir tame wel inough ere longe I warent thee
For he's fuch a churle waxen now of late that and he be
Neuer fo little angry he thums me out of all crie,
But in my minde firra the yongeft is a verie
Prettie wench, and if I thought thy maifter would
Not haue hir Ide haue a flinge at hir
My felfe, I'e fee foone whether twill be a match
Or no: and it will not Ile fet the matter
Hard for my felfe I warrant thee.

*Boy.* Sounes you flaue will you be a Riuall with
My maifter in his loue, fpeake but fuch
Another worde and Ile cut off one of thy legges.

*San.* Oh, cruell iudgement, nay then firra,
My tongue fhall talke no more to you, marry my
Timber fhall tell the truftie meffage of his maifter,
Euen on the very forehead on thee, thou abufious
Villaine, therefore prepare thy felfe.

*Boy.* Come hither thou Imperfeckfious flaue in
Regard of thy beggery, holde thee theres
Two fhillings for thee? to pay for the
Healing of thy left legge which I meane
Furioufly to inuade or to maime at the leaft.

*San.* O fupernodicall foule? well Ile take your
two fhillinges but Ile barre ftriking at legges.

*Boy.* Not I, for Ile ftrike any where.

*San.* Here here take your two fhillings again
Ile fee thee hangd ere Ile fight with thee,
I gat a broken fhin the other day,
Tis not, whole yet and therefore Ile not fight
Come come why fhould we fall out?

*Boy.* Well firray your faire words hath fomething
Alaied my Coller: I am content for this once
To put it vp and be frends with thee,

D But

367

*The taming of a Shrew.*

But foft fee where they come all from church,
Belike they be Married allredy.

Enter *Ferando and Kate and Alfonfo and Polidor
and Emelia and Aurelius and Philema.*

*Feran.* Father farwell, my *Kate* and I muft home,
Sirra go make ready my horfe prefentlie.

*Alfon.* Your horfe! what fon I hope you doo but ieft,
I am fure you will not go fo fuddainly.

*Kate.* Let him go or tarry I am refolu'de to ftay,
And not to trauell on my wedding day.

*Feran.* Tut *Kate* I tell thee we muft needes go home,
Villaine haft thou faddled my horfe?

*San.* Which horfe, your curtall?

*Feran.* Sounes you flaue ftand you prating here?
Saddell the bay gelding for your Miftris.

*Kate* Not for me: for Ile not go.                    (pence

*San.* The oftler will not let me haue him, you owe ten
For his meate, and 6 pence for ftuffing my miftris faddle.

*Feran.* Here villaine go pay him ftraight.

*San.* Shall I giue them another pecke of lauender.

*Feran.* Out flaue and bring them prefently to the dore.

*Alfon.* Why fon I hope at leaft youle dine with vs.

*San.* I pray you maifter lets ftay till dinner be don.

*Feran.* Sounes villaine art thou here yet? *Ex. Sander.*
Come *Kate* our dinner is prouided at home.

*Kate.* But not for me, for here I meane to dine.
Ile haue my will in this as well as you,
Though you in madding mood would leaue your frends
Defpite of you Ile tarry with them ftill.

*Feran.* I *Kate* fo thou fhalt but at fome other time,
When as thy fifters here fhall be efpoufd,
Then thou and I will keepe our wedding day,
In better fort then now we can prouide,

                                                        For

### *The taming of a Shrew.*

For here *I* promiſe thee before them all,
We will ere long returne to them againe,
Come *Kate* ſtand not on termes we will awaie,
This is my day, to morrow thou ſhalt rule,
And I will doo what euer thou commandes.
Gentlemen farwell, wele take our leues,
It will be late before that we come home.

*Exit Ferando and Kate.*

*Pol.* Farwell *Ferando* ſince you will be gone.

*Alfon.* So mad a cupple did I neuer ſee.

*Emel.* They're euen as well macht as I would wiſh.

*Phile.* And yet I hardly thinke that he can tame her.
For when he has don ſhe will do what ſhe liſt.

*Aurel.* Her manhood then is good I do beleeue.

*Pol.* *Aurelius* or elſe I miſſe my marke,
Her toung will walke if ſhe doth hold her handes,
*I* am in dout ere halfe a month be paſt
Hele curſe the prieſt that married him ſo ſoone,
And yet it may be ſhe will be reclaimde,
For ſhe is verie patient grone of late.

*Alfon.* God hold it that it may continue ſtill,
I would be loth that they ſhould diſagree,
But he I hope will holde her in a while.

*Pol.* Within this two daies I will ride to him,
And ſee how louingly they do agree.

*Alfon.* Now *Aurelius* what ſay you to this,
What haue you ſent to *Ceſtus* as you ſaid,
To certifie your father of your loue,
For I would gladlie he would like of it,
And if he be the man you tell to me,
*I* geſſe he is a Marchant of great wealth.
And *I* haue ſeene him oft at *Athens* here,
And for his ſake aſſure thee thou art welcome.

*Pol.* And ſo to me whileſt *Polidor* doth liue.

D 2　　　　　　　　　　　　*Aurelius*

369

*The taming of a Shrew.*

*Aurel.* I find it so right worthie gentlemen,
And of what worth your frendship I esteeme,
I leue censure of your seuerall thoughts,
But for requitall of your fauours past,
Rests yet behind, which when occasion serues
I vow shalbe remembred to the full,
And for my fathers comming to this place,
I do expect within this weeke at most.

*Alfon.* Inough *Aurelieus*? but we forget
Our Marriage dinner now the bride is gon,
Come let vs se what there they left behind. *Exit Omnes*

*Enter Sanders with two or three*
*seruing men*

*San.* Come sirs prouide all thinges as fast as you can,
For my Masters hard at hand and my new Mistris
And all, and he sent me before to see all thinges redy.

*Tom.* Welcome home *Sander* sirra how lookes our
New Mistris they say she's a plagie shrew.

*San.* I and that thou shalt find I can tell thee and thou
Dost not please her well, why my Maister
Has such a doo with hir as it passeth and he's euen
like a madman.

*Will.* Why *Sander* what dos he say.

*San.* Why Ile tell you what: when they should
Go to church to be maried he puts on an olde
Ierkin and a paire of canuas breeches downe to the
Small of his legge and a red cap on his head and he
Lookes as thou wilt burst thy selfe with laffing
When thou seest him: he's ene as good as a
Foole for me: and then when they should go to dinner
He made me Saddle the horse and away he came.
And nere tarried for dinner and therefore you had best
Get supper reddy against they come, for

They

### *The taming of a Shrew*

They be hard at hand *I* am fure by this time.

  *Tom.* Sounes fee where they be all redy.

          *Enter Ferando and Kate.*

  *Feran.* Now welcome *Kate:* wher'es thefe villains
Here, what? not fupper yet vppon the borde:
Nor table fpred nor nothing don at all,
VVheres that villaine that I fent before.

  *San.* Now, *adfum*, fir.

  *Feran.* Come hether you villaine Ile cut your nofe,
You Rogue:helpe me of with my bootes: wilt pleafe
You to lay the cloth? founes the villaine
Hurts my foote? pull eafely I fay; yet againe.

          *He beates them all.*
    *They couer the bord and fetch in the meate.*
Sounes? burnt and skorcht who dreft this meate?

  *Will.* Forfouth Iohn cooke.

        *He throwes downe the table and meate*
        *and all, and beates them.*

  *Feran.* Go you villaines bringe you me fuch meate,
Out of my fight I fay and beare it hence,
Come *Kate* wele haue other meate prouided,
Is there a fire in my chamber fir?

  *San.* I forfooth.         *Exit Ferando and Kate.*

  *Manent* feruingmen and eate vp all the meate.

  *Tom.* Sounes? I thinke of my confcience my Mafters
Mad fince he was maried.

  *Will.* I laft what a boxe he gaue *Sander*
For pulling of his bootes.

          *Enter Ferando* againe.

  *San.* I hurt his foote for the nonce man.

  *Feran.* Did you fo you damned villaine.

        *He beates them all out againe.*
This humor muft I holde me to a while,

                        To

## The taming of a Shrew

To bridle and hold backe my headstrong wife,
With curbes of hunger: ease: and want of sleepe,
Nor sleepe nor meate shall she inioie to night,
Ile mew her vp as men do mew their hawkes,
And make her gentlie come vnto the lure,
Were she as stuborne or as full of strength
As were the *Thracian* horse *Alcides* tamde,
That King *Egeus* fed with flesh of men,
Yet would I pull her downe and make her come
As hungry hawkes do flie vnto there lure.                    *Exit.*

Enter *Aurelius and Valeria.*
*Aurel.* *Valeria* attend: I haue a louely loue,
As bright as is the heauen cristalline,
As faire as is the milke white way of Ioue,
As chast as *Phœbe* in her sommer sportes,
As softe and tender as the asure downe,
That circles *Cithereas* siluer doues.
Her do *I* meane to make my louely bride,
And in her bed to breath the sweete content,
That *I* thou knowst long time haue aimed at.
Now *Valeria* it rests in thee to helpe
To compasse this, that *I* might ga ne my loue,
Which easilie thou maist performe at will,
If that the marchant which thou toldst me of,
Will as he sayd go to *Alfonsos* house,
And say he is my father, and there with all
Pas ouer certaine deedes of land to me,
That I thereby may gaine my hearts desire,
And he is promised reward of ine.
*Val.* Feare not my Lord Ile fetch him straight to you,
For hele do any thing that you command,
But tell me my Lord, is *Ferando* married then?
*Aurel.* He is: and *Polidor* shortly shall be wed,
And he meanes to tame his wife erelong.

                                                        *Valeria*

## *The taming of a Shrew.*

*Vale.* He faies fo.

*Aurel.* Faith he's gon vnto the taming fchoole.

*Val.* The taming fchoole, why is there fuch a place?

*Aurel.* I: and *Ferando* is the Maifter of the fchoole.

*Val.* Thats rare: but what *decorum* dos he vfe?

*Aurel.* Faith I know not: but by fom odde deuife
Or other, but come *Valeria* I long to fee the man,
By whome we muft comprife our plotted drift,
That I may tell him what we haue to doo.

*Val.* Then come my Lord and I will bring you to him
  ftraight.

*Aurel.* Agreed, then lets go.                *Exeunt*

  Enter *Sander and his Miftres.*

*San.* Come Miftris.

*Kate. Sander* I prethe helpe me to fome meate,
I am fo faint that I can fcarfely ftande.

*San.* I marry miftris but you know my maifter
Has giuen me a charge that you muft eate nothing,
But that which he himfelfe giueth you.

*Kate.* Why man thy Maifter needs neuer know it.

*San.* You fay true indede: why looke you Miftris,
What fay you to a peefe of beeffe and muftard now?

*Kate.* Why I fay tis excellent meate, canft thou
helpe me to fome?

*San.* I, I could helpe you to fome but that
I doubt the muftard is too collerick for you,
But what fay you to a fheepes head and garlick?

*Kate.* Why any thing, I care not what it be.

*San.* I but the garlike I doubt will make your breath
ftincke, and then my Maifter will courfe me for letting
You eate it: But what fay you to a fat Capon?

*Kate.* Thats meate for a King fweet *Sander* helpe
Me to fome of it.

*San.* Nay berlady then tis too deere for vs, we muft
                                                Not

### *The taming of a Shrew.*

Not meddle with the Kings meate.

*Kate* Out villaine doſt thou mocke me,
Take that for thy ſawſineſſe.

         *She beates him.*

*San.* Sounes are you ſo light fingerd with a murrin,
Ile keepe you faſting for it this two daies.

*Kate.* I tell thee villaine Ile teare the fleſh of
Thy face and eate it and thou prates to me thus.

*San.* Here comes my Maiſter now hele courſe you.

    Enter *Ferando* with a peece of meate vppon his
        daggers point and *Polidor* with him.

*Feran.* Se here *Kate* I haue prouided meate for thee,
Here take it: what iſt not worthie thankes,
Goe ſirra? take it awaie againe you ſhalibe
Thankefull for the next you haue.

*Kate* Why I thanke you for it.

*Feran.* Nay now tis not worth a pin go ſirray and take
It hence I ſay.

*San.* Yes ſir Ile Carrie it hence: Maiſter let her
Haue none for ſhe can fight as hungrie as ſhe is.

*Pol.* I pray you ſir let it ſtand, for Ile eate
Some with her my ſelfe.

*Feran.* Well ſirra ſet it downe againe.

*Kate.* Nay nay I pray you let him take it hence,
And keepe it for your owne diete for Ile none,
Ile nere be beholding to you for your Meate,
I tell thee flatlie here vnto the thy teethe
Thou ſhalt not keepe me nor feede me as thou liſt,
For I will home againe vnto my fathers houſe.

*Feran.* I, when you'r meeke and gentell but not
Before, I know your ſtomack is not yet come downe,
Therefore no maruell thou canſte not eate,
And I will goe vnto your Fathers houſe,
Come *Polidor* let vs goe in againe,

                        And

### *The taming of a Shrew.*

And *Kate* come in with vs I know ere longe,
That thou and I ſhall louingly agree.    *Ex. Omnes*

Enter Aurelius Valeria and Phylotus<br>
the Marchant.

*Aurel.* Now Senior *Phylotus*, we wil go
Vnto *Alfonſos* houſe, and be ſure you ſay
As I did tell you, concerning the man
That dwells in *Ceſtus*, whoſe ſon I ſaid I was,
For you doo very much reſemble him,
And feare not: you may be bold to ſpeake your mind.
   *Phylo.* I warrant you ſir take you no care,
Ile vſe my ſelfe ſo cunning in the cauſe,
As you ſhall ſoone inioie your harts delight.
   *Aurel.* Thankes ſweet *Phylotus*, then ſtay you here,
And I will go and fetch him hither ſtraight.
Ho, Senior *Alfonſo*: a word with you.

Enter Alfonſo.     (matter

*Alfon.* Whoſe there? what *Aurelius* whats the
That you ſtand ſo like a ſtranger at the doore?
   *Aurel.* My father ſir is newly come to towne,
And I haue brought him here to ſpeake with you,
Concerning thoſe matters that *I* tolde you of,
And he can certeſie you of the truth.
   *Alfon.* *Is* this your father? you are welcome ſir.
   *Phylo.* Thankes *Alfonſo*, for thats your name *I* geſſe,
I vnderſtand my ſon hath ſet his mind
And bent his liking to your daughters loue,
And for becauſe he is my only ſon,
And I would gladly that he ſhould doo well,
I tell you ſir, I not miſlike his choiſe,
If you agree to giue him your conſent,
He ſhall haue liuing to maintaine his ſtate,

E       Three

### *The taming of a Shrew.*

Three hundred poundes a yeere I will affure
To him and to his heyres, and if they do ioyne,
And knit themfelues in holy wedlock bande,
A thoufand maffie in gots of pure gold,
And twife as many bares of filuer plate,
I freely giue him, and in writing ftraight,
I will confirme what I haue faid in wordes.

   *Alfon.* Truft me I muft commend your liberall mind,
And louing care you beare vnto your fon,
And here I giue him freely my confent,
As for my daughter I thinke he knowes her mind,
And I will inlarge her dowrie for your fake.
And folemnife with ioie your nuptiall rites,
But is this gentleman of *Ceftus* too?

   *Aurel.* He is the *Duke* of *Ceftus* thrife renowned fon,
Who for the loue his honour beares to me:
Hath thus accompanied me to this place.

   *Alfonfo.* You weare to blame you told me not before,
Pardon me my Lord, for if I had knowne
Your honour had bin here in place with me,
I would haue donne my dutie to your honour.

   *Val.* Thankes good *Alfonfo*: but I did come to fee
When as thefe marriage rites fhould be performed,
And if in thefe nuptialls you vouchfafe,
To honour thus the prince of *Ceftus* frend,
In celebration of his fpoufall rites,
He fhall remaine a lafting friend to you,
What faies *Aurelius* father.

   *Phylo.* I humbly thanke your honour good my Lord,
And ere we parte before your honor here:
Shall articles of fuch content be drawne,
As twixt our houfes and poftefities,
Eternallie this league of peace fhall laft,
Inuiolat and pure on either part:

*Alfonfo*

*The taming of a Shrew.*

*Alfonso.* With all my heart, and if your honour please,
To walke along with vs vnto my houfe,
We will confirme thefe leagues of lafting loue.
*Val.* Come then *Aurelius* I will go with you. *Ex. omnes.*

Enter *Ferando and Kate and Sander.*
*San.* Mafter the haberdafher has brought my
Miftreffe home her cappe here.
*Feran.* Come hither firra: what haue you there?
*Habar.* A veluet cappe fir and it pleafe you.
*Feran.* Who fpoake for it? didft thou *Kate?*
*Kate.* What if I did, come hither firra, giue me
The cap, Ile fee if it will fit me.

She fets it one hir head.
*Feran.* O monftrous: why it becomes thee not,
Let me fee it *Kate:* here firra take it hence,
This cappe is out of fafhion quite.
*Kate* The fafhion is good inough: belike you,
Meane to make a foole of me.
*Feran.* Why true he meanes to make a foole of thee,
To haue thee put on fuch a curtald cappe,
firra begon with it.

Enter the *Taylor* with a gowne.
*San.* Here is the *Taylor* too with my Miftris gowne.
*Feran.* Let me fee it *Taylor:* what with cuts and iagges?
Sounes you villaine, thou haft fpoiled the gowne. (tion,
*Taylor.* Why fir I made it as your man gaue me direc-
You may reade the note here.
*Feran.* Come hither firra: *Taylor* reade the note.
*Taylor.* Item a faire round compaft cape.
*San.* I thats true.
*Taylor.* And a large truncke fleeue.

E 2                                     *Sander*

377

*The taming of a Shrew.*

*San.* Thats a lie maister, I sayd two truncke sleeues.

*Feran.* Well sir goe forward.

*Tailor.* Item a loose bodied gowne.

*San.* Maister if euer I sayd loose bodies gowne,
Sew me in a seame and beate me to death,
With a bottome of browne thred.

*Tailor.* I made it as the note bad me.

*San.* I say the note lies in his throate and thou too,
And thou sayst it.

*Taylor.* Nay nay nere be so hot sirra, for I seare you not.

*San.* Doost thou heare *Taylor*, thou hast braued
Many men: braue not me.
Thou'st faste many men.

*Taylor.* Well sir.

*San.* Face not me Ile nether be faste nor braued
At thy handes I can tell thee.

*Kate.* Come come I like the fashion of it well enough,
Heres more a do then needs Ile haue it I,
And if you do not like it hide your eies,
I thinke I shall haue nothing by your will.

*Feran.* Go I say and take it vp for your maisters vse.

*San.* Souns: villaine not for thy life touch it not,
Souns, take vp my mistris gowne to his
Maisters vse?

*Feran.* Well sir: whats your conceit of it.

*San.* I haue a deeper conceite in it then you
thin'e for, take vp my Mistris gowne
To his maisters vse?

*Feran.* *Tailor* come hether: for this time take it
Hence againe, and Ile content thee for thy paines.

*Taylor.* I thanke you sir.                    *Exit Taylor.*

*Feran.* Come *Kate* we now will go see thy fathers house
Euen in these honest meane abilliments,
Our purses shallbe rich, our garments plaine,

To

### *The taming of a Shrew.*

To fhrowd out bodies from the winter rage,
And thats inough, what fhould we care for more.
Thy fifters *Kate* to morrow muft be wed,
*And* I haue promifed them thou fhouldft be there
The morning is well vp lets haft away,
It will be nine a clocke ere we come there.

    *Kate.* Nine a clock, why tis allreadie paft two
In the after noone by all the clocks in the towne.

    *Feran.* I fay tis but nine a clock in the morning.

    *Kate.* I fay tis tow a clock in the after noone.

    *Feran.* It fhall be nine then ere we go to your fathers,
Come backe againe, we will not go to day.
Nothing but croffing of me ftill,
Ile haue you fay as I doo ere you go.     *Exeunt omnes.*


    Enter *Polidor, Emelia, Aurelius and Philema.*

    *Pol.* Faire *Emelia* fommers fun bright Queene,
Brighter of hew then is the burning clime,
Where *Phœbus* in his bright æquator fits,
Creating gold and preffious minneralls,
What would *Emelia* doo? if I were forft
To leaue faire *Athens* and to range the world.

    *Eme.* Should thou affay to fcale the feate of Ioue,
Mounting the futtle ayrie regions
Or be fnacht vp as erfte was *Ganimed,*
Loue fhould giue winges vnto my fwift defires,
And prune my thoughts that I would follow thee,
Or fall and perifh as did *Icarus.*

    *Aurel.* Sweetly refolued faire *Emelia,*
But would *Phylema* fay as much to me,
If I fhould afke a queftion now of thee,
What if the duke of *Ceftus* only fon,
Which came with me vnto your fathers houfe,
Should feeke to git *Phylemas* loue from me,

                   And

*The taming of a Shrew.*

And make thee Duches of that ſtately towne,
Wouldſt thou not then forſake me for his loue?

    *Phyle.* Not for great *Neptune*, no nor *Ioue* himſelfe,
Will *Phylema* leaue *Aurelius* loue,
Could he inſtall me *Empres* of the world,
Or make me Queene and guidres of the heauens,
Yet would *I* not exchange thy loue for his,
Thy company is poore *Philemas* heauen,
And without thee, heauen were hell to me.

    *Eme.* And ſhould my loue as erſte did *Hercules*
Attempt to paſſe the burning valtes of hell,
I would with piteous lookes and pleaſing wordes,
As once did *Orpheus* with his harmony,
And rauiſhing ſound of his melodious harpe,
Intreate grim *Pluto* and of him obtaine,
That thou mighteſt go and ſafe retourne againe.

    *Phyle.* And ſhould my loue as earſt *Leander* did,
Attempte to ſwimme the boyling heliſpont
For *Heros* loue: no towers of braſſe ſhould hold
But I would follow thee through thoſe raging flouds,
With lockes diſheuered and my breſt all bare,
With bended knees vpon *Abidas* ſhoore,
I would with ſmokie ſighes and briniſh teares,
Importune *Neptune* and the watry Gods,
To ſend a guard of ſiluer ſcaled *Dolphyns*,
With ſounding *Tritons* to be our conuoy,
And to tranſport vs ſafe vnto the ſhore,
Whilſt I would hang about thy louely necke,
Redoubling kiſſe on kiſſe vpon thy cheekes,
And with our paſtime ſtill the ſwelling waues.

    *Eme.* Should *Polidor* as great *Achilles* did,
Onely imploy himſelfe to follow armes,
Like to the warlike *Amazonian* Queene,
*Pentheſelea Hectors* paramore,

                                      Who

*The taming of a Shrew*

Who foyld the bloudie *Pirrhus* murderous greeke,
Ile thruſt my ſelfe amongſt the thickeſt throngs,
And with my vtmoſt force aſſiſt my loue.

*Phyle.* Let *Eole* ſtorme: be mild and quiet thou,
Let *Neptune* ſwell, be *Aurelius* calme and pleaſed,
I care not I, betide what may betide,
Let fates and fortune doo the worſt they can,
I recke them not: they not diſcord with me,
Whilſt that my loue and *I* do well agree·

*Aurel.* Sweet *Phylema* bewties mynerall,
From whence the ſun exhales his glorious ſhine,
And clad the heauen in thy reflected raies,
And now my lieſeſt loue, the time drawes nie,
That *Himen* mounted in his ſaffron robe,
Muſt with his torches waight vpon thy traine,
As *Hellens* brothers on the horned Moone,
Now *Iuno* to thy number ſhall I adde,
The faireſt bride that euer Marchant had.

*Pol.* Come faire *Emelia* the preeſte is gon,
And at the church your father and the reſte,
Do ſtay to ſee our marriage rites performde,
And knit in ſight of heauen this *Gordian* knot.
That teeth of fretting time may nere vntwiſt,
Then come faire loue and gratulate with me,
This daies content and ſweet ſolemnity.      *Ex. Omnes*

*Slie*  *Sim* muſt they be married now?
*Lord.* *I* my Lord.

Enter *Ferando and Kate and Sander.*

*Slie.* Looke *Sim* the foole is come againe now.
*Feran.* Sirra go fetch our horſſes forth, and bring
Them to the backe gate preſentlie.
*San.* I will ſir *I* warrant you,            *Exit Sander.*
*Feran.* Come *Kate* the Moone ſhines cleere to night
methinkes.                              *Kate.*

381

## *The taming of a Shrew*

*Kate.* The moone? why husband you are deceiud
It is the sun.

*Feran.* Yet againe: come backe againe it shall be
The moone ere we come at your fathers.

*Kate.* Why Ile say as you say it is the moone.

*Feran.* Iesus saue the glorious moone.

*Kate.* Iesus saue the glorious moone.

*Feran.* I am glad *Kate* your stomack is come downe,
I know it well thou knowest it is the sun,
But I did trie to see if thou wouldst speake,
And crosse me now as thou hast donne before,
And trust me *kate* hadst thou not named the moone,
We had gon back againe as sure as death,
But soft whose this thats comming here.

Enter the *Duke of Cestus* alone.

*Duke.* Thus all alone from *Cestus* am I come,
And left my princelie courte and noble traine,
To come to *Athens*, and in this disguise,
To see what course my son *Aurelius* takes,
But stay, heres some it may be Trauells thether,
Good sir can you derect me the way to *Athens*?

*Ferando* speakes to the olde man.
Faire louely maide yoong and affable,
More cleere of hew and far more beautifull,
Then pretious *Sardonix* or purple rockes,
Of *Amithests* or glistering *Hiasinthe*,
More amiable farre then is the plain,
Where glistring *Cepherus* in siluer boures,
Gaseth vpon the Giant *Andromede*,
Sweet *Kate* entertaine this louely woman.

*Duke.* I thinke the man is mad he calles me a woman.
*Kate*

### *The taming of a Shrew.*

*Kate.* Faire louely lady, bright and Chriſtalline,
Bewteous and ſtately as the eie-traind bird,
As glorious as the morning waſht with dew,
Within whoſe eies ſhe takes her dawningbeames,
And golden ſommer ſleepes vpon thy cheekes,
Wrap vp thy radiations in ſome cloud,
Leaſt that thy bewty make this ſtately towne,
Inhabitable like the burning Zone,
With ſweet reflections of thy louely face.

*Duke.* What is ſhe mad to? or is my ſhape transformd,
That both of them perſwade me I am a woman,
But they are mad ſure, and therefore Ile begon,
And leaue their companies for fear of harme,
And vnto Athens haſt to ſeeke my ſon.

*Exit Duke.*

*Feran.* Why ſo *Kate* this was friendly done of thee,
And kindly too: why thus muſt we two liue,
One minde, one heart, and one content for both,
This good old man dos thinke that we are mad,
And glad he is I am ſure, that he is gonne,
But come ſweet *Kate* for we will after him,
And now perſwade him to his ſhape againe.

*Ex. omnes.*

Enter Alfonſo and Phylotus and Valeria,
Polidor, Emelia, Aurelius and Phylema.

*Alfon.* Come louely ſonnes your marriage rites
performed,
Lets hie vs home to ſee what cheere we haue,
I wonder that *Ferando* and his wife
Comes not to ſee this great ſolemnitie.

*Pol.* No maruell if *Ferando* be away,
His wife I think hath troubled ſo his wits,

F             That

### *The taming of a Shrew.*

That he remaines at home to keepe them warme,
For forward wedlocke as the prouerbe sayes,
Hath brought him to his nightcappe long agoe.

   *Phylo.* But *Polidor* let my son and you take heede,
That *Ferando* say not ere long as much to you,
And now *Alfonso* more to shew my loue,
If vnto *Cestus* you do send your ships,
My selfe will fraught them with *Arabian* silkes,
Rich affrick spices *Arras* counter poines,
Muske *Cassia*: sweet smelling *Ambergreece*,
Pearle, curroll, christall, iett, and iuorie,
To gratulate the fauors of my son,
And friendly loue that you haue shone to him.

   *Vale.* And for to honour him and this faire bride,

         Enter the *Duke of Cestus.*

Ile yerly send you from my fathers courte,
Chests of refind suger seuerally,
Ten tunne of tunis wine, sucket sweet druges,
To celibrate and solemnise this day,
And custome free your marchants shall conuerse:
*And* interchange the profits of your land,
Sending you gold for brasse, siluer for leade,
Casses of silke for packes of woll and cloth,
To binde this friendship and confirme this league.

   *Duke.* I am glad sir that you would be so franke,
*Are* you become the *Duke* of *Cestus* son,
*And* reuels with my treasure in the towne,
Base villaine that thus dishonorest me.

   *Val.* Sounes it is the *Duke* what shall I doo,
Dishonour thee why, knowst thou what thou saist?

   *Duke.* Her's no villaine: he will not know me now,
But what say you? haue you forgot me too?

   *Phylo.* Why sir, are you acquainted with my son?

   *Duke.* With thy son? no trust me if he be thine,

                                I

## The taming of a Shrew.

Ipray you fir who am I?

*Aurel.* Pardon me father: humblie on my knees,
I do intreat your grace to heare me fpeake.

*Duke.* Peace villaine: lay handes on them,
A. d fend them to prifon ftraight.

> *Phylotus and Valeria* runnes away.
> Then *Slie* fpeakes.

*Slie.* I fay wele haue no fending to prifon.

*Lord.* My Lord this is but the play, theyre but in ieft.

*Slie.* I tell thee *Sim* wele haue no fending,
To prifon thats flat: why *Sim* am not I *Don Chrifto Vary?*
Therefore *I* fay they fhall not go to prifon.

*Lord.* No more they fhall not my Lord,
They be run away.

*Slie.* Are they run away *Sim?* thats well,
Then gis fome more drinke, and let them play againe.

*Lord.* Here my Lord.

> *Slie* drinkes and then falls a fleepe.

*Duke.* Ah trecherous boy that durft prefume,
To wed thy felfe without thy fathers leaue,
I fweare by fayre *Cintheas* burning rayes,
By *Merops* head and by feauen mouthed *Nile,*
Had I but knowne ere thou hadft wedded her,
Were in thy breft the worlds immortall foule,
This angrie fword fhould rip thy hatefull cheft,
And hewd thee fmaller then the *Libian* fandes,
Turne hence thy face: oh cruell impious boy,
*Alfonfo* I did not thinke you would prefume,
To mach your daughter with my princely houfe,
And nere make me acquainted with the caufe.

*Alfon.* My Lord by heauens I fweare vnto your grace,
*I* knew none other but *Valeria* your man,
Had bin the *Duke* of *Ceftus* noblefon,

F 2                                                            Not

385

### The taming of a Shrew.

Nor did my daughter I dare sweare for her.

*Duke.* That damned villaine that hath deluded me,
Whome I did send guide vnto my son,
Oh that my furious force could cleaue the earth,
That I might muster bands of hellish seendes,
To rack his heart and teare his impious soule.
The ceaselesse turning of celestiall orbes,
Kindles not greater flames in flitting aire,
Then passionate anguish of my raging brest,

*Aurel.* Then let my death sweet father end your griefe,
For I it is that thus haue wrought your woes,
Then be reuengd on me for here I sweare,
That they are innocent of what I did,
Oh had I charge to cut of *Hydraes* hed,
To make the toplesse *Alpes* a champion field,
To kill vntamed monsters with my sword,
To trauell dayly in the hottest sun,
And watch in winter when the nightes be colde,
I would with gladnesse vndertake them all,
And thinke the paine but pleasure that I felt,
So that my noble father at my returne,
Would but forget and pardon my offence,

*Phile.* Let me intreat your grace vpon my knees,
To pardon him and let my death discharge
The heauy wrath your grace hath vowd gainst him.

*Pol.* And good my Lord let vs intreat your grace,
To purge your stomack of this Melancholy,
Taynt not your princely minde with griefe my Lord,
But pardon and forgiue these louers faults,
That kneeling craue your gratious fauor here.

*Emel.* Great prince of *Cestus*, let a womans wordes,
Intreat a pardon in your lordly brest,
Both for your princely son, and vs my Lord.

*Duke.* Aurelius stand vp I pardon thee,

## The taming of a Shrew

I see that vertue will haue enemies,
And fortune willbe thwarting honour still,
And you faire virgin too I am content,
To accept you for my daughter since tis don,
And see you princely vsde in *Cestus* courte.

*Phyle.* Thankes good my Lord and I no longer liue,
Then *I* obey and honour you in all:

*Alfon.* Let me giue thankes vnto your royall grace,
For this great honor don to me and mine,
And if your grace will walke vnto my house,
I will in humblest maner I can, show
The eternall seruice I doo owe your grace.

*Duke* Thanks good *Alfonso*: but I came alone,
And not as did beseeme the *Cestian Duke*,
Nor would I haue it knowne within the towne,
That I was here and thus without my traine,
But as I came alone so will I go,
And leaue my son to solemnise his feast,
And ere't belong Ile come againe to you,
And do him honour as beseemes the son
Of mightie *Ierobell* the *Cestian Duke*,
Till when Ile leaue you, Farwell *Aurelius*.

*Aurel.* Not yet my Lord, Ile bring you to your ship.

*Exeunt Omnes.*

*Slie* sleepes.

*Lord.* Whose within there? come hither sirs my Lords
A sleepe againe: go take him easily vp,
And put him in his one apparell againe,
And lay him in the place where we did find him,
Iust vnderneath the alehouse side below,
But see you wake him not in any case.

*Boy.* It shall be don my Lord come helpe to beare him
hence,                                        *Exit.*

F3                                        Enter

## The taming of a Shrew.

Enter *Ferando, Aurelius and Polidor*
*and his boy and Valeria and Sander.*

*Feran.* Come gentlemen now that suppers donne,
How shall we spend the time till we go to bed?

*Aurel.* Faith if you will in triall of our wiues,
Who will come sownest at their husbands call.

*Pol.* Nay then *Ferando* he must needes sit out,
For he may call I thinke till he be weary,
Before his wife will come before she list.

*Feran.* Tis well for you that haue such gentle wiues,
Yet in this triall will I not sit out,
It may be *Kate* will come as soone as yours.

*Aurel.* My wife comes soonest for a hundred pound.

*Pol.* I take it: Ile lay as much to youres,
That my wife comes as soone as I do send.

*Aurel.* How now *Ferando* you dare not lay belike.

*Feran.* Why true I dare not lay indeede;
But how, so little mony on so sure a thing,
A hundred pound: why I haue layd as much
Vpon my dogge, in running at a Deere,
She shall not come so farre for such a trifle,
But will you lay fiue hundred markes with me,
And whose wife soonest comes when he doth call,
And shewes her selfe most louing vnto him,
Let him inioye the wager I haue laid,
Now what say you? dare you aduenture thus?

*Pol.* I weare it a thousand pounds I durst presume
On my wiues loue: and *I* will lay with thee.

### Enter *Alfonso.*

*Alfon.* How now sons what in conference so hard,
May I without offence, know where abouts.

*Aurelius*

## The taming of a Shrew

*Aurel.* Faith father a waighty caufe about our wiues
Fiue hundred markes already we haue layd,
And he whofe wife doth fhew moft loue to him,
He muft inioie the wager to himfelfe.

*Alfon.* Why then *Ferando* he is fure to lofe,
I promife thee fon thy wife will hardly come,
And therefore I would not wifh thee lay fo much.

*Feran.* Tufh father were it ten times more,
I durft aduenture on my louely *Kate*,
But if I lofe Ile pay, and fo fhall you.

*Aurel.* Vpon mine honour if I loofe Ile pay.

*Pol.* And fo will I vpon my faith I vow.

*Feran.* Then fit we downe and let vs fend for them.

*Alfon.* I promife thee *Ferando* I am afraid thou wilt lofe

*Aurel.* Ile fend for my wife firft, *Valeria*
Go bid your Miftris come to me.

*Val.* I will my Lord.

### Exit Valeria.

*Aurel.* Now for my hundred pound.
Would any lay ten hundred more with me,
I know I fhould obtaine it by her loue.

*Feran.* I pray God you haue not laid too much already.

*Aurel.* Truft me *Ferando* I am fure you haue,
For you I dare prefume haue loft it all.

### Enter *Valeria* againe.

Now firra what faies your miftris?

*Val.* She is fomething bufie but fhele come anon.

*Feran.* Why fo, did not I tell you this before,
She is bufie and cannot come.                    (fwere

*Aurel.* I pray God your wife fend you fo good an an-
She may be bufie yet fhe fayes fhele come.

*Feran.* Well well: *Polidor* fend you for your wife.

                                                  *Polidor*

## *The taming of a Shrew.*

*Pol.* Agreed *Boy* defire your miftris to come hither.
*Boy.* I will fir　　　　　　　　　　　　　　　*Ex. Boy.*
*Feran.* I fo fo he defiers her to come.
*Alfon. Polidor* I dare prefume for thee,
I thinke thy wife will not deny to come.
And I do marue'l much *Aurelius*,
That your wife carme not when you fent for her.

Enter the *Boy* againe.

*Pol.* Now wheres your Miftris?
*Boy.* She bad me tell you that fhe will not come,
And you haue any bufineffe, you muft come to her.
*Feran.* Oh monftrous intollerable prefumption,
Worfe then a blafing ftarre, or fnow at midfommer,
Earthquakes or any thing vnfeafonable,
She will not come: but he muft come to her.
*Pol.* Well fir *I* pray you lets here what
Anfwere your wife will make.
*Feran.* Sirra, command your Miftris to come
To me prefentlie.　　　　　　　　　　*Exit Sander.*
*Aurel.* I thinke my wife for all fhe did not come,
Will proue moft kinde for now I haue no feare,
For I am fure *Ferandos* wife, fhe will not come.
*Feran.* The mores the pittie: then I muft lofe.
Enter *Kate* and *Sander*.
But I haue won for fee where *Kate* doth come.
*Kate.* Sweet husband did you fend for me?
*Feran.* I did my loue I fent for thee to come,
Come hither *Kate*, whats that vpon thy head
*Kate.* Nothing husband but my cap I thinke.
*Feran.* Pull it of and treade it vnder thy feete,
*T*is foolifh I will not haue thee weare it.
She takes of her cap and treads on it.

　　　　　　　　　　　　　　　　　　*Polidor*

## *The taming of a Shrew.*

*Pol.* Oh wonderfull metamorphofis.

*Aurel.* This is a wonder: almoft paft beleefe.

*Feran.* This is a token of her true loue to me,
And yet Ile trie her further you fhall fee,
Come hither *Kate* where are thy fifters,

*Kate.* They be fitting in the bridall chamber.

*Feran.* Fetch them hither and if they will not come,
Bring them perforce and make them come with thee.

*Kate.* I will.

*Alfon.* I promife thee *Ferando* I would haue fworne,
Thy wife would nere haue donne fo much for thee.

*Feran.* But you fhall fee fhe will do more then this,
For fee where fhe brings her fifters forth by force.

Enter *Kate* thrufting *Phylema* and *Emelia* before her,
and makes them come vnto their husbands call.

*Kate* See husband I haue brought them both.

*Feran.* Tis well don *Kate*.

*Eme.* I fure and like a louing peece, your worthy
To haue great praife for this attempt.

*Phyle.* I for making a foole of her felfe and vs.

*Aurel.* Befhrew thee *Phylema*, thou haft
Loft me a hundred pound to night,
For I did lay that thou wouldft firft haue come.

*Pol.* But thou *Emelia* haft loft me a great deale more.

*Eme.* You might haue kept it better then,
Who bad you lay?

*Feran.* Now louely *Kate* before there husbands here,
I prethe tell vnto thefe hedftrong women,
What dutie wiues doo owe vnto their husbands.

*Kate.* Then you that liue thus by your pompered wills,
Now lift to me and marke what I fhall fay,
Theternall power that with his only breath,
Shall caufe this end and this beginning frame,

G                                    Not

## *The taming of a Shrew*

Not in time, nor before time, but with time, confusd,
For all the courfe of yeares, of ages, moneths,
Of feafons temperate, of dayes and houres,
Are tund and ftopt, by meafure of his hand,
The firft world was, a forme, without a forme,
A heape confusd a mixture all deformd,
A gulfe of gulfes, a body bodiles,
Where all the elements were orderles,
Before the great commander of the world,
The King of Kings the glorious God of heauen,
Who in fix daies did frame his heauenly worke,
And made all things to ftand in perfit courfe.
Then to his image he did make a man.
Olde *Adam* and from his fide a fleepe,
A rib was taken, of which the Lord did make,
The woe of man fo termd by *Adam* then,
Woman for that, by her came finne to vs,
And for her fin was *Adam* doomd to die,
As *Sara* to her husband, fo fhould we,
Obey them, loue them, keepe, and nourifh them,
If they by any meanes doo want our helpes,
Laying our handes vnder theire feete to tread,
If that by that we, might procure there eafe,
And for a prefident Ile firft begin,
And lay my hand vnder my husbands feete
     She laies her hand vnder her husbands feete.
  *Feran.* Inough fweet, the wager thou haft won,
And they I am fure cannot denie the fame.
  *Alfon.* I Ferando the wager thou haft won,
And for to fhew thee how *I* am pleafd in this,
A hundred poundes I freely giue thee more,
Another dowry for another daughter,
For fhe is not the fame fhe was before.
  *Feran.* Thankes fweet father, gentlemen godnight
                                                      For

*The taming of a Shrew.*

For *Kate* and *I* will leaue you for to night,
Tis *Kate* and I am wed, and you are sped.
And so farwell for we will to our beds.

*Exit Ferando and Kate and Sander.*

*Alfon.* Now *Aurelius* what say you to this?
*Aurel.* Beleeue me father I reioice to see,
*Ferando* and his wife so louingly agree.

*Exit Aurelius and Phylema and*
*Alfonso and Valeria.*

*Eme.* How now *Polidor* in a dump, what sayst thou
man?
*Pol.* *I* say thou art a shrew.
*Eme.* Thats better then a sheepe.
*Pol.* Well since tis don let it go, come lets in.

*Exit Polidor and Emelia.*

Then enter two bearing of *Slie* in his
Owne apparrell againe, and leaues him
Where they found him, and then goes out.
Then enter the *Tapster.*

*Tapster.* Now that the darkesome night is ouerpast,
And dawning day apeares in cristall sky,
Now must I hast abroad: but soft whose this?
What *Slie* oh wondrous hath he laine here allnight,
Ile wake him, I thinke he's starued by this,
But that his belly was so stuft with ale,
What how *Slie*, Awake for shame.
*Slie.* Sim gis some more wine: whats all the
Plaiers gon: am not I a Lord?
*Tapster.* A Lord with a murrin: come art thou
dronken still?
*Slie.* Whose this? *Tapster*, oh Lord sirra, I haue had
The brauest dreame to night, that euer thou
Hardest in all thy life.

*Tapster*

### *The taming of a Shrew.*

*Tapster*. I marry but you had best get you home,
For your wife will course you for dreming here to night,
   *Slie* Will she? I know now how to tame a shrew,
I dreamt vpon it all this night till now,
And thou hast wakt me out of the best dreame
That euer I had in my life, but Ile to my
Wife presently and tame her too
And if she anger me.
   *Tapster*. Nay tarry *Slie* for Ile go home with thee,
And heare the rest that thou hast dreamt to night.

*Exeunt Omnes.*

## FINIS.

# APPENDIX 4

## TWO *SHREWS*

*A Shrew* and *The Shrew* obviously know one another, a knowledge most pronounced in plot features – the Sly 'frame', the taming plot, the romantic subplot with Kate's sister – and similarities in narrative design, especially throughout the latter scenes. Yet although Gascoigne's *Supposes* lies behind both plays, many plot elements they share are not found in *Supposes*, which suggests some kind of dependence between the two plays rather than a double reliance on an existing literary source (see Miller, 23–31, 127–43; and pp. 19–23). Excepting the Sly ending (*AS*, 1599–626), each play contains fourteen scenes, with the first two (*AS*, 1–169/*TS* Ind.1–2) and the last three (*AS*, 1218–598/ *TS* 4.5–5.2) roughly equivalent. Parallels at the level of action and event also occur at *AS*, 312–63, 637–96 and 760–803 – comparable to *TS* 2.1 and 3.2 (the encounter between Kate and Ferando/Petruccio; the arrival at church; the couple's hasty exit from the wedding feast) – and the intersections between the taming plot and the subplot occur at relatively similar points in both. In *A Shrew*, however, each scene is more compressed than its equivalent in *The Shrew*; overall, *A Shrew* contains 1,550 to *The Shrew*'s 2,598 spoken lines (King, 81). The closest verbal parallels occur at *AS*, 925–8/*TS* 4.2.50–9, where, following Kate's wedding, a brief exchange between Valeria and Aurelius coincides rather precisely with the moment when Lucentio and Tranio tell Bianca that Hortensio will marry a widow and has gone to the taming school; and at *AS*, 938–94/*TS* 4.3.63–165, where Kate begs Sander/Grumio for food and, later, where the Haberdasher and the Tailor present their wares and the Tailor and Sander/Grumio argue over the bill (especially close are *AS*, 1072–122 and *TS* 4.3.117–65).

The two plays also share similarities at the level of dialogue: in a very few places, this approaches exact quotation; in others, imitation or echo. Both contain references to or quotations from popular plays: *A Shrew* borrows from Marlowe's *Doctor Faustus*[1] as well as *1 Tamburlaine*; *The Shrew* paraphrases Hieronimo's line from Kyd's *Spanish Tragedy* – 'Go by, Saint Jeronimy' (Ind.1.8) – and alludes, whether in brief phrases or patterned verse, to Marlowe and, in the heavy use of proverbs, to Lyly. Yet while *A Shrew*'s Marlovian borrowings occur throughout the text, *The Shrew*'s references to sixteenth-century tastes include plays and players associated with several acting companies and occur only in the Sly scenes.

The differences between the two plays comprise a longer list. Viewed from the perspective of *The Shrew*, the principal difference is that, rather than disappearing (or going to sleep) at the end of 1.1, in *A Shrew* Sly remains and continues to comment, in passages that serve to script the onstage audience into the play world, on the inset taming play. As though anticipating the behaviour of the Grocer and his Wife in Fletcher's *The Knight of the Burning Pestle* (*c*. 1607–11), he even intervenes at one moment to prevent the false father, Phylotus, and Valeria from being jailed, announcing, from his (theatrically given) authority as a 'lord', that 'they shall not go to prison' (1329–93). *A Shrew* is set in Athens, not Padua; aside from Sly and Kate, *A Shrew*'s characters have different names: Petruccio is Ferando; Grumio's equivalent, Sander, becomes a principal comic role; and in the subplot, Kate has two sisters, Phylema

---

1   An example suggests how closely *A Shrew* follows Marlowe: 'Now that the gloomy shadow of the night, / Longing to view Orion's drizzling look, / Leaps from th'Antarctic world unto the sky, / And dims the welkin with her pitchy breath, / Faustus, begin thine incantations' (*Faustus*, 1.3.1–5, B-text (1616), cited in Miller, 61n.); 'Now that the gloomie shaddow of the night, / Longing to view Orions drizzling lookes, / Leapes from th'antarticke World unto the skie, / And dims the Welkin with her pitchie breath, / And darksome night oreshades the christall heauens, / Here breake we off our hunting for tonight' (*AS*, 17–22).

and Emelia, and each has a suitor – Aurelius, son to the Duke of Sestos, and Polidor, a student; there is no equivalent for *The Shrew*'s Gremio. In *A Shrew*'s secondary plot, as in Gascoigne's *Supposes*, the block to Phylema's and Aurelius' marriage is class-inflected, complicated more by their unequal social rank than, as in *The Shrew*, by disguisings and shifting identities; in this respect, *A Shrew* is closer to *The Two Gentlemen of Verona*. While *The Shrew*'s taming plot overshadows the subplot, *A Shrew* not only treats the taming somewhat summarily but also: considerably expands the romantic plot; stages Kate's music lesson (519–60); adds several comic turns between Sander and his Boy, both containing references to marriage between unequal partners (405–35, 698–759); and, just before the double wedding of Kate's sisters, includes a moment where Aurelius tests Phylema's love (1151–8), ensuring that she loves him not for his title or wealth but for himself. Consistently, too, *A Shrew* signals confrontations and events that are to come,[1] a feature which also impacts on individual roles, as characters announce their motives. Among these, the most prominent distinctions occur when Kate, after complaining that her father has given her to 'this brainsick man', delivers an aside indicating her willingness to marry Ferando – 'But yet I will consent and marrie him, / For I methinkes have liude too long a maid, / And match him to, or else his manhoods good' (348–50) – and when Ferando explains why he arrives at his wedding 'basely attired' – 'For when my wife and I am married once, / Shee's such a shrew, if we should once fal out / Sheele pul my costlie sutes ouer mine eares' (644–6). Finally, significant differences in content as well as ideology mark Kate's last speech (*AS*, 1546–67/*TS* 5.2.142–85). While *A Shrew*, drawing heavily from the French Protestant poet Guillaume de Salluste Du Bartas, replicates the biblical argument that woman's creation from Adam's rib (the

---

1   The word 'presently' occurs with unusual frequency to set up *A Shrew*'s next event: 'a usage that would much recommend itself to someone making things up as he went along with little regard for stylistic variety or control' (RP).

'woe of man') confirms her subordinate status,[1] *The Shrew* relies on language drawn from the *Book of Common Prayer*, the *Homily of the State of Matrimony* and the *Homily against Disobedience and Wilful Rebellion*. As with the theatrical references mentioned above, *A Shrew* here appears to evoke official Elizabethan rhetoric on women's status, while *The Shrew* more closely resembles Jacobean positions on the relations between women and men within marriage. Those differences in particular open up the question of what revisions might have occurred between 1594 and 1616 (if not 1622). To what version or *Shrew*-play was Fletcher responding in *Tamer Tamed* (see Marcus, *Unediting*, 123–4)?

1    See H.W. Crundell, 'Notes on *The Taming of the Shrew*', *N&Q*, 163 (1932), 309–10; George C. Taylor, 'Two notes on Shakespeare', *Philological Quarterly*, 20 (1941), 371–6; and Miller, 147–52.

# APPENDIX 5

## CASTING

*The Taming of the Shrew*, so David Bradley conjectures, could be performed by fifteen to seventeen players, a number within the range of the average required by plays performed between 1580 and 1642 (233, 47). By contrast, Richard Hosley's estimate of twelve to thirteen players, which supports his hypothesis that *The Shrew* had no 'Sly epilogue', seems possible, though somewhat sparse ('Epilogue', esp. 30–1); and T.J. King's hypothesis of twenty-four players, which includes non-speaking parts (81), is probably excessive. Although F's initial entry SD for 5.2 (TLN 2534–7) – *The Shrew*'s most crowded scene – omits Katherina, Petruccio and Hortensio, clearly they are required, bringing the total number of players in the scene to thirteen (without counting 'Attendants', a flexible category). Adding two more would account for the Servants who appear first in Baptista's household, then in Petruccio's and finally in Lucentio's. And although F's entry SD for 3.2 (TLN 1387–8) omits Lucentio, since he appears later in the scene (TLN 1521), his presence is required.

Both the Induction, which requires at least eight players, and the inset play might also be staged with fifteen players. Those playing the Lord's Huntsmen in Ind.1 could double as 1 and 2 Servant in Ind.2; together with Ind.2's 3 Servant, these three players could also double as Servants in Baptista's, Petruccio's and Lucentio's households (Mahood, 46, 269–70). Although the Casting Chart (which accounts for those players who speak in a given scene) notes five appearances for a Servant who appears first at the end of 1.1 (TLN 558–9) and subsequently at 1.2, 2.1, 3.1 ('Messenger') and 4.1, Hibbard's assumption that the Lord doubles as a Servant at the end of 1.1 seems reasonable (see 1.1.247n.), as does conjecturing that this role was later shared out among the players of 1, 2 and 3 Servant. These three busy players also might double as the Tailor, the Haberdasher (two roles that may be conflated, and often have been in modern performances), Curtis and the Officer (who may or may not appear); 1 and 2 Player might be doubled with two principals from the inset play. Other doublings between the Sly scenes and the inset play might include the following (or some combination thereof): Sly/Petruccio, Sly/Vincentio, Sly/Merchant or Sly/Grumio; Hostess/Katherina or Hostess/Curtis/Widow (a triple); Lord/Petruccio or Lord/Vincentio; Bartholomew/Hostess or Bartholomew/Grumio. Although it might be possible to stage *The Shrew* with a minimum of fourteen players, a total of fifteen would have eased performance considerably on the early modern stage. If, however, Sly, Bartholomew and the Lord (or Servant) do indeed follow F's '*They sit and marke.*' (TLN 564), seventeen or even eighteen players would be required.

Although there are exceptions, most modern performances include more players, typically in 1.1, 3.2, 4.1, 5.1 and 5.2. Yet even where more players are available to flesh out these scenes, doubling regularly occurs. Elizabeth Schafer's stage history provides a range of commentary mentioning some options cited above as well as others (79–81 and *passim*). In some modern performances, the Sly scenes are not staged (e.g. Doran, 2003), but when they are, doubling Katherina/Hostess and Petruccio/Sly often occurs – perhaps most notably in Bogdanov, 1978. However, practice varies widely, and also depends on whether Sly remains onstage and whether *A Shrew*'s so-called epilogue is imported to frame the action. In addition, since the SD at Ind.1.77 (TLN 86) does not specify the number of players, the entire troupe might enter here (e.g. Alexander, 1992): when 'stars' or well-known actors are cast in some or most of the principal parts in the inset play, such a strategy makes their forthcoming roles in the inset play immediately apparent.

| Roles and scenes | | Ind.1 | Ind.2 | 1.1 | 1.2 | 2.1 | 3.1 | 3.2 | 4.1 | 4.2 | 4.3 | 4.4 | 4.5 | 5.1 | 5.2 |
|---|---|---|---|---|---|---|---|---|---|---|---|---|---|---|---|
| Christopher Sly | 3 | x | x | x | | | | | | | | | | | |
| Hostess | 1 | x | | | | | | | | | | | | | |
| Lord | 3 | x | x | x | | | | | | | | | | | |
| 1 Huntsman | 1 | x | | | | | | | | | | | | | |
| 2 Huntsman | 1 | x | | | | | | | | | | | | | |
| Servant | 5 | | | x | x | x | x | | x | | | | | | |
| 1 Player | 1 | x | | | | | | | | | | | | | |
| 2 Player | 1 | x | | | | | | | | | | | | | |
| 1 Servant | 1 | | x | | | | | | | | | | | | |
| 2 Servant | 1 | | x | | | | | | | | | | | | |
| 3 Servant | 1 | | x | | | | | | | | | | | | |
| Bartholomew (page) | 2 | | x | x | | | | | | | | | | | |
| Lucentio | 9 | | | x | x | x | x | x | | x | | x | | x | x |
| Tranio | 8 | | | x | x | x | | x | | x | | x | | x | x |
| Baptista Minola | 6 | | | x | | x | | x | | | | x | | x | x |
| Katherina Minola | 8 | | | x | | x | | x | x | | x | | x | x | x |
| Bianca Minola | 7 | | | x | x | x | x | x | | x | | | | x | x |

| Roles and scenes | | Ind.1 | Ind.2 | 1.1 | 1.2 | 2.1 | 3.1 | 3.2 | 4.1 | 4.2 | 4.3 | 4.4 | 4.5 | 5.1 | 5.2 |
|---|---|---|---|---|---|---|---|---|---|---|---|---|---|---|---|
| Gremio | 6 | | | x | x | x | x | x | | | | | | x | x |
| Hortensio | 9 | | | x | x | x | x | x | | x | x | | x | | x |
| Biondello | 8 | | | x | x | x | | x | | x | | x | | x | x |
| Petruccio | 8 | | | | x | x | | x | x | | x | | x | x | x |
| Grumio | 6 | | | | x | | | x | x | | x | | | x | x |
| Curtis | 1 | | | | | | | | x | | | | | | |
| Nathaniel | 1 | | | | | | | | x | | | | | | |
| Philip | 1 | | | | | | | | x | | | | | | |
| Joseph | 1 | | | | | | | | x | | | | | | |
| Nicholas | 1 | | | | | | | | x | | | | | | |
| Merchant | 4 | | | | | | | | | x | | x | | x | x |
| Tailor | 1 | | | | | | | | | | x | | | | |
| Haberdasher | 1 | | | | | | | | | | x | | | | |
| Vincentio | 3 | | | | | | | | | | | | x | x | x |
| Officer | 1 | | | | | | | | | | | | | x | |
| Widow | 1 | | | | | | | | | | | | | | x |
| Attendants | misc. | | | | | | | misc. | | | | | | misc. | misc. |

# ABBREVIATIONS AND REFERENCES

Quotations from and references to *The Taming of the Shrew* are keyed to this edition. All other references to works by Shakespeare are taken from the most recently published Arden editions: for *AC*, *Ham*, *1H4*, *H5*, *2H6*, *H8*, *KL*, *LLL*, *MA*, *Oth*, *Per*, *TC* and *TGV*, the individual Arden 3 volumes; for all others, *The Arden Shakespeare: Complete Works*, gen. eds Richard Proudfoot, Ann Thompson and David Scott Kastan (revised edn, 2001). Line references to *The Taming of a Shrew* conform to the Malone Society Reprint edition by Stephen Roy Miller, with Richard Proudfoot and R.V. Holdsworth (Oxford, 1998). A facsimile of the Huntington Library copy (RB 69594), which the Malone Society Reprint also reproduces, appears in this volume as Appendix 3. Biblical citations are from the Bishop's Bible (1576) unless otherwise indicated. Place of publication or performance is London unless otherwise indicated.

## ABBREVIATIONS

### ABBREVIATIONS USED IN NOTES

| | |
|---|---|
| conj. | conjectured by |
| LR | list of roles |
| LN | long note |
| n. | note |
| om. | omitted |
| opp. | opposite |
| SD | stage direction |
| SP | speech prefix |
| subst. | substantially |
| this edn | a reading adopted for the first time in this edition |
| TLN | through line numbering in *First Folio* |
| t.n. | textual note |
| * | precedes commentary notes involving readings altered from the text on which this edition is based |
| ( ) | enclosing a reading in the textual notes indicates F spelling; enclosing an editor's or scholar's name indicates a conjectural reading |

## WORKS BY AND PARTLY BY SHAKESPEARE

| | |
|---|---|
| *AC* | *Antony and Cleopatra* |
| *AW* | *All's Well That Ends Well* |
| *AYL* | *As You Like It* |
| *CE* | *The Comedy of Errors* |
| *Cor* | *Coriolanus* |
| *Cym* | *Cymbeline* |
| *E3* | *King Edward III* |
| *Ham* | *Hamlet* |
| *1H4* | *King Henry IV, Part 1* |
| *2H4* | *King Henry IV, Part 2* |
| *H5* | *King Henry V* |
| *1H6* | *King Henry VI, Part 1* |
| *2H6* | *King Henry VI, Part 2* |
| *3H6* | *King Henry VI, Part 3* |
| *H8* | *King Henry VIII* |
| *JC* | *Julius Caesar* |
| *KJ* | *King John* |
| *KL* | *King Lear* |
| *LC* | *A Lover's Complaint* |
| *LLL* | *Love's Labour's Lost* |
| *Luc* | *The Rape of Lucrece* |
| *MA* | *Much Ado About Nothing* |
| *Mac* | *Macbeth* |
| *MM* | *Measure for Measure* |
| *MND* | *A Midsummer Night's Dream* |
| *MV* | *The Merchant of Venice* |
| *MW* | *The Merry Wives of Windsor* |
| *Oth* | *Othello* |
| *Per* | *Pericles* |
| *PP* | *The Passionate Pilgrim* |
| *PT* | *The Phoenix and Turtle* |
| *R2* | *King Richard II* |
| *R3* | *King Richard III* |
| *RJ* | *Romeo and Juliet* |
| *Son* | *Sonnets* |
| *STM* | *Sir Thomas More* |
| *TC* | *Troilus and Cressida* |
| *Tem* | *The Tempest* |
| *TGV* | *The Two Gentlemen of Verona* |
| *Tim* | *Timon of Athens* |
| *Tit* | *Titus Andronicus* |

| TN | *Twelfth Night* |
| TNK | *The Two Noble Kinsmen* |
| TS | *The Taming of the Shrew* |
| VA | *Venus and Adonis* |
| WT | *The Winter's Tale* |

# REFERENCES

## EDITIONS OF SHAKESPEARE COLLATED
## OR REFERRED TO

| Alexander | *Works*, ed. Peter Alexander (1951) |
| Ard[1] | *The Taming of the Shrew*, ed. R. Warwick Bond, Arden Shakespeare first series (1904; 2nd edn, 1929) |
| Ard[2] | *The Taming of the Shrew*, ed. Brian Morris, Arden Shakespeare second series (1981) |
| Bell | *Bell's Edition of Shakespeare's Plays, as They are Now Performed at the Theatres Royal in London*, 9 vols (1773–4) |
| Bevington | *The Taming of the Shrew*, ed. David Bevington, Bantam Shakespeare (New York, 1988) |
| Bond | See Ard[1] |
| Boswell-Stone | *The Taming of the Shrew*, ed. W.G. Boswell-Stone, Old Spelling Shakespeare (1908) |
| Cam | *Works*, ed. William George Clark, John Glover and William Aldis Wright, 9 vols (Cambridge, 1863–6) |
| Cam[1] | *The Taming of the Shrew*, ed. Arthur Quiller-Couch and John Dover Wilson (Cambridge, 1928; 2nd edn 1953) |
| Cam[2] | *The Taming of the Shrew*, ed. Ann Thompson (Cambridge, 1984; 2nd edn 2003) |
| Capell | *Comedies, Histories, and Tragedies*, ed. Edward Capell, 10 vols (1768) |
| Capell[2] | *Plays*, ed. Edward Capell, 6 vols (Dublin, 1771) |
| Collier | *Works*, ed. J.P. Collier, 8 vols (1842–4) |
| Craig | *Works*, ed. Hardin Craig (Chicago and New York, 1951) |
| Daly | *The Taming of the Shrew, First Produced at Daly's Theatre, January 18th, 1887*, ed. Augustin Daly (New York, 1887) |
| Dolan | *The Taming of the Shrew*, ed. Frances E. Dolan, Bedford Texts and Contexts (Boston, 1996) |
| Dyce | *Works*, ed. Alexander Dyce, 6 vols (1857) |
| Dyce[2] | *Works*, ed. Alexander Dyce, 9 vols (1864–7) |
| F | *Comedies, Histories, and Tragedies*, The First Folio (1623) |
| F2 | *Comedies, Histories, and Tragedies*, The Second Folio (1632) |

| | |
|---|---|
| F3 | *Comedies, Histories, and Tragedies*, The Third Folio (1664) |
| F4 | *Comedies, Histories, and Tragedies*, The Fourth Folio (1685) |
| Folg | *The Taming of the Shrew*, ed. Barbara A. Mowat and Paul Werstine, New Folger Shakespeare Library (New York, 1992) |
| Freeman | *The Applause First Folio of Shakespeare in Modern Type*, ed. Neil Freeman (New York, 2001) |
| Gollancz | *The Taming of the Shrew*, ed. Israel Gollancz, Temple Shakespeare (1923) |
| Halliwell | *Works*, ed. James O. Halliwell, 16 vols (1853–65) |
| Hanmer | *Works*, ed. Thomas Hanmer, 6 vols (Oxford, 1743–4) |
| Harbage | *The Complete Pelican Shakespeare*, ed. Alfred Harbage (Baltimore, Md., 1969) |
| Harrison | *The Taming of the Shrew*, ed. G.B. Harrison, Penguin Shakespeare (Harmondsworth, England, 1951) |
| Herford | *Works*, ed. Charles H. Herford, Eversley edn, 10 vols (1899) |
| Hibbard | *The Taming of the Shrew*, ed. G.R. Hibbard, New Penguin Shakespeare (Harmondsworth, England, 1968) |
| Hosley | *The Taming of the Shrew*, ed. Richard Hosley, New Pelican Shakespeare (Baltimore, Md.,1964) |
| Hudson | *Works*, ed. Henry N. Hudson, 11 vols (Boston, 1851–6) |
| Hudson[2] | *Works*, ed. Henry N. Hudson, Harvard edn, 20 vols (Boston, 1880–1) |
| Irving | *Works*, ed. Henry Irving and Frank A. Marshall, The Irving Shakespeare, 6 vols (1900–9) |
| Johnson | *Plays*, ed. Samuel Johnson, 8 vols (1765) |
| Keightley | *Plays*, ed. Thomas Keightley, 6 vols (1864) |
| Kittredge | *Works*, ed. George Lyman Kittredge (Boston, 1936) |
| Knight | *Works*, ed. Charles Knight, 8 vols (1838–43) |
| Malone | *Plays and Poems*, ed. Edmund Malone, 10 vols (1790) |
| Malone–Boswell | *Plays and Poems*, ed. Edmund Malone and James Boswell, 21 vols (1821) |
| Morris | See Ard[2] |
| Neilson | *Works*, William Allan Neilson (Boston and New York, 1906) |
| Oliver | See Oxf[1] |
| Oxf | *The Oxford Shakespeare, The Complete Works*, ed. Stanley Wells, Gary Taylor, John Jowett and William Montgomery (Oxford, 1986) |
| Oxf[1] | *The Taming of the Shrew*, ed. H.J. Oliver (Oxford, 1982) |
| Pope | *Works*, ed. Alexander Pope, 6 vols (1723–5) |

| | |
|---|---|
| Pope[2] | *Works*, ed. Alexander Pope, 6 vols (1728) |
| Q | *A Witty and Pleasant Comedy Called, The Taming of the Shrew*, The Quarto (1631) |
| Rann | *Dramatic Works*, ed. Joseph Rann, 6 vols (Oxford, 1786–[94]) |
| Reed | *Plays*, ed. Isaac Reed, 21 vols (1803) |
| Ridley | *The Taming of the Shrew*, ed. M.R. Ridley, New Temple Shakespeare (1934) |
| Riv | *The Riverside Shakespeare*, 2nd edn, ed. G. Blakemore Evans and Harry Levin (Boston, Mass., 1974 rev. edn 1997) |
| Rowe | *Works*, ed. Nicholas Rowe, 6 vols (1709) |
| Rowe[2] | *Works*, ed. Nicholas Rowe, 2nd edn, 6 vols (1709) |
| Rowe[3] | *Works*, ed. Nicholas Rowe, 3rd edn, 8 vols (1714) |
| Schafer | *The Taming of the Shrew*, ed. Elizabeth Schafer, Cambridge Shakespeare in Production (Cambridge, 2002) |
| Singer | *Plays*, ed. Samuel Weller Singer, 10 vols (1826) |
| Sisson | *Complete Works*, ed. C.J. Sisson (1954) |
| Steevens | *Plays*, ed. Samuel Johnson and George Steevens, 10 vols (1773) |
| Stockdale | *Stockdale's Edition of Shakespeare*, ed. Samuel Ayscough (1784) |
| Theobald | *Works*, ed. Lewis Theobald, 7 vols (1733) |
| Thompson | See Cam[2] |
| Warburton | *Works*, ed. William Warburton, 8 vols (1747) |
| White | *Works*, ed. Richard Grant White, 12 vols (Boston, 1857–66) |
| Wilson | See Cam[1] |

## OTHER WORKS CITED

| | |
|---|---|
| Aarne–Thompson | Antti Amatus Aarne, *The Types of the Folktale: A Classification and Bibliography*, trans. and enlarged by Stith Thompson, 2nd edn (Helsinki, 1961) |
| Abbott | E.A. Abbott, *A Shakespearian Grammar*, 3rd edn (1870) |
| Abel | Richard Abel, *The Red Rooster Scare: Making Cinema American, 1900–1910* (Berkeley, Calif., 1999) |
| ACS | *A Companion to Shakespeare*, ed. David Scott Kastan (Oxford and Malden, Mass., 1999) |
| Ady | Thomas Ady, *A Candle in the Dark* (1655) |
| Aebischer | Pascale Aebischer, 'Shrewd or shrewish? "Steal[ing] out o' th' old plays" in John Lacy's *Sauny the Scott: or The Taming of the Shrew*', *Restoration and 18th Century Theatre Research*, 16.1 (2001), 24–41 |

| | |
|---|---|
| *Aeneid* | Virgil, *The Aeneid*, trans. Robert Fitzgerald (New York, 1990) |
| Alexander, 'Original' | Peter Alexander, 'The original ending of *The Taming of the Shrew*', *SQ*, 20.2 (1969), 111–16 |
| Alexander, '*Shrew*' | Peter Alexander, '*The Taming of A Shrew*', *TLS*, 16 September 1926, 614 |
| Allen & Muir | *Shakespeare's Plays in Quarto: A Facsimile Edition*, ed. Michael J.B. Allen and Kenneth Muir (Berkeley, Calif., 1981) |
| AR | Amy Rodgers, private communication |
| Arnold | Janet Arnold, *Queen Elizabeth's Wardrobe Unlock'd* (2001) |
| *AS* | *The Taming of a Shrew*, facsimile, ed. Stephen Roy Miller, with Richard Proudfoot and R.V. Holdsworth, Malone Society Reprints, vol. 160 (Oxford, 1998) |
| Aspinall | *The Taming of the Shrew: Critical Essays*, ed. Dana E. Aspinall (New York and London, 2002) |
| Baldwin | Thomas Whitfield Baldwin, *William Shakespeare's Small Latine and Lesse Greeke*, 2 vols (Urbana, Ill., 1944) |
| Barkan | Leonard Barkan, 'What did Shakespeare read?', in de Grazia & Wells, 31–48 |
| Baskervill | Charles Read Baskervill, *The Elizabethan Jig and Related Song Drama* (Chicago, 1929) |
| Bate | Jonathan Bate, *Shakespeare and Ovid* (Oxford, 1993) |
| Bate & Jackson | *Shakespeare: An Illustrated Stage History*, ed. Jonathan Bate and Russell Jackson (Oxford, 1996) |
| BBC | British Broadcasting Corporation |
| *BCP* | *The Book of Common Prayer, 1559*, ed. John E. Booty (Charlottesville, Va., 1976) |
| Bean | John C. Bean, 'Comic structure and the humanizing of Kate in *The Taming of the Shrew*', in Carolyn Ruth Swift Lenz, Gayle Green and Carol Thomas Neely (eds), *The Woman's Part: Feminist Criticism of Shakespeare* (Urbana, Ill., 1980), 65–78 |
| Beauman | Sally Beauman, *The Royal Shakespeare Company: A History of Ten Decades* (Oxford, 1982) |
| Beaumont & Fletcher | Francis Beaumont and John Fletcher, *The Dramatic Works in the Beaumont and Fletcher Canon*, gen. ed. Fredson Bowers, 9 vols (Cambridge, 1966–92) |
| Becon | *The Catechism of Thomas Becon* (1560), ed. John Ayre (New York, 1968) |
| Benson | Constance Benson, *Mainly Players: Bensonian Memories* (1926) |

| | |
|---|---|
| Bentley | Gerald Eades Bentley, *The Jacobean and Caroline Stage*, 7 vols (Oxford, 1941–68) |
| Bergeron | David M. Bergeron, 'The Wife of Bath and Shakespeare's *The Taming of the Shrew*', *University Review*, 35 (1969), 279–86 |
| Berry | Herbert Berry, *The Boar's Head Playhouse* (Washington, DC, and London, 1986) |
| Blamires | Alcuin Blamires, 'Beneath the pulpit', in Carolyn Dinshaw and David Wallace (eds), *The Cambridge Companion to Medieval Women's Writing* (Cambridge, 2003), 141–60 |
| Blayney, 'Introduction' | Peter W.M. Blayney, 'Introduction to the second edition', in *First Folio*, xxvii–xxxvii |
| Blayney, 'Publication' | Peter W.M. Blayney, 'The publication of playbooks', in Cox & Kastan, 383–422 |
| Blumenthal | Eileen Blumenthal, *Julie Taymor, Playing with Fire: Theater, Opera, Film* (New York, 1995) |
| Boas | *'The Taming of a Shrew': Being the Original of Shakespeare's 'Taming of the Shrew'*, ed. F.S. Boas (1908) |
| Boccaccio | Giovanni Boccaccio, *The Decameron*, trans. Mark Musa and Peter Dondanella (New York, 1982) |
| Bogdanov, *Shakespeare* | Michael Bogdanov, *Shakespeare: The Director's Cut*, 2 vols (Edinburgh, 2003) |
| Bond, *Early* | *Early Plays From the Italian*, ed. R. Warwick Bond (New York, 1967) |
| Boose, 'Husbandry' | Lynda E. Boose, '*The Taming of the Shrew*, good husbandry, and enclosure', in Russ McDonald (ed.), *Shakespeare Reread: The Texts in New Contexts* (Ithaca, NY, 1994), 193–225 |
| Boose, 'Scolding' | Lynda E. Boose, 'Scolding brides and bridling scolds: taming the woman's unruly member', *SQ*, 42.2 (1991), 179–213 |
| Bowers, *Dramatists* | Fredson Bowers, *On Editing Shakespeare and the Elizabethan Dramatists* (Philadelphia, Pa., 1955) |
| Bowers, *Editing* | Fredson Bowers, *On Editing Shakespeare* (Charlottesville, Va., 1966) |
| Bradbrook | M.C. Bradbrook, 'Dramatic role as social image: a study of *The Taming of the Shrew*', *Shakespeare Jahrbuch*, 94 (1958), 132–50 |
| Bradley | David Bradley, *From Text to Performance in the Elizabethan Theatre* (Cambridge, 1992) |
| Brooks | Ann Brooks, *Post-feminisms: Feminism, Cultural Theory and Cultural Forms* (London and New York, 1997) |
| Brown | Pamela Allen Brown, *Better a Shrew than a Sheep: Women, Drama, and the Culture of Jest in Early Modern England* (Ithaca, NY, 2003) |

| | |
|---|---|
| BRS | Bruce R. Smith, private communication |
| Brunvand, 'Folktale' | Jan Harold Brunvand, 'The folktale origin of *The Taming of the Shrew*', *SQ*, 17.4 (1966), 345–59 |
| Brunvand, *Oral* | Jan Harold Brunvand, *The Taming of the Shrew: A Comparative Study of Oral and Literary Versions* (New York, 1991) |
| Bryson | Anna Bryson, *From Courtesy to Civility: Changing Codes of Conduct in Early Modern England* (Oxford, 1998) |
| Bullock | Christopher Bullock, *The Cobbler of Preston* (1716) |
| Bullough | Geoffrey Bullough, *Narrative and Dramatic Sources of Shakespeare*, 8 vols (New York, 1957–75) |
| Burke | Kenneth Burke, 'Antony in behalf of the play', in *The Philosophy of Literary Form: Studies in Symbolic Action*, 3rd edn (Berkeley, Calif., 1973) |
| Burnett | Mark Thornton Burnett, *Masters and Servants in English Renaissance Drama and Culture: Authority and Obedience* (New York, 1997) |
| Burns | Margie Burns, 'The ending of *The Shrew*', in Aspinall, 84–105 |
| Burt | Richard A. Burt, 'Charisma, coercion and comic form in *The Taming of the Shrew*', *Criticism*, 26.4 (1984), 295–311 |
| Burton | Richard Burton, *The Anatomy of Melancholy*, ed. Thomas C. Faulkner, Nicolas K. Kiessling and Rhonda L. Blair, 5 vols (1989–2000) |
| *Calendar* | *Calendar of State Papers and Manuscripts, Relating to English Affairs, Existing in the Archives and Collections of Venice*, ed. Allen B. Hinds, vol. 15 (1909) |
| Capp | Bernard Capp, *When Gossips Meet: Women, Family, and Neighbourhood in Early Modern England* (Oxford, 2003) |
| Carlson | Susan Carlson, 'The suffrage Shrew: the Shakespeare Festival, "A man's play," and new women', in Jonathan Bate, Jill L. Levenson and Dieter Mehl (eds), *Shakespeare and the Twentieth Century: The Selected Proceedings . . . Los Angeles, 1996* (1998), 85–102 |
| Carroll | *The Two Gentlemen of Verona*, ed. William C. Carroll, Arden Shakespeare third series (2004) |
| Castiglione | Baldassare Castiglione, *The Book of the Courtier* (1528), trans. Thomas Hoby, 4 vols (1561) |
| Cavell | Stanley Cavell, *Pursuits of Happiness: The Hollywood Comedy of Remarriage* (Cambridge, Mass., 1981) |
| CG | Chris Goodwin, private communication |
| Chambers, *Shakespeare* | E.K. Chambers, *William Shakespeare: A Study of Facts and Problems*, 2 vols (Oxford, 1930) |

| Chambers, *Stage* | E.K. Chambers, *The Elizabethan Stage*, 4 vols (Oxford, 1923) |
| Chaucer | *The Riverside Chaucer*, ed. Larry D. Benson, 3rd edn (Boston, 1987) |
| Christensen | Ann C. Christensen, 'Of household stuff and homes: the stage and social practice in *The Taming of the Shrew*', *Explorations in Renaissance Culture*, 22 (1996), 127–45 |
| Chudleigh | Lady Mary Chudleigh, *The Poems and Prose of Mary, Lady Chudleigh*, ed. Margaret J.M. Ezell (New York and Oxford, 1993) |
| Clark, *Demons* | Stuart Clark, *Thinking with Demons: The Idea of Witchcraft in Early Modern Europe* (Oxford, 1997) |
| Clark, *Plays* | Sandra Clark, *The Plays of Beaumont and Fletcher: Sexual Themes and Dramatic Representation* (New York, 1994) |
| Cohen | Ralph Alan Cohen, 'Looking for Cousin Ferdinand: the value of F1 stage directions for a production of *The Taming of the Shrew*', in Laurie E. Maguire and Thomas L. Berger (eds), *Textual Formations and Reformations* (Newark, NJ, 1998), 264–80 |
| Cohn | Ruby Cohn, *Modern Shakespeare Offshoots* (Princeton, NJ, 1976) |
| Collins | Michael J. Collins (ed.), *Shakespeare's Sweet Thunder: Essays on the Early Comedies* (Newark, NJ, 1997) |
| Corbet | Gordon Corbet, *The Terrestrial Mammals of Western Europe* (Philadelphia, Pa., 1966) |
| Cordner, 'Actors' | Michael Cordner, 'Actors, editors, and the annotation of Shakespearean playscripts', *SS* 55 (2002), 181–98 |
| Cordner, 'Scripts' | Michael Cordner, '"To show our simple skill": scripts and performances in Shakespearean comedy', *SS* 56 (2003), 167–83 |
| Coulton | G.G. Coulton, *Social Life in Britain From the Conquest to the Reformation* (Cambridge, 1918; repr. 1938) |
| Cousin | Geraldine Cousin, 'The touring of the *Shrew*', *New Theatre Quarterly*, 2.7 (1986), 275–81 |
| Cox | John D. Cox, 'Open stage, open page? Editing stage directions in early dramatic texts', in Lukas Erne and Margaret Jane Kidnie (eds), *Textual Performances: The Modern Reproduction of Shakespeare's Drama* (Cambridge, 2004), 178–93 |
| Cox & Kastan | John D. Cox and David Scott Kastan (eds), *A New History of Early English Drama* (New York, 1997) |
| CR | Carol Chillington Rutter, private communication |

411

| | |
|---|---|
| Craig | Edward Gordon Craig, *On the Art of the Theatre* (1911; repr. 1957) |
| Creizenach | Wilhelm Michael Anton Creizenach, *The English Drama in the Age of Shakespeare*, trans. Cécile Hugon (1916) |
| Crocker | Holly A. Crocker, 'Affective resistance: performing passivity and playing a-part in *The Taming of the Shrew*', *SQ*, 54.2 (2003), 142–59 |
| Croft | P.J. Croft, 'The "friar of order gray" and the nun', *RES*, 32 (1981), 1–16 |
| Crosse, *Diaries* | Gordon Crosse, *The Gordon Crosse Theatrical Diaries 1890–1953*, 20 vols, facsimile MS at The Shakespeare Institute library, Stratford-upon-Avon, UK |
| Crosse, *Fifty* | Gordon Crosse, *Fifty Years of Shakespearean Playgoing* (1940) |
| Crosse, *Playgoing* | Gordon Crosse, *Shakespearean Playgoing, 1890–1952* (1953) |
| Crowcroft | Peter Crowcroft, *The Life of a Shrew* (1957) |
| Crystal & Crystal | David Crystal and Ben Crystal, *Shakespeare's Words: A Glossary and Language Companion* (2002) |
| Cunningham | Karen Cunningham, 'Female fidelities on trial: proof in the Howard Attainder and *Cymbeline*', *RD*, 25 (1994), 1–31 |
| Dam | B.A.P. van Dam, '*The Taming of a Shrew* and *The Taming of the Shrew*', *ES*, 10 (1928), 97–106 |
| Daniel | P.A. Daniel, *A Time Analysis of the Plots of Shakspere's Plays*, Transactions of the New Shakspere Society, 1877–9, Series I (1879) |
| Daniell | David Daniell, 'The good marriage of Katherine and Petruchio', *SS 37* (1984), 23–31 |
| Danks | K.B. Danks, '*A Shrew* and *The Shrew*', *N&Q*, 200 (1955), 331–2 |
| David | Alfred David, 'The ownership and use of the Ellesmere Manuscript', in Martin Stevens and Daniel Woodward (eds), *The Ellesmere Chaucer: Essays in Interpretation* (San Marino, Calif., 1997), 307–26 |
| Davies, *Garrick* | Thomas Davies, *Memoirs of the Life of David Garrick*, 2 vols (1818) |
| Davies, *Works* | Sir John Davies, *The Poetical Works* (1773) |
| Davis | Philip Davis, *Shakespeare Thinking* (2007) |
| de Grazia & Wells | Margreta de Grazia and Stanley Wells (eds), *The Cambridge Companion to Shakespeare* (Cambridge, 2001), 31–48 |
| Dent | R.W. Dent, *Shakespeare's Proverbial Language: An Index* (1981) |
| Dessen | Alan C. Dessen, *Rescripting Shakespeare: The Text, the Director and Modern Productions* (Cambridge, 2002) |

| | |
|---|---|
| Dessen & Thomson | Alan C. Dessen and Leslie Thomson, *A Dictionary of Stage Directions in English Drama, 1580–1642* (Cambridge, 1999) |
| Detmer | Emily Detmer, 'Civilizing subordination: domestic violation and *The Taming of the Shrew*', *SQ*, 48.3 (1997), 273–94 |
| Dobson | Michael Dobson, *The Making of the National Poet: Shakespeare, Adaptation and Authorship, 1660–1769* (Oxford and New York, 1992) |
| Dod & Cleaver | John Dod and Robert Cleaver, *A Godly Form of Household Government: For the Ordering of Private Families* (1621) |
| Dolan, 'Household' | Frances E. Dolan, 'Household chastisements: gender, authority, and "domestic violence"', in Patricia Fumerton and Simon Hunt (eds), *Renaissance Culture and the Everyday* (Philadelphia, Pa., 1999), 204–28 |
| Dolan, *Marriage* | Frances E. Dolan, *Marriage and Violence: The Early Modern Legacy* (Philadelphia, Pa., 2008) |
| Dolan, 'Plot' | Frances E. Dolan, 'The subordinate('s) plot: petty treason and the forms of domestic rebellion', *SQ*, 43.3 (1992), 317–40 |
| Dolan, *Shrew* | See Dolan (under Editions of Shakespeare collated or referred to) |
| 'Dramatic records' | 'Dramatic records of the City of London', ed. E.K. Chambers and W.W. Greg, *Malone Society Collections*, 1 (1907), 43–92 |
| Dusinberre | Juliet Dusinberre, *Shakespeare and the Nature of Women* (Basingstoke, 1975; 3rd edn 2003) |
| Duthie | G.I. Duthie, '*The Taming of a Shrew* and *The Taming of the Shrew*', *RES*, 19 (1943), 337–56 |
| Dutschke | C.W. Dutschke *et al.* (eds), *Guide to Medieval and Renaissance Manuscripts in the Huntington Library*, 2 vols (San Marino, Calif., 1989) |
| Eccles | Mark Eccles, 'Elizabethan actors IV: S–Z', *N&Q*, 238 (1993), 168–9 |
| Eco | Umberto Eco, *The Open Work*, trans. Anna Cancogni with an introduction by David Robey (Cambridge, Mass., 1989) |
| Elsom | John Elsom, ed., *Is Shakespeare Still Our Contemporary?* (London, 1989) |
| Elyot, *Castle* | Sir Thomas Elyot, *The Castle of Health* (1539) |
| Elyot, *Governor* | Sir Thomas Elyot, *The Book Named the Governor*, ed. S.E. Lehmberg (1962) |
| *ES* | *English Studies* |
| Fava | Antonio Fava, *The Comic Mask in the Commedia dell'Arte* (Chicago, 2007) |

| Felheim | Marvin Felheim, *The Theater of Augustin Daly: An Account of the Late Nineteenth Century American Stage* (Cambridge, Mass., 1956) |
|---|---|
| Ferguson | Margaret Ferguson, 'The tutors' nicknames', paper presented at MLA conference, Chicago, 2007 |
| Fineman | Joel Fineman, 'The turn of the shrew', in Patricia Parker and Geoffrey Hartmann (eds), *Shakespeare and the Question of Theory* (New York, 1985), 138–59 |
| *First Folio* | *The First Folio of Shakespeare: The Norton Facsimile*, ed. Charlton Hinman and Peter W.M. Blayney, 2nd edn (New York, 1996) |
| Fleay | F.G. Fleay, *A Chronicle History of the London Stage, 1559–1642* (1890) |
| Fleming | Juliet Fleming, 'The Ladies' Shakespeare', in Dympna Callaghan (ed.), *A Feminist Companion to Shakespeare* (Malden, Mass., 2000), 3–20 |
| Fletcher | Anthony Fletcher, *Gender, Sex and Subordination in England 1500–1800* (New Haven, Conn., 1999) |
| Florio | John Florio, *Florio's First Fruits* (1578) and *Florio's Second Fruits* (1591) |
| *FQ* | Edmund Spenser, *The Faerie Queene*, ed. A.C. Hamilton (Harlow, 2001) |
| *Frederyke of Jennen* | *Here Beginneth a Proper Treatise of a Merchant's Wife, that Afterward Went Like a Man and Became a Great Lord, and was Called Frederyke of Jennen* (*c*. 1560) |
| Freed | Amy Freed, *The Beard of Avon* (New York, 2004) |
| Freedman, *Gaze* | Barbara Freedman, *Staging the Gaze: Postmodernism, Psychoanalysis, and Shakespearean Comedy* (Ithaca, NY, 1991) |
| Friedan | Betty Friedan, *The Feminine Mystique* (New York, 1963) |
| Furnivall | F.J. Furnivall, 'Sir John Harington's Shakespeare quartos', *N&Q*, 229 (1890), 282–3 |
| Gabrieli & Melchiori | Anthony Munday *et al.*, *Sir Thomas More*, ed. Vittorio Gabrieli and Giorgio Melchiori (Manchester, 1990) |
| Galey | Alan Galey, 'Signal to noise: designing a digital edition of *The Taming of a Shrew* (1594)', *College Literature*, 36.1 (2009), 40–66 |
| Garner | Shirley Nelson Garner, '*The Taming of the Shrew*: inside or outside of the joke?', in Maurice Charney (ed.), *'Bad' Shakespeare: Revaluations of the Shakespeare Canon* (Rutherford, NJ, and London, 1988), 105–19 |
| Garrick | David Garrick, *Catharine and Petruchio* (1756) |

| | |
|---|---|
| Gascoigne | George Gascoigne, *Supposes* (1566), in Frederick S. Boas (ed.), *Five Pre-Shakespearean Comedies* (1934) |
| Gaw | Allison Gaw, 'John Sincklo as one of Shakespeare's actors', *Anglia*, 49 (1926), 289–303 |
| Gay | Penny Gay, *As She Likes It: Shakespeare's Unruly Women* (1994) |
| George | David George, 'Shakespeare and Pembroke's Men', *SQ*, 32.3 (1981), 305–23 |
| Gilbert | Miriam Gilbert, 'Performance as deflection', in Barbara Hodgdon and W.B. Worthen (eds), *A Companion to Shakespeare and Performance* (Malden, Mass., and Oxford, 2005), 319–34 |
| Glenn | Susan A. Glenn, *Female Spectacle: The Theatrical Roots of Modern Feminism* (Cambridge, Mass., 2000) |
| *Gorgeous* | *A Gorgeous Gallery of Gallant Inventions (1578)*, ed. Hyder E. Rollins (New York, 1971) |
| Gower | John Gower, *Confessio Amantis*, ed. Russell A. Peck (Toronto, 1997) |
| Greenblatt | Stephen Greenblatt, 'Invisible bullets: Renaissance authority and its subversion, *Henry IV* and *Henry V*', in Jonathan Dollimore and Alan Sinfield (eds), *Political Shakespeare: New Essays in Cultural Materialism* (Manchester, 1985), 18–47 |
| Greene | Robert Greene, *The Defence of Cony-Catching* (1593), ed. G.B. Harrison (New York, 1966) |
| Greenfield | Thelma N. Greenfield, *The Induction in Elizabethan Drama* (Eugene, Ore., 1969) |
| Greg, *Bibliography* | W.W. Greg, *A Bibliography of the English Printed Drama to the Restoration*, 4 vols (1939–59) |
| Greg, *Documents* | W.W. Greg, *Dramatic Documents From the Elizabethan Playhouses*, 2 vols (Oxford, 1931) |
| Greg, *Folio* | W.W. Greg, *The Shakespeare First Folio: Its Bibliographical and Textual History* (Oxford, 1955) |
| Grigely | Joseph Grigely, *Textualterity: Art, Theory, and Textual Criticism* (Ann Arbor, Mich., 1995) |
| Gurr, *Company* | Andrew Gurr, *The Shakespeare Company, 1594–1642* (Cambridge, 2004) |
| Gurr, 'Maximal' | Andrew Gurr, 'Maximal and minimal texts: Shakespeare v. the Globe', *SS 52* (1999), 68–87 |
| Gurr, *Playing* | Andrew Gurr, *The Shakesperian Playing Companies* (Oxford, 1996) |
| Gurr, *Stage* | Andrew Gurr, *The Shakespearean Stage, 1574–1642*, 3rd edn (Cambridge, 1992) |

| | |
|---|---|
| Gurr, 'Work' | Andrew Gurr, 'The work of Elizabethan plotters, and *2 The Seven Deadly Sins*', *Early Theatre*, 10.1 (2007), 67–87 |
| GZ | Georgianna Zeigler, private communication |
| Hackel | Heidi Brayman Hackel, '"The great variety of readers" and early modern reading practices', in *ACS*, 139–57 |
| Haring-Smith | Tori Haring-Smith, *From Farce to Metadrama: A Stage History of 'The Taming of the Shrew', 1594–1983* (Westport, Conn., 1985) |
| Harington | Sir John Harington, *A New Discourse of a Stale Subject, Called the Metamorphosis of Ajax* (1596), ed. Elizabeth Story Donno (New York, 1962) |
| Harman | Thomas Harman, *A Caveat for Common Cursitors Vulgarly Called Vagabonds* (1567) |
| Harris | Bernard Harris, 'Goldsmith in the theatre', in Andrew Swarbrick (ed.), *The Art of Oliver Goldsmith* (London and Totowa, NJ, 1984), 144–67 |
| Harrison, *Description* | William Harrison, *The Description of England* (1587), ed. Georges Edelen (Toronto and London, 1994) |
| Hartwig | Joan Hartwig, 'Horses and women in *The Taming of the Shrew*', *Huntington Library Quarterly*, 45.4 (1982), 285–94 |
| Hattaway | Michael Hattaway, *Elizabethan Popular Theatre: Plays in Performance* (1982) |
| Hazlitt | W.C. Hazlitt, *Shakespeare's Library*, 2nd edn, 6 vols (1875) |
| Heilman | Robert B. Heilman, 'The *Taming* untamed, or, The Return of the Shrew', in Aspinall, 45–57 |
| Helmers | Helmer Jon Helmers, 'Some unknown Shrews', paper presented at '"Shrews" on the Renaissance stage' conference, York, 2006 |
| Henderson, 'Revisited' | Diana Henderson, 'A *Shrew* for the times, revisited', in Richard Burt and Lynda E. Boose (eds), *Shakespeare the Movie II: Popularizing the Plays on Film, TV, Video, and DVD* (London and New York, 2003), 120–39 |
| Henderson, 'Times' | Diana Henderson, 'A *Shrew* for the times', in Lynda E. Boose and Richard Burt (eds), *Shakespeare the Movie: Popularizing the Plays on Film, TV, and Video* (London and New York, 1997), 148–68 |
| Henslowe | *Henslowe's Diary*, ed. R.A. Foakes, 2nd edn (Cambridge, 2002) |
| Herbert | Sir Henry Herbert, *The Control and Censorship of Caroline Drama: The Records of Sir Henry Herbert, Master of the Revels 1623–73*, ed. N.W. Bawcutt (Oxford, 1996) |

Heywood, *Ovid*     Thomas Heywood, *The Art of Love: The First Complete English Translation of Ovid's Ars Amatoria*, ed. M.L. Stapleton (Ann Arbor, Mich., 2000)

Heywood, *Proverbs*     *John Heywood's Works. A Dialogue Containing the Number of the Effectual Proverbs in the English Tongue* (1566)

Hibbard, 'Social'     George R. Hibbard, '*The Taming of the Shrew*: a social comedy', in Alwin Thaler and Norman Sanders (eds), *Shakespearian Essays* (Knoxville, Tenn., 1964), 15–28

Hickson     Samuel Hickson, '*The Taming of the Shrew*', *N&Q*, 22 (1850), 345–7

Hinman, 'Introduction'     Charlton Hinman, 'Introduction to the first edition', in *First Folio*, ix–xxvi

Hinman, *Printing*     Charlton Hinman, *Printing and Proof-Reading of the First Folio of Shakespeare*, 2 vols (Oxford, 1963)

Hodgdon, 'Bound'     Barbara Hodgdon, 'Katherina bound; or, play(K)ating the strictures of everyday life', *PMLA*, 107.3 (1992), 538–53

Hodgdon, 'Bride-ing'     Barbara Hodgdon, 'Bride-ing the *Shrew*: costumes that matter', *SS 60* (2007), 72–83

Hodgdon, 'New'     Barbara Hodgdon, 'New collaborations with old plays: the (textual) politics of performance commentary', in Lukas Erne and Margaret Jane Kidnie (eds), *Textual Performances: The Modern Reproduction of Shakespeare's Drama* (Cambridge, 2004), 210–23

Hodgdon, *Trade*     Barbara Hodgdon, *The Shakespeare Trade: Performances and Appropriations* (Philadelphia, Pa., 1998)

Hodgdon, 'Who'     Barbara Hodgdon, 'Who is performing "in" these texts?; or, *Shrew*-ing around', in Ann Thompson and Gordon McMullan (eds), *In Arden: Editing Shakespeare* (2003), 95–110

Hodgdon, 'Wooing'     Barbara Hodgdon, 'Wooing and winning (or not): film/Shakespeare/comedy and the syntax of genre', in Jean E. Howard and Richard Dutton (eds), *Blackwell Companion to Shakespearean Comedy* (Oxford, 2003)

Hodges     C. Walter Hodges, *The Globe Restored: A Study of the Elizabethan Theatre* (1953)

Hoenselaars     A.J. Hoenselaars, 'Italy staged in English Renaissance drama', in Michele Marrapodi *et al.* (eds), *Shakespeare's Italy: Functions of Italian Locations in Renaissance Drama* (Manchester and New York, 1993), 30–48

Holderness     Graham Holderness, *The Taming of the Shrew*, Shakespeare in Performance Series (Manchester, 1989)

Holderness & Loughrey     *The Taming of a Shrew*, ed. Graham Holderness and Bryan Loughrey (Lanham, MD, 1992)

417

| | |
|---|---|
| Holland, *English* | Peter Holland, *English Shakespeares: Shakespeare on the English Stage in the 1990s* (Cambridge, 1997) |
| Holland, 'Shakespeare' | 'Shakespeare in the twentieth-century theatre', in de Grazia & Wells, 199–216 |
| Holt | Emily S. Holt, *Ye Olden Times: English Customs in the Middle Ages* (1971) |
| *Homilies* | *The Second Tome of Homilies. Of such matters as were promised, and entituled in the former part of Homilies. Set out by the authority of the Queens Majesty and to be read in every Parish Church agreeably* (1595) |
| Honigmann, 'Lost' | E.A.J. Honigmann, 'Shakespeare's "lost source-plays"', *Modern Language Review*, 49.3 (1954), 293–307 |
| Honigmann, 'New' | E.A.J. Honigmann, 'The new bibliography and its critics', in Lukas Erne and Margaret Jane Kidnie (eds), *Textual Performances: The Modern Reproduction of Shakespeare's Drama* (Cambridge, 2004), 77–93 |
| Honigmann & Brock | *Playhouse Wills, 1558–1642: An Edition of Wills by Shakespeare and His Contemporaries in the London Theatre*, ed. E.A.J. Honigmann and Susan Brock (Manchester and New York, 1993) |
| Hope | Jonathan Hope, *Shakespeare's Grammar* (2003) |
| Hopkins | Matthew Hopkins, *The Discovery of Witches* (1647) |
| Horace | Horace, *Odes III: Dulce Periculum*, ed. David West (Oxford, 2002) |
| Hosley, 'Epilogue' | Richard Hosley, 'Was there a "dramatic epilogue" to *The Taming of the Shrew*?', *SEL*, 1.2 (1961), 17–34 |
| Hosley, 'Formal' | Richard Hosley, 'The formal influence of Plautus and Terence', in John Russell Brown and Bernard Harris (eds), *Elizabethan Theatre*, Stratford-upon-Avon Studies 9 (1966), 131–45 |
| Hosley, 'Sources' | Richard Hosley, 'Sources and analogues of *The Taming of the Shrew*', *Huntington Library Quarterly*, 27.3 (1964), 289–308 |
| Houk | Raymond A. Houk, 'The evolution of *The Taming of the Shrew*', *PMLA*, 57.4 (1942), 1009–38 |
| Howard | Jean E. Howard, Introduction to *The Taming of the Shrew*, in Stephen Greenblatt *et al.* (eds), *The Norton Shakespeare* (New York, 1997), 133–40 |
| Howard-Hill | T.H. Howard-Hill, 'The compositors of Shakespeare's Folio comedies', *SB*, 26 (1973), 61–106 |
| Hulme | Hilda M. Hulme, *Explorations in Shakespeare's Language: Some Problems of Lexical Meaning in the Dramatic Text* (1962) |

| | |
|---|---|
| Hunt | Margaret Hunt, 'Wife-beating, domesticity and women's independence in eighteenth-century London', *Gender & History*, 4.1 (1992), 10–33 |
| Huston | J. Dennis Huston, *Shakespeare's Comedies of Play* (New York, 1981) |
| Hutcheon | Linda Hutcheon, *A Theory of Adaptation* (London and New York, 2006) |
| Hutson | Lorna Hutson, *The Usurer's Daughter: Male Friendship and Fictions of Women in Sixteenth-Century England* (1994) |
| Ingram | Martin Ingram, '"Scolding women cucked or washed": a crisis in gender relations in early modern England?', in Jenny Kermode and Garthine Walker (eds), *Women, Crime, and the Courts in Early Modern England* (Chapel Hill, NC, 1994), 48–80 |
| JA | Jane Armstrong, private communication |
| Jardine | Lisa Jardine, *Worldly Goods* (1996) |
| Jayne | Sears Jayne, 'The dreaming of *The Shrew*', *SQ*, 17.1 (1966), 41–56 |
| Jeaffreson | John Cordy Jeaffreson, *Brides and Bridals*, 2 vols (1872) |
| Jones & Stallybrass | Ann Rosalind Jones and Peter Stallybrass, *Renaissance Clothing and the Materials of Memory* (Cambridge, 2000) |
| Jonson | *The Complete Plays of Ben Jonson*, ed. G.A. Wilkes, 4 vols (Oxford, 1981) |
| Kahn | Coppélia Kahn, *Man's Estate: Masculine Identity in Shakespeare* (Berkeley, Calif., 1981) |
| Kaplan & Stowell | Joel H. Kaplan and Sheila Stowell, *Theatre and Fashion: Oscar Wilde to the Suffragettes* (Cambridge, 1994) |
| Kathman, 'Grocers' | David Kathman, 'Grocers, goldsmiths, and drapers: freemen and apprentices in the Elizabethan theater', *SQ*, 55.1 (2004), 1–49 |
| Kathman, 'Index' | David J. Kathman, 'Biographical index of English drama before 1660' (http://shakespeareauthorship.com/bd/) |
| Kathman, 'Reconsidering' | David Kathman, 'Reconsidering *The Seven Deadly Sins*', *Early Theatre*, 7.1 (2004), 13–44 |
| Kemble | John Philip Kemble, *Shakespeare's Katharine and Petruchio . . . Revised by J.P. Kemble . . . as it is Acted at the Theatre Royal in Covent Garden* (1815) |
| Kidnie, *Problem* | Margaret Jane Kidnie, *Shakespeare and the Problem of Adaptation: Forms of Possibility* (London and New York, 2009) |
| Kidnie, 'Staging' | Margaret Jane Kidnie, 'The staging of Shakespeare's drama in print editions', in Lukas Erne and Margaret Jane Kidnie (eds), *Textual Performances: The Modern Reproduction of* |

419

|  | *Shakespeare's Drama* (Cambridge, 2004), 158–77 |
| Kidnie, 'Text' | Margaret Jane Kidnie, 'Text, performance, and the editors: staging Shakespeare's drama', *SQ*, 51.4 (2000), 456–73 |
| King | T.J. King, *Casting Shakespeare's Plays: London Actors and Their Roles, 1590–1642* (Cambridge, 1992) |
| Kirschbaum | Leo Kirschbaum, 'A census of bad quartos', *RES*, 14 (1938), 20–43 |
| Klein | Joan Larsen Klein (ed.), *Daughters, Wives, and Widows: Writings by Men about Women and Marriage in England, 1500–1640* (Urbana, Ill., 1992) |
| *Knack* | *A Knack to Know a Knave* (1594), ed. G.R. Proudfoot (Oxford, 1964) |
| Knutson, 'Knows' | Roslyn Lander Knutson, '"Everybody knows . . . ": the *Shrew* plays and conventional wisdom', paper presented at SAA conference, Dallas, Texas, 2008 |
| Knutson, 'Pembroke's' | Roslyn Lander Knutson, 'Pembroke's Men in 1592–3: their repertory and touring schedule', *Early Theatre*, 4 (2001), 129–38 |
| Knutson, *Playing* | Roslyn Lander Knutson, *Playing Companies and Commerce in Shakespeare's Time* (Cambridge, 2001) |
| Knutson, *Repertory* | Roslyn Lander Knutson, *The Repertory of Shakespeare's Company, 1594–1613* (Fayetteville, Ariz., 1991) |
| Knutson, 'Shakespeare's' | Roslyn Lander Knutson, 'Shakespeare's repertory', in *ACS*, 346–61 |
| Kökeritz | Helge Kökeritz, *Shakespeare's Pronunciation* (New Haven, Conn., 1953) |
| Korda | Natasha Korda, *Shakespeare's Domestic Economies: Gender and Property in Early Modern England* (Philadelphia, Pa., 2002) |
| Kostihová | Marcela Kostihová, 'Katherina "humanized": abusing the shrew on the Prague stage', in Sonia Massai (ed.), *World-Wide Shakespeares: Local Appropriations in Film and Performance* (London and New York, 2005), 72–9 |
| Lanier | Douglas Lanier, 'Julie Taymor', in John Russell Brown (ed.), *A Routledge Companion to Directors' Shakespeare* (London and New York, 2008), 457–73 |
| Latham | Simon Latham, *Latham's Falconry, or the Falcon's Lure and Cure* (1614) |
| Leggatt | Alexander Leggatt, *Shakespeare's Comedy of Love* (1974) |
| LEM | Laurie E. Maguire, private communication |
| Levenson | *Romeo and Juliet*, ed. Jill Levenson (Oxford, 2000) |

| | |
|---|---|
| Levin | Richard Levin, 'Grumio's "rope-tricks" and the nurse's "ropery"', *SQ*, 22.1 (1971), 82–6 |
| Linthicum | Marie Channing Linthicum, *Costume in the Drama of Shakespeare and His Contemporaries* (Oxford, 1936) |
| LM | Leah Marcus, private communication |
| Long, 'Factor' | William B. Long, 'Stage-directions: a misinterpreted factor in determining textual trovenance', *TEXT*, 2 (1985), 121–37 |
| Long, 'Precious' | William B. Long, '"Precious few": English manuscript playbooks', in *ACS*, 414–33 |
| Lyly | *The Complete Works of John Lyly*, ed. R. Warwick Bond, 3 vols (Oxford, 1902) |
| Lynch | Kathryn L. Lynch, 'East meets West in Chaucer's Squire's and Franklin's Tales', in Kathryn L. Lynch (ed.), *Chaucer's Cultural Geography* (New York, 2002), 76–101 |
| MacDonald, 'Haymarket' | Jan MacDonald, '*The Taming of the Shrew* at the Haymarket Theatre, 1844 and 1847', in Kenneth Richards and Peter Thomson (eds), *Essays on Nineteenth Century British Theatre* (1971), 157–70 |
| MacDonald, 'Unholy' | Jan MacDonald, '"An Unholy Alliance": William Poel, Martin Harvey, and *The Taming of the Shrew*', *Theatre Notebook*, 36.2 (1982), 64–72 |
| McEachern | *Much Ado About Nothing*, ed. Claire McEachern, Arden Shakespeare third series (2006) |
| Machiavelli | Niccolò Machiavelli, *The History of Florence*, 8 vols (trans. 1595, pub. 1680) |
| McKerrow | R.B. McKerrow, 'A suggestion regarding Shakespeare's manuscripts', *RES*, 11.44 (1935), 459–65 |
| McLuskie | Kathleen McLuskie, 'The patriarchal bard: feminist criticism and Shakespeare: *King Lear* and *Measure for Measure*', in Jonathan Dollimore and Alan Sinfield (eds), *Political Shakespeare: New Essays in Cultural Materialism* (Manchester, 1985), 88–108 |
| McMillin, 'Building' | Scott McMillin, 'Building stories: Greg, Fleay, and the plot of *2 Seven Deadly Sins*', *Medieval and Renaissance Drama in England*, 4 (1989), 53–62 |
| McMillin, 'Casting' | Scott McMillin, 'Casting for Pembroke's Men: the *Henry VI* quartos and *The Taming of a Shrew*', *SQ*, 23.2 (1972), 141–59 |
| McMillin, *More* | Scott McMillin, *The Elizabethan Theatre and 'The Book of Sir Thomas More'* (Ithaca, NY, 1987) |
| McMillin & MacLean | Scott McMillin and Sally-Beth MacLean, *The Queen's Men and Their Plays* (Cambridge and New York, 1998) |

McMullan     *King Henry VIII*, ed. Gordon McMullan, Arden Shakespeare (2000)

Magnusson     Lynne Magnusson, *Shakespeare and Social Dialogue: Dramatic Language and Elizabethan Letters* (Cambridge and New York, 1999)

Maguire, 'Cultural'     Laurie E. Maguire, 'Cultural control in *The Taming of the Shrew*', *RD*, 26 (1995), 83–104

Maguire, 'Household'     Laurie E. Maguire, '"Household Kates": chez Petruchio, Percy, and Plantagenet', in S.P. Cerasano and Marion Wynne-Davies (eds), *Gloriana's Face: Women, Public and Private, in the English Renaissance* (New York, 1992), 129–65

Maguire, *Names*     Laurie E. Maguire, *Shakespeare's Names* (Oxford, 2007)

Maguire, 'Petruccio'     Laurie E. Maguire, 'Petruccio and the barber's shop', *SB*, 51 (1998), 117–26

Maguire, *Suspect*     Laurie E. Maguire, *Shakespearean Suspect Texts: The 'Bad' Quartos and Their Contexts* (New York, 1996)

Mahood     M.M. Mahood, *Bit Parts in Shakespeare's Plays* (Cambridge, 1992)

Makaryk     Irena R. Makaryk, *Shakespeare in the Undiscovered Bourn: Les Kurbas, Ukrainian Modernism, and Early Soviet Cultural Politics* (Toronto, 2004)

Manley, *Literature*     Lawrence Manley, *Literature and Culture in Early Modern London* (Cambridge, 1995)

Manley, 'Reconsidering'     Lawrence Manley, 'Reconsidering David Kathman's "Reconsidering *The Seven Deadly Sins*"', paper presented at SAA conference, Bermuda, 2005

Manningham     *The Diary of John Manningham of the Middle Temple, 1602–1603*, ed. Robert Parker Sorlien (Hanover, NH, 1976)

Marcus, 'Editor'     Leah S. Marcus, 'The shrew as editor/editing *Shrews*', paper presented at '"Shrews" on the Renaissance stage' conference, York, 2006

Marcus, *Unediting*     Leah S. Marcus, *Unediting the Renaissance: Shakespeare, Marlowe, Milton* (1996)

Marinis     Marco de Marinis, *The Semiotics of Performance*, trans. Áine O'Healy (Bloomington, Ind., 1993)

Marino, 'Anachronistic'     James J. Marino, 'The anachronistic *Shrews*', *SQ*, 60.1 (2009), 25–46

Marino, 'Oldcastle'     James J. Marino, 'William Shakespeare's Sir John Oldcastle', *RD*, 30 (2001), 93–114

Marino, *Owning*     James J. Marino, *Owning Shakespeare: The King's Men and Their Intellectual Property* (Philadelphia, Pa., 2011)

Marlowe     Christopher Marlowe, *The Complete Plays*, ed. J.B. Steane (1986)

Marlowe, *Works*     *The Complete Works of Christopher Marlowe*, ed. Fredson
                     Bowers, 2nd edn, 4 vols (Cambridge, 1981)

Marowitz, *Shrew*    Charles Marowitz, *The Marowitz Shakespeare: Adaptations
                     and Collages of 'Hamlet', 'Macbeth', 'The Taming of the
                     Shrew', 'Measure for Measure', and 'The Merchant of
                     Venice'* (New York and London, 1978), 132–80

Marston, *Malcontent* John Marston, *The Malcontent*, ed. Bernard Harris
                     (1967)

Martin               Randall Martin, 'Kates for the table and Kates of the
                     mind: a social metaphor in *The Taming of the Shrew*',
                     *English Studies in Canada*, 17.1 (1991), 1–20

*Mary Magdalene*     *Mary Magdalene (Digby)*, in David Bevington, ed.,
                     *Medieval Drama* (Boston, 1975)

Massai, *Rise*       Sonia Massai, *Shakespeare and the Rise of the Editor*
                     (Cambridge, 2007)

Massai, 'Shakespeare' Sonia Massai, 'Shakespeare, text and paratext', paper
                     presented at SAA conference, Washington, DC, 2009

Masten               Jeffrey Masten, *Textual Intercourse: Collaboration,
                     Authorship and Sexualities in Renaissance Drama*
                     (Cambridge, 1997)

Maurer               Margaret Maurer, 'The Rowe editions of 1709/1714 and
                     3.1 of *The Taming of the Shrew*', in Joanna Gondris (ed.),
                     *Reading Readings: Essays on Shakespeare Editing in the
                     Eighteenth Century* (Madison, NJ, and London, 1998),
                     244–6

Maurer & Gaines      Margaret Maurer and Barry Gaines, 'Putting the silent
                     woman back into the Shakespearean *Shrew*', paper pre-
                     sented at '"Shrews" on the Renaissance Stage' conference,
                     York, 2006

Maxwell              J.C. Maxwell, '*The Shrew* and *A Shrew*: the suitors and the
                     sisters', *N&Q*, 15 (1968), 130–1

Mazer                Cary M. Mazer, *Shakespeare Refashioned: Elizabethan
                     Plays on Edwardian Stages* (Ann Arbor, Mich., 1981)

MC                   Michael Cordner, private communication

Meisel               Martin Meisel, *Realizations: Narrative, Pictorial, and
                     Theatrical Arts in Nineteenth-Century England* (Princeton,
                     NJ, 1983)

Mendelson &          Sara Mendelson and Patricia Crawford, *Women in Early
    Crawford         Modern England 1550–1720* (Oxford, 1998)

*Merry Jest*         *A Merry Jest of a Shrewd and Curst Wife, Lapped in Morel's
                     Skin, for Her Good Behaviour* (*c.* 1550), in Hazlitt, 4.415–48

Metlitzki            Dorothee Metlitzki, *The Matter of Araby in Medieval
                     England* (New Haven, Conn., 1977)

| | |
|---|---|
| Middleton | *Thomas Middleton: The Collected Works*, ed. Gary Taylor and John Lavagnino (Oxford, 2007) |
| Mikesell | Margaret Lael Mikesell, '"Love wrought these miracles": marriage and genre in *The Taming of the Shrew*', *RD*, 20 (1989), 141–67 |
| Miller | *The Taming of a Shrew: The 1594 Quarto*, ed. Stephen Roy Miller (Cambridge, 1998) |
| Mincoff | Marco Mincoff, 'The dating of *The Taming of the Shrew*', *ES*, 54 (1973), 554–65 |
| Miola | Robert S. Miola, 'The influence of New Comedy on *The Comedy of Errors* and *The Taming of the Shrew*', in Collins, 21–34 |
| MLA | Modern Language Association |
| Moisan | Thomas Moisan, '"What's that to you?" or, facing facts: anti-paternalistic chords and social discords in *The Taming of the Shrew*', in Aspinall, 255–76 |
| Moore | William H. Moore, 'An allusion in 1593 to *The Taming of the Shrew*?', *SQ*, 15.1 (1964), 55–60 |
| Mowat | Barbara A. Mowat, 'The reproduction of Shakespeare's texts', in de Grazia & Wells, 13–30 |
| Muir | Kenneth Muir, *The Sources of Shakespeare's Plays* (New Haven, Conn., 1977) |
| *N&Q* | *Notes and Queries* |
| Neely | Carol Thomas Neely, *Broken Nuptials in Shakespeare's Plays* (New Haven, Conn., 1985) |
| Newman | Karen Newman, *Fashioning Femininity and English Renaissance Drama* (Chicago, 1991) |
| Novy, *Argument* | Marianne Novy, *Love's Argument: Gender Relations in Shakespeare* (Chapel Hill, NC, 1984) |
| Novy, *Re-Visions* | Marianne Novy (ed.), *Women's Re-Visions of Shakespeare: On Responses of Dickinson, Woolf, Rich, H.D., George Eliot, and Others* (Urbana, Ill., 1990) |
| Nungezer | Edwin Nungezer, *A Dictionary of Actors . . . in England Before 1642* (New Haven, Conn., 1929) |
| Nuttall | A.D. Nuttall, *Shakespeare the Thinker* (New Haven, Conn., 2007) |
| O'Connor | John O'Connor, 'Compositors D and F of the Shakespeare First Folio', *SB*, 28 (1975), 81–117 |
| Odell | George C.D. Odell, *Shakespeare from Betterton to Irving*, 2 vols (New York, 1920) |
| *Odyssey* | Homer, *The Odyssey*, trans. Robert Fitzgerald (New York, 1990) |

OED     *Oxford English Dictionary; OED Online*, ed. John Simpson, Edmund Weiner and Michael Proffitt (Oxford, 2007), http://dictionary.oed.com/

Ong, *Orality*     Walter J. Ong, *Orality and Literacy: The Technologizing of the Word* (London and New York, 1982)

Ong, *Rhetoric*     Walter J. Ong, *Rhetoric, Romance and Technology: Studies in the Interaction of Expression and Culture* (Ithaca, NY, 1971)

Orlin     Lena Cowen Orlin, 'The performance of things in *The Taming of the Shrew*', *Yearbook of English Studies*, 23 (1993), 167–88

Osborne     Laurie E. Osborne, 'Rethinking the performance editions: theatrical and textual productions of Shakespeare', in James C. Bulman (ed.), *Shakespeare, Theory and Performance* (London and New York, 1996), 168–86

Ovid, *Ars*     *The Art of Love: Ovid's Ars Amatoria*, trans. B.P. Moore (1935)

Ovid, *Heroides*     *Heroides and Amores*, trans. Grant Showerman (Cambridge, Mass., 1977)

Ovid, *Met.*     *The Metamorphoses*, trans. Arthur Golding (1567), ed. Madeleine Forey (Baltimore, Md., 2002); see also Heywood, *Ovid*

Ovid, *Remedy*     *Ovidius Naso his Remedy of Love. Translated and Entitled to the Youth of England* (1600)

Parker, 'Construing'     Patricia Parker, 'Construing gender: mastering Bianca in *The Taming of the Shrew*', in Dympna Callaghan (ed.), *The Impact of Feminism in English Renaissance Studies* (Basingstoke, 2007), 193–209

Parker, *Margins*     Patricia Parker, *Shakespeare From the Margins: Language, Culture, Context* (Chicago, 1996)

Partridge     Eric Partridge, *Shakespeare's Bawdy*, 3rd edn (London and New York, 1968)

Peacham     Henry Peacham, *The Garden of Eloquence* (1593)

Pearson & Uricchio     Roberta E. Pearson and William Uricchio, 'How many times shall Caesar bleed in sport: Shakespeare and the cultural debate about moving pictures', *Screen*, 31.3 (1990), 243–61

Pepys     *The Diary of Samuel Pepys*, ed. Robert Latham and William Matthews, 11 vols (1970–83)

Perret     Marion D. Perret, 'Petruchio: the model wife', *SEL*, 23.2 (1983), 223–35

Planché     J.R. Planché, *The Recollections and Reflections of J.R. Planché, A Professional Autobiography*, 2 vols (1872)

| | |
|---|---|
| Plautus | *The Haunted House (Mostellaria)*, trans. Erich Segal, in *Three Comedies* (New York, 1969) |
| *PMLA* | *Publications of the Modern Language Association of America* |
| Pollard | A.W. Pollard, *Shakespeare Folios and Quartos: A Study in the Bibliography of Shakespeare's Plays, 1594–1685* (1909) |
| PP | Patricia Parker, private communication |
| Praz | Mario Praz, 'Shakespeare's Italy', *SS* 7 (1954), 95–106 |
| Proudfoot | Richard Proudfoot, 'Marlowe and the editors', in J.A. Downie and J.T. Parnell (eds), *Constructing Christopher Marlowe* (Cambridge, 2000), 41–54 |
| Quilligan | Maureen Quilligan, 'Staging gender: William Shakespeare and Elizabeth Cary', in James Grantham Turner (ed.), *Sexuality and Gender in Early Modern Europe: Institutions, Texts, Images* (Cambridge, 1993), 208–32 |
| Race | Sydney Race, 'Manningham's diary: the case for re-examination', *N&Q*, 199 (1954), 380–3 |
| Radway | Janice A. Radway, *Reading the Romance: Women, Patriarchy, and Popular Literature* (Chapel Hill, NC, 1984) |
| Rainolds | John Rainolds, *The Overthrow of Stage-Plays* (1599) |
| Ranald, 'Performance' | Margaret Loftus Ranald, 'The performance of feminism in *The Taming of the Shrew*', *Theatre Research International*, 19.3 (1994), 214–25 |
| Ranald, *Social* | Margaret Loftus Ranald, *Shakespeare and His Social Context* (New York, 1987) |
| Rasmussen, 'Revision' | Eric Rasmussen, 'The revision of scripts', in Cox & Kastan, 441–60 |
| Rasmussen, *Textual* | Eric Rasmussen, *A Textual Companion to 'Doctor Faustus'* (Manchester, 1993) |
| *RD* | *Renaissance Drama* |
| Rehan | Ada Rehan, 'Introduction', in *The Taming of the Shrew*, Players' Edition (New York, 1900) |
| *RES* | *Review of English Studies* |
| Richmond | *Henry VIII*, ed. Hugh M. Richmond, Shakespeare in Performance Series (Manchester, 1994) |
| RJ | Russell Jackson, private communication |
| Roach | Joseph Roach, *Cities of the Dead: Circum-Atlantic Performance* (New York, 1996) |
| Roberts | Jeanne Addison Roberts, 'Horses and hermaphrodites: metamorphoses in *The Taming of the Shrew*', *SQ*, 34.2 (1983), 159–71 |
| Rowlands | Samuel Rowlands, *A Whole Crew of Kind Gossips, All Met to Be Merry* (1609) |

| | |
|---|---|
| RP | Richard Proudfoot, private communication |
| RS | Robert Shaughnessy, private communication |
| RSC | Royal Shakespeare Company |
| Rutter, *Clamorous* | Carol Chillington Rutter, with Sinead Cusack *et al.*, *Clamorous Voices: Shakespeare's Women Today* (1989) |
| Rutter, 'Kate' | Carol Chillington Rutter, 'Kate, Bianca, Ruth, and Sarah: playing the woman's part in *The Taming of the Shrew*', in Collins, 176–215 |
| Rutter, 'Learning' | Carol Chillington Rutter, 'Learning Thisby's part – or – what's Hecuba to him?', *Shakespeare Bulletin*, 22.3 (2004), 5–30 |
| SAA | Shakespeare Association of America |
| Saccio | Peter Saccio, 'Shrewd and kindly farce', *SS 37* (1984), 33–40 |
| Salgado | Gamini Salgado, *Eyewitnesses of Shakespeare: First Hand Accounts of Performance, 1590–1890* (New York, 1975) |
| Salingar | Leo Salingar, *Shakespeare and the Traditions of Comedy* (London and New York, 1974) |
| Sams, *Real* | Eric Sams, *The Real Shakespeare: Retrieving the Early Years, 1564–1594* (New Haven, Conn., 1995) |
| Sams, 'Timing' | Eric Sams, 'The timing of the Shrews', *N&Q*, 230 (1985), 33–45 |
| *Sauny* | John Lacey, *Sauny the Scot; or, The Taming of the Shrew* (1698) |
| *SB* | *Studies in Bibliography* |
| Schafer, *Ms-Directing* | Elizabeth Schafer, *Ms-Directing Shakespeare: Women Direct Shakespeare* (New York, 2000) |
| Schoenbaum | S. Schoenbaum, *William Shakespeare: A Documentary Life* (Oxford, 1975) |
| Schroeder | John W. Schroeder, '*The Taming of a Shrew* and *The Taming of the Shrew*: a case reopened', *Journal of English and Germanic Philology*, 57 (1958), 424–53 |
| Schuler | Robert M. Schuler, 'Bewitching *The Shrew*', *Texas Studies in Literature and Language*, 46.4 (2004), 387–431 |
| *SEL* | *Studies in English Literature, 1500–1900* |
| Seneca | *Seneca and His Tenne Tragedies*, ed. Thomas Newton (1581), facsimile rpt (New York, 1967) |
| Seronsy | Cecil C. Seronsy, '"Supposes" as the unifying theme in *The Taming of the Shrew*', *SQ*, 14.1 (1963), 15–30 |
| Sewell | William H. Sewell, Jr., 'The concept(s) of culture', in Gabrielle M. Spiegel (ed.), *Practicing History: New Directions in Historical Writing After the Linguistic Turn* (New York, 2005), 76–96 |

Shand, 'Guying'    G.B. Shand, 'Guying the guys and girling *The Shrew*: (post)feminist fun at Shakespere's Globe', in Barbara Hodgdon and W.B. Worthen (eds), *A Companion to Shakespeare and Performance* (Malden, Mass., and Oxford, 2005), 550–63

Shand, 'Reading'    G.B. Shand, 'Reading power: classroom acting as close reading', in Milla Cozart Riggio (ed.), *Teaching Shakespeare Through Performance* (New York, 1999), 244–55

Shand, 'Romancing'    G.B. Shand, 'Romancing *The Shrew*: recuperating a comedy of love', in Karen Bamford and Ric Knowles (eds), *Shakespeare's Comedies of Love: Essays in Honour of Alexander Leggatt* (Toronto, 2008), 228–45

Shapiro    Michael Shapiro, 'Framing the taming: metatheatrical awareness of female impersonation in *The Taming of the Shrew*', *Yearbook of English Studies*, 23 (1993), 143–66

Shaw    George Bernard Shaw, *Shaw on Shakespeare: An Anthology of Bernard Shaw's Writings on the Plays and Production of Shakespeare*, ed. Edwin Wilson (New York, 1961)

Shershow    Scott Cutler Shershow, *Puppets and 'Popular' Culture* (Ithaca, NY, 1995)

Silver    Brenda R. Silver, '"Anon" and "The Reader": Virginia Woolf's last essays', *Twentieth Century Literature*, 25.3/4 (1979), 356–441

Sinfield    Alan Sinfield, *Faultlines: Cultural Materialism and the Politics of Dissident Reading* (Berkeley, Calif., 1992)

Sisson, *New*    C.J. Sisson, *New Readings in Shakespeare*, 2 vols (Cambridge, 1956)

Skura    Meredith Anne Skura, *Shakespeare the Actor and the Purposes of Playing* (Chicago, 1993)

Smallwood    Robert Smallwood, ed., *Players of Shakespeare 4* (Cambridge, 1998)

Smith, *Commedia*    Winifred Smith, *The Commedia dell'arte: A Study in Italian Popular Comedy*, 3 vols (New York, 1912), vol. 3

Smith, 'Exits'    Irwin Smith, 'Their exits and reentrances', *SQ*, 18.1 (1967), 7–16

Smith, 'Response'    Molly Easo Smith, 'John Fletcher's response to the gender debate: *The Woman's Prize* and *The Taming of the Shrew*', *Papers on Language and Literature*, 31.1 (1995), 38–60

Smith, 'Review'    Peter J. Smith, review of Ed Hall's 2006 RSC *The Taming of the Shrew*, in *Cahiers Élizabéthains*, 72 (2007), 65–6

SMT    Shakespeare Memorial Theatre, Stratford-upon-Avon

Somerset                J.A.B. Somerset, 'The Lords President, their activities
                        and companies: evidence from Shropshire', *Elizabethan
                        Theatre*, 10 (1988), 93–111
Soule                   Lesley Wade Soule, 'Tumbling tricks: presentational
                        structure and *The Taming of the Shrew*', *New Theatre
                        Quarterly*, 20.2 (2004), 164–79
*Spanish Tragedy*       Thomas Kyd, *The Spanish Tragedy*, ed. J.R. Mulryne
                        (1989)
Speaight                Robert Speaight, *Shakespeare on the Stage: An Illustrated
                        History of Shakespearian Performance* (London, 1973)
Spencer                 Hazelton Spencer, *Shakespeare Improved: The Restoration
                        Versions in Quarto and on the Stage* (Cambridge, Mass.,
                        1927)
Spivak                  Gayatri Spivak, 'Displacement and the discourse of
                        woman', in Anthony Easthope and Kate McGowan (eds),
                        *A Critical and Cultural Theory Reader* (Toronto, 1992),
                        162–80
Sprague, *Actors*       Arthur Colby Sprague, *Shakespeare and the Actors: The
                        Stage Business in His Plays, 1660–1905* (Cambridge, Mass.,
                        1944)
Sprague, *Restoration*  Arthur Colby Sprague, *Beaumont and Fletcher on the
                        Restoration Stage* (Cambridge, Mass., 1926)
*SQ*                    *Shakespeare Quarterly*
SR                      Sasha Roberts, private communication
*SS*                    *Shakespeare Survey*
*S.St*                  *Shakespeare Studies*
Staves                  Susan Staves, *Players' Scepters: Fictions of Authority in the
                        Restoration* (Lincoln, Nebr., 1979)
STC                     Short-Title Catalogue. *A Short-Title Catalogue of Books
                        Printed in England, Scotland, & Ireland and of English
                        Books Printed Abroad 1475–1640*, A.W. Pollard and G.R.
                        Redgrave, ed. W.A. Jackson, F.S. Ferguson and Katherine
                        F. Pantzer, 2nd rev. and enlarged edn, 3 vols (1976–91)
Stern                   Tiffany Stern, 'Re-patching the play', in Peter Holland and
                        Stephen Orgel (eds), *From Script to Stage in Early Modern
                        England* (Basingstoke and New York, 2004), 151–80
Stopes                  Charlotte Carmichael Stopes, *The Life of Henry, Third Earl
                        of Southampton, Shakespeare's Patron* (Cambridge, 1922)
Stow                    John Stow, *A Survey of the Cities of London and Westminster
                        . . . Very Much Enlarged . . . by John Strype*, 2 vols (1720)
Stubbes                 *Phillip Stubbes's Anatomy of the Abuses in England in
                        Shakespeare's Youth, A.D. 1583*, ed. Frederick J. Furnivall,
                        2 vols (1877–82)

| | |
|---|---|
| Summers | Montague Summers, *Shakespeare Adaptations* (1922) |
| *Tamer Tamed* | John Fletcher, *The Woman's Prize; or, The Tamer Tamed* (*c.* 1611), ed. George B. Ferguson (London and The Hague, 1966) |
| Taylor | John Taylor, *Divers Crabtree Lectures* (1639) |
| Taylor & Jowett | Gary Taylor and John Jowett, *Shakespeare Reshaped, 1606–1623* (Oxford, 1993) |
| Terence | *Terence: The Comedies*, trans. Peter Brown (Oxford and New York, 2006) |
| Thompson, *Chaucer* | Ann Thompson, *Shakespeare's Chaucer: A Study in Literary Origins* (New York, 1978) |
| Thorn-Drury | G. Thorn-Drury, *Some Seventeenth Century Allusions to Shakespeare and His Works, not Hitherto Collected* (1920) |
| *Three Lords* | R.W., *The Three Lords and Three Ladies of London* (1590), ed. H.S.D Mithal (New York, 1988) |
| Tilley | Morris Palmer Tilley, *A Dictionary of the Proverbs in England in the Sixteenth and Seventeenth Centuries* (Ann Arbor, Mich., 1950) |
| Tilley, *Lore* | Morris Palmer Tilley, *Elizabethan Proverb Lore in Lyly's 'Euphues' and in Pettie's 'Petite Pallace'* (New York, 1926) |
| *TLS* | *The Times Literary Supplement* |
| *Tongue* | *The Anatomy of a Woman's Tongue Divided into Five Parts* (1638), in *The Harleian Miscellany*, 12 vols (1808–11), 4.267–85 |
| Topsell | Edward Topsell, *The History of Four-Footed Beasts* (1607) |
| Trewin, *Benson* | J.C. Trewin, *Benson and the Bensonians* (1960) |
| Trewin, *Going* | J.C. Trewin, *Going to Shakespeare* (London, 1970) |
| TWC | T.W. Craik, private communication |
| *TxC* | Stanley Wells and Gary Taylor, with John Jowett and William Montgomery, *William Shakespeare: A Textual Companion* (Oxford, 1987) |
| Tyrwhitt | Thomas Tyrwhitt, *Observations and Conjectures Upon Some Passages of Shakespeare* (Oxford, 1766) |
| Underdown | David Underdown, 'The taming of the scold: the enforcement of patriarchal authority in early modern England', in Anthony Fletcher and John Stevenson (eds), *Order and Disorder in Early Modern England* (Cambridge, 1985), 116–36 |
| Vickers, *Artistry* | Brian Vickers, *The Artistry of Shakespeare's Prose* (1968) |
| Vickers, 'Kyd' | Brian Vickers, 'Thomas Kyd, secret sharer', *TLS*, 18 April 2008, 13–15 |
| Vives | Juan Luis Vives, *The Instruction of a Christian Woman* (1523), trans. Richard Hyde (1557) |

| | |
|---|---|
| VW | Valerie Wayne, private communication |
| Waldo & Herbert | Tommy Ruth Waldo and T.W. Herbert, 'Musical terms in *The Taming of the Shrew*', *SQ*, 10.2 (1959), 185–99 |
| Walker | William Sidney Walker, *Shakespeare's Versification and its Apparent Irregularities, Explained by Examples from Early and Late English Writers* (1854) |
| Warton | Thomas Warton, *The History of English Poetry*, 4 vols (1774–81) |
| Weimann | Robert Weimann, *Author's Pen and Actor's Voice: Playing and Writing in Shakespeare's Theatre* (Cambridge, 2000) |
| Weiss | Susan Forscher Weiss, 'The singing hand', in Claire Richter Sherman (ed.), *Writing on Hands: Memory and Knowledge in Early Modern Europe* (Carlisle, Pa., and Washington, DC, 2001), 35–5 |
| Wells | Stanley Wells, *Re-Editing Shakespeare for the Modern Reader* (Oxford, 1984) |
| Wells & Taylor | Stanley Wells and Gary Taylor, 'No shrew, *A Shrew* and *The Shrew*: internal revision in *The Taming of the Shrew*', in Bernhard Fabian and Kurt Tetzeli von Rosador (eds), *Shakespeare: Text, Language, Criticism: Essays in Honour of Marvin Spevack* (Hildesheim and New York, 1987), 351–70 |
| Wentersdorf | Karl P. Wentersdorf, 'The original ending of *The Taming of the Shrew*: a reconsideration', *SEL*, 18.2 (1978), 201–15 |
| Werner | Sarah Werner, *Shakespeare and Feminist Performance: Ideology on Stage* (London and New York, 2001) |
| Werstine, 'Close' | Paul Werstine, 'Close contrivers: nameless collaborators in early modern London plays', in A.L. Magnusson and C.E. McGee (eds), *Elizabethan Theatre XV* (Toronto, 2002), 3–20 |
| Werstine, 'Compositor' | Paul Werstine, 'Compositor B of the Shakespeare First Folio', *Analytical and Enumerative Bibliography*, 2 (1978), 241–63 |
| Werstine, 'Narratives' | Paul Werstine, 'Narratives about printed Shakespeare texts: "foul papers" and "bad" quartos', *SQ*, 41.1 (1990), 65–86 |
| Werstine, 'Quartos' | Paul Werstine, 'A century of "bad" Shakespeare quartos', *SQ*, 50.3 (1999), 310–33 |
| Werstine, 'Suggestion' | Paul Werstine, 'McKerrow's "Suggestion" and twentieth-century textual criticism', *RD*, 19 (1988), 149–73 |
| West | Michael West, 'The folk background of Petruchio's wooing dance: male supremacy in *The Taming of the Shrew*', *SSt*, 7 (1974), 65–74 |

| | |
|---|---|
| Whately | William Whately, *A Bride-Bush. Or, A Direction for Married Persons* (1623) |
| White | Mary Frances White, *Fifteenth Century Misericords in the Collegiate Church of Holy Trinity, Stratford-Upon-Avon* (Stratford-upon-Avon, 1974) |
| WI | William Ingram, private communication |
| Wiles | David Wiles, *Shakespeare's Clown* (Cambridge and New York, 1987) |
| Williams | Gordon Williams, *A Dictionary of Sexual Language and Imagery in Shakespearean and Stuart Literature* (Atlantic Highlands, NJ, and London, 1994) |
| Wilson, *Art* | Thomas Wilson, *The Art of Rhetoric*, ed. Peter E. Medine (University Park, Pa., 1994) |
| Wiltenburg | Joy Wiltenburg, *Disorderly Women and Female Power in the Street Literature of Early Modern England and Germany* (Charlottesville, Va., 1992) |
| Winter, *England* | William Winter, *Shakespeare's England: An Account of the Life and Manners of His Age* (1893, rev. edn 1917) |
| Winter, *Rehan* | William Winter, *Ada Rehan: A Study* (London and New York, 1898) |
| Winter, *Stage* | William Winter, *Shakespeare on the Stage*, Second Series (New York, 1915) |
| Woodbridge | Linda Woodbridge, *Women and the English Renaissance: Literature and the Nature of Womankind, 1540 to 1620* (Urbana, Ill., 1984) |
| Worsdale | James Worsdale, *A Cure for a Scold. As it is Now Acting at the Theatres in London and Dublin, with Universal Applause* (Dublin, 1735) |
| Worthen | William B. Worthen, 'Texts, tools, and technologies of performance: a quip modest, in response to R.A. Foakes', *Shakespeare*, 2.2 (2006), 208–19 |
| Woudhuysen | *Love's Labour's Lost*, ed. H.R. Woudhuysen, Arden Shakespeare third series (1998) |
| Yachnin | Paul Yachnin, 'The populuxe theatre', in Anthony B. Dawson and Paul Yachnin, *The Culture of Playgoing in Shakespeare's England: A Collaborative Debate* (Cambridge, 2001), 38–68 |

## STAGE PRODUCTIONS

| | |
|---|---|
| Alexander, 1992 | RSC, Royal Shakespeare Theatre, Stratford-upon-Avon, directed by Bill Alexander; Amanda Harris, Anton Lesser |

| | |
|---|---|
| Antoon, 1990 | New York Public Theatre, directed by A.J. Antoon; Tracy Ullman, Morgan Freeman |
| Ball, 1973 | American Conservatory Theatre, San Francisco, directed by William Ball; Fredi Olster, Marc Singer (televised 1976) |
| Barton, 1960 | SMT, Stratford-upon-Avon, directed by John Barton; Peggy Ashcroft, Peter O'Toole |
| Benthall, 1948 | SMT, Stratford-upon-Avon, directed by Michael Benthall; Diana Wynyard, Anthony Quayle |
| Benson, 1889 | SMT, Stratford-upon-Avon, directed by Frank Benson; Constance Benson, Frank Benson |
| Bogdanov, 1978 | RSC, Royal Shakespeare Theatre, Stratford-upon-Avon, directed by Michael Bogdanov; Paola Dionisotti, Jonathan Pryce |
| Bridges-Adams, 1933 | SMT, Stratford-upon-Avon, directed by W. Bridges-Adams; Madge Compton, Anew McMaster |
| Cass, 1935 | Old Vic Company, Sadler's Wells, directed by Henry Cass; Cathleen Nesbitt, Maurice Evans |
| Daly, 1887 | Daly's Theatre, New York, directed by Augustin Daly; Ada Rehan, John Drew |
| Devine, 1953 | SMT, Stratford-upon-Avon, directed by George Devine; Yvonne Mitchell, Marius Goring |
| Dews, 1981 | Stratford, Ontario, directed by Peter Dews; Sherry Flett, Len Cariou |
| Doran, 2003 | RSC, Stratford-upon-Avon, Royal Shakespeare Theatre, directed by Gregory Doran; Alexandra Gilbreath, Jasper Britton |
| Edwards, 1995 | RSC, Royal Shakespeare Theatre, Stratford-upon-Avon, directed by Gale Edwards; Josie Lawrence, Michael Siberry |
| Erten, 1986 | venue unknown, Turkey, directed by Yücel Erten; actors unknown |
| Freed, 2003 | *The Beard of Avon*, New York Theatre Workshop, directed by Doug Hughes; Mary Louise Wilson (Queen Elizabeth), Tim Blake Nelson (Shakespeare) |
| Garrick, 1756 | *Catharine and Petruchio*, Drury Lane, directed by David Garrick; Kitty Clive, Henry Woodward |
| Gribble, 1935 | Guild Theatre, New York, directed by H.W. Gribble; Lynn Fontanne, Alfred Lunt |
| Gurney, 1937 | New Theatre, directed by Claud Gurney; Edith Evans, Leslie Banks |

| | |
|---|---|
| Hall, 2006–7 | Propeller, Courtyard, Stratford-upon-Avon, directed by Edward Hall; Simon Scardifield, Dugald Bruce-Lockhart |
| Harvey, 1913 | His Majesty's, directed by Martin Harvey; Nina de Silva, Martin Harvey |
| Jackson, 1928 | Court Theatre, London, directed by H.K. Ayliff and Barry Jackson; Eileen Beldon, Scott Sunderland |
| Kemble, 1810 | *Katherine and Petruchio*, Covent Garden, directed by J.P. Kemble; Mrs Charles Kemble, J.P. Kemble |
| *Kiss Me, Kate*, 1948 | New Century Theatre, New York, musical by Cole Porter, directed by John C. Wilson; Patricia Morison, Alfred Drake |
| Kyle, 1982 | RSC, Royal Shakespeare Theatre, Stratford-upon-Avon, directed by Barry Kyle; Sinead Cusack, Alun Armstrong |
| Leach, 1978 | Delacorte Theater, New York, directed by Wilford Leach; Meryl Streep, Raul Julia |
| Lloyd, 2003 | Shakespeare's Globe, directed by Phyllida Lloyd; Kathryn Hunter, Janet McTeer |
| Marowitz, 1974 | Open Space Theatre, directed by Charles Marowitz; Thelma Holt, Malcolm Tierney (first performed at the Hot Theatre, The Hague, 1973) |
| Miller, 1987 | RSC, Royal Shakespeare Theatre, Stratford-upon-Avon, directed by Jonathan Miller; Fiona Shaw, Brian Cox |
| Monette, 1988 | Stratford Festival Theatre, Ontario, Canada, directed by Richard Monette; Lucy Peacock, Colm Fiore |
| Nunn, 1967 | RSC, Royal Shakespeare Theatre, Stratford-upon-Avon, directed by Trevor Nunn; Janet Suzman, Michael Williams |
| Potter, 2003 | Stratford Festival Theatre, Ontario, Canada, directed by Miles Potter; Seana McKenna, Graham Abbey |
| Sothern & Marlowe, 1905 | Knickerbocker Theater, New York, directed by E.H. Sothern and Julia Marlowe; Julia Marlowe, E.H. Sothern |
| Taymor, 1988 | Theatre for a New Audience, New York, directed by Julie Taymor; Sheila Dabney, Sam Tsoustsouvras |
| Trevis, 1985–6 | RSC, Warehouse, Stratford-upon-Avon, directed by Di Trevis; Sian Thomas, Alfred Molina |
| Ultz, 1985 | Theatre Royal Stratford East, *The Taming of the Shrew: The Women's Version*, directed by David Ultz; Susan Cox, Fiona Victory |
| Webster, 1844 | Haymarket, directed by Benjamin Webster; Louisa Nisbett, Benjamin Webster |
| Williams, 1931 | Old Vic, directed by Harcourt Williams; Phyllis Thomas, Ralph Richardson |

## PROMPTBOOKS

| | |
|---|---|
| Alexander, 1992 | Shakespeare Centre Library |
| Asche, 1916 | Shakespeare Centre Library |
| Barton, 1960 | Shakespeare Centre Library |
| Benson, 1890 | Shakespeare Centre Library |
| Bogdanov, 1978 | Shakespeare Centre Library |
| *Cure*, 1735 | *Cure for a Scold*, Folger Shakespeare Library |
| Devine, 1953 | Shakespeare Centre Library |
| Edwards, 1995 | Shakespeare Centre Library |
| Jewett, 1915 | Folger Shakespeare Library |
| Kemble, 1874 | Folger Shakespeare Library |
| Miller, 1987 | Shakespeare Centre Library |
| Nunn, 1967 | Shakespeare Centre Library |
| Sauny, 1735 | *Sauny the Scott*, Folger Shakespeare Library |

## FILM, TELEVISION AND RADIO PRODUCTIONS

| | |
|---|---|
| Ford, 1952 | Republic Pictures, *The Quiet Man*, directed by John Ford; Maureen O'Hara, John Wayne |
| Gottlieb, 1940 | CBS, Columbia Workshop, *The Taming of the Shrew*, musical adapted by Joseph Gottlieb, music by Irvin Graham; Nan Sunderland, Carleton Young |
| Junger, 1999 | Jaret/Mad Chance/Touchstone, *10 Things I Hate About You*, directed by Gil Junger; Julia Stiles, Heath Ledger |
| Miller, 1980–1 | BBC TV, directed by Jonathan Miller; Sarah Badel, John Cleese |
| *Moonlighting*, 1986 | ABC, 'Atomic Shakespeare' (episode), directed by Will MacKenzie; Cybill Shepherd, Bruce Willis |
| Richards, 2005 | BBC TV, *Shakespeare Retold*, directed by David Richards; Shirley Henderson, Rufus Sewell |
| Selig, 1911 | Selig Polyscope, *The Cow Boy and the Shrew* (silent film), director unknown; Herbert Rawlinson |
| Sidney, 1953 | MGM, *Kiss Me Kate*, film of Cole Porter musical, directed by George Sidney; Kathryn Grayson, Howard Keel |
| Taylor, 1929 | United Artists, directed by Sam Taylor; Mary Pickford, Douglas Fairbanks |
| Zeffirelli, 1967 | Columbia Pictures, directed by Franco Zeffirelli; Elizabeth Taylor, Richard Burton |

# INDEX

This index covers the Introduction, the commentary notes and the Appendices; it excludes references in the textual notes and references to the *OED*. The abbreviation 'n.' is used only for footnotes in the Introduction and Appendices; it is not used for commentary notes.

# Index